W9-AFB-399

ADVANCES IN
EXPERIMENTAL
SOCIAL PSYCHOLOGY

VOLUME 19

CONTRIBUTORS TO VOLUME 19

Robert S. Baron

John T. Cacioppo

Jeffrey D. Fisher

Dieter Frey

Arie Nadler

Richard E. Petty

David P. Phillips

Ivan D. Steiner

David A. Wilder

ADVANCES IN

Experimental

Social Psychology

EDITED BY

Leonard Berkowitz
DEPARTMENT OF PSYCHOLOGY
UNIVERSITY OF WISCONSIN—MADISON
MADISON, WISCONSIN

VOLUME 19

 1986

ACADEMIC PRESS, INC.
Harcourt Brace Jovanovich, Publishers

Orlando   San Diego   New York   Austin
London   Montreal   Sydney   Tokyo   Toronto

301.151
A244
v.19

COPYRIGHT © 1986 BY ACADEMIC PRESS, INC.
ALL RIGHTS RESERVED.
NO PART OF THIS PUBLICATION MAY BE REPRODUCED OR
TRANSMITTED IN ANY FORM OR BY ANY MEANS, ELECTRONIC
OR MECHANICAL, INCLUDING PHOTOCOPY, RECORDING, OR
ANY INFORMATION STORAGE AND RETRIEVAL SYSTEM, WITHOUT
PERMISSION IN WRITING FROM THE PUBLISHER.

ACADEMIC PRESS, INC.
Orlando, Florida 32887

United Kingdom Edition published by
ACADEMIC PRESS INC. (LONDON) LTD.
24–28 Oval Road, London NW1 7DX

LIBRARY OF CONGRESS CATALOG CARD NUMBER: 64-23452

ISBN 0–12–015219–3
ISBN 0–12–000010–5 (paperback)

PRINTED IN THE UNITED STATES OF AMERICA

86 87 88 89   9 8 7 6 5 4 3 2 1

CONTENTS

N.C. WESLEYAN COLLEGE LIBRARY   71745

The Elaboration Likelihood Model of Persuasion

Richard E. Petty and John T. Cacioppo

Natural Experiments on the Effects of Mass Media Violence on Fatal Aggression: Strengths and Weaknesses of a New Approach

David P. Phillips

Paradigms and Groups

Ivan D. Steiner

Social Categorization: Implications for Creation and Reduction of Intergroup Bias

David A. Wilder

CONTRIBUTORS

Numbers in parentheses indicate the pages on which the authors' contributions begin.

Robert S. Baron (1), *Department of Psychology, University of Iowa, Iowa City, Iowa 52242*

John T. Cacioppo (123), *Department of Psychology, University of Iowa, Iowa City, Iowa 52242*

Jeffrey D. Fisher (81), *Department of Psychology, University of Connecticut, Storrs, Connecticut 06268*

Dieter Frey (41), *Department of Psychology, Christian-Albrechts-University, Kiel, Federal Republic of Germany*

Arie Nadler (81), *Department of Psychology, Tel-Aviv University, Ramat-Aviv, Israel 69978*

Richard E. Petty (123), *Department of Psychology, University of Missouri, Columbia, Missouri 65211*

David P. Phillips (207), *Department of Sociology, University of California, San Diego, La Jolla, California 92093*

Ivan D. Steiner (251), *Department of Psychology, University of Massachusetts, Amherst, Massachusetts 01002*

David A. Wilder (291), *Department of Psychology, Rutgers, The State University of New Jersey, New Brunswick, New Jersey 08903*

DISTRACTION–CONFLICT THEORY: PROGRESS AND PROBLEMS

Robert S. Baron

DEPARTMENT OF PSYCHOLOGY
UNIVERSITY OF IOWA
IOWA CITY, IOWA

I. Background and Theory

Over a decade ago Glenn Sanders and I first offered distraction–conflict theory as an explanation for why species mates might elevate drive in social facilitation research (Baron, Sanders, & Baron, 1974; Sanders & Baron, 1975). This theory suggested that attentional conflict might be the key mediator of drive

1

ADVANCES IN EXPERIMENTAL
SOCIAL PSYCHOLOGY, VOL. 19

Copyright © 1986 by Academic Press, Inc.
All rights of reproduction in any form reserved.

in such research settings. This notion and subsequent theoretical refinements suggested by myself, Sanders, and Dan Moore have since been subjected to a good deal of research attention. This article reviews this research and argues that, despite a good deal of corroborating data for some of the major contentions of distraction–conflict theory, attentional mechanisms may offer a more parsimonious account of social facilitation phenomena than does a drive perspective. Moreover, this attentional emphasis suggests that distraction (and environmental stressors in general) may have a variety of effects on cognition, attitude change, and social behavior (cf. Cohen, 1978).

A. HISTORY AND EMPIRICAL FEATURES OF SOCIAL FACILITATION

Social facilitation refers to the fact that the presence of others tends to energize certain performances. It is one of the oldest documented effects in social psychology. Triplett (1898), in one of social psychology's first experiments, observed that children turned fishing reels faster if faced with a live competitor. This study was prompted by Triplett's observation that bicycle racers achieved better times in live heats than when racing against the clock. Other corroborating reports of social facilitation soon followed. These early effects were quite exciting since they seemed to document the impact on behavior of a purely social manipulation, i.e., the mere presence of others. This finding accelerated research on the phenomenon. Research was also encouraged by the generality of the effect. Social facilitation has been found in a wide range of species (ants, rats, dogs, cats, chicks, humans, cockroaches, etc.) and across a wide range of behaviors (in humans: pursuit rotor, copying, memorization, running; in animals: escape, nest building, eating, sexual behavior). Unfortunately, this encouraging pattern of results was soon complicated by emerging reports that social impairment occurred on certain tasks. For example, birds took longer to master a complex maze under social conditions; Harvard undergraduates performed more poorly on a difficult epigram task when working with others (for reviews see Allport, 1924; Zajonc, 1965; Geen & Gange, 1977; Bond & Titus, 1983). After years of conflicting research and various attempts at theoretical integration (e.g., Allport, 1924), Zajonc (1965) proposed his now well-known and elegant integration of these conflicting data in terms of Hull–Spence drive theory. According to Zajonc, social conditions increased drive/arousal. This in turn facilitated simple, well-learned, dominant responses, but impaired complex, counterinstinctual, subordinate responses. Thus, according to Zajonc (1965), whether social facilitation or social impairment occurred in a given study depended upon whether the researcher focused on a dominant or a subordinate response.

Zajonc's theory elicited an intense research effort, which provided a good deal of support for Zajonc's view (Geen & Gange, 1977). Most of this research carefully delineates the dominant and subordinate response and finds that both audiences and coactors facilitate dominant responding while impairing subordinate responses. This, of course, is quite in accord with Zajonc's drive theory. Moreover, Geen and Gange (1977) point out that memory effects associated with drive also occur under social conditions.

These basic observations are supplemented by several other empirical findings. First, at least a few investigators report that social facilitation/impairment occurs where audiences are nonevaluative or where coactors are noncompetitive (e.g., Markus, 1978). These *mere presence* effects are somewhat controversial in that they have not been consistently replicated (Cottrell, Wack, Sekerak, & Rittle, 1968), but they clearly must be included as part of the social facilitation data base.

Secondly, a good number of studies report that increasing the salience of competitive pressure (Martens & Landers, 1972) heightens social facilitation/impairment as does increasing evaluative pressure from an audience (Henchy & Glass, 1968). These findings are commonly accepted by most social facilitation researchers (cf. Geen & Gange, 1977), but they must be qualified. A meta-analysis of 241 studies by Bond and Titus (1983) concludes that evaluative/competitive pressure does not increase the overall *magnitude* of the social facilitation effect. This analysis will undoubtedly encourage further research. At this point, it seems safe to conclude that at least in *some* research settings evaluative/competitive pressure can increase social facilitation/impairment phenomena. Finally, social facilitation has been produced in some studies just by telling the subject he is being observed (from behind one-way glass or via videotape), even though no audience is physically present (Cohen & Davis, 1973).

B. DISTRACTION–CONFLICT THEORY

The theoretical perspective reviewed in this article—distraction–conflict theory—attempts to integrate and explain this body of empirical data as well as the subhuman research findings on social facilitation. Early statements of distraction–conflict theory (Baron *et al.,* 1974; Sanders & Baron, 1975; Baron, Moore, & Sanders, 1978; Sanders, Baron, & Moore, 1978) proposed a unique explanation for why social conditions might elevate drive as Zajonc argued. According to distraction–conflict theory, both audiences and coactors (even their mere presence) can elevate drive by provoking attentional conflict. The distraction–conflict model can easily be broken down into a series of causal steps. These are outlined below.

1. *Others are distracting.* As numerous writers have noted, species mates are very provocative stimuli (e.g., Zajonc, 1980). They may attract our attention for a variety of reasons: They mediate very powerful social reinforcements and punishments; they are unpredictable; they provide sexual and social cues we may wish to respond to; they often offer social comparison information. As such, species mates will generally be very attractive targets of attention.

2. *Distraction can lead to attentional conflict.* Attending to others will often be incompatible with task demands. This can create attentional conflict, i.e., a form of response conflict regarding what attentional response one should make. This problem of attentional conflict, of course, will exist in a social facilitation setting only when the subject has a fairly strong inclination to attend to *both* his species mates and the task. Stating this differently, distraction–conflict theory does *not* assume distraction will invariably create attentional conflict. Attentional conflict is conceptualized as a tendency, desire, or requirement to attend to two (or more) mutually exclusive inputs. As such, it represents a variety of approach–approach conflict in which the organism has difficulty determining how to allocate attention. Not all distractions will lead to such conflict. We view distraction as something that directs attention away from some ongoing activity. Such shifts in attention will not always lead to noticeable conflict (i.e., difficulty allocating attention). If one is washing dishes, a surprise visit from an out-of-town best friend could easily draw attention completely from the drudgery of dishwashing without producing any attentional conflict. Stated simply, in this case there is no contest between the ongoing activity and the distracting stimulus. We feel that one precondition for strong attentional conflict is that pressure to attend to rival inputs should be substantial and roughly equal. This can be due to such factors as time pressure, instructional set, curiosity (intrinsic interest),[1] threat, or reinforcement pressure. In addition, if there is reason to attend to multiple inputs, a conflict is likely to occur only in settings where the organism either has inadequate attentional capacity or inadequate physical capacity to attend to both inputs or task requirements. Settings where such conflict is quite likely are those involving what Kahneman (1973) refers to as *structural interference.* Structural interference occurs when one is required (or strongly tempted) to attend to two inputs involving the same physiological–neural mechanisms, e.g., attending to two simultaneous visual signals located several feet apart. A second situation where one might have conflict over attention allocation is described by Kahneman as *capacity interference.* According to Kahneman, even where attentional responses are not in structural conflict, there will be numerous cases where attentional capacity will be inadequate for performing more than one task, particularly if at least one of the tasks is difficult. Here there is more ambiguity concerning when the tasks are taxing enough for

---

[1]This would include attentional shifts associated with orienting responses.

such "capacity" interference to occur. But when such interference does take place, again the organism lacks the ability to perform all that is required of her/him and again attentional decisions must be made. An example of such conflict would be requiring someone to do difficult mental arithmetic while juggling. Even though juggling and math would seem to involve different and nonoverlapping physiological–neural mechanisms,[2] most of us would find the experience frustrating and would probably suffer impaired performance on at least one of the tasks. Our point is that distraction–conflict theory only predicts that distraction will lead to drivelike effects when the subject is faced with an attentional conflict stemming from either structural or capacity interference.[3]

3. *Attentional conflict elevates drive.* A number of theorists have argued that attentional conflict of the type described above will elevate drive/arousal (Thibaut & Kelley, 1959; Kimble, 1961; Brown & Farber, 1951). There are several reasons why attentional conflict might elevate drive level. Indecision or uncertainty about what attentional response to make might stress the organism and elevate arousal or drive. The overload of attempting to attend to and process multiple inputs also could elevate stress/arousal/drive. Finally, frustration due to delay of reinforcement caused by response conflict could also elevate drive (Brown & Farber, 1951). In short, attentional conflict is hypothesized to produce the same drivelike effects long associated with such forms of behavioral conflict as approach–approach conflict and approach–avoidance conflict (e.g., Kimble, 1961).

Distraction–conflict theory is outlined graphically in Fig. 1A.

C. ASSUMPTIONS AND IMPLICATIONS OF DISTRACTION– CONFLICT THEORY

1. A major hypothesis of distraction–conflict theory is that inducing any form of attentional conflict will produce *drivelike*[4] effects on task performance and motor behavior, e.g., facilitation of simple responses and impairment of

---

[2]Kahneman (1973) suggests an empirical procedure for assessing whether or not two tasks are structurally related. Assuming Task A = Task B in difficulty, then performing Task A and Task C together should equal performing Task B and Task C together if there is no structural relationship between Task A and Task C and Task B and Task C. If, in fact, an inequality results, this could imply either structural interference on one side of the equation or structural facilitation on the other side.

[3]From this it follows that distraction–conflict theory does not predict that drivelike behavior is caused by distraction or task interruption per se or even by paying attention to others during a task. Distraction that lures attention away from a very low priority task would not produce conflict, nor should conflict occur if there is ample time to attend to both distraction and task without cost or if attending to both inputs can be done easily without inducing either structural or capacity interference.

[4]We use the term *drivelike* to indicate our recognition that nondrive mechanisms may mediate the task effect produced by mechanical distractions, conflict manipulations, and social presence (see discussion below and Section III).

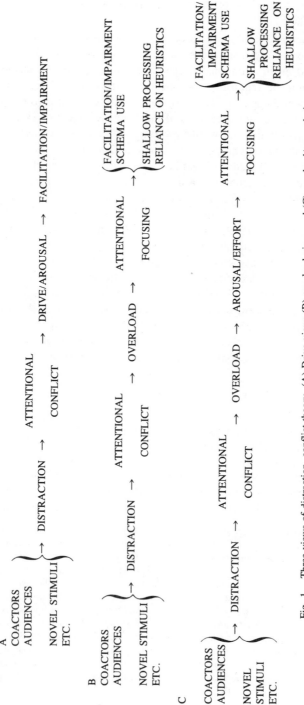

Fig. 1. Three views of distraction–conflict theory. (A) Drive view; (B) overload view; and (C) overload/arousal view.

complex responses (referred to hereafter as facilitation/impairment). This attentional conflict can be due to mechanical or social distraction during a task or simply to having multiple tasks to perform. Early suggestions that conflict can lead to drive (e.g., Kimble, 1961; Brown & Farber, 1951) were based primarily on considerations of approach–avoidance (i.e., behavioral) conflict. Our contention is that *attentional* conflict produces drivelike behavior as well.

As noted above, such conflict is likely to occur, we feel, when (1) the distraction is very interesting and/or hard to ignore, (2) there is pressure to complete the task quickly and accurately, and (3) attending to the task and the distracter simultaneously is difficult or impossible. Note that, according to this hypothesis, we predict that under certain circumstances both social or mechanical distracters could increase or facilitate task performance on certain tasks. Note, however, this prediction is not expected to hold for intense levels of distraction. Distraction–conflict theory recognizes that even if distraction does elevate drive, it also diverts attention from the task. While increasing drive should have a beneficial effect on simple task performance, diverting attention from the task should have a disruptive effect. Therefore, if distraction is to facilitate simple task performance, the beneficial effects of increased drive must outweigh the disruptive effects of the distraction. This is unlikely to occur if distraction is extremely intense. Stated differently, according to distraction–conflict theory, the intensity of distraction during a simple task should be related in a curvilinear fashion to task performance (Sanders & Baron, 1975; Sanders, 1981a).[5]

2. Distraction–conflict theory explicitly assumes that in settings in which there is pressure to perform a task quickly and well, attentional conflict can be created not only by external distractions but also by internal distractions, i.e., cognitive activity that is not directly relevant to task solution (see discussion in Sanders *et al.,* 1978, p. 292). While such distracting cognitions can take any form, we feel that frequently they will involve ruminations regarding the adequacy of task performance and the consequences of task success and failure (cf. Sarason, 1980, for a related notion). This may explain why unseen but evaluative audiences can trigger social facilitation effects. Our argument would be that, although the audiences cannot be directly observed, they trigger ruminative activity that distracts the subject from ongoing task activity thereby creating attentional conflict.

3. A very common reason others are distracting in task settings is because individual performers are attempting social comparison. That is, we feel per-

---

[5]It seems likely that task difficulty, task pressure, and/or the interest value of the task and the distracter will affect the slopes of this curvilinear relationship and the point at which distraction becomes too intense to benefit performance. Thus, for a given task and distraction, it would be wise to determine this inflection point empirically by parametric variation of distraction intensity in initial pilot research.

formers are quite interested in gaining information regarding the adequacy of their own performance (and perhaps tips that can be applied to performing the task). This information can be gleaned either by comparing one's own performance to that of coactors or examining the evaluative reactions of the audience to one's performance, thereby comparing the audience's opinion of the performance to one's own.

It follows from this assumption that one way to heighten social facilitation phenomena is to increase subjects' desire for social comparison information and to make sure that adequate social comparison information is being provided by coactors or the audience. This is not to state that social comparison pressure is the only way to cause distraction, attentional conflict, or social facilitation. It seems indisputable that on occasion coactors and audiences may lure attention from the task for a variety of reasons that have nothing to do with social comparison such as bizarre appearance or behavior, sexual attraction, overt overtures of friendship, and social interaction.

Rajecki, Ickes, Corcoran, and Lenerz (1977), for example, produced "social facilitation" using a mannequin as an audience. While this seems puzzling at first, a photo revealed that the mannequin was fairly startling in appearance, having no facial detail (no lips, nostrils, or facial lines) and yet dressed in wool cap, clothing, and dark sunglasses. It seems likely that such a sight was capable of luring attention from the task if only by provoking internal rumination and bewilderment regarding why such an incongruous object was present in a psychology experiment. In a similar fashion, the late Brad Groff once jokingly proposed that as a test of distraction–conflict theory we induce social facilitation by having his small, well-trained dog, Banana, hop on a lab chair, assume a begging posture, and observe subjects as they attempted to complete a drive-sensitive task. Groff felt this test would illustrate that the mere presence of "species mates" was hardly a necessary condition to elicit "social" facilitation.

4. Distraction–conflict theory offers one explanation for why evaluative and/or competitive pressure has been found to heighten social facilitation phenomena at least in some studies. An evaluative/competitive setting probably increases the pressure to work diligently on the primary task, as well as increasing the pressure to attend to coactors and/or the audience in order to check the adequacy of one's progress. Feeling both pressures simultaneously should elevate the level of conflict experienced by subjects. Of course, it is possible that nonevaluative audiences and noncompetitive coactors may still be distracting enough to trigger attentional conflict and consequent facilitation/impairment.

This last point, in turn, may explain why in some studies the mere presence of others has been sufficient to provoke social facilitation even when they are nonevaluative or noncompetitive. This bears upon the controversy in the social facilitation literature regarding whether evaluative or competitive pressure is a necessary and sufficient condition for eliciting social facilitation phenomena.

Zajonc (1980) and associates (e.g., Markus, 1978) favor a mere presence view arguing that evaluative pressure is not a necessary condition. Others (e.g., Cottrell *et al.*, 1968) argue that evaluative pressure is a necessary condition to obtain the effect. While some studies lend support to Zajonc's argument, roughly an equal number find that social facilitation phenomena do not occur reliably when evaluative/competitive pressure is low (for reviews see Geen & Gange, 1977; Geen, 1980). One post hoc explanation for these inconsistent data is that in the latter studies, for some reason, the presence of nonevaluative or noncompetitive others may not have been sufficiently distracting to trigger attentional conflict, whereas in the "mere presence" studies, distraction was effectively created by the presence of others. In the absence of distraction data from these studies, this must remain post hoc speculation, but certainly this fairly glaring inconsistency in the social facilitation data lends itself easily to an integration in terms of distraction–conflict theory (Baron & Byrne, 1981).

   5. One clear advantage of distraction–conflict theory is that it offers a parsimonious explanation for social facilitation effects observed among animals as well as among humans. That is, it seems safe to assume that subhumans are as interested in the activities of their species mates as human beings are interested in the activities of their fellow human beings. In subhuman species this interest is probably more due to concerns about competition, safety, or sexual interest than it is in social comparison, but, nevertheless, attending to other animals while simultaneously engaging in some other task should provoke attentional and/or behavioral conflict in these animals, and as other theorists over the years have pointed out, such conflict theoretically should elevate drive (Brown & Farber, 1951). If so, this readily accounts for the fact that subhuman species from cockroaches to pigeons have exhibited drivelike responding under social conditions.

   6. Distraction–conflict theory also reconciles the social facilitation effect with recent findings on social loafing. From one perspective these two phenomena contradict one another. Social facilitation research assumes working with others heightens motivation thereby facilitating simple task performance. *Social loafing* research documents that working with others lowers motivation and reduces output on seemingly simple tasks such as rope pulling, yelling, clapping, etc. (cf. Latane, Williams, & Harkins, 1979). The major difference between these two research arenas is that social loafing tends to occur on tasks where subjects cannot accurately assess their relative output, i.e., there is no accurate individual feedback. This should dramatically reduce if not eliminate social comparison thereby reducing the tendency to attend to others. Moreover, social loafing research tends to employ simple motor tasks (on which attending to co-workers does not conflict with attending to the task) (see Petty, Harkins, & Williams, 1980, for an exception). For instance, one can easily attend to others while clapping. In short, social loafing tends to occur in settings where the

presence of co-workers seems unlikely to trigger attentional conflict. Indeed, in one study where social comparison was possible and attending to co-workers was structurally incompatible with the primary task (competitive swimming), Latane, Harkins, and Williams (1980) report that group testing conditions produced social facilitation of performance. In contrast, when social comparison was impossible, group testing on this same task produced social loafing. The social facilitation observed in the first condition and the absence of social facilitation in the latter condition is, of course, just the effect predicted by distraction–conflict theory.

7. One implication of distraction–conflict theory is somewhat unsettling. One of the major assumptions of distraction–conflict theory is that attending to others provokes drive primarily because it conflicts with task demands. This suggests that some of the very tasks used to assess drive may be *creating* drive in that they represent task activity that puts the organism into conflict. This is a difficult issue to resolve so long as we rely on behavioral tasks as our assessments of drive. Unfortunately, the inconsistent results obtained with psychophysiological measures (see Section II,F) hamper attempts to deviate from this methodology.

II.   Research on Distraction–Conflict Theory

A.   NONSOCIAL DISTRACTION PRODUCES FACILITATION/IMPAIRMENT EFFECTS

The first aspect of distraction–conflict theory subjected to empirical test was the counterintuitive hypothesis that moderate nonsocial distraction would lead to facilitation of simple task performance as well as impairment of complex task performance. Complex impairment, of course, would not be a very surprising outcome given the fact that distraction lures a subject's attention away from the task. Finding that distraction facilitated simple task performance, however, seemed to be a more provocative and difficult prediction to substantiate. In fact, there were some preliminary empirical indications that distraction might indeed facilitate simple task performance. For example, in one early experiment, Pessin (1933) trained his subjects to memorize nonsense syllables under one of three conditions: mechanical distraction, isolation, or under occasional experimenter scrutiny. Not surprisingly, the isolation condition produced the fastest learning with both mechanical distraction (buzzers and bells) and occasional experimenter evaluation producing slower rates of learning. Pessin then waited until subjects had learned the nonsense lists to criterion and then reintroduced the experimental conditions. He found that in this measure of well-learned performance, both mechanical distraction and occasional experimenter observation produced superior recall of the nonsense syllables (see Table I).

In short, Pessin demonstrated that both an audience and a mechanical distraction produced similar effects, specifically impairment of initial learning relative to the isolated group (i.e., the alone controls), and then, later, facilitation of performance once the correct response was well learned. This, of course, is precisely the pattern of results one would expect if mechanical distraction and audiences were indeed elevating drive. Unfortunately, there are certain methodological problems with Pessin's early research. The most provocative finding (i.e., the facilitation of well-learned performance under distraction) is open to the criticism that subjects in both the mechanical and audience cells took more trials to originally learn the material and therefore had a longer exposure time to the material, and this rather than heightened drive may have facilitated their later performance.

There are at least six other studies, however, that have reported that distraction has facilitated arousal-related performance. Houston (1969), Hartley and Adams (1974), Houston and Jones (1967), and O'Malley and Poplawsky (1971) all found that noise increased speed of response on the Stroop task. Since this is just the effect other forms of arousal (e.g., fear) have on this task (Agnew & Agnew, 1963; Tecce & Happ, 1964; Calloway, 1959), it seems plausible that this facilitation of response speed under noise reflects elevated arousal.[6] Similarly, McBain (1961) and Zuercher (1965) have also found facilitation of fairly simple responses under distracting conditions.

In addition to this evidence, there are at least eight studies demonstrating that distraction impairs performances that are complex or poorly learned (e.g., Woodhead, 1965; Eschenbrenner, 1971). Finally, there are some five studies indicating that apparent attentional conflict elevates physiological activity (Helper, 1957; Ryan, Cottrell, & Bitterman, 1950; Teece & Cole, 1976). Ryan *et al.* (1950) found, for instance, that presenting a visual distracter during a task elevated electromyographic (EMG) responding, while a series of studies by Tecce and associates (cf. Tecce & Cole, 1976) indicates that distraction occurring during reaction time tasks elevates tonic heart rate levels.

These various physiological and behavioral results are complemented by Sanders and Baron (1975), who conducted two studies to assess the impact of distraction on task performance using tasks that were drive validated (shown to be responsive to other forms of drive). In these experiments subjects worked on copying tasks that were either simple or complex. One complex task, for example, required subjects to write letters upside down and backwards. A simple task required them simply to write numbers as they appeared on the page. Subjects in

---

[6]These Stroop data, however, are not necessarily consistent with a drive theory interpretation (see Section III).

TABLE I

RECALL OF WELL-LEARNED NONSENSE SYLLABLES[a]

Condition	Group 1, after 1 day[b] (N = 20)	Group 2, after 2 days[b] (N = 20)	Group 3, after 3 days[b] (N = 20)
Mechanical	43.82	54.67	51.65
Social	46.39	46.59	53.06
Control	36.59	40.43	37.57

[a]Taken from Pessin (1933).
[b]Days refer to the number of days since learning material to criterion.

the distracted condition worked on these copying tasks for 40-sec periods. During these periods they received either zero, two, four, six, or eight signals which required them to look at a target (an "X") on the laboratory wall. Subjects in the nondistracted control condition simply worked for 40 sec on the copying tasks without interruption.

In both Studies 1 and 2 the interaction predicted by drive theory was significant. Specifically, in the distraction conditions simple task performance was facilitated, and complex performance was impaired relative to the nondistricted controls. In addition to these interaction effects, a supplementary analysis compared the nondistracted controls and the distracted subjects only on those few trials where no distraction occurred (i.e., where distraction was omitted on a given 40-sec trial). This analysis assumed that distracted subjects would still show facilitation/impairment effects if the distraction on surrounding trials had, in fact, elevated drive since drive is thought to carry over for at least a few minutes (Spence, 1956). This subanalysis was interesting because on these "zero signal" trials both the subjects who had just been distracted and the nondistracted controls had equal time to work on the task. On the other trials distracted subjects have less time available for task activity.

This time confound, of course, makes it harder to document simple task facilitation since when distraction becomes high enough (i.e., eight signals in 40 sec), no amount of response energization is likely to compensate for the amount of lost time.[7] Contrariwise, the fact that less time is available in distraction cells makes the prediction of complex task impairment in distracted cells somewhat trivial. As a result, equating cells on the time they had available to work provides a most interesting test of our key hypothesis. In Study 1 the simple task was

[7]As noted above (see Assumption I, Section I,C), distraction is expected to have a curvilinear effect on simple task performance. At a high enough rate of distraction, no amount of heightened motivation will be able to compensate for the low amount of time available for task behavior (see Table II).

TABLE II

Mean Performance Broken Down by Number of Distraction Signals Delivered[a,b]

Task	No-distraction controls	Number of distraction signals				
		0	2	4	6	8
Simple: Number copying	73.13	81.38	77.75	76.63	74.63	72.50
Complex: Reverse letter copying	28.88	23.79	21.25	21.63	20.50	18.38

[a]During a single trial. Taken from Study 2 of Sanders and Baron (1975), *Journal of Personality and Social Psychology*, **32**, 956–963. Copyright 1975 by the American Psychological Association.

[b]All cells to the right of the no-distraction controls data are related; that is, the same subjects contributed data to all levels of distraction signals for a given task.

indeed facilitated by (previous) distraction on these zero signal trials, but an order effect weakened the effects of the treatment on the complex task. This was remedied in Study 2 where distraction again facilitated simple task performance and this time impaired complex task performance as well (see Table II).

In short, there seem to be at least 16 studies that demonstrate that distraction can either facilitate simple task performance, increase performance on tasks facilitated by other stressors, or impair complex task performance. In addition, some five studies show that distraction during a task elevates physiological responding. This provides encouraging support for the notion that moderate distraction produces drivelike effects so commonly associated with social facilitation/impairment phenomena.

B. ARE OTHERS DISTRACTING?—RECALL AND SELF-REPORT DATA

The second aspect of distraction–conflict theory that we subjected to empirical test was the notion that in social facilitation settings the presence of others, whether as coactors or audiences, would in fact distract attention from the ongoing primary task. Our first attempt to address this issue involved monitoring subjects' eye movements, direction of gaze, etc. This research strategy did not prove fruitful, and our second strategy was simply to rely on a variety of questionnaire probes to assess subjects' feelings of distraction and the extent to which they focused attention on various parts of the experimental situation. For example, Baron et al. (1978) replicated a fairly well-known social facilitation study. After exposing subjects to the original procedure, Baron et al. (1978) administered a questionnaire asking subjects where they directed their attention and how well they recalled certain key task features. As in the original study, audiences produced facilitation of simple task performance and impairment of complex task performance. Subjects also were less likely to recall key aspects of the task if they worked before an audience and were more likely to say that they focused attention on something other than the task.[8] Note that this was true even in the simple task cells, i.e., where performance was *superior* in the audience cells. At least three other studies conceptually replicate this basic pattern of self-report finding (Sanders *et al.*, 1978; Gastorf, Suls, & Sanders, 1980; Strube, Miles, & Finch, 1981). Sanders *et al.* (1978), for example, used self-reports of attention and recall to assess distraction and found it to be higher in coaction cells where social facilitation/impairment occurred.

In addition to self-report measures of attention and recall, Sanders *et al.* (1978) asked subjects to gauge the progress of their coactors. They found that when social facilitation occurred, subjects were more accurate at gauging their coactors' performance, supporting the idea that some of their attention was directed at coactors. Two of the studies in this series extend these data by demonstrating that social facilitation occurs only when the presence of others produces distraction (Sanders *et al.*, 1978; Gastorf *et al.*, 1980).

Strube *et al.* (1981) also provide self-report evidence that others can lead to distraction in task settings and that this distraction is related to social facilitation. A first substudy indicated that jogging speed at an indoor track was facilitated by the presence of an attentive spectator but not by an inattentive spectator. In a second substudy Strube *et al.* found that awareness of an attentive spectator was more distracting than awareness of an inattentive spectator, and that direct self-reports of distraction in the attentive spectator cell were negatively correlated with lap time ($r = -.42$).

C. ARE OTHERS DISTRACTING?—BEHAVIORAL AND PHYSIOLOGICAL DATA

These findings involving self-reports of attention, distraction, and recall all tend to confirm distraction–conflict theory's argument that distraction is often produced by the presence of others in task settings and that this contributes to social facilitation/impairment. These findings, however, all rely on a post hoc

---

[8]Direct verbal measures of distraction (How distracted were you during the task?) tended to be nonsensitive in this experiment as well as in several other experiments (Glass & Singer, 1972; Sanders, Baron, & Moore, 1978). It is not immediately clear why this is so. Perhaps subjects are poor monitors of their attentional activity (Nisbett & Wilson, 1977). Alternatively, this particular item may have surplus meaning. It is true, however, that in several studies, including those done by Glass and Singer (1972), direct measures of distraction have not proved to be sensitive despite compelling evidence that distraction or shifts in attention did indeed occur. Gastorf *et al.* (1980) did successfully use a direct measure of distraction; however, this experiment used a within design. Perhaps this type of sensitivity is needed because the item has a good deal of error variance associated with it.

questionnaire methodology and are, therefore, somewhat suspect. Are people accurately reporting the actual levels of distraction they experienced *during* the task, or are they responding to demand or some other forms of bias in the questionnaire? Since posttreatment questionnaire responses are poorly suited for establishing the temporal occurrence or location of a mediating state (such as distraction), it is fortunate that these self-report findings are nicely complemented by studies involving task behavior and physiological responding.

The strategy in this research is simply to compare the impact of a nonsocial distraction with that of an audience or a coactor. If audiences and/or coactors are in fact distracting, they should have the same impact on behavior and physiology as any nonsocial/mechanical distraction. Two studies report data of this type. Pessin (1933; see Section II,A) found that mechanical distraction (lights and buzzers) and an audience (the experimenter) produced very similar effects on both initial learning and subsequent performance on a verbal learning task relative to an isolated control. This, of course, suggests a certain functional equivalence between the mechanical distraction and the audience. Moore, Baron, Logel, Sanders, and Weerts (1984) noted that in the reaction time literature, certain physiological changes typically occur during the period between the warning ("get ready") stimulus and the imperative ("go") stimulus. In this interstimulus interval (ISI), heart rate decelerates, while spontaneous skin conductance and certain forms of cortical activity increase (e.g., Tecce & Cole, 1976; Lacey & Lacey, 1970; Bower & Tate, 1976). These physiological changes are not usually interpreted as drive or arousal effects but are described instead as task-specific physiological reactions associated with preparing to make a motor response (Obrist, 1976; Edelberg, 1972). (In this paradigm a more appropriate indication of tonic levels of arousal is the physiological activity occurring *between* trials. These data on tonic arousal are reported below in Section II,F.) A key additional finding in the constant foreperiod reaction time literature is that distraction dampens many of the physiological changes that occur during the ISI (Tecce & Cole, 1976; Lacey & Lacey, 1970). In addition, distraction slows reaction time (Tecce & Scheff, 1969). In short, distraction during this specific period is seen as disrupting attention to the task and the preparation to respond, thereby slowing reaction time. This gives us a means of assessing our primary hypothesis. If distraction affects physiological responding during the ISI, it follows that if others are distracting, their presence during this preparation period (between get ready and go signals) should produce effects on reaction time, heart rate, and skin conductance that closely resemble the effects of a mechanical distraction.

One is tempted to predict that reaction time would decrease if distraction was producing drive in this setting. We did not offer this prediction since prior research on reaction time has produced mixed evidence regarding the effect of drive/arousal on reaction time latency (Kamin & Clark, 1957; Farber & Spence,

TABLE III

Mean Cardiac Deceleration during the ISI[a] and Reaction Times[b]

		Condition	
	Alone	Mechanical distraction	Audience
Cardiac deceleration (beats/min)	−4.25	−2.36	−2.83
Reaction time (sec)	.352	.449	.437

[a]The ISI (interstimulus interval) is the period between the warning and imperative stimuli.

[b]Taken from Moore et al. (1984). Data are given for the first block of trials.

1956; Tecce & Cole, 1976). Indeed, there are some data indicating that, on this particular reaction time task, reaction time is *slower* when arousal is high (Tecce & Cole, 1976). As a result of this confusion, our focus regarding reaction time was simply empirical. Did an audience produce reaction time effects which were functionally equivalent to those of mechanical distraction?

To test this, Moore et al. (1984) used the same constant foreperiod reaction time paradigm typically employed in this literature. Subjects worked alone, with a flashing light, or in the presence of an evaluating audience (a graduate student). The distracting light and the audience produced very similar effects during the ISI on all three key measures (Table III; Fig. 2) and these effects closely resembled the classical pattern associated with mechanical distracters in this paradigm.

In short, whether one examines recall scores, attentional self-report regarding attention, or parallel effects between mechanical distractions and social conditions on behavior and physiological response, the data all suggest that audiences and coactors are capable of distracting attention away from task activity simply due to their passive[9] presence.

D. SOCIAL COMPARISON AND DISTRACTION–CONFLICT
    THEORY

We have suggested that an important reason that audiences and coactors are distracting in task settings is because they provide important sources of social comparison. This is not to say that social comparison is a necessary condition for

[9]We emphasize the word *passive* here to delineate this prediction from the more obvious and trivial case in which an audience or coactors might create distraction by actively yelling, screaming, jumping up and down, or otherwise intrusively badgering a performer.

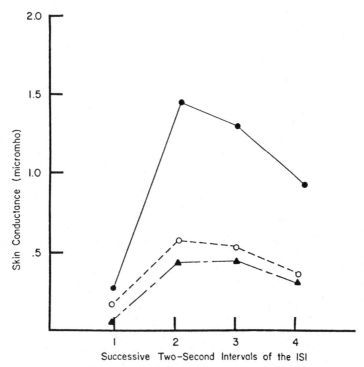

Fig. 2.   Mean skin conductance responses (micromho) for each condition during successive 2-sec intervals of the interstimulus interval. (●——●), Alone; (○---○), mechanical distraction; (▲—·—▲), audience. Taken from Moore *et al.* (1984).

distraction, conflict, or social facilitation. We recognize that there are many reasons that subjects might be distracted. But all things being equal, if a subject can gain a great deal of social comparison information and if he strongly desires such information, we would expect that the presence of coactors or an observing audience would be a tempting target for his attention. This in turn should lead to the attentional conflict that we feel mediates social facilitation/impairment effects.

This emphasis on social comparison is somewhat less central to distraction–conflict theory than most of our other hypotheses. We are assuming that social comparison is a frequent reason for distraction and that heightening social comparison pressure, needs, or availability will heighten that distraction. It is conceivable, however, that under certain circumstances social comparison information might not be highly distracting. For example, social comparison information might be presented so unequivocally during the early parts of the task session that the subject no longer needs to attend to such cues as the task progresses. To the extent that social comparison does not produce distraction, distraction–conflict theory would have to predict that under those conditions social comparison pressure might not necessarily lead to heightened degrees of conflict and social facilitation. This is basically an empirical issue that can be ascertained with appropriate measures of distraction under varying social comparison manipulations. Our hunch, however, is that in most instances social comparison cues will represent stimuli that direct attention away from the task.

There are a number of studies that bear on this general set of issues. In Study 1 of Sanders et al. (1978), social facilitation was found to occur only in conditions where subjects were concerned about their relative task performance (i.e., a condition that should heighten concerns with social comparison). In a control cell where subjects thought they were working on a pilot project (where their personal traits were presumably not reflected in task performance), social facilitation did not occur.

In Study 2 of Sanders et al. (1978), coacting subjects worked either on the same task or on different tasks. Since subjects knew of this fact before the task period began, subjects in the "different task" cell had much less reason to engage in social comparison. The data indicated that, relative to alone controls, social facilitation/impairment occurred only when subjects were working with coactors engaged on the same task. In addition, it was found that in that cell task recall was lower than in the other cells and subjects were more accurate in gauging the progress of their coactors than in other cells. Indeed, in this particular experiment, there was no evidence of any social facilitation in the cells where subjects worked with coactors who were engaged in different tasks (i.e., where social comparison needs were probably less pronounced) (see Table IV). This certainly supports our contention that social comparison enhances social facilitation.

TABLE IV

MEAN NUMBER OF DIGITS COPIED CORRECTLY AND INCORRECTLY[a]

Task difficulty	Alone ($n = 20$)	Together–different ($n = 10$)	Together–same ($n = 10$)
Digits copied correctly			
Simple	151.65_c	158.60_c	179.60_d
Complex	78.70_c	81.90_c	78.00_c
Digits copied incorrectly			
Simple	0.25_c	0.60_c	0.60_c
Complex	0.60_c	0.50_c	3.90_d

[a]Taken from Study 2 of Sanders et al. (1978, p. 299).
[b]Cells having different subscripts within a row differ significantly at $p < .05$, using two-tailed t tests with common error terms.

The study conducted by Gastorf *et al.* (1980) also supports this view. Gastorf *et al.* divided subjects into Type A and Type B coronary-prone patterns and observed that social facilitation effects occurred only among Type A subjects. Gastorf *et al.* (1980) also found that it was these subjects who provided indications that they were more distracted under social conditions (see Table V). The authors predicted these results on the assumption that Type A individuals would be generally more competitive and concerned with social comparison information. Seta (1982) also has reported data supporting the view that social comparison is an important component of social facilitation phenomena. Thus, data from a variety of research strategies all generally corroborate the notion that social comparison often plays a role in social facilitation effects.

E. CONFLICT AND SOCIAL FACILITATION

The data reviewed above all strongly imply that social facilitation effects are mediated at least in part by the distraction created by the presence of others in task settings. Mechanical distraction produces the very same facilitation/ impairment on drive-sensitive tasks usually associated with social facilitation. Mechanical distraction and social manipulations produce very similar effects on behavior and physiology. Finally, there are various indications that the presence of others is distracting. There is a gap in this data base, however.

First, one cannot be sure that the distraction created by the presence of others is of the same type or intensity as the mechanical distractions that have been found to create facilitation/impairment. Secondly, while these data suggest that distraction can create drivelike effects on behavior (facilitation/impairment), there is no evidence bearing on the role of attentional conflict as a mediator of these effects. While it seems empirically true that distraction is capable of creat-

TABLE V

MEAN TASK PERFORMANCE DIFFERENCE SCORE[a,b]

Subjects	Simple task		Complex task	
	Alone	Similar coactor	Alone	Similar coactor
A's	140.75_a	199.90_b	63.00_d	49.25_e
B's	$149.65_{a,f}$	159.05_f	62.45_d	56.90_d

[a]Taken from Gastorf, Suls, & Sanders (1980), *Journal of Personality and Social Psychology*, **38**, 773–780. Copyright 1980 by the American Psychological Association.

[b]The higher the score, the greater the number of digits copied. Means with the same subscript are not significantly different from each other; other comparisons, $p < .01$.

ing facilitation/impairment, it would be comforting to rule out the possibility that such effects are due to such mechanisms as startle responses and novelty.

One way to address both of these problems is to assess facilitation/ impairment effects after manipulating whether or not attending to the audience or coactors conflicts with task demands. By manipulating attentional conflict within a social facilitation setting in this way, one can assess the role of attentional conflict as well as increasing one's confidence that the distracting effects *of others* are sufficient to generate the drive effects associated with social facilitation. The prediction from distraction–conflict theory is clear: Others should increase social facilitation/impairment only when attending to them conflicts with task demands. This prediction runs counter to those of most other theoretical formulations. Those who favor an evaluation apprehension view of social facilitation (e.g., Geen, 1979; Cottrell *et al.*, 1968) would predict that social facilitation should occur even in low-conflict settings, so long as evaluative pressure is substantial. Similarly, Zajonc's (1980) view that the mere presence of others increases drive (based on the notion that others elevate uncertainty) also predicts social facilitation in both high- and low-conflict settings so long as in both settings an audience is physically present. Thus, research manipulating attentional conflict not only investigates a key assumption of distraction–conflict theory, it also provides some basis for distinguishing between competing theoretical positions.

We found it difficult for a while to construct manipulations of attentional conflict in a social facilitation setting that didn't confound such factors as boredom, evaluation apprehension, or differences in task stimuli. We finally adopted the strategy of using a person perception video task where the target of perception could be either the evaluative audience or some other individual (Groff, Baron, & Moore, 1983). Groff *et al.* (1983) had subjects watch the face of an individual portrayed on a TV screen. The subject's job was to periodically rate the face for how positive or negative it appeared. Subjects received an innocuous signal (a quiet tone) each time they were to make a rating (a check mark in a plus or minus column). In addition to making this rating, subjects were required to squeeze a soft plastic bottle with each signal.[10]

The latency and intensity of this squeeze response were the primary measure of response facilitation. As drive increased, the intensity and speed of such simple ergographic responses should increase (Woodworth & Schlossberg, 1954). Subjects first made a series of ratings (and squeeze responses) alone. The stimulus person being rated was a confederate. After this baseline period, *control* subjects continued to work alone, this time observing a second stimulus individual on the TV screen. Subjects in the *high-conflict* cell also made ratings of

---

[10]Subjects were told that the purpose of this part of the procedure would be explained during the debriefing.

this confederate, but they did so while they were observed by an individual introduced as a graduate student who would be evaluating the subject's performance. This audience–confederate sat just enough to the subject's right of the TV monitor so that the subject could not examine the audience–confederate without shifting his/her gaze from the TV monitor. Thus, attending to the audience conflicted with the primary task demand to monitor the TV. In a final *low-conflict* cell, subjects were also monitored by the audience–confederate during the postbaseline trials, but here the face being rated on the TV was the face of the audience–confederate which was broadcast live on the TV monitor via a video camera (located next to the subject in all cells but only aimed and turned on in this cell). The rationale for describing this as a low-conflict cell is that attending to the audience does not conflict with the primary task demand (rating the audience reaction). Both actions can be accomplished by attending to the TV monitor (or attending directly to the audience) without any attendant conflict.

The results basically substantiate the predictions of distraction–conflict theory. The only evidence of facilitation on the squeeze response relative to baseline was in the high-conflict cells. The alone and low-conflict cells did not differ. No other performance effects or rating effects proved to be significant, despite the fact that the audience was described as moderately evaluative[11] (see Fig. 3).

One major strength of the Groff *et al.* study is that it assessed the impact of attentional conflict within a social facilitation paradigm. Since social facilitation occurred only when attending to the audience conflicted with task demands, it elevates our confidence that such attentional conflict contributes to social facilitation phenomena just as distraction–conflict theory contends. According to distraction–conflict theory, moreover, this particular form of attentional conflict (i.e., conflict between attending to an audience and a task) is only one way of producing facilitation/impairment effects. Distraction–conflict theory predicts that any form of attentional conflict should produce drivelike effects on task performance (facilitation/impairment).

Study 2 of Groff *et al.* (1983) verified this prediction. Subjects in all cells were asked to work on two (drive-sensitive) tasks during the task period: writing letters upside down and backwards (Taylor & Rechtschaffen, 1959) and an anagram task in which subjects are trained to respond with animal names (Cohen & Davis, 1973).

Subjects in the choice–high-conflict cell had to choose from moment to moment which of these two tasks they would work on. Each task was presented on a teaching machine located on its own desk. These desks were adjacent and formed a right angle. In order to switch from one task to another, subjects simply turned 90° on a swivel chair and faced the other desk. The performance of these

---

[11]The response energization found by Groff *et al.* did not persist on the last block of trials. This lack of persistence has been noted on other tests of social facilitation using motor behavior (cf. Groff *et al.*, 1983).

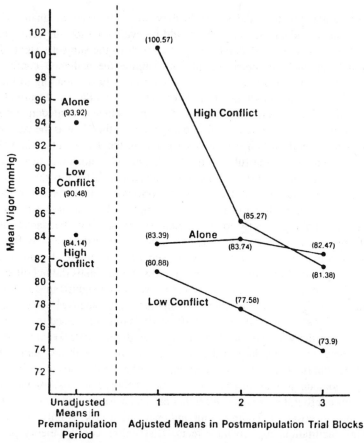

Fig. 3. Adjusted mean vigor (mmHg) during postmanipulation trial blocks with unadjusted premanipulation means. In the premanipulation period all subjects respond alone. Taken from Groff *et al.* (1983, p. 366).

high-conflict subjects was compared to the performance of low-conflict controls who were signaled when to work in each task (i.e., these control subjects had no choice about task attention). Each low-conflict control subject was yoked to a subject in the high-conflict cell such that the amount of time on each task and the precise sequence of switching from task to task was constant in the two cells. Thus, in the high-conflict cells subjects had to decide how to allocate their attention between the demands of two conflicting tasks, while in the low-conflict cell subjects had no such conflict to resolve.

As predicted by distraction–conflict theory, on both tasks, dominant responses were significantly more likely in the high-conflict cell than in the low-conflict cell (see Table VI). That is, high-conflict subjects copied fewer letters

TABLE VI

Task Performance[a]

	Dominant responses (hidden-word task)	Subordinate responses (hidden-word task)	Total letters copied (reverse copying task)	Errors (reverse copying task)
Choice–conflict cell	11.80	5.33	8.13	4.60
Yoked–control cell	7.40	6.60	12.73	3.40
$t(14)$	1.94	<1	2.91	1.41
p Value	<.04, one-tailed	ns[b]	<.01, one-tailed	<.10, one-tailed

[a]Taken from Study 2 of Groff et al. (1983, p. 375).
[b]ns, Not significant.

upside down and backwards and were more likely to persist in constructing animal names even when other solutions became possible. In this study there were no questionnaire differences between conditions on such items as perceived evaluation, task adequacy, or negative affect.

These data nicely complement the data from Groff et al. Study 1. Together, Studies 1 and 2 document distraction–conflict theory's claim that attentional conflict produces the drivelike phenomena so closely associated with social facilitation. Moreover, Study 1 directly demonstrates that in an actual social facilitation setting, attentional conflict is an important mediator of facilitation/impairment effects. As such, Groff et al. (1983) represent some of the most compelling data we know of establishing an empirical link between attentional conflict and social facilitation. What is not clear is whether or not attentional conflict has such effects because it elevates drive. Indeed, other mechanisms are possible and these are described in the sections below.

F. SOCIAL FACILITATION AND PSYCHOPHYSIOLOGY

Not surprisingly, a good number of social facilitation investigators began to examine psychophysiological responding following Zajonc's (1965) argument that social facilitation phenomena were mediated by drive/arousal effects. Zajonc (1965) did not distinguish between drive and arousal, using the terms pretty much interchangeably (e.g., Zajonc, 1980, p. 39). Unfortunately, these data constitute some of the weakest and most contradictory evidence regarding Zajonc's assertions (cf. Moore & Baron, 1983; Bond & Titus, 1983). Bond and Titus (1983) conclude in a meta-analysis of social facilitation that evidence of increased physiological activity under social conditions occurs only when complex tasks are employed. Moreover, even these positive results are evident only when palmar sweat is employed as the measure of "arousal." Heart rate and galvanic skin response (GSR) yield negative results regardless of task according to Bond and Titus. These results complement a narrative review, which focused on social facilitation studies that employ various psychophysiological measures (Moore & Baron, 1983). Moore and Baron (1983) first noted that the majority of the studies included in their review do not report evidence favoring Zajonc's (1965) "arousal" hypothesis, even when "arousal" is liberally construed as any change in physiological activity. Note that most of these studies do report behavioral evidence of social facilitation. It is the psychophysiological data that is weak. For example, Henchy and Glass (1968) found evidence of social facilitation on a pseudo-recognition task under certain audience conditions but found no evidence of either heightened heart rate or skin conductance in these cells. In accord with Bond and Titus's (1983) observations, Moore and Baron (1983) note that positive results (of increased physiological activity under social conditions) are most likely to occur on certain key electrodermal measures (palmar sweat and skin resistance) and least likely to occur on skin conductance and heart rate. Even in palmar sweat and skin resistance studies, however, positive results ($n = 4$) occur in less than 50% of the studies ($n = 9$). While these positive results on palmar sweat and skin resistance could reflect arousal or excitement, it also is possible that they reflect other processes, such as threat (Fowles, 1980) or preparation to make a motor response (Edelberg, 1972). Thus, Moore and Baron (1983), in agreement with Bond and Titus (1983), conclude that, aside from these electrodermal data, physiological evidence does not reliably corroborate Zajonc's notion that social facilitation effects are mediated by arousal (see Geen & Gange, 1977, for an opposing viewpoint).

There are some data from the reaction time literature indicating that distraction during a task elevates tonic levels of heart rate (Tecce & Cole, 1976), but even these data have not always been replicated. When Moore et al. (1984) assessed tonic levels of heart rate and skin conductance (in between reaction time trials), there was no evidence of heightened tonic levels of arousal in mechanical distraction or audience cells. In a related finding, Glass and Singer (1972) found little evidence of tonic arousal in their research on noise.

These disappointing empirical conclusions are complemented by some conceptual confusion as well. Classic drive theorists did not equate drive and arousal (cf. Spence, 1956), preferring instead to view drive as a hypothetical construct having no necessary psychophysiological concomitants (cf. Geen & Gange, 1977, p. 1273). As a result, at least one social facilitation researcher argues that psychophysiological data are more or less irrelevant to the notion that social facilitation is mediated by drive (Sanders, 1981b). This, of course, does not jibe with Zajonc's (1965) original statement of the drive/arousal view of social facilitation, but it is a defensible position. Nevertheless, it does not help much in interpreting the existing psychophysiological data since from this perspective one cannot even view the data as a disconfirming pattern. Complicating this debate are general criticisms of the arousal concept, such as Lacey's (1967) observation that the various indices of "arousal" tend to correlate poorly and that on occasion they are negatively correlated. This perhaps explains, in part, the inconsistency among studies examining whether or not social conditions heighten physiological activity.

III. Conceptual Problems and Future Research

This review of available evidence indicates that a good deal of progress has been made evaluating the causal chain described by distraction–conflict theory. The available data support most of the links in this causal sequence, implying that attentional conflict is at least a partial cause of social facilitation phenomena. That is, (1) others have been found to be distracting (particularly when social comparison is likely); (2) distraction does trigger facilitation/impairment effects; (3) in at least one study, the presence of others induces social facilitation only when attending to these others conflicts with the primary task; and finally (4) nonsocial forms of attentional conflict lead to facilitation/impairment effects closely associated with social facilitation.

The one exception to this corroborating pattern are the data relating to whether or not the effects of attentional conflict on social facilitation are mediated by drive. As indicated in Section II,F, the physiological data have not proved very helpful in substantiating the drive link. Moreover, alternative views suggested from attentional theory provide a nondrive explanation for why attentional conflict might produce facilitation/impairment. These and other conceptual issues are discussed in this section.

A. CAN DISTRACTION–CONFLICT THEORY BE DISPROVED?

One important issue concerns the complexity of the causal sequence specified by distraction–conflict theory and the difficulty of corroborating the existence of distraction and attentional conflict in any given situation. These problems are particularly troublesome in post hoc analyses of studies not explicitly designed to test distraction–conflict theory. For example, if one presented data showing that a distracting display during a task did not heighten social facilitation effects, an apologist for distraction–conflict theory might claim that (1) the manipulation failed—i.e., subjects were not distracted by the display; or (2) the

N.C. WESLEYAN COLLEGE LIBRARY   71745

display was noticed but it did not create attentional conflict. This could be because the display was easy to screen out or alternatively because attending to it did not conflict with task demands (perhaps because there was more than ample time in the task period to attend to both the distraction and the task). Such issues are hard to resolve unless sensitive measures of attention and conflict are included in the research. While self-report indices of attention have been employed in some studies (see Section II,B), measures of attentional conflict are not easy to conceptualize.

In some cases, subjects might be asked directly if they had problems allocating attention, but since the allocation process is probably quasi-conscious in many cases, subjects may be unable to reliably report on their attention-allocation strategies (cf. Nisbett & Wilson, 1977). While measuring conflict seems difficult, it nevertheless is true that when conflict is directly manipulated drivelike effects are noted. It does seem clear from such results that attentional conflict does contribute to the drivelike effects associated with social facilitation. Perhaps we will have to satisfy ourselves by inferring the presence of conflict by parametrically manipulating such factors as task pressure, distraction level, and/or the compatibility of attending to both (as in Groff *et al.*, 1983). In short, the complexity of distraction–conflict theory and the difficulty of measuring the key construct of attentional conflict must be considered drawbacks to the formulation. Nevertheless, despite this complexity, it is quite clear that there is still a wide variety of outcomes that would firmly contradict the theory. For example, distraction–conflict theory argues that when social facilitation occurs, it is due at least in part to the fact that others are distracting. If research repeatedly demonstrated that social facilitation effects occurred independently of distraction, it would be hard to argue that attentional conflict is an important cause of social facilitation.

Similarly, as noted in Section I, distracting individuals during an important (well-learned) task should produce a curvilinear pattern, i.e., facilitation of task performance at low to moderate levels of distraction with task impairment occurring at sufficiently intense levels of distraction (e.g., Table II). Here, too, disconfirmation seems quite possible. In addition, distraction–conflict theory would be hard pressed to account for why distraction that conflicts with an important task does not elevate facilitation/impairment effects any more than a distraction that does not conflict in this way.

Admittedly, it may be tricky to be certain that the distraction employed in a particular study is intense enough to create attentional conflict, but one can grapple with this issue either by pretesting or by employing different levels of distraction within a given research endeavor. In short, conclusive disconfirmation does seem quite possible even given the fact that distraction–conflict theory does involve some complex nonobservable constructs that are difficult to assess. Certainly it is not the only theory in this area to have such a characteristic.

B. AN INFORMATION PROCESSING VIEW OF DISTRACTION–CONFLICT

A second important issue concerns whether the effects of attentional conflict are in fact mediated by drive/arousal. One reason to at least question this view is the conflicting and generally nonconvincing psychophysiological evidence discussed above. A second reason we feel compelled to consider nondrive mechanisms is a desire to integrate distraction–conflict theory with other areas of distraction research (e.g., distraction and persuasion—Baron, Baron, & Miller, 1973; Petty, Wells, & Brock, 1976; distraction and stress—Glass & Singer, 1972; Cohen, Glass, & Singer, 1973; distraction and information processing—Boggs and Simon, 1968). The research in these areas suggests that distraction somehow taxes attentional capacity thereby disrupting cognitive processing. Distraction–persuasion research, for example, indicates that distraction disrupts cognitive reactions to persuasive messages (Petty *et al.*, 1976). Implicit in this view is the notion that distracted individuals do not have the capacity to deeply consider the message (counterargue and proargue) as well as attend to the distraction. In accord with this view, in the processing literature, distraction leads to poorer performance on low-priority tasks (Boggs & Simon, 1968), again suggesting that individuals have less capacity to attend to all their various task demands under distracting conditions. Notions such as these led to us consider whether the social facilitation phenomena, too, might be explained in terms of some form of attentional capacity mechanism.

More recent papers (Moore & Baron, 1983; Baron *et al.*, 1978; Groff *et al.*, 1983) have recognized that there is at least one attention-related mechanism that may explain why distraction and attentional conflict may facilitate simple responses and impair complex responses. This nondrive mechanism is derived from attentional theories (Kahneman, 1973; Cohen, 1978; Broadbent, 1971) and assumes that attentional conflict threatens the organism with attentional overload.[12] Attentional theories argue that overload leads to a restriction in cognitive focus in which the individual attends more to cues that are most central to the task (or alternatively most central geographically in the display) at the expense of more peripheral cues. The attention literature contains a large body of data consistent with this argument (see reviews by Kahneman, 1973; Cohen, 1978). For example, Youngling (1967) had subjects work on both a (primary) tracking task and a (secondary) light-detection task. As target speed increased on the tracking task, deterioration occurred only on the light-detection task and was

[12]Settings that provoke attentional conflict could lead to overload for several reasons. First, simply attempting to process multiple stimulus inputs should frequently tax attentional capacity. Secondly, trying to *decide* which input to attend to and wondering whether the choice was correct should also tax attentional capacity.

most pronounced for peripherally located lights, thereby indicating a narrowing in the range of attention.

The essence of the attentional capacity view is that the individual faced with overload creates an attentional priority system and as a result attends to a narrower range of stimuli. Cohen (1978) suggests that this restricted focus may produce just the task effects usually viewed as evidence of drive. Cohen (1978) argues that on complex tasks a wide range of stimuli generally must be processed for adequate performance. Therefore, restricting attentional focus leaves out certain crucial stimuli, thereby impairing performance. On simple tasks, however, only a few cues are presumed relevant and restricting focus aids performance by screening out nonessential (distracting) stimuli that would only take time away from the task (see Geen & Gange, 1977, p. 1284, for a related argument).[13] Thus, Cohen (1978) argues that overload may lead to facilitation/impairment phenomena. Moreover, this involves an attentional mechanism rather than a motivational construct.

At a superficial level, it would seem that examining physiological data provides a means of differentiating a drive/arousal view of social facilitation from the attention view suggested by Cohen. Unfortunately, the confusing pattern of physiological data in this area (cf. Moore & Baron, 1983; see Section II,F) does little to clarify issues. Moreover, some writers (Kahneman, 1973) have suggested that overload triggers momentary increases in effort/arousal. If so, any observed increases in arousal could be explained from an attentional standpoint.

One possible strategy for differentiating these two perspectives is to focus on poorly learned, complex tasks that involve only a few key stimuli. Here an overload perspective predicts that distraction should facilitate performance, while a drive perspective predicts impairment. There are some initial data of this type. O'Malley and Poplawsky (1971), Hartley and Adams (1974), Houston (1969), and Houston and Jones (1967) all report that performance on the Stroop color–word task is facilitated by noise distraction. On this task subjects must report what color letters are used to form the names of colors. Here it is usually assumed that reading the color name (rather than reporting the letter colors) is the dominant response, and as such, drive theory predicts that heightened drive should impair performance. From an overload perspective, the obtained data occur because narrowing one's focus (under distracting conditions) allows one to

---

[13]One possible objection to Cohen's reasoning is that one can think of "complex tasks" that are impaired under high drive that seem to involve only a few central cues (reverse copying). In order to claim that such tasks involve a "wide range of cues," one must argue that such cues include proprioceptive bodily feedback involved in making the correct motor responses. One must also assume that these cues are more important to attend to on complex tasks since the behavior is not automatic or well learned. This argument is not entirely satisfying and it remains to be seen how well Cohen's assumptions about simple/complex task characteristics stand up to empirical test.

screen out the incorrect semantic cues and focus more exclusively on the letter color cues (e.g., Cohen, 1978). From this perspective, then, these results offer some preliminary support for an attentional capacity explanation of distraction effects.

In favor of a drive view, a great deal of the research that favors a drive interpretation of social facilitation research explicitly uses tasks, settings, and measures that were designed a priori to test drive predictions. While attentional theory can accommodate most of these data quite well, this explanation is post hoc. Thus, drive theory must be given the credit that is due any theory that confirms a priori predictions. Adopting the attentional perspective, however, has some important heuristic advantages. One advantage noted above is that it integrates the research on distraction and social facilitation with the prior research on distraction (cf. Baron *et al.,* 1973; Glass & Singer, 1972). In all these research areas, distraction can be viewed as a manipulation that taxes attentional capacity leading the organism to make priorities, take cognitive shortcuts, and ignore certain stimuli and tasks.

C. COGNITIVE ECONOMY

A second heuristic advantage of the attentional explanation is that it leads to a number of new predictions that are only indirectly implied by a drive view. Specifically, overload of attentional capacity should encourage the organism to take various cognitive shortcuts. Indeed, establishment of attentional priorities and the focusing of available attention alluded to by theorists such as Kahneman (1973) can be viewed simply as cognitive shortcuts aimed at conserving the organism's limited attentional capacity.[14] If so, overload should affect a wide range of social behaviors that seem to contribute to cognitive economy. These include the careless encoding of events and inaccurate word-of-mouth communication that characterize rumor transmission (Allport & Postman, 1947); the use of heuristics such as availability and stimulus salience when attributing causality (Taylor & Fiske, 1978; Fiske & Taylor, 1984); the reliance on past overall

[14]Some research on human attention suggests that the conditions that precipitate overload may vary as a function of training. Several studies (e.g., Underwood, 1974; Spelke, Hirst, & Neisser, 1976) have found that the ability of subjects to perform two tasks (e.g., copying words and reading stories) more or less simultaneously increases substantially over prolonged training (e.g., 20 weeks). Indeed, Spelke *et al.* (1976) trained subjects to the point that no performance decrements existed when attention was divided. The authors argue that these effects demonstrate that prolonged training can increase one's attentional capacity. Thus, no debilitation occurred on task performance because the increased capacity after training prevented and/or minimized overload. These data have interesting implications for those faced with chronic attentional overload situations (switchboard operators, air traffic controllers, waitresses), although it leaves open the issue of whether undetected stress effects may still be occurring despite the absence of task impairment (cf. Glass & Singer, 1972).

evaluations and underutilization of actual behavior events in person perception (Carlston, 1980); engaging in rationalization rather than attitude change when confronted with inconsistent data; and even relying on social influence rather than careful personal investigation when making judgments. All of these phenomena seem to represent cognitive shortcuts. An additional "shortcut" would be to rely on prior expectancies, stereotypes, and social schemata in social judgment and interaction. Still another capacity-saving strategy is to generally engage in less effortful and/or shallower levels of information processing (Schneider & Shiffrin, 1977). For example, in a persuasion context, overload should heighten the tendency for subjects to engage in what Petty and Cacioppo (1981) refer to as peripheral processing—basing one's reaction to the message on such cues as audience reaction, communicator credibility, emotional reaction, and the number of arguments as opposed to a careful consideration of the pros and cons of the message (central processing). From an attentional perspective, all of these phenomena should be more likely to occur in distracting or stressful settings that tax attentional capacity.

D. PHYSIOLOGICAL ACTIVITY AND ATTENTION— AN INTERACTIVE MODEL

A related point that warrants some thought when discussing the drive versus attention issue is the possibility that physiological activity, i.e., arousal, *and* attentional mechanisms interact to affect behavior. In the preceding sections we have discussed drive/arousal and overload as mutually exclusive alternative explanations for social facilitation, either one of which could be triggered by attentional conflict (see Figs. 1A,B). It seems conceivable, however, that conflict could trigger both overload *and* arousal (i.e., changes in physiological activity) and that these mechanisms might interact in some fashion. In fact, one can easily derive one such model from the general standpoint outlined by Kahneman (1973). Kahneman suggests that when attention allocation becomes difficult (say, because of the attentional conflict produced by either structural or capacity interference), there is an involuntary increase in effort/arousal, which, in turn, produces cue utilization (i.e., focusing) (1973, p. 16). Kahneman feels (1) that this increase in effort is often inadequate to meet the increased attentional demands of difficult tasks and (2) that a variety of task effects occur because of cue utilization. This model is outlined in Fig. 1C.[15]

[15]Moore and Baron (1983) have proposed a related notion. In Moore and Baron's model, arousal and overload are seen as roughly simultaneous consequences of attentional conflict. Moore and Baron also suggest that arousal and its attendent internal (drive?) stimuli may provoke rumination, worry, problem solving, and assessment (i.e., attribution), which can themselves absorb capacity and heighten overload, thereby creating a feedback loop.

A fair amount of data are consistent with the type of interactive model depicted in Fig. 1C. First, there are some data indicating that conditions fostering attentional overload also elevate motivation (effort) and physiological activity in accord with an interactive model. Kahneman (1973, Chapter 2) reviews a good deal of data which suggest that when organisms are threatened with overload they heighten their task efforts (drive?) and show various signs of physiological change, most specifically, pupillary dilation and increases in skin conductance. Similarly, Tecce and Cole (1976) conclude after a review of the reaction time literature that distraction elevates tonic heart rate.[16]

Secondly, several literature reviews (e.g., Geen & Gange, 1977) suggest that heightened drive produces just the type of restricted attentional focusing alluded to by the attention theorists when the latter discuss overload, i.e., heightened attention to central inputs. If we assume that these drive manipulations generally elevate "arousal," these data are consistent with the view that arousal leads to focusing as Kahneman suggests. For example, several studies generally support the claim that manipulations involving anxiety narrow perceptual focus (e.g., Mueller, 1976). Indeed, Bruning, Capage, Kozuh, Young, and Young (1968) and Geen (1976) have indicated that an audience manipulation can trigger this form of attentional focusing. In these studies, focusing was assessed by seeing how well people ignored stimuli presented during a task that were either relevant or irrelevant to the task. Subjects in the audience cells were less affected by both forms of stimuli than control subjects. Thus, there is some empirical basis to the claims that (1) arousal could be affecting attentional processing (as argued by Fig. 1C) and (2) that this process occurs as a function of audience presence.

A study by Moore and Baron (1984) supplements this research. Rather than investigating the relationship between arousal and attentional focusing, Moore and Baron examined the tendency of aroused subjects to be biased by a preexisting schema. As noted above, overload should lead subjects to adopt various cognitive shortcuts. Relying on stereotyping and schemata can be viewed as such shortcuts. Quite simply, Moore and Baron found that when individuals had their blood pressure increased via a short period (1.5 min) of vigorous cycling exercise, they were more influenced in a memory task by a preestablished schema than less-aroused subjects. Following the strategy used by Kuiper and Rogers (1979), Moore and Baron (1984) asked subjects to decide whether various adjec-

---

[16]Admittedly, research on the overload–arousal link is not all consistent. Glass and Singer (1972), for example, generally found little evidence of prolonged physiological change under noise (often referred to as an arousal manipulation), when examining measures such as GSR and finger vasoconstriction. Similarly, Moore et al. (1984) did not find distraction to elevate heart rate in a reaction time study. Moreover, it is not clear whether the changes in pupillary dilation relied on heavily in most of Kahneman's research are symptomatic of the widespread activity in the autonomic nervous system, which is usually associated with the arousal concept.

tives described the experimenter after they first provided subjects with a schema (i.e., a description) of the experimenter. Moore and Baron found high-exercise subjects remembered more trait adjectives that were consistent with the schema and fewer adjectives that were inconsistent with the schema than low-exercise subjects (see Table VII). As a result, these data support the view that drive/ arousal triggers the type of attentional shortcuts alluded to by attentional theorists (as depicted in Fig. 1C).

A study by White and Carlston (1983) also bears on the model depicted in Fig. 1C. In this study subjects were placed in attentional conflict by being required to monitor two separate conversations on stereo headphones with one conversation broadcast on the right channel and the other broadcast on the left. Subjects could select which conversation to attend to by moving a switch. Each conversation involved different individuals. The subject was asked to make judgments about one specific individual in each conversation. In one cell subjects were given preexisting schemata about one of these target individuals, while in other cells no information was given. White and Carlston found that subjects in this task situation definitely utilized schemata when they were provided. When subjects had schemata about a target individual on one channel, they spent much more of their time attending to the *other* channel, only periodically checking on the individual they already had descriptive information about. This tendency, however, was counteracted when that target individual emitted a series of behaviors that flagrantly violated the schema. Thus, so long as the schema seemed valid, subjects placed in clear attentional conflict relied upon it as a shortcut strategy in an impression formation task. Since conflict was not manipulated in this particular study, the results do not establish that attentional conflict heightens schema utilization, but it does show that schemata are at least relied upon in situations involving task conflict consistent with Fig. 1C.

These results, of course, are quite preliminary. Moreover, establishing that some links in the arousal–overload models depicted in Fig. 1C have empirical

TABLE VII

RECALL OF TRAIT ADJECTIVES BY AROUSAL AND TRAIT CATEGORY[a,b,c]

Subject category	Extroverted adjectives	Introverted adjectives	Unrelated adjectives	Row marginal total recall
No exercise	3.17_a	4.33_a	3.17_a	10.67
Moderate exercise	3.50_a	3.83_a	$2.75_{a,b}$	10.08
Heavy exercise	4.58_b	3.08_b	2.25_b	9.91

[a]Taken from Moore and Baron (1984).

[b]Subjects were given an extroverted schema regarding the stimulus person.

[c]Means in the same column that do not share a common subscript differ significantly at the .05 level, using preplanned comparisons.

validity in no way establishes the validity of the overall models nor excludes other theoretical possibilities. As a result, these models are frankly speculative and offered more as a guide for future research and as a tentative integration for emerging findings. Because Fig. 1C explains existing research on the relationship between drive and attentional focusing and also suggests that conflict, drive manipulations, and arousal should have impact on something other than task facilitation/impairment (e.g., person perception, rumor transmission, memory, and attitude change), we feel this model has substantial heuristic value that warrants continued research.

E. STRONG AND WEAK VERSIONS OF DISTRACTION–CONFLICT THEORY

One last interesting unresolved issue is whether one should subscribe to a strong or weak version of distraction–conflict theory. The strong version (referred to below as D/C-Strong) is that distraction–conflict theory is the sole explanation for social facilitation phenomena, i.e., that attentional conflict is the necessary and sufficient condition for facilitation/impairment effects. A weak version (D/C-Weak) is that attentional conflict is a sufficient but not a necessary mediator. The weak version implies that other mediators such as evaluation apprehension or self-awareness may also contribute to social facilitation effects. The exchange between Sanders (1981a), Geen (1981), and Markus (1981) touches on this issue.

According to D/C-Strong, those manipulations used to heighten social facilitation effects do so *only* because they increase either the probability of producing attentional conflict or the strength of this conflict. Thus, evaluative pressure could simultaneously increase the desire to work diligently at a primary task and also the desire to take time away from the task to ascertain the progress of coactors or the reactions of the audience, thereby increasing the intensity of attentional conflict. Similarly, manipulations used to heighten self-awareness (mirrors, video cameras) could be interpreted as potent distracters that trigger attentional conflict.

One advantage of the strong version of distraction–conflict theory is that it makes several clear predictions that distinguish it from rival explanations. For example, if the strong version of distraction–conflict theory is true, treatments such as social presence, evaluative pressure, or the presence of a mirror should trigger social facilitation/impairment *only* when attentional conflict seems likely. Two of our studies, in fact, reveal such a data pattern. In Sanders *et al.* (1978) and Groff *et al.* (1983), subjects in all "social" conditions were placed under more evaluative pressure than alone controls. Sanders *et al.* (1978, Study 2), for example, told alone subjects that their task was a nonevaluative warm-up exercise for an upcoming task, while subjects working with coactors were told the task would be carefully evaluated. This evaluative pressure only heightened drivelike behavior above the alone baseline in the one condition in which attentional conflict seemed likely, i.e., where subjects were likely to repeatedly divert attention from the task to coactors for purposes of social comparison (similar-tasks cell) (see Table IV). Of course, one would need to replicate this finding with a wide range of evaluation manipulations before confidently concluding that D/C-Strong was the most plausible explanation for "evaluation effects." Nevertheless, these data provide at least some preliminary data supporting this view.

Another strategy for assessing D/C-Strong is to manipulate the presence or absence of a behavioral task while assessing physiological response or perhaps behavioral signs of tension (cf. Paul, 1966, for a checklist of "tension behaviors"). As noted, Zajonc's (1980) mere presence position predicts that, even in the absence of task activity, social presence should heighten tonic levels of arousal (i.e., over and above any initial orienting response). D/C-Strong would not predict such an outcome.

Hopefully, future research will allow a fuller assessment of D/C-Strong. My own feeling at present is that the weaker version of distraction–conflict theory is more plausible. Certainly strong forms of social threat (be it physical threat, e.g., a bully; or evaluative threat, e.g., a parent) would seem capable of altering physiological response and heightening motivation in the total absence of attentional conflict. Thus, if either arousal or motivational systems play a role in social facilitation, it seems likely that attentional conflict will not be a necessary condition for such phenomena. Alternatively, if attentional mechanisms are completely mediating social facilitation, one might produce social facilitation phenomena by any manipulation that either reduces attentional capacity or elevates attentional demands. While most of the latter manipulations could be said to involve attentional conflict, certain capacity-reducing manipulations seem to not involve conflict (e.g., fatigue).[17] If so, here, too, conflict would not be a necessary condition. The weaker version of distraction–conflict theory generally would predict that social facilitation phenomena would be more robust when attentional conflict was likely but that social facilitation/impairment could still occur under other conditions.

Finally, evidence favoring other theoretical explanations would not necessarily invalidate the claim made by D/C-Weak that attentional conflict is a partical cause of social facilitation phenomena. This, of course, is at best a mixed blessing since it makes it more difficult to disconfirm such a theory. Nevertheless, even with D/C-Weak disconfirming outcomes are possible. If conditions that foster attentional conflict did not increase the strength of social facilita-

---

[17]Cook and Baron (1984) report that 36 hours of sleep deprivation does, in fact, reduce performance primarily on low-priority tasks in a multiple-task paradigm.

tion phenomena, for example, all versions of distraction–conflict theory would be embarrassed. In addition, despite our preference and arguments favoring D/C-Weak, it is quite possible that the mechanisms specified by distraction–conflict theory do totally explain the outcome of the vast majority of social facilitation studies. For example. while intense social threat may be capable of elevating motivation and affecting task performance, intense social threat is hardly ever present in such research. Empirical research will have to resolve such issues.

IV. Conclusion

The major distinguishing feature of distraction–conflict theory as an explanation for social facilitation phenomena is the hypothesis that attentional conflict is at least a partial mediator of such phenomena. Distraction–conflict theory assumes that in social facilitation research social comparison pressure is a common cause of distraction but that distraction can occur for other reasons as well, including internal (task-irrelevant) rumination by the subject. The strong version of distraction–conflict theory holds that attentional conflict is the sole mediator of social facilitation phenomena and that social facilitation effects represent just a subclass of attentional conflict. While this strong version of distraction–conflict theory seems somewhat implausible, it may be valid at least for the typical social facilitation study in which evaluative pressure is not extraordinary and social threat is fairly minimal. Future research will hopefully clarify these points.

Distraction–conflict theory can account post hoc for the findings that indicate that (1) evaluative/competitive pressure heightens social facilitation/impairment; (2) "mere presence" occasionally produces social facilitation in the absence of evaluative/competitive pressure; (3) social loafing can occur on simple well-learned tasks; and (4) hidden audiences produce social facilitation.

Distraction–conflict theory makes predictions that differentiate it from Zajonc's (1980) social uncertainty view as well as from evaluation apprehension models (Geen, 1979) and self-awareness theories (e.g., Carver & Scheier, 1981). For example, distraction–conflict theory predicts that nonsocial distracters should trigger drivelike task effects and that social presence should not elevate signs of drive if attentional conflict can be avoided (e.g., Groff *et al.*, 1983). Moreover, it offers a parsimonious account for social facilitation/impairment in human and nonhuman populations, a difficult problem for self-awareness and evaluation apprehension views.

Distraction–conflict theory does *not* predict that distraction, task interruption, or paying attention to others invariably elevates drivelike behavior, since distraction and attentional confflict are not seen as synonymous. Finally, distraction–conflict theory is not viewed exclusively as a drive theory. We recognize that attentional conflict may trigger perceptual and information processing mechanisms associated with attentional overload as well as elevating drive and physiological activity. Indeed, most of our empirical reports document the importance of distraction, attentional conflict, and social comparison as elements of social facilitation and do not bear directly on whether attentional versus motivational mechanisms mediate the observed effects. Adopting the perspective suggested by an attentional mechanism has some heuristic advantage. This perspective integrates the research on distraction and message impact (Baron *et al.*, 1973; Petty *et al.*, 1976) and distraction as a stressor (e.g., Glass & Singer, 1972) with that of social facilitation, and suggests that manipulations of drive, arousal, and attentional conflict should have specific impact on memory, person perception, and attitude change—topics that have been largely ignored by researchers in this area who typically have taken a motivational perspective.

ACKNOWLEDGMENTS

This article was wrtten while the author was on sabbatical leave at the Department of Psychology at the University of Southern California, Los Angeles. I would like to thank the members of the USC faculty for their support. I would also like to especially thank Danny L. Moore, University of Florida, for his suggestions, and Becky Huber, for her excellent secretarial assistance.

REFERENCES

Agnew, N., & Agnew, M. (1963). Drive level effects in tasks of narrow and broad attention. *Quarterly Journal of Experimental Psychology, 15,* 58–62.

Allport, F. H. (1924). *Social psychology.* Boston: Houghton.

Allport, G. W., & Postman, L. J. (1947). *The psychology of rumor.* New York: Holt.

Baron, R. A., & Byrne, D. (1981). *Social psychology: Understanding human interaction* (3rd ed.). Boston: Allyn & Bacon.

Baron, R. S., Baron, P. H., & Miller, N. (1973). The relation between distraction and persuasion. *Psychological Bulletin, 80,* 310–323.

Baron, R. S., Moore, D., & Sander, G. S. (1978). Distraction as a source of drive in social facilitation research. *Journal of Personality and Social Psychology, 36,* 816–824.

Baron, R. S., Sanders, G. S., & Baron, P. H. (1974). *Social comparison reconceptualized: Implications for choice shifts, averaging effects, and social facilitation.* Unpublished manuscript, The University of Iowa, Iowa City.

Boggs, D. H., & Simon, J. R. (1968). Differential effect of noise on tasks of varying complexity. *Journal of Applied Psychology, 52,* 148–153.

Bond, C. F., Jr., & Titus, L. J. (1983). Social facilitation: A meta-analysis of 241 studies. *Psychological Bulletin, 94,* 265–292.

Bower, A. C., & Tate, D. L. (1976). Cardiovascular and skin conductance correlates of a fixed-foreperiod reaction time task in retarded and nonretarded youth. *Psychophysiology, 13,* 1–9.

Broadbent, D. E. (1971). *Decision and stress.* New York: Academic Press.

Brown, J. S., & Farber, I. E. (1951). Emotions conceptualized as intervening variables—With suggestions toward a theory of frustration. *Psychological Bulletin,* **48,** 465–495.

Bruning, J. L., Capage, J. E., Kozuh, J. F., Young, P. F., & Young, W. E. (1968). Socially induced drive and range of cue utilization. *Journal of Personality and Social Psychology,* **9,** 242–244.

Calloway, E. (1959). The influence of amobarbital (amylobarbitone) and metamphetamine on the focus of attention. *Journal of Mental Science,* **105,** 382–392.

Carlston, D. (1980). The recall and use of traits and events in social inference processes. *Journal of Experimental Social Psychology,* **16,** 303–328.

Carver, C. S., & Scheier, M. F. (1981). The self-attention-induced feedback loop and social facilitation. *Journal of Experimental Social Psychology,* **17,** 545–568.

Cohen, J. L., & Davis, J. H. (1973). Effects of audience status, evaluation, and time of action on performance with hidden-word problems. *Journal of Personality and Social Psychology,* **27,** 74–85.

Cohen, S. (1978). Environmental load and the allocation of attention. In A. Baum, J. E. Singer, & S. Valins (Eds.), *Advances in environmental psychology: Volume 1. The urban environment* (pp. 1–29). Hillsdale, NJ: Erlbaum.

Cohen, S., Glass, D. C., & Singer, J. E. (1973). Apartment noise, auditory discrimination, and reading ability. *Journal of Experimental Social Psychology,* **9,** 407–422.

Cook, M. S., & Baron, R. S. (1984). *Sleep deprivation, and attentional processing.* Unpublished manuscript, The University of Iowa, Iowa City.

Cottrell, N. B., Wack, D. L., Sekerak, G. J., & Rittle, R. H. (1968). Social facilitation of dominant responses by the presence of an audience and the mere presence of others. *Journal of Personality and Social Psychology,* **9,** 245–250.

Edelberg, R. (1972). Electrodermal recovery rate, goal-orientation and aversion. *Psychophysiology,* **9,** 512–520.

Eschenbrenner, A. J. (1971). Effects of intermittent noise on the performance of a complex psychomotor task. *Human Factors,* **13,** 59–63.

Farber, I. E., & Spence, K. W. (1956). Effects of anxiety, stress, and task variables on reaction time. *Journal of Personality,* **25,** 1–18.

Fiske, S. T., & Taylor, S. E. (1984). *Social cognition.* Reading, MA: Addison-Wesley.

Fowles, D. C. (1980). The three arousal model: Implications of Gray's two-factor learning theory for heart rate, electrodermal activity, and psychopathy. *Psychophysiology,* **17,** 87–104.

Gastorf, J. W., Suls, J., & Sander, G. S. (1980). Type A coronary-prone behavior pattern and social facilitation. *Journal of Personality and Social Psychology,* **38,** 773–780

Geen, R. G. (1976). Test anxiety, observation, and range of cue utilization. *British Journal of Social and Clinical Psychology,* **15,** 253–259.

Geen, R. G. (1979). Effects of being observed on learning following success and failure experiences. *Motivation and Emotion,* **3,** 355–371.

Geen, R. G. (1980). The effects of being observed on performance. In P. B. Paulus (Ed.), *Psychology of group influence* (pp. 61–98). Hillsdale, NJ: Erlbaum.

Geen, R. G. (1981). Evaluation apprehension and social facilitation: A reply to Sanders. *Journal of Experimental Social Psychology,* **17,** 252–256.

Geen, R. G., & Gange, J. J. (1977). Drive theory of social facilitation: Twelve years of theory and research. *Psychological Bulletin,* **84,** 1267–1288.

Glass, D. C., & Singer, J. E. (1972). *Urban stress: Experiments on noise and social stressors.* New York: Academic Press.

Groff, B. D., Baron, R. S., & Moore, D. L. (1983). Distraction, attentional conflict, and drivelike behavior. *Journal of Experimental Social Psychology,* **19,** 359–380.

Hartley, L. R., & Adams, R. G. (1974). The effect of noise on the Stroop test. *Journal of Experimental Psychology, 102*, 62–66.

Helper, M. M. (1957). *The effects of noise on work output and physiological activation.* (U.S. Army Medical Research Laboratory Reports, No. 270.) Washington D.C.: U.S. Government Printing Office.

Henchy, T., & Glass, D. C. (1968). Evaluation apprehension and the social facilitation of dominant and subordinate responses. *Journal of Personality and Social Psychology, 10*, 446–454.

Houston, B. K., & Jones, T. M. (1967). Distraction and Stroop color–word performance. *Journal of Experimental Psychology, 74*, 54–56.

Houston, B. K., & Jones, T. M. (1967). Distraction and Stroop color--word performance. *Journal of Experimental Psychology, 74*, 54–56.

Kahneman, D. (1973). *Attention and effort.* Engelwood Cliffs, NJ: Prentice-Hall.

Kamin, L. J., & Clark, J. W. (1957). The Taylor scale and reaction time. *Journal of Abnormal and Social Psychology, 54*, 262–263.

Kimble, G. A. (1961). *Hilgard and Marquis' conditioning and learning* (2nd ed.). New York: Appleton.

Kuiper, N. A., & Rogers, T. B. (1979). Encoding of personal information: Self–other differences. *Journal of Personality and Social Psychology, 37*, 499–514.

Lacey, J. I. (1967). Somatic response patterning and stress: Some revisions of activation theory. In M. H. Appley & R. Trumbull (Eds.), *Psychological stress: Issues in research.* New York: Appleton.

Lacey, J. I., & Lacey, B. C. (1970). Some autonomic–central nervous system interrelationships. In P. Black (Ed.), *Physiological correlates of emotion.* New York: Academic Press.

Latane, B., Harkins, S. G., & Williams, K. (1980). *Many hands make light the work: Social loafing as a social disease.* Unpublished manuscript, Ohio State University, Columbus. Awarded the 1980 Socio-Psychological prize by the American Association for the Advancement of Science.

Latane, B., Williams, K., & Harkins, S. (1979). Many hands make light the work: The causes and consequences of social loafing. *Journal of Personality and Social Psychology, 37*, 822–832.

Markus, H. (1978). The effect of mere presence on social facilitation. *Journal of Experimental Social Psychology, 14*, 389–397.

Markus, H. (1981). The drive for integration: Some comments. *Journal of Experimental Social Psychology, 17*, 257–261.

Martens, R., & Landers, D. M. (1972). Evaluation potential as a determinant of coaction effects. *Journal of Experimental Social Psychology, 8*, 347–359.

McBain, W. N. (1961). Noise, the "arousal hypothesis," and monotonous work. *Journal of Applied Psychology, 45*, 390–397.

Moore, D. L., & Baron, R. S. (1983). Social facilitation: A psychophysiological analysis. In J. T. Cacioppo & R. E. Petty (Eds.), *Social psychophysiology: A sourcebook.* New York: Guilford.

Moore, D. L., & Baron, R. S. (1984). *Social schemata, exercise-induced arousal, and memory.* Unpublished manuscript, The University of Iowa, Iowa City.

Moore, D. L., Baron, R. S., Logel, M. L., Sanders, G. S., & Weerts, T. C. (1984). *Are audiences distracting? Behavioral and physiological data.* Unpublished manuscript, The University of Iowa, Iowa City.

Mueller, J. M. (1976). Anxiety and cue utilization in human learning and memory. In M. Zuckerman & C. D. Spielberger (Eds.), *Emotions and anxiety: New concepts, methods, and applications.* Hillsdale, NJ: Erlbaum.

Nisbett, R. E., & Wilson, T. D. (1977). Telling more than we know: Verbal reports on mental processes. *Psychological Review, 84*, 231–259.

Obrist, P. A. (1976). The cardiovascular–behavioral interaction—As it appears today. *Psychophysiology, 13*, 95–107.

O'Malley, J. J., & Poplawsky, A. (1971). Noise induced arousal and breadth of attention. *Perceptual and Motor Skills,* **33,** 887–890.

Paul, G. L. (1966). *Insight vs. densensitization in psychotherapy: An experiment in anxiety reduction.* Stanford, CA: Stanford University Press.

Pessin, J. (1933). The comparative effects of social and mechanical stimulation on memorizing. *American Journal of Psychology,* **45,** 263–270.

Petty, R. E., & Cacioppo, J. T. (1981). *Attitudes and persuasion: Classic and contemporary approaches.* Dubuque, IA: Wm. C. Brown.

Petty, R., Harkins, S., & Williams, K. (1980). The effects of group diffusion of cognitive effort on attitudes: An information processing view. *Journal of Personality and Social Psychology,* **39,** 81–92.

Petty, R. E., Wells, G. L., & Brock, T. C. (1976). *Distraction can enhance or reduce yielding to propaganda: Thought disruption versus effort justification. Journal of Personality and Social Psychology,* **34,** 874–884.

Rajecki, D. W., Ickes, W., Corcoran, C., & Lenerz, K. (1977). Social facilitation of human performance: Mere presence effects. *Journal of Social Psychology,* **102,** 297–310.

Ryan, T. A., Cottrell, C. L., & Bitterman, M. E. (1950). Muscular tension as an index of effort: The effect of glare and other disturbances in visual work. *American Journal of Psychology,* **63,** 317–341.

Sanders, G. S. (1981a). Driven by distraction: An integrative review of social facilitation theory and research. *Journal of Experimental Social Psychology,* **17,** 227–251.

Sanders, G. S. (1981b). Toward a comprehensive account of social facilitation: Distraction/conflict does not mean theoretical conflict. *Journal of Experimental Social Psychology,* **17,** 262–265.

Sanders, G. S., & Baron, R. S. (1975). The motivating effects of distraction on task performance. *Journal of Personality and Social Psychology,* **32,** 956–963.

Sanders, G. S., Baron, R. S., & Moore, D. L. (1978). Distraction and social comparison as mediators of social facilitation effects. *Journal of Experimental Social Psychology,* **14,** 291–303.

Sarason, I. G. (Eds.) (1980). *Text anxiety: Theory, research and applications.* Hillsdale, NJ: Erlbaum.

Schneider, W., & Shiffrin, R. M. (1977). Controlled and automatic human information processing: I. Detection, search, and attention. *Psychological Review,* **84,** 1–66.

Seta, J. J. (1982). The impact of comparison processes on coactors' task performance. *Journal of Personality and Social Psychology,* **42,** 281–291.

Spelke, E. S., Hirst, W. C., & Neisser, U. (1976). Skills of divided attention. *Cognition,* **4,** 215–230.

Spence, K. W. (1956). *Behavior theory and conditioning.* New Haven, CT: Yale University Press.

Strube, M. J., Miles, M. E., & Finch, W. H. (1981). The social facilitation of a simple task: Field tests of alternative explanations. *Personality and Social Psychology Bulletin,* **7,** 701–707.

Taylor, J. A., & Rechtschaffen, A. (1959). Manifest anxiety and reversed alphabet printing. *Journal of Abnormal and Social Psychology,* **58,** 221–224.

Taylor, S. E., & Fiske, S. T. (1978). Salience, attention, and attribution: Top of the head phenomena. In L. Berkowitz (Ed.), *Advances in experimental social psychology* (Vol. 11, pp. 249–288). New York: Academic Press.

Tecce, J. J., & Cole, J. O. (1976). The distraction–arousal hypothesis, CNV, and schizophrenia. In D. I. Mostofsky (Ed.), *Behavior control and modification of physiological activity.* Engelwood Cliffs, NJ: Prentice-Hall.

Tecce, J. J., & Happ, S. J. (1964). Effects of shock-arousal on a card-sorting test of color–inferences. *Perceptual and Motor Skills,* **19,** 905–906.

Tecce, J. J., & Scheff, N. M. (1969). Attention reduction and suppressed direct-current potentials in the human brain. *Science, 164,* 331–333.

Thibaut, J. W., & Kelley, H. H. (1959). *The social psychology of groups.* New York: Wiley.

Triplett, N. (1898). The dynamogenic factors in pacemaking and competition. *Journal of Psychology, 9,* 507–533.

Underwood, G. (1974). Moray vs. the rest: The effect of extended shadowing practice. *Quarterly Journal of Experimental Psychology, 26,* 368–372.

White, J. D., & Carlston, D. E. (1983). Consequences of schemata for attention, impressions, and recall in complex social interactions. *Journal of Personality and Social Psychology, 45,* 538–549.

Woodhead, M. M. (1965). The effects of bursts of noise on an arithmetic task. *American Journal of Psychology, 77,* 627–633.

Woodworth, R. S., & Schlossberg, H. (1954). *Experimental psychology* (rev. ed.). New York: Holt.

Youngling, E. W. (1967). The effects of thermal environments and sleep deprivation upon concurrent central and peripheral tasks. *Dissertation Abstracts International, 1,* 348-B.

Zajonc, R. B. (1965). Social facilitation. *Science, 149,* 269–274.

Zajonc, R, B. (1980). Compresence. In P. B. Paulus (Ed.), *Psychology of group influence* (pp. 35–60). Hillsdale, NJ: Erlbaum.

Zuercher, J. D. (1965). The effects of extraneous stimulation on vigilance. *Human Factors, 7,* 101–105.

RECENT RESEARCH ON SELECTIVE EXPOSURE TO INFORMATION

Dieter Frey

DEPARTMENT OF PSYCHOLOGY
CHRISTIAN-ALBRECHTS-UNIVERSITY
KIEL, FEDERAL REPUBLIC OF GERMANY

I. Introduction

The term *selective exposure* implies several assumptions concerning the decision-making process. First, it assumes that the seeking out of decision-

41

Copyright © 1986 by Academic Press, Inc.
All rights of reproduction in any form reserved.

relevant information does not cease once a decision is made. Rather, this search continues during a postdecisional period during which the person confronts and weighs the various decision alternatives and their respective advantages and disadvantages. Second, this notion also implies that this postdecisional information seeking and evaluation is not impartial but, rather, is biased by certain factors activated during the decision-making process. The research discussed in this paper is concerned with determining the nature and source of these biasing factors.

To take a concrete example, suppose a person has committed himself to buying a certain house and afterwards becomes aware of additional pieces of information, some supportive and others nonsupportive of the decision he made. Some of his friends, for example, may tell him that the house is too expensive or too old, some may say that it is too ugly, and others that it is beautiful and nice. Assuming that our homeowner cannot revise his decision, and given the equal availability of information opposed to and supportive of his choice, a question arises as to which kind of information will he give greater attention?

There are at least three possibilities: (1) the homeowner may prove equally attentive to the two information types, (2) he may favor information supporting his choice (i.e., a confirmatory strategy), or, conversely, (3) he may favor information opposing it (disconfirmatory strategy). A fourth possibility is that he may pay no attention to either kind of decision-relevant information. Although logically each of these information-seeking strategies seems possible and plausible, social psychologists have shown a particular interest in the second one. The reason, of course, is that this is the reaction emphasized by Festinger's (1957) influential theory of cognitive dissonance.

According to dissonance theory, people prefer information that supports their decisions (hypotheses, beliefs, standpoints, etc.) and avoid information that contradicts these cognitions. In terms of our example, this means that the homeowner will search out information favorable to his new house and/or the deal he made and avoid information to the effect that he had "been had."

Selective exposure to information is a particularly suitable illustration of the active, creative processes implied by many discussions of this phenomenon (e.g., Lowin, 1969). Assume for a moment that a person is in a state of tension regarding a recent decision about a future profession. Information telling this person that he has chosen wrongly clearly blocks the reduction of the tension state. Which kind of thinking might the person then engage in? According to cognitive dissonance theory, one can assume that the person constructs his cognitions to support the decision and to further his goal-directed activity. That is, the person would refuse information that contradicts the chosen course. Such situations were observed in most of the new experiments described later in detail.

Research on selective exposure is one of the classic testing grounds for dissonance theory. It is of special interest because, unlike other dissonance-implied research areas (e.g., forced compliance or postdecisional dissonance), the simple predictions outlined above concerning selective exposure effects have met with rather shaky empirical support. Indeed, up to 1965 research on selective exposure seemed so discouraging for dissonance theory that Freedman and Sears (1965) concluded that dissonance theory was inapplicable to selective exposure phenomena. That this conclusion was widely accepted at the time led to an eventual loss of interest in selective exposure research (for further reviews of the earlier research on selective exposure see Mills, 1968; Sears, 1968; Sears & Abeles, 1969; McGuire, 1968; Katz, 1968).

Freedman and Sears's (1965) pessimism should not, however, prevent us from redirecting our attention to selective exposure phenomena, especially since Festinger's subsequent revision of dissonance theory (Festinger, 1964) provides a basis for deriving new predictions concerning selective exposure phenomena. Furthermore, methodologically improved experiments have generated results that are more supportive of dissonance theory than the earlier investigations. In short, the time seems ripe for a renewed overview of selective exposure research, one that takes up where Freedman and Sears (1965) left off, and that is open to the possibility of reaching completely different conclusions.

I will begin by briefly discussing the fundamental theses of dissonance theory as it relates to selective exposure and giving a short overview regarding the early research. Then I shall briefly discuss the controversy raised by Freedman and Sears (1965). Then, in Section III, I will describe new research including our own experiments designed to specify those factors most important in influencing informational selectivity: the effects of choice and commitment on selective information seeking, selectivity and refutability of arguments, the amount of available information and its usefulness, the usefulness of decision reversibility, as well as the intensity of dissonance. Finally, results on some additional variables—cost of information, reliability of dissonant information, and the effects of personality—are reported.

II. Early Research and Theory

A. THE THEORY OF COGNITIVE DISSONANCE: HYPOTHESES CONCERNING SELECTIVE EXPOSURE IN FESTINGER'S (1957) VERSION

In this section the fundamentals of dissonance theory will be covered, only to the extent that it is necessary for our present purposes. (For recent overviews see Frey, 1978a; Frey, Irle, Möntmann, Kumpf, Ochsmann, & Sauer, 1982; Irle & Möntmann, 1978; Wicklund & Brehm, 1976.)

According to Festinger (1957), cognitive dissonance exists when two cognitions have opposing implications for behavior. Dissonance exists, for example, when a person has made a decision, because the negative aspects of the chosen alternative are incompatible with having chosen it, while the positive aspects of the nonchosen alternative are inconsistent with having passed it up. Since dissonance is considered to be a negative drive state, an individual will be driven to reduce it whenever it is aroused, with the intensity of the drive varying positively with the intensity of dissonance. The intensity of dissonance depends on the relative proportion of dissonant and consonant cognitions in the person's cognitive system as well as on the cognitions' relative importance. Dissonance can be reduced by the addition of new consonant cognitions, by elimination of dissonant cognitions, or by a combination of the two.

Reduction of cognitive dissonance following a decision can be attained by selectively looking for decision-consonant information and avoiding contradictory information. This search can occur either within the cognitive system (memory, etc.) or outside of it. In all cases, the objective is to reduce the discrepancy between the cognitions, but the specification of which strategy will be chosen (i.e., under which condition subjects utilize their own cognitions and when they will go "outside" to get additional information) is not explicitly addressed by dissonance theory. One can assume, however, that people will choose that strategy which most perfectly guarantees a reduction of the experienced dissonance. This may depend mostly on the quantity and quality of the information available inside and outside the cognitive system.

Early research on selective exposure dealt primarily with the search for *new* information from the external environment. The general hypothesis was that the search should differ according to whether it occurs before or after the commitment is made. Prior to a decision, people should be relatively unbiased in their seeking and evaluation of information. Once the decision has been made, however, selectivity sets in: People search for decision-supporting (consonant) information and avoid decision-contrary (dissonant) information. This same bias is evident as well in the manner in which people evaluate the information found: Items of information that support the decision are often considered to be more credible and reliable than contrary information (cf. Grabitz & Grabitz-Gniech, 1972; Kozielecki, 1966).

As an additional hypothesis not strictly derived from the main part of the theory, Festinger (1957, p. 131) argued that these selective tendencies will diminish as the amount of dissonance approaches a maximum. There is a sort of ceiling effect here where, after a given point, the person considers it to be more effective to revise rather than retain his original decision, and therefore prefers information arguing against the original decision.

For reversible decisions, then, Festinger postulated a curvilinear relationship between the strength of cognitive dissonance and the tendency to selectively search for and avoid information. Dissonance reduction via selectivity is presumably most pronounced at moderate levels of dissonance.

Within the area of postdecisional effects, there is an important difference between evaluative change (which was measured in most dissonance research, i.e., attitude change, change in cognitions) and selective exposure effects. Evaluative change does not demand any new behavior or learning experiences of the individual; the dissonance reduction processes are generated from within. Selective exposure, on the other hand, does require additional behavior. In this case, the person is called upon to delve into previously unexplored information; to obtain, evaluate, react to, and perhaps even to learn this information. In short, dissonance reduction via selective exposure necessitates a considerable buildup of relevant cognitions by drawing selectively upon the environment, whereas evaluative change necessitates nothing but a change in one's own cognitions.

Given that selective exposure typically requires additional behavior, factors other than the existence of cognitive dissonance will have an impact on exposure. This is because the behavior to be performed (exposure) is unfamiliar and is subject to whatever influences are normally present when someone is about to move in a previously unexplored direction. Then, too, an individual must react to possibly threatening stimuli, and make decisions about dealing with these new events. Evaluative change as a mode of dissonance reduction, on the other hand, may also have multiple determinants, but the problem is not of an imposing quality. This is primarily because evaluative change comes entirely from within the person and is a function of relevant cognitions already in his possession.

B.   SHORT REVIEW OF SELECTIVE EXPOSURE RESEARCH
     PRIOR TO 1965

Freedman and Sears's (1965) above-mentioned pessimism concerning dissonance theory's relevance for selective exposure is based on their assessment of research using two basic paradigms. In this section we will briefly consider each of these paradigms and the results that led Freedman and Sears to their conclusions.

1. *Failure to Find Selective Exposure Effects:*
   Feather and Brock's Research Program about
   the Selectivity of Information by Smokers
   and Nonsmokers

Feather (1962, 1963) and Brock (1965) investigated whether smokers, as compared to nonsmokers, look more intensely for information that casts doubt on the relationship between smoking and lung cancer, and less for information that corroborates this smoking–cancer relationship. In two separate studies, Feather (1962, 1963) found that smokers were more interested (according to desirability ratings) in articles both consistent and inconsistent with their continued smoking than were nonsmokers. However, Feather (1963) did not find (as Feather, 1962, did) that, in the smoker group, information which denied the relationship between smoking and cancer was preferred to information that corroborated such a linkage.

Brock (1965) partly replicated the experiments by Feather (1962, 1963). As a dependent variable, he let his subjects rank order their degree of interest in reading pro-smoking and contra-smoking information (described by the titles of articles). One group of subjects was told explicitly that they had to read the article they ranked first (required exposure condition), while the other subjects did not get such explicit information (no required exposure condition). Under the latter condition (which had also been used by Feather, 1962, 1963) there was no difference between smokers and nonsmokers regarding their interest in reading material expressing either point of view. In contrast to this result, smokers in the required exposure condition preferred information that denied the relationship. Neither experiment clearly demonstrated, however, that smokers had a stronger tendency to *avoid* information that argued in favor of a connection between smoking and cancer. It should be noted, however, that the measure of avoidance in these experiments is derived indirectly from the preference ratings: Subjects were not asked (either in these or in later experiments) which articles they would actually avoid.

2. Failure to Find Selective Exposure
for Consonant Information: The Research
Program of Sears and Freedman

In nearly all of the Sears and Freedman studies, information seeking was operationalized by having subjects choose one of two possible items of information (one consonant and one dissonant). For example, Freedman's (1965a) subjects heard an interview with a fellow student who had applied for a job. Some of the subjects heard a very good evaluation of this person, while other students listened to a very bad assessment. All subjects then had to decide whether it was justified that the student got the job. Finally, subjects had the opportunity to read one of two evaluations that other persons had written about the job applicant, one agreeing with the subject, the other disagreeing. Contrary to what one would predict on the basis of dissonance theory, Freedman found a clear preference for dissonant information.

In a similar study, Sears (1965) had subjects play the role of a judge and decide whether a person was guilty or not guilty. After their decision, the subjects were given a chance to receive information that either supported or did not support their decision. There was a strong preference for the nonsupporting information.

From the results of these and other experiments Freedman and Sears (1965) concluded that dissonance theory does not apply to selective exposure phenomena. Because of a lack of further research in this field, social psychologists generally accepted this conclusion. As a consequence, very few articles were published in this field after the article of Freedman and Sears (1965) appeared in the *Advances* series. All of the studies mentioned up to now undoubtedly established limits to the general validity of the predictions derived from Festinger's (1957) version of dissonance theory.

C. FESTINGER'S (1964) VERSION OF DISSONANCE THEORY

Developments in the area of dissonance theory—especially in the forced compliance area—have revealed two necessary preconditions for the existence of dissonance: Choice and commitment (see Brehm and Cohen, 1962). Although there has not been much research on the role of these two variables in selective exposure, it seems probable that their influence is important. Neglect of these variables can help explain the failure to find selective exposure effects in experiments. Festinger's (1964) version of dissonance theory is even more important for selective exposure.

In his revised version of dissonance theory, Festinger (1964) argued that dissonant information is not always avoided and consonant information is not always preferred. He specified the following conditions under which dissonant information is presumably desired.

1. *When dissonant information is perceived as easily refutable.* If a person feels confident that the incoming belief-contradictory information can easily be refuted or resisted, he may actually seek out such information in order to reduce whatever dissonance exists by means of counterarguments. If, on the other hand, the person thinks the dissonance-producing information cannot be defended against so easily, such dissonant information will be avoided. Thus, the decisive factor here is the person's confidence in his ability to refute the dissonant information.

2. *When the dissonant information is useful for future decisions.* If a person believes that ignoring the dissonant information could result in bad future decisions and therefore produce in the long run an even greater amount of cognitive dissonance, he will not avoid, and may even seek out, this information.

3. Also not explicitly, though implicitly, it is assumed that *under states of high dissonance and when revision of the decision is possible,* dissonant information is preferred. Although Festinger (1964) did not emphasize the curvilinear

relationship between amount of cognitive dissonance and information seeking, this last point is readily derivable from dissonance theory once an ad hoc assumption is made that at high dissonance levels people ultimately decide to reverse their first decision and want information that would help them change their mind and thus lessen their unpleasant dissonance.

Festinger thus postulated in his revision that the consistency of a cognitive system can be maintained by avoidance (avoid-only strategy) or by seeking and counterarguing against dissonant information (approach–avoid strategy). Both strategies are based on the assumption of an ability to refute the incoming information. The probability of avoid-only strategies being used is greater the more difficult it is to argue against the dissonant information. "Approach–avoid" strategies, however, are more likely to be used the easier it is to counter the dissonant information. [1]

To summarize, there seem to be two fundamental positions with regard to the selectivity of *postdecisional* information seeking.

1. Freedman and Sears (1965) maintained that such selectivity seldom (if ever) occurs, and if it does that it can be traced back to mediating mechanisms other than those postulated by dissonance theory (e.g., defacto selectivity).

2. On the other hand, Festinger stressed (1957, 1964) that people avoid dissonant and/or approach consonant information after having made a decision. But he also added that if people consider the dissonant information useful for other purposes, such as for regarding decision revision or future decisions, and/or if they are confident of being able to refute the dissonant information, they will search out or at least not avoid this kind of information.

In the following sections we will discuss in more detail the empirical evidence relevant to these two positions.

D. INTERPRETATIONS OF THE EARLY RESEARCH WITHIN THE 1964 VERSION OF DISSONANCE THEORY

From the perspective of the revised formulation of dissonance theory, Feather's and Brock's failure to support the original dissonance predictions with smokers and nonsmokers may have been due to smokers actually wanting infor-

---

[1]Of course, Festinger (1957) did not deny that such factors as curiosity or intellectual fairness play an important role in information seeking; however, he neglects these factors in his analysis, because he is interested mainly in dissonance effects.

mation about the relationship between smoking and lung cancer in order to be able to refute it. Indeed, this possibility is in line with another of Feather's (1963) results. He found that smokers were more apt to deny the validity of information that emphasized the relationship between smoking and lung cancer than non-smokers were. Additionally, smokers in the Brock experiment (1965) may have considered it useful to expose themselves to dissonant information in order to test how convincing these arguments are.

The results obtained by Mills, Aronson, and Robinson (1959) and by Rosen (1961) can also be reinterpreted in terms of the revised dissonance theory notions regarding counterarguments. In these experiments dissonance was produced by having college students decide whether they preferred essay exams or multiple choice tests in their courses before they selected articles about each type of exam. The students had had experience with both kinds of examinations and had knowledge (and therefore some self-confidence) about their performance. It was then easy for them to argue in their minds against the dissonant information, and they therefore weren't selective in which articles they wanted to read.

The 1964 version of dissonance theory can also account for the findings from the Sears and Freedman research. In the study of Freedman (1965a), for example, it was found as mentioned above that subjects always preferred the dissonant to the consonant information after deciding whether a student should get a job or not. From the content of the experimental story, however, one can argue that subjects may *have been so confident* in the validity of their judgments (the job interviews that they heard being clearly favorable or unfavorable) that they tried to reduce their dissonance by seeking out and counterarguing against the dissonant article. (In addition, the existence of an evaluation that was incongruent with their own would not have been at all dissonance arousing but would have rather aroused their curiosity for the other side as well as the salience of a fairness norm.)

The same reasoning applies to Sears (1965). In his study, subjects were to decide whether a person was innocent or guilty after having heard a very one-sided story. Of course the one-sided story produced a decision in line with the story, however, subjects always preferred the dissonant information. The reason for this result (counter to dissonance theory) may be quite simple: Because the report of the subjects' innocence or guilt was so one-sided the subjects felt confident and could therefore expose themselves to counter-information. Again there was a strong norm for "fairness" in trial settings that would have contributed to the subjects' readiness to hear dissenting opinions. Besides the confidence and the fairness norm argument, in most experiments by Sears and Freedman one can assume that the resulting dissonance was only minimal because the decision had nearly no consequence for the subjects (see also Wicklund & Brehm, 1976).

III. Research after 1965

Despite the pessimistic conclusion offered by Freedman and Sears (1965), research on selective exposure continued slowly over the next years. Much of this research sought to isolate the conditions under which selective exposure effects may occur. In the following, this research will be integrated into the reformulated theory of cognitive dissonance. First, the relevance of the factors choice and commitment is discussed as mentioned by Brehm and Cohen's (1962) version of dissonance theory. Then we will discuss research in which the central variables relevant for the newly reformulated theory of cognitive dissonance are tested. The relevance of new research for dissonant theory is especially highlighted and discussed. It should be emphasized, however, that most of the research since 1965 has concentrated mainly on selective *seeking* rather than avoiding.

A. THE EFFECT OF CHOICE ON SELECTIVE
    INFORMATION SEEKING

It has been found consistently in research on evaluative change within the framework of dissonance theory that subjects who engage in some activity opposed to their beliefs are much more likely to display dissonance reduction effects when they have freely (or relatively freely) chosen this activity (e.g., Cohen & Latané, 1962; Cohen, Terry, & Jones, 1959; Frey & Irle, 1972; Frey, Irle, & Hochgürtel, 1979; Linder, Cooper, & Jones, 1967; Sogin & Pallak, 1976; Zanna & Cooper, 1974) than when they were forced to do so. Frey and Wicklund (1978) hypothesized that selective exposure to supportive information and the concomitant avoidance of nonsupportive information would take place primarily after the subjects were given freedom of choice. To test these hypotheses the following experiment was conducted. As in numerous other forced-compliance experiments, subjects were asked to perform a dull task (writing random numbers) under high or low choice conditions. High-choice subjects were told that it was completely up to them to do this assignment whereas low-choice subjects heard that doing the task was part of the experiment. After subjects had worked at the task, they received a list of titles of articles, each supposedly one page long. Half of the titles appeared supportive of the choice to write random numbers, and the other half appeared nonsupportive.

In general, the effect of choice was clearly in the predicted direction: Subjects' preference for supportive over nonsupportive articles was higher under the choice than under the no-choice condition. In one condition subjects were asked not only which three items they wanted, but also which three they definitely did not want. If there had been an active avoidance process, choice subjects should have shown a particularly strong aversion to nonsupportive information, and, indeed, choice subjects did exhibit a stronger avoidance tendency than no-choice subjects. In a replication of the Frey and Wicklund (1978) experiment, Cotton and Hieser (1980) also found that high-choice subjects desired consonant information more and dissonant information less than did low-choice subjects. Thus, both studies demonstrate that when one takes a traditional dissonance paradigm and manipulates the person's choice to engage in the belief-incompatible activity (a factor first proposed by Brehm & Cohen, 1962, and accepted by Festinger, 1964, as a necessary condition for dissonance arousal), then a clear selective exposure effect exists.

B. THE EFFECTS OF COMMITMENT

According to both Brehm and Cohen (1962) and Festinger (1964) cognitive dissonance arises only when there is a high degree of commitment to one of the opposing cognitions. Selective exposure effects should therefore be strongest when subjects are committed to a certain decision or position. There are several experiments in which subjects' commitment was manipulated and their selective preference for information was tested.

In an experiment by Brock and Balloun (1967), committed church-goers were confronted with audiotaped information that supported the value system about church and religion, or with information that did not support this value system. The communication was "mixed" with white noise, which the subjects could eliminate from the message by pressing a button.[2] It was found that subjects clarified the communication more when it was consistent with their commitment than when it was inconsistent. Brock and Balloun (1967) replicated this with smokers and nonsmokers, finding that smokers clarified the pro-smoking communication more, whereas nonsmokers showed a stronger tendency to clarify the anti-smoking communication. These results demonstrate how people will expend effort to invest, maintain, or restore cognitive consonance.

In an investigation by Sweeney and Gruber (1984), the selective exposure hypothesis was also tested using the natural issues surrounding the Watergate affair. Subjects who were committed (a) Nixon supporters, (b) McGovern supporters, or (c) who were Undecided in their preferences participated in the survey. Answers to questions that proved subjects' interest in and attention to Watergate-related matters gave support to the selective exposure hypotheses: Relative to the McGovern supporters and Undecideds, Nixon supporters reported less interest in and paid less attention to Watergate-related matters. Also, the

---

[2]Thus, Brock and Balloun (1967) tested the selectivity hypothesis by measuring subject's *actual* exposure to consonant and dissonant information, instead of indicating which of the available information they wanted to read.

Nixon supporters appeared to know less about the committee proceedings than the Undecideds and McGovern supporters.

In an experiment by Schwarz, Frey, and Kumpf (1980) the commitment variable was manipulated under full experimental control. Subjects in the high-commitment condition wrote an essay on an issue which they generally favored (the introduction of a mandatory social service year for women), while low-commitment subjects wrote an essay on an irrelevant topic. There also was a control group who didn't write any essay but only indicated their attitude toward the year of social service. Subjects' interest in information was measured by their preference for further information opposing and supporting this proposal. The results are in accord with expectations: Subjects who wrote the supporting essay (that is, the high-commitment subjects) were more selective in wanting favorable information than subjects who wrote an irrelevant essay (low-commitment subjects), while control group subjects showed an equal preference for both kinds of information.

A second experiment by Frey and Stahlberg (1986) also tested the effects of commitment on information preference. Subjects making a behavioral commitment (counter to their existing attitude regarding the legalization of marijuana) were compared with a control group who only indicated their attitude on the issue of legalizing marijuana (which was negative). Afterwards subjects could choose pro and contra articles on this topic. Whereas control group subjects showed no differential preference, there was a clear bias in the preferences for behavior-supporting information when subjects had made a behavioral commitment. Under these conditions, subjects clearly preferred pro-legalization arguments compared to contra-legalization arguments in order to justify their behavior commitment.

C. SELECTIVITY AND REFUTABILITY OF ARGUMENTS

According to Festinger (1964), there are two possible ways to justify a decision: The addition of new, consonant elements to the pool of available decision-relevant information and the refutation of already available dissonant elements. The refutation of dissonant information can be a more effective strategy (1) when a person anticipates that the dissonant information is easy to refute, (2) when it is attributed to a source of low competence and low credibility, and (3) when a person has high decision certainty and/or a lot of decision-supporting information. Research touching upon each of these three eventualities will be discussed in the following.

1. Weak versus Strong Arguments

A field study by Lowin (1967) tested the effect of argument strength on selective exposure. During the 1964 United States presidential election, subjects preferring either Johnson or Goldwater were confronted with either weak (relatively unconvincing) or strong (plausible and convincing) statements attributed to either candidate. Consonant information was provided by positive statements about the preferred candidate, dissonant information was provided by negative statements, while strength was varied according to the convincingness of the arguments as rated by judges. Four conditions were established this way: (1) weak consonant–weak dissonant; (2) strong consonant–strong dissonant; (3) weak dissonant–strong consonant; or (4) strong dissonant–weak consonant information. Weak consonant or dissonant information should be seen as not very reliable and therefore easy to refute, whereas strong information should be perceived as much more reliable and therefore harder to refute. The four groups of subjects received letters stating the titles of two brochures that were available to them. This material varied in type (consonant/dissonant) of information and strength (strong/weak) of argument. The subjects were then asked to choose between the brochures.

The question was whether the percentage of subjects who chose consonant information would be different among the four groups. The results were as follows: (1) weak dissonant information was preferred at the same rate as strong, consonant information. (2) Interest in brochures with strongly positive arguments for the preferred presidential candidate (consonant information) was far greater than the interest in corresponding strongly positive material about the opposing candidate. (3) The interest in strongly negative arguments about the opposing candidate was greater than the interest in strongly negative arguments about the preferred candidate.

The results thus show that despite an overall preference for consonant information, weak dissonant information was also highly favored, a result that can be explained by dissonance theory if one assumes that subjects expected to be able to argue against the weak dissonant information in their minds.

Kleinhesselink and Edwards (1975) investigated the effect of the refutability of consonant and dissonant information of selective exposure using the Brock and Balloun "de-jamming" paradigm described above. In this study subjects were strongly committed to an anti-marijuana attitude. They were then confronted with attitude-discrepant or attitude-convergent communications about the legalization of marijuana and were told that the arguments were either easy or difficult to refute. Kleinhesselink and Edwards found that subjects clarified the message more often when the difficult-to-refute arguments were supportive instead of nonsupportive. However, when the arguments were easily refutable (weak supportive and weak nonsupportive), subjects clarified the nonsupportive information more than the supportive. These results together with those of Lowin (1967) support the refutability notion. Subjects in general prefer supportive information—but when dissonant information is weak, it is chosen with comparable frequency to strong supportive information.

2. Competence of the Source

Another way to operationalize refutability of an argument is to attribute the arguments to a source of high or low credibility. This was first done in a study by Lowin (1969), in which the hypothesis tested again was that persons would prefer dissonant information that is perceived as being easily refutable (i.e., that comes from a low-competence source) to consonant information.

Lowin used the same procedure as that followed by Canon (1964) and Freedman (1965b). Subjects were first asked to make decisions concerning five case studies and were then given the "correct" decision after each choice. They also were asked to justify the decision they had made by writing an essay. After this was done, they were given the opportunity to read either supportive or nonsupportive articles to assist them in their task, the articles being attributed to either high- or low-competence authors.

Lowin's predictions concerning refutability were confirmed: Dissonant information was preferred when the source of information was low in credibility. For a highly credible source, however, consonant information was preferred.

Lowin's design contained only two out of four possible combinations of the two factors, source competence and information type, thus ruling out the possibility of detecting any interaction between them. Frey (1981a) reported two studies designed to eliminate this problem. In one of these studies (Frey, 1981a, Experiment 2), subjects were asked to choose their profession six months before graduation from high school. (Needless to say, this was a decision of far more personal importance than those used in other experiments.) One week later, subjects received five positive and five negative pieces of information about their chosen profession, which were again attributed to either high- or low-competence sources (career advisers or laymen), and were asked to indicate how much they were interested in reading the articles.

The results of this experiment (see Table 1) are very similar to those obtained by Lowin (1969). Greater selective exposure was found when both sources' credibility was high than when it was low. In addition, dissonant information coming from a highly competent source was preferred to consonant information from a low-competence source. This effect is easily explained when one considers that the choice of a profession was still reversible and it may have therefore been useful in the long run to have highly competent advice regardless of its direction. However, the influence of competence was far greater for consonant than for dissonant information, thus suggesting that the present findings, as well as those of Lowin's (1969), are due exclusively to the effect of the competence of the source on the preference for decision-supporting information.

In Experiment 1, Frey (1981a) used a different decision situation, one similar to the approach used by Canon (1964), Freedman (1965b), and Lowin (1969). Once their decison was made, subjects rated how much they wanted to

TABLE I

MEAN READING DESIRABILITY OF DECISION-SUPPORTING AND
DECISION-OPPOSING INFORMATION[a,b]

	Competence of decision-opposing information source	
	High	Low
A. Desirability of decision-supporting information		
High-competence source of decision-supporting information	7.47	7.33
Low-competence source of decision-supporting information	6.29	7.14
B. Desirability of decision-opposing information		
High-competence source of decision-supporting information	5.04	4.44
Low-competence source of decision-supporting information	6.34	6.12
C. Difference (A − B)		
High-competence source of decision-supporting information	+2.43	+2.89
Low-competence source of decision-supporting information	−0.05	+1.02

[a]From Frey (1981a, Experiment 2).
[b]The higher the score the higher the reading desirability (score could vary from 0 to 10).

read each of six pieces of information (three decision supporting and three decision opposing) (Table II). Again it was found that preferences for decision-supporting over decision-opposing information were greater when sources of both types of information were highly competent than when they were not. Also, the study showed that information was rated as generally more desirable if it supported the prior decision than if it opposed this decision. This difference was much greater when the competence of the source of the supporting information was high than when it was low. Source competence for decision-opposing information, on the other hand, had little effect. Again, the only cell in which there was a preference for dissonant over consonant information was in the condition in which the competence of the source of dissonant information was high and the competence of the source of consonant information was low.

Both experiments reported above demonstrate that source competence does have an effect on the selective exposure paradigm and that this variable's influence is most marked for decision-supporting information. One explanation may be the following: Subjects who are interested in obtaining information that is useful to them in supporting a decision to which they are committed may initially

TABLE II

Mean Reading Desirability of Decision-Supporting and
Decision-Opposing Information[a,b]

	Competence of decision-opposing information source	
	High	Low
A. Desirability of decision-supporting information		
High-competence source of decision-supporting information	88.66	77.31
Low-competence source of decision-supporting information	60.75	67.22
B. Desirability of decision-opposing information		
High-competence source of decision-supporting information	44.81	57.29
Low-competence source of decision-supporting information	66.75	61.15
C. Difference (A − B)		
High-competence source of decision-supporting information	+43.85	+20.01
Low-competence source of decision-supporting information	−6.00	+6.06

[a]From Frey (1981a, Experiment 1).
[b]The higher the score the higher the reading desirability (score could vary from 0 to 120).

prefer supportive (consonant) information. If the supportive information available to them comes from a highly credible source, they decide it *is* in fact useful in reducing their cognitive dissonance and so they express a strong desire to read it and a low desire to read opposing information, regardless of the source of this latter information. If, however, the supportive information comes from a low-credibility source, and is therefore not assumed to be useful, subjects may reject this information (express low desire to read it), and thus increase their preference for opposing information by default, perhaps hoping that they can refute it regardless of the nature of its source.

The results thus suggest a relatively rational information-seeking process oriented toward the usefulness of the information for dissonance reduction, with the limitation that consonant information has a certain "credibility credit." In the first experiment, for example, such an approach on the part of the subjects would have been particularly sensible, since they could revise their decisions. In short, it seems that subjects show selective preference for information that supports their decision in the sense of being in the "right direction" and being trustworthy. Noncredible information in accord with their decision does not fulfill this double requirement (and in fact, may even undermine the decision), and thus elicits no selective preference.

3. Refutability and Stability of the Cognitive System

One can argue that the stability of the cognitive system depends on the number of consonant (decision-supporting) elements that it contains. Upon receiving decision-supporting information the number of these elements increases and the cognitive system becomes increasingly stable. A person with a *stable* cognitive system can expose himself more readily to dissonant information, with the possibility of arguing against this information in his mind. A cognitive system *destabilized* by the reception of dissonant, decision-opposing information would, on the other hand, stand in need of additional, consonant elements to "shore itself up." One might therefore expect selective exposure to be stronger following the reception of decision-opposing information than it is following the reception of decision-supporting information (see also Sears & Freedman, 1965).

It is also interesting to ask what happens when subjects receive *both* decision-supporting and decision-opposing information or receive no additional information after a decision. A study by Frey (1981a, Experiment 3) addressed this issue by allowing subjects access to different amounts of decision-supporting and/or -opposing information and then measuring their preferences for further information. In this study subjects first made a decision about whether or not the contract of a manager should be extended. Afterward, they were confronted with either (1) two pieces of information supporting this decision; (2) two pieces of information opposing this decision; (3) one supporting and one opposing piece of information; or (4) no information. They then could choose either (in one condition) 3 or (in another condition) an unlimited number of additional pieces of information from a pool of 10 pieces of information, 5 of which supported their decision and 5 of which opposed it.

The results show, in line with earlier research, that subjects who received consonant (decision-supporting) information subsequently preferred dissonant over consonant information. This finding is in line with Berlyne's (1960, 1968) contention that people are drawn to stimuli that represent moderate levels of novelty. However, subjects who had previously received information on both sides of the issue or no information at all subsequently exhibited a clear preference for consonant over dissonant information, the effect being strongest in the no-information condition.

The Schwarz *et al.* (1980) experiment mentioned in Section III,B is also relevant here. Besides varying the subjects' commitment, another variable was manipulated in that study. After writing the essay, subjects read an article that either supported or opposed their own expressed decision concerning the desirability of a social service year for women. The results are in accord with expectations: Subjects who had read an opposing (dissonant) essay were more selective than those who had read a supportive essay. One can assume that dissonance is highest when subjects are committed to their own position and receive an opposing essay, and that the selectively seeking out of consonant information is a means for reducing it. Under low commitment, however, dissonance will be less pronounced and hence the need for selective information seeking lower.

On the whole, the results of both experiments show that subjects who encounter consonant material after they make a decision show a relatively weak tendency to seek out further consonant information. They are certain about the correctness of their decision and thus are willing to expose themselves to information opposing their decision.

D.   THE AMOUNT OF INFORMATION FROM WHICH
TO CHOOSE

As already mentioned, there are two strategies for dealing with dissonant information. Theoretically, the number of available pieces of selective information plays a role in deciding upon one strategy or the other. With *one* piece of dissonant information the subject can eliminate all dissonant information by selecting and refuting it. However, when more dissonant information exists, selection and refutation of only one aspect of the information have no effect because other (unrefuted) dissonant information remains. Therefore, in this case, it makes more sense to look for consonant information. Frey (1985) reported four experiments investigating the effect of the amount of available information on selective exposure. Subjects had to make a decision on some issue, for example, as to whether a fictitious manager's contract ought to be renewed or not, or whether or not a certain industrial concern should invest in a developing country. Before the subjects decided, they received items of information in which the advantages of the respective decision alternatives were discussed. *After* the decision had been made, the subjects could request *one* item from a pool of decision-supporting and decision-contrary information. This pool consisted either of 10 items (5 supporting and 5 contrary) or 2 items (1 supporting and 1 contrary).

The results of the four experiments were very similar. Under the low availability of information (two items) condition, 40–50% of the subjects chose the consonant information. In the 10-item conditions, on the other hand, between 80 and 95% of the subjects chose the consonant information exclusively. Besides the decision to select dissonant or consonant information, in addition, subjects in all experiments had to state on 10-point scales how much they would be interested in reading each item. This measure also showed that the preference for consonant over dissonant information was greater in the high-availability (10 items) condition than in low-availability (2 items) conditions.

A possible explanation for these findings is that a person who has to choose between only one piece of consonant and one piece of dissonant information will choose the dissonant one because all the existing dissonance can be eliminated by arguing against and refuting this one piece of information. When, however, there are a great number of dissonant elements available, refuting only one will do little in the way of dissonance reduction, because unrefuted, dissonant information will remain. Another possible explanation is that the greater is the availability of dissonant information, the stronger is the person's uncertainty about the correctness of his/her decision, and, therefore, the greater will be the need for additional consonant information. Either explanation, however, has the selective exposure effect increasing with the general availability of information.

E. USEFULNESS OF INFORMATION

In the Frey (1981a) experiments discussed above (Section III,C,2), it was found that dissonant information from a highly credible source was favored over decision-consonant information from a low-credibility source. This reversal of selective exposure is understandable when one considers that the subjects were students who anticipated being able to modify their decision after having read the information in question. In this situation, information from a highly "credible" source, whatever its orientation, would be more useful than information from a source in whom one could have little confidence.

It should be noted that "usefulness" is one of the central variables in Festinger's (1964) reformulated theory of cognitive dissonance, and is relevant to the notion of a *long-term* avoidance of cognitive dissonance. To avoid cognitive dissonance in the long run, it is often best to deliberately expose oneself to dissonant information, especially when a decision revision in the near future is possible and when further similar decisions are anticipated.

The first experiment in which "usefulness" was explicitly introduced as a factor was carried out by Canon (1964) and replicated with slight modifications by Freedman (1965b). Canon's subjects were given five business problems with two possible solutions each. Their task was to indicate which solution they thought to be the right one. For the key, fifth problem, subjects were told either that they would have to defend their decision later in a debate, or that they would have to write an essay defending their position.

After this decision, however, and before they engaged in this justification, subjects were given an opportunity to read two or three articles from a set of five (two pro, two contra, one neutral) that commented on the problem at hand. The

title of each article indicated which side of the problem the given article advocated.

Canon (1964) predicted that subjects who anticipated the debate would
prefer dissonant arguments, while those anticipating having to write an essay
would prefer consonant ones. The reason for this—although not explicitly stated
in these terms by Canon (1964)—was that in order to give a good self-presentation, it is helpful to know the dissonant arguments in advance of the debate, in
order to be familiar with them in the discussion. On the other hand, if an essay is
to be written, it is more useful to have more supporting information so that it
would be easier to justify the decision that had been taken.

The results confirmed the predictions: Subjects who expected to have to
defend their standpoint in a discussion were more likely to prefer dissonant
information, whereas subjects who only expected to write an explanation for
their decisions were more likely to prefer consonant information.

A study by Freedman (1965b) varied usefulness over three levels: In the
"consonant more useful" condition, subjects were to justify their decisions in
written essays; in the "dissonant more useful" condition, they expected to be
confronted with a number of opposing arguments that they would have to refute
in writing; and in the condition "consonant and dissonant useful" the subjects
only had to give their opinion of decisions made by others. Freedman's results
(1965b) supported the prediction that the selectivity of information seeking varied with its usefulness.

F. USEFULNESS FOR DECISION REVERSIBILITY

The discussion in the preceding sections suggests that a decision's reversibility is an important determinant of selectivity in subsequent information
seeking. Subjects are presumably more open to dissonant information following
reversible than irreversible decisions. For reversible decisions, revising the decision is one way of reducing dissonance, and dissonant information can be useful
in reevaluating one's conclusion. Yet, revision of a previously made decision
should occur only when dissonance is high. Under low-dissonance conditions,
selective exposure should still occur.

A study by Frey (1981b) tested the effect of decision reversibility. In this
experiment a standard paradigm (cf. Brehm, 1956; Greenwald, 1969) was used
in which subjects first had to rank order a series of decision alternatives (books)
and then make a choice, either reversible or irreversible, between two of the
alternatives designated by the experimenter.

In order to manipulate the amount of aroused dissonance independently of
the reversibility factor, a second independent variable was introduced in the
design: Similarity of attractiveness of alternatives. In the "high similarity"

condition, subjects chose between alternatives that they had ranked second and third, while "moderate similarity" was introduced by giving subjects a choice between the second and seventh ranked alternatives and "low similarity" by a choice between the second and thirteenth.

Once subjects had made their choice, the experimenter told them that he had collected some pertinent articles regarding the books from magazines, newspapers, and scientific journals which they could read. There were 12 brief articles per book, 6 positive and 6 negative. The subjects were asked to indicate which 3 articles they wanted to read regarding the chosen book and, after that, the 3 comments (out of 12) they wanted to read regarding the nonchosen alternative. In addition, they were asked to indicate which three articles concerning the chosen and nonchosen alternatives they wouldn't care to read at all. The results are shown in Table III.

As predicted, subjects showed a stronger preference for decision-supporting information following irreversible decisions than they did following reversible ones, as one would expect if such information were useful for bolstering the decision to which they were committed. Also, as expected, the preference for decision-supporting information after an irreversible decision increased as the two decision alternatives became more similar. For reversible decisions, the predicted negative linear relationship was obtained: the more similar the decision alternatives, the *less* was the search for consonant information. As we reasoned above, the greater the similarity of the alternatives, the less certainty there should be about which is best and, hence, the greater the likelihood of decisional revision.

In another experiment (Frey & Rosch, 1984), besides the reversibility factor, the novelty of information was manipulated by telling subjects after they expressed a decision (whether or not to prolong a manager's contract) that the information from which they could select was either newer or older than the material they had previously seen in formulating their decision. The main dependent variables were the amount and kind of information chosen. As in the Frey (1981b) experiment described above, it was found (see Table IV) that preference

TABLE III

NUMBER OF POSITIVE COMMENTS ABOUT THE CHOSEN ALTERNATIVE[a]

	Similarity in attractiveness		
Reversibility of decision	High	Medium	Low
Irreversible	2.00	1.50	1.41
Reversible	1.13	1.23	1.67

[a]From Frey (1981b).

TABLE IV

INFORMATION SEEKING AS A FUNCTION OF INFORMATION FAMILIARITY AND DECISION REVERSIBILITY[a]

Decision	Old information				New information			
	Total[b]	Supportive[c]	Nonsupportive[c]	Difference[c]	Total[b]	Supportive[c]	Nonsupportive[c]	Difference[c]
Reversible	3.65	2.29	1.36	0.93	5.20	2.70	2.50	+0.20
Irreversible	4.25	2.60	1.65	0.95	4.84	3.19	1.65	+1.54

[a]From Frey and Rosch (1984).
[b]Total score could vary from 0 to 10 pieces of information.
[c]The score for each individual kind of information could vary from 0 to 5.

for consonant over dissonant information was greater following irreversible decisions than following reversible ones.

The results also showed an interaction between reversibility and information novelty: The selective exposure effect was greater following irreversible than reversible decisions when the information was new, but for old information, decision reversibility had no effect. This greater preference for new consonant over new dissonant information in the irreversible decision condition may be due to the fact that learning new things *opposing* an irreversible decision is especially dissonance arousing, while new consonant information could provide additional cognitive support. Following reversible decisions, on the other hand, subjects are not only less interested in stabilizing their prior decision but are also more willing to consider new decision-dissonant facts in order to possibly revise their earlier decisions. Thus, under new information conditions, utility considerations are relevant and can counter the dissonance-reduction processes.

In general, the results show that under irreversible conditions there is a considerable selective exposure effect, while under the reversible decision condition there is neither a bias in favor of decision-supporting information nor even a small preference for dissonant information. These findings can be seen as a conceptual replication of previous research. Studies by Frey (1981b) and Goethals and Cooper (1972) show that dissonance processes are not (or at least, less) invoked if the decision is not final or binding (see Frey, Kumpf, Irle, & Gniech, 1984; Wicklund & Brehm, 1976, for a review).

G. INTENSITY OF COGNITIVE DISSONANCE

Dissonance theory implies that selectivity should vary positively with the intensity of dissonance, at least up to the point where the dissonance exceeds the resistance to changing the decision and people begin to think about a decision revision. In this latter case, the search for consonant information should diminish, and people should begin searching for information supporting the opposing point of view. Thus, over the full range of possible dissonance intensity, the theory postulates a curvilinear relationship between dissonance and information selectivity, the latter reaching its peak at moderate levels of dissonance. Of course, a prerequisite here is that the decisions are reversible. For irreversible decisions positive linear effects can be expected, selectivity increasing with increasing dissonance.

The experiments presented so far in this article have shown that increased dissonance is paralleled by stronger selective exposure effects. None of these experiments, however, varied dissonance intensity over more than two levels. This is essentially also the case in nearly all the early studies (except Cohen, Brehm, & Latané, 1959; Festinger, 1957; Rhine, 1967) examining Festinger's original and revised versions of dissonance theory, thus rendering them inadequate for testing the hypothesized curvilinear relationship.

In what follows research is presented in which more than two levels of dissonance were established. Frey (1982) tested the curvilinear relationship between amount of dissonance and the seeking of consonant and avoidance of dissonant information. The procedure used was similar to those in the classical experiments of Festinger (1957) and Cohen, Brehm, and Latané (1959). After having chosen the role of a player A or B, subjects participated in a card game involving 30 trials in which they could win or lose money. As in the original Festinger experiment, it was assumed that the higher the loss in the card game, the greater the dissonance as a result of having chosen position A or B.

Following the twelfth trial, the experimenter told the subjects that there would be a short break in which the subject could read short essays written by players who had taken part in previous sessions of the experiment. The 12 essays either supported position A or B. Subjects were asked to indicate which three essays they wanted to read (information seeking) and which three they didn't want to read (information avoidance).

As predicted, the effect of amount of winning/losing was significant and supported the hypothesized curvilinear relationship between amount of dissonance (money lost or won) and the amount of consonant information sought over the whole win/lose distribution (see Table V). The amount of consonant information chosen was largest when subjects neither won nor lost a large amount of money.[3] Also as expected, measured decision certainty decreased and probability of revision increased with the amount of loss. The higher the probability of decision revision, the less consonant information was chosen and the less dissonant information was avoided.

In general, one can assume that two processes may be operating: A dissonance process that produces increasing search for consonant items, and a tendency to seek information that will help to make future decisions as to whether to change one's position. The latter tendency becomes stronger and the former inclination weaker as losses increase, leading to a net decrease in preference for consonant information. It is, of course, difficult to predict exactly at which point of the scale the search for consonant information decreases. For example, in the Festinger (1957) experiment, the greatest amount of selective information seeking occurred in the more extreme loss zones and not when subjects had either lost or won a lot of money. (However, other situational factors, e.g., the amount of money one must pay for changing sides, may determine the precise point at which the maximum selectivity occurs.)

[3]Concerning the avoidance of dissonant information, it was shown that more dissonant than consonant information was avoided in each experimental condition. Dissonant information was avoided the most when subjects had neither won nor lost money; however, the differences across gain and loss intervals were too small to reach statistical significance.

TABLE V

MEANS OF THE DEPENDENT VARIABLES[a]

Item	Gain zone			Loss zone		
	81–∞ pfennigs ($n = 24$)	41–80 pfennigs ($n = 10$)	1–40 pfennigs ($n = 15$)	0–40 pfennigs ($n = 24$)	41–80 pfennigs ($n = 22$)	81–∞ pfennigs ($n = 22$)
Number of consonant pieces of information chosen	1.54	1.40	2.00	1.67	1.27	1.09
Number of dissonant pieces of information avoided	1.64	1.70	1.87	1.88	1.64	1.70
Desirability ratings						
Consonant information						
Favoring chosen alternative	4.75	5.33	5.62	4.46	4.46	4.85
Opposing rejected alternative	3.71	4.63	4.73	3.75	4.22	3.40
M	4.23	4.88	4.88	4.11	4.01	4.13
Dissonant information						
Opposing chosen alternative	3.88	3.69	2.78	2.71	4.17	5.03
Favoring rejected alternative	3.71	4.64	4.57	4.05	4.21	4.63
M	3.48	4.16	3.66	3.38	4.13	4.83
Difference score	+.75	+.82	+1.31	+.73	−.18	−.70
Decision certainty ratings						
First measure	61.75	60.00	63.27	62.04	59.50	66.32
Second measure	69.93	62.00	64.66	49.13	50.00	43.91
Difference	8.18	2.44	1.40	−12.92	−9.50	−23.14
Probability of decision revision	15.00	25.00	31.33	25.79	38.96	52.74

[a]From Frey (1982).

Frey (1981c) further tested this same hypothesis using a different paradigm. In this experiment subjects were asked to estimate their own intelligence after they had taken an intelligence test but had not yet received the results (cf. Frey, 1978b). They then were provided with fictitious intelligence test results which were either 7, 15, 25, or 33 points less than the score the subjects believed they would obtain in the first session. Information seeking was measured by giving subjects the opportunity to choose among 10 articles, 5 containing arguments for the validity and 5 for the invalidity of intelligence tests, and having them indicate how much they wanted to read these articles.

According to the curvilinear hypothesis, one would expect an increasing amount of selective exposure with an increasing discrepancy from the expected score, at least up to a point of extreme discrepancy, where this tendency should decrease. Our reasoning also implies, however, that subjects would change their self-ratings about their own intelligence more in the extreme discrepancy condition. Thus, the more subjects change their self-ratings toward the implications of the test results, the less they should prefer information that disparages the test. In other words, there should be a negative correlation between changes in self-estimation and selective exposure.

The results supported both the curvilinearity hypothesis as well as the correlation hypothesis. Consonant information was preferred to dissonant under conditions of moderate discrepancy, regardless of whether the dependent variable was active information seeking or rating of reading desirability. There was also a highly negative correlation ($r = -.50$) between change in judgment of one's own intelligence and selective exposure.

The experiment thus offers some evidence of a postulated curvilinear relationship between amount of cognitive dissonance and the selective preference for *consonant* information. Additionally, it could be shown that those subjects who changed their self-evaluations under extreme discrepancy showed a considerably smaller amount of selective exposure than those who did not change their self-evaluations, thus supporting the speculations mentioned above concerning the mediation of these selective exposure effects by a change in self-concept.

H. ADDITIONAL VARIABLES

1. Cost of Information

In numerous studies of predecisional information seeking it has been found that the cost of information influenced the *amount* of information seeking (see Frey, Kumpf, Raffee, Sauter, & Silberer, 1976; Lanzetta, 1963; Lanzetta & Kanareff, 1962; Silberer & Frey, 1980). Little research has been done, however, on the effect of the cost variable on the *direction* of information seeking. An experiment already mentioned (see Frey, 1981c) was performed in which different amounts of information which were negatively discrepant from one's own self-evaluation of intelligence were introduced and the effects on information seeking tested. Subjects received fictitious intelligence test results that were lower than their self-evaluation. They were then given the opportunity to choose among several articles containing information that either derogated intelligence tests (test-disparaging information) or argued for their validity (test-supporting information).

The cost of this information was also manipulated in order to investigate the influence of this variable on the amount and kind of information subjects chose and desired to read. Subjects were told either that the information was free or that each piece of information cost 50 pfennig (about 25¢ at the time of the investigation). It seemed reasonable to suppose that when the cost of obtaining information was high, the subjects would think more carefully about their selections and put relatively greater weight on the information they preferred most. Therefore, their relative preference for self-supporting (i.e., consonant) over self-threatening (i.e., dissonant) information should be greater when the cost of the information is high than when it is low. The data showed, as expected, and in accordance with the ideas of Lanzetta (1963), that cost decreased the search for both types of information. Fewer articles supporting as well as disparaging intelligence tests were chosen in the cost compared to the no-cost condition. More importantly, for reading desirability, the experiment showed that subjects rated the desirability of test-disparaging (consonant) information higher than the desirability of test-supporting (dissonant) information. Moreover, this difference was greater when the information cost money than when it was free. Increased financial cost produced a stronger tendency to prefer consonant over dissonant information.

The effects of cost on information selectivity parallel "cost" results in the field of predecisional information processing (see, for example, Pitz, Downing, & Reinhold, 1967). In these experiments it was found that information that supported a hypothesis or judgment was evaluated higher in its diagnostic value (i.e., reliability) than information that contradicted a hypothesis or judgment. This preference in reliability judgments (called inertia effect) was more pronounced when the information cost money than when it did not. Thus, it seems that as the cost of information increases, the selective exposure effect increases.

2. The Effect of Perceived Validity or Reliability of Dissonant Information on Selective Exposure

One can assume that the amount of dissonance produced by a dissonant information depends on its perceived validity or reliability. This was tested in two experiments by Frey and Stahlberg (1986) using the "intelligence test paradigm" of Frey (1978b) mentioned above. Subjects in both experiments received fictitious intelligence test results which were always negatively discrepant from their self-evaluations but varied in degree of dissonance or seriousness.

In Experiment I, amount of dissonance was manipulated by giving subjects along with their test results either some information that devaluated intelligence tests or by giving no further information about intelligence tests at all. In Experiment II subjects were told either that their intelligence test results were reliably scored, or that there exists a certain, though not great, possibility that their results were incorrect because the scoring may have been erroneous. Subjects were then given the opportunity to choose among several articles containing information which emphasized either the validity or invalidity of intelligence tests.

It was hypothesized that subjects in the two reliable test result conditions experienced more dissonance when confronted with a negative intelligence test feedback and, therefore, were more prone to search selectively for information disparaging intelligence tests, compared to subjects in the less reliable test result conditions. Data in both experiments were in accordance with this hypothesis. In addition, measures of cognitive change showed that subjects under the reliable test score conditions rated being highly intelligent as less important than subjects under the potentially noncredible conditions. Thus, one can assume that the perceived reliability of a dissonant piece of information has important consequences for the amount of existing dissonance and thus for the amount of selective seeking of information. It should be added that the intelligence test paradigm could be interpreted equally well with the dissonance theory as with the self-esteem framework (see Frey, Fries, & Osnabrügge, 1983; Frey & Stahlberg, 1986; Fries & Frey, 1980; Wyer & Frey, 1983).

3.   Selectivity and Personality Variables

Do certain personality types differ in their patterns of information seeking? As already mentioned, Canon (1964) found that people with low self-confidence were more likely to prefer decision-supportive information, whereas people with high self-confidence preferred nonsupportive information. Canon (1964) did not measure his subjects' self-confidence directly, but instead manipulated[4] this confidence by giving the subjects either positive or negative feedback about their success in a problem-solving task. It seems likely, however, that people with differences in measured self-confidence will also show different kinds of information-seeking behavior.

Besides self-confidence, other personality variables investigated with respect to their effects on selective exposure are dogmatism, field dependence,

[4]Neither Canon (1964) nor Freedman (1965b) and Lowin (1969), who induced both high and low self-esteem, found a difference between the groups. On the other hand, Rosnow, Gitter, and Holz (1968) found self-confidence results that were highly similar to Canon's.

manifest anxiety, and repressor–sensitizer, among others. Clarke and James (1967), for example, found a high correlation between dogmatism and selectivity; highly dogmatic people were more prone to seek out consonant and avoid dissonant information. Kleck and Wheaton (1967) obtained similar results; their chronically "closed-minded" subjects showed a greater preference for consonant information than did the open-minded ones.

Olson and Zanna (1979) observed how long subjects categorized as repressors and sensitizers looked at two objects that they had previously chosen or rejected. They found that subjects looked more at the chosen than the nonchosen alternative and that the selective exposure effect was more pronounced in repressors than in sensitizers.

One of the author's own experiments (Frey, Stahlberg, & Fries, 1986) tested the influence of the degree of manifest anxiety on selective exposure. Subjects received feedback about their performance in an intelligence test, which was either negatively or positively discrepant from their expectations. After having learned of their test results, subjects were offered some pieces of information which either supported or criticized the use of intelligence tests. Subjects with high manifest anxiety had a higher preference for test-disparaging information than those with low manifest anxiety when the results were below their expectations, and a greater preference for test-supporting information when their results were unexpectedly favorable. High anxiety subjects thus seem driven to lessen the effect of the negative information and to increase the effect of positive information.

As in other areas of dissonance theory (and of course in the whole field of social psychology), there is relatively little research on the effects of personality variables, and, as we have seen, the results are not always very convincing (e.g., for the effects of self-confidence, category width, etc.). Commenting on this state of affairs, Wicklund and Brehm (1976) noted that it is difficult to make any predictions for personality variables because a personality variable can have an influence on the threshold of dissonance, on the amount of perceived dissonance, as well as on the kind of strategy chosen for dissonance reduction.

I. RESULTS CONCERNING INFORMATION AVOIDANCE

Dissonance theory postulates that, in addition to selectively searching for consonant information, people who experience dissonance try to avoid receiving further dissonant information. Our own research provides clear support for this notion. In some experiments in which subjects were asked which pieces of information they did not want to see, there was a significantly greater tendency to avoid dissonant as opposed to consonant information. Unlike selective information seeking, however, the magnitude of avoidance in general did not vary as a function of any of the variables discussed above. In only one of our experiments (Frey & Wicklund, 1978) was there a significant difference between high- and low-dissonance conditions on the avoidance measure. Subjects under the choice (high-dissonance) condition avoided dissonant information more than subjects in the no-choice (low-dissonance) condition. When, however, dissonance was manipulated over more than two levels (Frey, 1982), avoidance proved to be independent of the amount of dissonance induced.[5]

There would appear to be at least two reasons why selective avoidance is weaker than selective information seeking. First, avoidance of further dissonant information merely hinders any increase in the existing dissonance. It does not, however, decrease the dissonance itself. Secondly, general avoidance of all dissonant information would not be effective for the cognitive system because the subject can never exclude the possibility that some items of dissonant information might be useful for future decisions.

A third possible reason for the general weakness of observed selective avoidance effects has to do with an experimental artifact. In most experiments on selective information seeking, first the selective seeking and then the selective avoidance of information was measured. It is thus possible that whatever dissonance reduction was to be done was already accomplished before the measurement of selective avoidance took place. Research by Götz-Marchand, Götz, and Irle (1974), for example, shows that there is a higher probability that variables at the beginning of a questionnaire produce more significant dissonance reduction effects compared to those at the end of the questionnaire. Future research should therefore test the avoidance hypothesis either by measuring avoidance only or by at least counterbalancing for any possible order effect among dependent variables.

IV. Other Theoretical and Empirical Approaches

Snyder and co-workers (Snyder & Campbell, 1980; Snyder & Cantor, 1979; Snyder & Uranowitz, 1978; Snyder & Swann, 1978a,b; for an overview see Snyder, 1981) have examined the strategies that individuals formulate to test hypotheses about other people with whom they anticipate social interaction. In

---

[5]Within the whole range of research on selective exposure there are only a few experiments in which avoidance effects were found: Rhine (1967) was the only one who found a *curvilinear* relationship between the amount of cognitive dissonance and the avoidance of dissonant information; Mills (1965a) also found avoidance effects dependent on different levels of dissonance. However, in most experiments, separate avoidance measures were not taken (for an overview see also Mills, 1965b, 1968).

most of their experiments, the experimenter informed participants that they would take part in an investigation of how people come to know and understand each other. The experimenter explains that one way to learn about other people is to ask them questions about their likes and dislikes, their favored activities, their life experiences, and their feelings about themselves.

The subjects are then provided with hypotheses about other individuals (introverted or extroverted individuals) and asked to test the hypotheses by planning a series of questions for what they believed was to be a forthcoming interview. Subjects were asked to select a certain number of questions out of a pool of 12, some of which were clearly oriented toward extroverts and others toward introverts.

The experiments provided clear evidence that individuals systematically formulate confirmatory strategies for testing hypotheses about other people. For example, to test their hypotheses that their targets were extroverted, participants were particularly likely to choose to ask precisely those questions that one typically asks people already known to be extroverts. Similarly, to test the hypotheses that their targets were introverts, participants were particularly likely to ask precisely those questions that one typically asks people already known to be introverts.

Snyder and Swann tested the influence of a series of independent variables (origins of the hypotheses being tested, knowledge of the likelihood that the hypotheses could prove accurate or inaccurate, incentive of accuracy, etc.) but found no noticeable effect on the kind of hypothesis-testing strategies chosen. In all cases, participants engaged in confirmatory strategies.

Although it was not mentioned by Snyder and Swann or by their co-workers, there is no reason why dissonance theory cannot account for these results. When an individual has formulated a (tentative) hypothesis (suggested from outside) about another person he tries to support this hypothesis by selectively choosing questions. Of course, Festinger's (1957, 1964) original formulation of dissonance theory cannot easily be made to apply to this particular research setting. However, numerous reformulations of dissonance theory (Frey, 1978a, 1981d; Irle, 1975; Janis, 1968) argue that dissonance theory is applicable also for tentative decisions, although the effects may be weaker.

Finally, some of the research results on selective exposure can be explained by the ideas of Kruglanski (1980) about lay epistemology. In making predictions about epistemological behavior they argue that one must consider *three* personal needs: Fear of invalidity, need for structure, and conclusional needs. Fear of invalidity means that people are afraid of making invalid judgments or decisions and therefore hestitate to stop information seeking. Transferring this to the problem of selective exposure, they show a high preference for dissonant information (when the decision is reversible!) in order to minimize the possibility of making a wrong decision. Festinger's postulate that dissonant information will be searched for if the person feels that it may prove useful for future decisions can be conceptualized in these terms.

Attending the need for structure, people have a tendency to stop information seeking in order to establish a structured and predictable world. Dominance of this need will result in a higher preference for consonant information in order to quickly establish a structure. Conclusional needs refer to a drive to conserve a certain information status either if it has some hedonistic value or if further information seeking is expected to lead to self-threatening information. In short, that information is preferred that fulfills an important need or motive.

According to Kruglanski (1980), one could assume that there is a tendency toward nonbiased or even nonsupporting information search when subjects have a high fear of invalidity while a tendency for supporting information should be seen when there is a high need for structure. It may be that the differences found for the personality variables of dogmatism and closed-mindedness can be explained by different degrees of need for structure, and that fear of invalidity can explain the effects of decision reversibility. Future research is necessary in order to evaluate whether the theoretical framework of Kruglanski is a better explanation than Festinger's modified dissonance theory.

V.   Theoretical Conclusions

Selective exposure to information is a particularly suitable illustration of active creative processes. According to the thinking of Lewin and Festinger (see Wicklund & Frey, 1981), one can assume that the person constructs cognitions around a decision in order to further his goal-directed activity; that is, one refuses information that contradicts the chosen course of action and seeks out information that supports the chosen course of action. Most of the recent experiments clearly illustrate the highly active state that characterizes a person whose cognitions contradict an on-going behavioral tendency. The research we have summarized calls attention to the active quality of dissonance reduction and makes it salient that one cannot reconcile or explain this realm of human functioning with the nomenclature of nonmotivational theories (such as, for example, self-perception theory). The selective exposure effect has been viewed as the strongest motivational aspect of dissonance theory, yet it received weak empirical support during the first years after Festinger's publication. This lack of support for the selective exposure hypothesis has often been cited as a strong argument against the motivational concept of dissonance. We think that shortcomings in experimental designs of previous research have largely been responsible for the lack of conclusive results in the earlier studies.

Results of selective exposure experiments done since 1965 show, however, that the original assumptions of the theory of cognitive dissonance by Festinger (1957, 1964) cannot be maintained. There are a variety of conditions under which consonant information is not preferred to dissonant information and some in which dissonant information is preferred to consonant. These latter conditions can be enumerated as follows: (1) When subjects are able to counterargue dissonant information; (2) when dissonant information is useful in the long run, e.g., because future comparable decisions are anticipated or a decision revision is possible; this is especially the case at extreme levels of cognitive dissonance; (3) when the person is highly familiar with consonant information; or (4) when a norm of fairness exists (as in most of the experiments about jury cases) (Sears, 1965).

Expressed more abstractly, this means, that selective exposure is small or dissonant information is searched for (1) when the cognitive system is so stable that the dissonant information can be easily integrated (for example, by refuting it), thereby accomplishing further stabilization of the cognitive system, and/or (2) when the cognitive system is so unstable that the addition of consonant information will be seen as being, in the long run, less effective in reducing dissonance than would be changing the cognitive system.

The predicted curvilinear relationship between the intensity of cognitive dissonance and selective exposure to and avoidance of information does not apply in all situations. The necessary prerequisite for this relationship is that the decision, attitude, or action be perceived as being reversible. In cases of *irreversibility,* selectivity increases linearly with increasing dissonance.

Festinger's (1957, 1964) version of dissonance theory, as far as the selective exposure effect is concerned, must also be reversed when active avoidance effects are being considered. Festinger supposed that more dissonant than consonant information is avoided and that this effect increases curvilinearly with increasing dissonance. Most of the research presented, however, showed that avoidance effects did not clearly depend on the intensity of dissonance. We explained these results by the fact that avoidance of dissonant information does not effectively reduce dissonance.

In making predictions about the selective exposure hypothesis, the person's entire cognitive system must be considered, since what might seem at first to be dissonant information may prove relevant for a person who wishes to optimally inform himself in order to make future decisions. The person's failure to consider such information could result in arousal of more intense dissonance in the long run (cf. Mills *et al.,* 1959).

It is clear that the reformulated theory of cognitive dissonance cannot explain all the research conducted until now. As mentioned before, utility, curiosity, fairness norms, and other factors must be considered in order to explain all the results completely. Nevertheless, the present research demonstrates the defensive character of people's information processing. People are relatively open to new information (supporting and opposing their belief or decision of hypotheses) as long as they see a possibility for revision. When, for varying reasons (e.g., external constraints, internal resistance to change), this possibility is not seen to exist, subjects tend to ignore nonsupportive information and increase their preferences for information that lends them support.

In the author's opinion, there is at present no theoretical alternative to the reformulated theory of cognitive dissonance able to explain the experimental results more precisely.

In recent social cognitive theorizing there has been a strong tendency to cast human beings as mere cognitive organisms and to rule out human drives, motivations, and tensions as explanatory devices. In contrasting purely cognitive approaches with more complex motivational tension theories, we hope to show that cognitive processes without a motivational component do not suffice to explain the voluminous empirical evidence available. I hope that the research presented here increases the trend to characterize human beings as seen from a Lewinian or Festingerian perspective.

The present research on selective exposure to information has not only produced new knowledge, but has also opened a broad range of new questions and problems, some of which are discussed at the end of this article.

VI. Implications for Future Research

1. Theoretical Improvements

Future research in the area of selective exposure to information will hopefully stimulate ideas about the theoretical links between dissonance theory and confirmation bias notions (see Snyder, 1981), Kruglanski's ideas (see Kruglanski, 1980), the incongruity adaption level approach of Streufert and Streufert (1978), and the choice–certainty theory (see Mills, 1968; Mills & Ross, 1964). Although I believe that dissonance theory is the best theoretical approach for explaining the existing data on selective exposure, it may be worthwhile to integrate dissonance theory and the other notions into a broader theoretical framework.

2. Field Research

Although there are some experiments made outside the laboratory, there is a lack of field investigations. For example, it would be interesting to study the information-seeking activities of doctors, politicians, or managers (after real investment decisions), especially when these decisions proved to be wrong.

3. Sequential Effects

Whereas there is enough evidence for a selective exposure effect, there are only a few items of empirical evidence depicting avoidance of dissonant information (see Section III,I). Because the avoidance measure was always taken *after* the seeking measure, the lack of avoidance effects could be due partially to a sequential effect. Götz-Marchand *et al.* (1974), for example, showed that dissonance is reduced by measures offered first, but not those offered later. Future research should eliminate such sequential effects by measuring the active avoidance of dissonant information first.

4. Selective Seeking and Selective Forgetting

While there are a large number of studies that investigated the seeking of dissonant and consonant information, no research exists that tests the remembering or forgetting of such information, i.e., is consonant information retained better than dissonant information? A first experiment in this direction was done by Wyer and Frey (1983). This was, however, not done in the context of selective exposure to information. Wyer and Frey gave their subjects negatively discrepant test results on an intelligence test. Subjects were then given test-supporting and test-disparaging material to read and then asked to reproduce the articles they had read. It was found that subjects remembered the dissonant (test-supporting) material better than the consonant (test-disparaging) material. This was explained by the fact that subjects made more efforts to counterargue this kind of information—that they are forced to deal with this kind of information more intensely and that they therefore remembered it easier. Future research should concentrate more on what kind of information is forgotten or remembered when subjects are confronted with consonant or dissonant material.

5. Sequential Information Seeking

In the selective exposure experiments performed up to now subjects were confronted with the titles of the information and were then asked to indicate how many articles and which of them they wanted to read. A theoretically interesting extention in this paradigm would be to investigate sequences of information seeking. What happens when a subject articulates a preference and is granted his preference, i.e., when he receives the requested information and is then asked to state a new preference? To date, this kind of sequential information-seeking activity has not been explicitly tested.

6. Misattribution of Arousal

Throughout this article, we have emphasized the relevance of motivational processes for information seeking. Therefore it may be useful to test the consequences for misattribution of arousal on information seeking. Until now only evaluative changes were measured (see, for example, Frey *et al.*, 1983; Fries & Frey, 1980; Zanna & Cooper, 1974). Future research should investigate how much stronger the selective exposure effect is when additional arousal states are added to the dissonance-produced arousal state. Also, whether the selective exposure effect is eliminated when the dissonance arousal produced by the decision is attributed to other (dissonant-irrelevant) causes (misattribution) should be tested.

7. Time Pressure

Finally, unresolved is the effect of reading the material under time pressure after making a decision. In the experiments on selective exposure done so far, no explicit time pressure was presented. That is, the subjects could take as much time as they wanted in choosing between the information offered, and the subjects also anticipated as much time as they wanted for reading their chosen information. What would happen if the subjects are pressured for time?—i.e., when they have only a limited time available for selecting or reading the material? I expect that time pressure would produce stronger selective exposure effects [similar to our cost variable (see Section III,H,1), which also increased the selective exposure effect].

8. Group Information Seeking

All experiments have been done with individuals. It would be interesting—especially for practical reasons—to study group decisions and group information-seeking activities. Do groups have selective exposure tendencies similar to those of individuals or do they expose themselves unbiased to all kinds of decision-supporting and decision-nonsupporting information?

ACKNOWLEDGMENTS

I would like to express my appreciation to the following persons for helpful suggestions in revising the manuscript: Len Berkowitz, Peter Gollwitzer, Joanna Harms, Stefan Hormuth, Martin Irle, Larry Katz, Arie Kruglanski, Martin Kumpf, Anne Maass, Randolph Ochsmann, Gabriele Osnabrügge, Norbert Schwarz, Dagmar Stahlberg, Fritz Strack, Bob Wicklund, and Bob Wyer, Jr.

REFERENCES

Berlyne, D. E. (1960). *Conflict, arousal, and curiosity.* New York: McGraw-Hill.
Berlyne, D. E. (1968). The motivational significance of collative variables and conflict. In R. P. Abelson, E. Aronson, W. J. McGuire, T. M. Newcomb, M. J. Rosenberg, & P. H. Tannenbaum (Eds.), *Theories of cognitive consistency: A sourcebook* (pp. 257–274). Chicago: Rand McNally.

Brehm, J. W. (1956). Postdecision changes in the desirability of alternatives. *Journal of Abnormal and Social Psychology*, **52**, 384–389.

Brehm, J. W., & Cohen, A. R. (1962). *Explorations in cognitive dissonance*. New York: Wiley.

Brock, T. C. (1965). Commitment to exposure as a determination of information receptivity. *Journal of Personality and Social Psychology*, **2**, 10–19.

Brock, T. C., & Balloun, J. C. (1967). Behavioral receptivity to dissonant information. *Journal of Personality and Social Psychology*, **6**, 413–428.

Canon, L. K. (1964). Self-confidence and selective exposure to information. In L. Festinger (Ed.), *Conflict, decision, and dissonance* (pp. 83–96). Stanford, CA: Stanford University Press.

Clarke, P., & James, J. (1967). The effects of situation, attitude-intensity, and personality on information seeking. *Sociometry*, **30**, 235–245.

Cohen, A. R., Brehm, J. W., & Latané, B. (1959). Choice of strategy and voluntary exposure to information under public and private conditions. *Journal of Personality*, **27**, 63–73.

Cohen, A. R., & Latané, B. (1962). An experiment on choice in commitment to counterattitudinal behavior. In J. W. Brehm & A. R. Cohen (Eds.), *Explorations in cognitive dissonance* (pp. 88–91). New York: Wiley.

Cohen, A. R., Terry, H. I., & Jones, C. B. (1959). Attitudinal effects of choice in exposure to counter-propaganda. *Journal of Abnormal and Social Psychology*, **58**, 388–391.

Cotton, J. L., & Hieser, R. A. (1980). Selective exposure to information and cognitive dissonance. *Journal of Research in Personality*, **14**, 518–527.

Feather, N. T. (1962). Cigarette smoking and lung cancer: A study of cognitive dissonance. *Australian Journal of Psychology*, **14**, 55–64.

Feather, N. T. (1963). Cognitive dissonance, sensitivity, and evaluation. *Journal of Abnormal and Social Psychology*, **66**, 157–163.

Festinger, L. (1957). *A theory of cognitive dissonance*. Stanford, CA: Stanford University Press.

Festinger, L. (1964). *Conflict, decision, and dissonance*. Stanford, CA: Stanford University Press.

Freedman, J. L. (1965a). Preference for dissonant information. *Journal of Personality and Social Psychology*, **2**, 287–289.

Freedman, J. L. (1965b). Confidence, utility, and selective exposure: A partial replication. *Journal of Personality and Social Psychology*, **2**, 778–780.

Freedman, J. L., & Sears, D. O. (1965). Selective exposure. In L. Berkowitz (Ed.), *Advances in experimental social psychology* (Vol. 2, pp. 57–97). New York: Academic Press.

Frey, D. (1978a). Die Theorie der kognitiven Dissonanz. In D. Frey (Ed.), *Kognitive Theorien der Sozialpsychologie* (pp. 243–292). Bern: Huber.

Frey, D. (1978b). Reactions to success and failure in public and private conditions. *Journal of Experimental Social Psychology*, **14**, 172–179.

Frey, D. (1981a). Postdecisional preferences for decision-relevant information as a function of the competence of its source and the degree of familiarty with this information. *Journal of Experimental Social Psychology*, **17**, 621–626.

Frey, D. (1981b). Reversible and irreversible decisions: Preference for consonant information as a function of attractiveness of decision alternatives. *Personality and Social Psychology Bulletin*, **7**, 621–626.

Frey, D. (1981c). The effect of negative feedback about oneself and cost of information on preferences for information about the source of this feedback. *Journal of Experimental Social Psychology*, **17**, 42–50.

Frey, D. (1981d). *Informationssuche und Informationsbewertung bei Entscheidungen*. Bern: Huber.

Frey, D. (1982). Different levels of cognitive dissonance, information seeking and information avoidance. *Journal of Personality and Social Psychology*, **43**, 1175–1183.

Frey, D. (1985). *Amount of available information and selective exposure*. Unpublished manuscript, Christian-Albrechts-University, Kiel.

Frey, D., Fries, A., & Osnabrügge, G. (1983). Reactions of failure after taking a placebo: A study of dissonance reduction. *Personality and Social Psychology Bulletin,* **9**, 481–488.

Frey, D., & Irle, M. (1972). Some conditions to produce a dissonance and an incentive effect in a "forced-compliance" situation. *European Journal of Social Psychology,* **2**, 45–54.

Frey, D., Irle, M., & Hochgürtel, G. (1979). Performance of an unpleasant task: Effects of over vs. under-payment on perception of adequacy of rewards and attractiveness of the task. *Journal of Experimental Social Psychology,* **15**, 275–284.

Frey, D., Irle, M., Möntmann, V., Kumpf, M., Ochsmann, R., & Sauer, C. (1982). Cognitive dissonance: Experiments and theory. In M. Irle (Ed.), *Studies in decision-making* (pp. 281–310). New York: de Gruyter.

Frey, D., Kumpf, M., Irle, M., & Gniech, G. (1984). Re-evaluaton of decision alternatives dependent upon the reversibility of a decision and the passage of time. *European Journal of Social Psychology,* **14**, 447–450.

Frey, D., Kumpf, M., Raffee, H., Sauter, B., & Silberer, G. (1976). Informationskosten und Reversibilität des Entschlusses als Determinanten der Informationsnachfrage vor Entscheidungen. *Zeitschrift für experimentelle und angewandte Psychologie,* **23**, 569–585.

Frey, D., & Rosch, M. (1984). Information seeking after decisions: The roles of novelty of information and decision reversibility. *Personality and Social Psychology Bulletin,* **10**, 91–98.

Frey, D., & Stahlberg, D. (1986). *Information-seeking and attitude change after attitude-discrepant behavior*. Unpublished manuscript, Christian-Albrechts-University, Kiel.

Frey, D., & Stahlberg, D. (1986). Selection of information after receiving more or less reliable self-threatening information. *Personality and Social Psychology Bulletin,* in press.

Frey, D., Stahlberg, D., & Fries, A. (1986). Reactions of high and low anxiety subjects to positive and negative self-relevant feedback. *Journal of Personality,* in press.

Frey, D., & Wicklund, R. (1978). A clarification of selective exposure: The impact of choice. *Journal of Experimental Social Psychology,* **14**, 132–139.

Fries, A., & Frey, D. (1980). Misattribution of arousal and self-threatening information. *Journal of Experimental Social Psychology,* **16**, 405–416.

Goethals, G. R., & Cooper, J. (1972). Role of intention and postbehavioral consequence in the arousal of cognitive dissonance. *Journal of Personality and Social Psychology,* **23**, 298–301.

Götz-Marchand, B., Götz, J., & Irle, M. (1974). Preference of dissonance reduction modes as a function of their order, familiarity, and reversibility. *European Journal of Social Psychology,* **4**, 201–228.

Grabitz, H.-J., & Grabitz-Gniech, G. (1972). Der Inertia-Effekt in Abhängigkeit vom diagnostischen Wert einer Information. *Zeitschrift für experimentelle und angewandte Psychologie,* **19**, 364–375.

Greenwald, H. J. (1969). Dissonance and relative versus absolute attractiveness of decision alternatives. *Journal of Personality and Social Psychology,* **11**, 328–333.

Irle, M. (1975). *Lehrbuch der Sozialpsychologie*. Göttingen: Hogrefe.

Irle, M., & Möntmann, V. (1978). Die Theorie der kognitiven Dissonanz: Ein Resumee ihrer theoretischen Entwicklung und empirischen Ergebnisse 1957–1976. In L. Festinger (Ed.), *Theorie der kognitiven Dissonanz* (pp. 274–365). Bern: Huber.

Janis, I. L. (1968). Stages in decision-making process. In R. P. Abelson, E. Aronson, W. J. McGuire, T. M. Newcomb, M. J. Rosenberg, & P. H. Tannenbaum (Eds.), *Theories of cognitive consistency: A sourcebook* (pp. 577–588). Chicago: Rand McNally.

Katz, E. (1968). On reopening the question of selectivity in exposure to mass communications. In R. P. Abelson, E. Aronson, W. J. McGuire, T. M. Newcomb, M. J. Rosenberg, & P. H.

Tannenbaum (Eds.), *Theories of cognitive consistency: A sourcebook* (pp. 788–796). Chicago: Rand McNally.

Kleck, R. E., & Wheaton, J. (1967). Dogmatism and responses to opinion consistent and opinion inconsistent information. *Journal of Personality and Social Psychology, 5,* 249–253.

Kleinhesselink, R. R., & Edwards, R. E. (1975). Seeking and avoiding belief-discrepant information as a function of its perceived refutability. *Journal of Personality and Social Psychology, 31*(5), 787–790.

Kozielecki, J. (1966). *The mechanism of self-confirmation of hypothesis in a probabilistic situation.* International Congress of Psychology, Symposium 25: Heuristic processes of thinking, Moscow, 1966.

Kruglanski, A. W. (1980). Lay epistemologie process and contents. *Psychological Review, 87,* 70–87.

Lanzetta, J. T. (1963). Information acquisition in decision making. In O. J. Harvey (Ed.), *Motivation and social interaction* (pp. 239–265). New York: Ronald.

Lanzetta, J. T., & Kanareff, V. T. (1962). Information cost, amount of payoff, and level of aspiration as determinants of information seeking in decision making. *Behavioral Science, 7,* 459–473.

Linder, D. E., Cooper, J., & Jones, E. E. (1967). Decision freedom as a determinant of the role of incentive magnitude in attitude change. *Journal of Personality and Social Psychology, 6,* 245–254.

Lowin, A. (1967). Approach and avoidance: Alternative modes of selective exposure to information. *Journal of Personality and Social Psychology, 6,* 1–9.

Lowin, A. (1969). Further evidence for an approach–avoidance interpretation of selective exposure. *Journal of Experimental and Social Psychology, 5,* 265–271.

McGuire, W. J. (1968). Selective exposure: A summing up. In R. P. Abelson, E. Aronson, W. J. McGuire, T. M. Newcomb, M. J. Rosenberg, & P. H. Tannenbaum (Eds.), *Theories of cognitive consistency: A sourcebook* (pp. 797–800). Chicago: Rand McNally.

Mills, J. (1965a). Avoidance of dissonant information. *Journal of Personality and Social Psychology, 2,* 589–593.

Mills, J. (1965b). Effect of certainty about a decision upon postdecision exposure to consonant and dissonant information. *Journal of Personality and Social Psychology, 2,* 749–752.

Mills, J. (1968). Interest in supporting and discrepant information. In R. P. Abelson, E. Aronson, W. J. McGuire, T. M. Newcomb, M. J. Rosenberg, & P. H. Tannenbaum (Eds.), *Theories of cognitive consistency: A sourcebook* (pp. 771–776). Chicago: Rand McNally.

Mills, J., Aronson, E., & Robinson, H. (1959). Selectivity in exposure to information. *Journal of Abnormal and Social Psychology, 59,* 250–253.

Mills, J., & Ross, A. (1964). Effects of commitment and certainty upon interest in supporting information. *Journal of Abnormal and Social Psychology, 68,* 552–555.

Olson, J. M., & Zanna, M. P. (1979). A new look at selective exposure. *Journal of Experimental Social Psychology, 15,* 1–15.

Pitz, G. F., Downing, L., & Reinhold, H. (1967). Sequential effects in the revision of subjective probabilities. *Canadian Journal of Psychology, 21,* 381–393.

Rhine, R. J. (1967). The 1964 presidential election and curves of information seeking and avoiding. *Journal of Personality and Social Psychology, 5,* 416–423.

Rosen, S. (1961). Postdecision affinity for incompatible information. *Journal of Abnormal and Social Psychology, 63,* 188–190.

Rosnow, R. L., Gitter, A. G., & Holz, R. F. (1968). *Some determinants of postdecisional information preferences.* Unpublished manuscript.

Schultz, C. B. (1974). The effect of confidence on selective exposure: An unresolved dilemma. *Journal of Social Psychology, 94,* 64–69.

Schwarz, N., Frey, D., & Kumpf, M. (1980). Interactive effects of writing and reading a persuasive essay on attitude change and selective exposure. *Journal of Experimental Social Psychology,* **16,** 1–17.

Sears, D. O. (1965). Biased indoctrination and selectivity of exposure to new information. *Sociometry,* **28,** 420–426.

Sears, D. O. (1968). The paradox of de facto selective exposure without preferences for supportive information. In R. P. Abelson, E. Aronson, W. J. McGuire, T. M. Newcomb, M. J. Rosenberg, & P. H. Tannenbaum (Eds.), *Theories of cognitive consistency: A sourcebook* (pp. 777–787). Chicago: Rand McNally.

Sears, D. O., & Abeles, D. P. (1969). Attitudes and opinions. *Annual Review of Psychology,* **20,** 253–288.

Sears, D. O., & Freedman, J. L. (1965). The effects of expected familiarity with arguments upon opinion change and selective exposure. *Journal of Personality and Social Psychology,* **2,** 420–426.

Silberer, G., & Frey, D. (1980). Experimentelle Untersuchungen zur Informationsbeschaffung bei der Produktauswahl. In H. Raffee & G. Silberer (Eds.), *Informationsverhalten des Konsumenten* (pp. 63–68). Wiesbaden: Gabler Verlag.

Snyder, M. (1981). On the self-perpetuating nature of social stereotypes. In D. L. Hamilton (Ed.), *Cognitive processes in stereotyping and intergroup behavior* (pp. 277–303). Hillsdale, NJ: Erlbaum.

Snyder, M., & Campbell, B. H. (1980). Testing hypotheses about other people: The role of the hypothesis. *Personality and Social Psychology Bulletin,* **6,** 421–426.

Snyder, M., & Cantor, N. (1979). Testing hypotheses about other people: The use of historical knowledge. *Journal of Experimental Social Psychology,* **15,** 330–342.

Snyder, M., & Swann, W. B., Jr. (1978a). Behavioral confirmation in social interaction: From social perception to social reality. *Journal of Experimental Social Psychology,* **14,** 148–162.

Snyder, M., & Swann, W. B., Jr. (1978b). Hypothesis-testing processes in social interaction. *Journal of Personality and Social Psychology,* **36,** 1202–1212.

Snyder, M., & Uranowitz, S. W. (1978). Reconstructing the past: Some cognitive consequences of person perception. *Journal of Personality and Social Psychology,* **36,** 941–950.

Sogin, S. R., & Pallak, M. S. (1976). Bad decisions, responsibility, and attitude change: Effects of volition, foreseeability, and locus of causality of negative consequences. *Journal of Personality and Social Psychology,* **33,** 300–306.

Streufert, S., & Streufert, S. C. (1978). *Behavior in the complex environment.* Unpublished manuscript.

Sweeney, P. D., & Gruber, K. L. (1984). Selective exposure: Voter information preferences and the Watergate Affair. *Journal of Personality and Social Psychology,* **46,** 1208–1221.

Wicklund, R. A., & Brehm, J. W. (1976). *Perspectives on cognitive dissonance.* Hillsdale, NJ: Erlbaum.

Wicklund, R. A., & Frey, D. (1981). Cognitive consistency: Motivational vs. non-motivational perspectives. In J. Forgas (Ed.), *Social cognition: Perspectives on everyday understanding* (pp. 141–163). New York: Academic Press.

Wyer, R. S., Jr., & Frey, D. (1983). The effects of feedback about the self and others on the recall and judgments of feedback-relevant information. *Journal of Experimental Social Psychology,* **19,** 540–549.

Zanna, M. P., & Cooper, J. (1974). Dissonance and the pill: An attribution approach to studying the arousal properties of dissonance. *Journal of Personality and Social Psychology,* **29,** 703–709.

THE ROLE OF THREAT
TO SELF-ESTEEM AND PERCEIVED
CONTROL IN RECIPIENT REACTION
TO HELP: THEORY DEVELOPMENT
AND EMPIRICAL VALIDATION

Arie Nadler

DEPARTMENT OF PSYCHOLOGY
TEL-AVIV UNIVERSITY
RAMAT-AVIV, ISRAEL

Jeffrey D. Fisher

DEPARTMENT OF PSYCHOLOGY
UNIVERSITY OF CONNECTICUT
STORRS, CONNECTICUT

I. Introduction and Objectives

The study of prosocial behavior has recently taken a previously untraveled route, and has started to explore recipient reactions to aid (for a complete review

ADVANCES IN EXPERIMENTAL
SOCIAL PSYCHOLOGY, VOL. 19

Copyright © 1986 by Academic Press, Inc.
All rights of reproduction in any form reserved.

of this literature, see Fisher, Nadler, & Whitcher-Alagna, 1982). This development reflects an awareness that reactions to aid are complex phenomena, and that helpers may elicit negative as well as positive responses. As with many areas of social psychology, researchers have come to realize what was well understood by accumulated cultural wisdom. For example:

1. Maimonides (a twelfth-century Jewish scholar) outlined eight different types of aid ranging from help that must be solicited by the recipient to help given without a request being made and in such a way that it promotes self-sufficiency. Each kind of help was assumed to elicit a different reaction in the beneficiary (Joffe, 1949).

2. An Indian proverb states "Why do you hate me—I never even helped you?"

3. The Koran admonishes "A charitable deed must be done as a duty which man owes to man, so that it conveys no idea of the superiority of the giver or the inferiority of the receiver . . ." (2:262).

4. In the Hindu culture it is said that "The mind of the man who receives gifts is acted on by the mind of the giver, so the receiver is likely to become degenerate. Receiving gifts is prone to destroy the independence of mind and encourage slavishness. Therefore accept no gifts" [Raja Yoga, quoted in Kuppuswamy (1978)].

5. Similar beliefs about aid being a "mixed blessing" are reflected in the Christian religions, and in the Eskimo and Filipino cultures, among others (see Greenberg, 1980).

The mixed effects of aid have now been demonstrated across several domains, and in both naturalistic observations and experimental research. These effects are apparent in observations made in clinical and rehabilitational psychology (e.g., Fischer, Winer, & Abramowitz, 1983; Ladieu, Hanfman, & Dembo, 1947; Nadler, Sheinberg, & Jaffe, 1981), in analyses of the consequences of foreign aid programs (e.g., Gergen & Gergen, 1974, 1983), in the gerontology literature (e.g., Kalish, 1967; Lipman & Sterne, 1962), and in writings on social welfare programs (e.g., Briar, 1966; Pettigrew, 1983). Also, an increasing amount of experimental research has documented negative as well as positive reactions to help in laboratory studies and simulations (e.g., Fisher & Nadler, 1974; Nadler, Fisher, & Streufert, 1974).

In all these diverse contexts the receipt of help may be either a self-threatening or self-supportive experience for the recipient (Fisher et al., 1982). Aid may be threatening because of the implied inferiority, inadequacy, and dependency inherent in the role of someone needing help. Amplifying this self-threat is the fact that dependency is contrary to the norm of self-reliance, which is so well ingrained in Western civilization (Merton, 1968). However, the receipt of help may also contain positive, supportive aspects (i.e., material gain, signs of the donor's caring and concern). Our theoretical model suggests that aid which is supportive typically elicits positive/nondefensive recipient reactions, whereas threatening help tends to evoke negative/defensive reactions (Fisher *et al.*, 1982).

The term *recipient reactions to aid* is not a unidimensional concept. It refers to a set of related phenomena that are multidimensional and dynamic. Conditions associated with the receipt of help affect how the receipient feels, evaluates, and behaves with respect to the self and others. Under certain conditions the recipient may "bite the hand that feeds him," suffer a loss in self-esteem, and try to engage in immediate reciprocity. In other circumstances, reactions may be dominated by gratitude, good feelings, and little sense of obligation. Beyond the immediate consequences of receiving help, there is the issue of its long-term effectiveness. Help may be effective in motivating the recipient to regain independence or it may be ineffective, constituting the first link in a chain of passivity and dependency. This article considers both the immediate and long-term consequences of receiving help within a single conceptual framework, the threat to self-esteem model of reactions to aid.

The article has a number of related objectives. The first is to provide the reader with a short summary of the major empirical findings in extant research, and the conceptual approaches that have proved most useful (Section II). Second, we focus on one theoretical orientation—the threat to self-esteem model of reactions to aid—with the goal of introducing a conceptual development to it (Section III). We discuss the basic postulates of the original Fisher *et al.* (1982) formulation, then examine the implications for it of a related literature on models of effective helping and coping (e.g., Brickman, Rabinowitz, Karuza, Coates, Cohn, & Kidder, 1982; Janoff-Bulman, Madden, & Timko, 1983; Silver & Wortman, 1980; Wortman, 1983). From this, we derive a refinement in our model involving the distinction between controllable and uncontrollable threat in aid. In Section IV we discuss how the findings of our research on donor–recipient similarity support our theoretical postulates. Section V considers the applied implications of our research, and Section VI its place within the context of social psychology.

The importance of furthering our knowledge of recipient reaction to aid cannot be overstated. Conceptually, it should produce a better understanding of the prosocial interaction in its entirety. Previous social psychological research on helping has focused on *helping behavior* (e.g., factors that enhance an individual's willingness to help others) (Rushton & Sorrentino, 1981). The present emphasis on recipient reaction to help and the long-term effectiveness of assistance shifts attention to the entire range of *helping relations*. As will become evident in our presentation, this domain of interpersonal behavior provides an arena where predictions from several theoretical orientations toward human behavior (e.g., social comparison theory, equity theory, learned helplessness) can be put to a test. The implications of this research seem obvious on an applied level as well. To cite one example, knowing the aid-related conditions likely to promote future recipient independence is important for constructing effective helping relations.

II. Past Research and Theory

We may proceed in either of two directions in reviewing work on reactions to help. First, the empirical findings may be discussed, organized in terms of the major variables under study (e.g., the effect of the level of donor resources, or the amount of help given, on recipient reaction to aid). For a detailed presentation along these lines, see Fisher, DePaulo and Nadler (1981). A second approach would organize a review in terms of each of the several theoretical perspectives used to conceptualize reaction to aid. For such a detailed discussion, see Gross, Wallston, and Piliavin (1979) or Fisher *et al.* (1982). Since at least a selective exposition of past empirical and conceptual work is necessary to provide background for the discussion in this chapter, we will proceed along both of these paths briefly, in turn.

A. AN EMPIRICAL REVIEW

Past research has focused on how recipient reactions to aid are affected by situational conditions (characteristics of the *help* and the *helper*), and the personality of the *recipient*. The recipient's responses should properly be viewed as a function of the interaction among all three of these elements (cf. Nadler, Fisher, & Streufert, 1976; Nadler & Mayseless, 1983). Yet, for the sake of clarity and because much of the research approaches these factors taken alone, the following overview separates the three independent variables.

Distinctions should also be drawn among the types of dependent variables (i.e., recipient reactions). Characteristics of the help, the helper, and the recipient may affect recipient *external perceptions* (e.g., evaluations of the donor and the aid), *self-perceptions* (e.g., evaluations of oneself; affective state after being helped), and *behaviors* (e.g., reciprocity toward the donor). Although a particular situational condition or recipient personality characteristic is likely to affect all three response classes, an examination of past research indicates a covariation between independent and dependent variables. Research within a given category of independent variables (e.g., characteristics of the help) tends to center on one, or at most two, classes of dependent measures (e.g., recipient evaluation of the helper). The need for studying the joint effects of help, helper, and recipient characteristics on a broad spectrum of recipient reactions exists, and will be made more apparent in following sections.

1. Characteristics of the Help

This research has mostly been concerned with how aspects of the aid offer, in and of itself, affect the recipient's external perceptions and externally directed behaviors. One group of studies varied the amount of help given, and observed that greater amounts of help are more often accepted (e.g., Rosen, 1971), and lead to stronger perceptions that the helper is motivated by true concern for the recipient (e.g., Greenberg & Frisch, 1972). Similarly, recipients generally expressed a stronger desire to interact with helpers who gave them a relatively large amount of aid (e.g., Freeman, 1977), and reported more attraction to them (e.g., Berkowitz & Friedman, 1967). On the behavioral level, greater amounts of help lead to more reciprocity (e.g., DePaulo, Brittingham, & Kaiser, 1983; Greenberg & Bar-Tal, 1976; Kahn & Tice, 1973; Stapleton, Nacci, & Tedeschi, 1973).

Other studies investigated the effects of the perceived cost of help to the donor and found this to be a major determinant of recipient reactions. Recipients impute more caring to a donor whose help is viewed as representing a relatively greater sacrifice, and evaluate him or her more positively (Fisher & Nadler, 1976; Gergen, Ellsworth, Maslach, & Seipel, 1975). Finally, when aid is given with "strings attached" (i.e., when stipulations are put on the use of aid), it is less likely to be accepted (e.g., Gergen, Morse, & Kristeller, 1973), and the donor is evaluated less favorably than the donor of "nonrestrictive" aid (e.g., Ladieu et al., 1947).

2. Characteristics of the Helper

A sizable body of research has investigated the effects of helper-related variables on recipient reactions. These studies ask whether individuals respond differentially to help from different sorts of helpers. Available data indicate an affirmative answer.

Two major lines of study exist. One focuses on whether the favorability of the preexisting donor-recipient relationship affects recipient evaluation of the donor and the aid, as well as reciprocity. For example, do individuals react differently to help from a close friend or relative than from a stranger (e.g., Bar-Tal, Zohar, Greenberg, & Hermon, 1977)? This line of research is unique in several ways. First, it deals with a generic variable—overall quality of donor–recipient relations. Thus, it tackles questions with considerable theoretical and applied importance, but does not tend to pinpoint the psychological processes responsible for the effects. It has also been heterogeneous in its use of theoretical constructs. Concepts from attribution theories (Nadler et al., 1974), Goffmanian analyses of human action (Clark & Mills, 1979), and role theories (Bar-Tal et al., 1977) have been used.

These studies indicate that help from someone with whom there is a positive relationship (e.g., a friend) is a positive interpersonal event. Relative to aid from a stranger or from one with whom there is an unfavorable relation, this assistance produces more positive attributions of donor intent (Nadler *et al.*, 1974), a lower "tension of obligation" (Bar-Tal *et al.*, 1977; Clark & Mills, 1979), greater willingness to accept aid (DePaulo, 1982), and a more favorable evaluation of the helper (Nadler *et al.*, 1974). (For a detailed description of this research, see Nadler and Fisher, 1984.)

The second line of investigation assesses the effect of degree of donor–recipient similarity on reaction to help. Compared to the former research, it is distinguishable by several features. It deals with a specific rather than a generic variable, and is concerned with identifying the psychological mechanism responsible for the effects. Also, it is unique in considering the effect of help on recipient self-perception (i.e., affect and self-evaluation), and self-related behavior (i.e., self-help efforts). This emphasis on self-oriented reactions can be traced to the homogeneous conceptual underpinnings of the research. The studies proceed from the assumption [explicitly made in the threat to self-esteem model (Fisher *et al.*, 1982)] that help contains a mixture of positive and negative self-related information (e.g., positive signs of donor concern; negative information about one's inferiority and dependency). Since much of the latter part of this article is devoted to our work on donor–recipient similarity, we will not offer a more detailed presentation at this point.

3. Characteristics of the Recipient

Other research has sought to delineate the ways in which recipient characteristics (e.g., personality, demographics) affect reactions to help. In the case of personality factors, a major variable for study has been the recipient's level of self-esteem. In line with a consistency approach (cf. Bramel, 1968), high self-esteem individuals (who conceive of themselves as competent and self-reliant) are more sensitive to the self-threatening implications involved in receiving help (e.g., information about inferiority and dependency) than are those with low self-esteem (e.g., DePaulo, Brown, Ishii, & Fisher, 1981; DePaulo, Brown, & Greenberg, 1983; Nadler *et al.*, 1976; Nadler, Altman, & Fisher, 1979; Nadler & Mayseless, 1983).

Related research has examined links between other conceptually relevant personality variables and *help-seeking*. Although this research has not directly assessed recipient reactions to receiving help, its implications are important for understanding that phenomenon.[1] Thus far, locus of control, degree of authoritarianism (Fischer & Turner, 1970), and need for achievement (Tessler & Schwartz, 1972), among other variables, have been reported to predict the willingness to seek help. Externals, high authoritarians, and those with high achieve-

---

[1]For example, in some cases the same personality characteristics associated with low help-seeking may predispose one to respond negatively to an offer to help, or to help which is "imposed" on one (cf. Tessler & Schwartz, 1972; Nadler *et al.*, 1976).

ment motivation are more negative toward seeking help and/or are relatively unlikely to seek it. (For a more detailed review, see Nadler, 1983.)

Another group of recipient characteristics affecting reactions to help are demographic variables associated with internalized values about dependency. Consistent with the idea that, relative to females, males are socialized to be more self-reliant and independent (e.g., Weitzman, 1979), men are less favorably disposed than women toward seeking (e.g., Anderson & Anderson, 1972; De-Paulo, 1978, 1982; Fischer & Turner, 1970; McMullin & Gross, 1983; Nadler, Shapira, & Ben-Itzhak, 1982) and receiving help (Nadler, Maler, & Friedman, 1984). Cross-cultural differences in willingness to seek help have also been observed (Nadler & Eshet, 1983). Individuals socialized in a communal social system (the Israeli Kibbutz) sought more help to perform group than individual-oriented tasks, while the reverse was true of city children socialized in an individual achievement-oriented context.

Since the literature on how recipient characteristics affect reactions to help is reviewed by Nadler and Mayseless (1983) and Nadler (1983), we will not discuss it further. Overall, it seems that high self-esteem and internalized values of independence and self-reliance lead to greater sensitivity to the possible self-threatening aspects of help.

B. CONCEPTUAL REVIEW

Thus far we have provided an empirical summary of the area. An overview of the major conceptual approaches which have served heuristic and explanatory purposes will also prove helpful. The distinction between empirical efforts and their conceptual underpinnings is arbitrary and artificial, but is made for clarity of presentation. Research on reactions to aid involves a wide array of behavioral manifestations, and most of the theoretical concepts used in past work were borrowed from other areas of social psychology. Although these theories generally were not developed to explain reactions to aid, they have proved useful in this endeavor. Equity, reactance, attribution, and threat to self-esteem notions have been employed by researchers. Each is more applicable in some domains than others (e.g., for dealing with particular classes of independent and/or dependent variables). In this section, we discuss briefly how researchers have adapted and applied equity, reactance, and attribution conceptualizations to the issues at hand. In Section III we focus on the threat to self-esteem model of reactions to aid.

1. Equity Theories

Equity theories (e.g., Adams, 1963; Hatfield, Walster, & Piliavin, 1978) maintain that people aspire to maintain equity in social relations, and find inequitable relationships aversive. When inequity occurs, people are motivated to restore actual equity through an adjustment of outputs or inputs, or to establish psychological equity by cognitively distorting outputs or inputs. One of the consequences often associated with the receipt of help is a state of inequity, since, by definition, one party (the recipient) has a more favorable ratio of outputs to inputs than the other (the helper). In line with extensions of the equity principle to helping relations (Greenberg & Westcott, 1983; Hatfield & Sprecher, 1983), recipients find nonreciprocal helping psychologically disturbing (Clark, Gotay, & Mills, 1974; Morris & Rosen, 1973), and therefore invest efforts to restore equity via direct reciprocity (e.g., Greenberg & Frisch, 1972). If opportunities for direct reciprocity do not exist, people often restore equity through psychological means (e.g., derogating the helper) (e.g., Castro, 1974).

2. Reactance Theory

Another approach used to explain phenomena associated with the receipt of help is *reactance theory* (Brehm, 1966; Brehm & Brehm, 1981). Its use is linked to the fact that help can pose explicit or implicit restrictions on the recipient's freedom for future action (cf. Briar, 1966). Reactance theory suggests that to the extent that these restrictions exist (e.g., the helper specifies how help is to be used, or the recipient feels he or she has to act kindly toward the benefactor), a negative affective state (reactance) is aroused. Reactance presumably leads to attempts by the recipient to reestablish his or her freedom. These attempts may include making unfavorable evaluations of the helper or the help, and/or a general unwillingness to accept or repay aid (e.g., Brehm & Cole, 1966; Gergen *et al.*, 1973; Goldin, Perry, Margolin, & Stotsky, 1972).

3. Attribution Theories

A cursory scan of social psychology since 1965 reveals that hardly any area has failed to note the heuristic implications of *attribution theories* (e.g., Jones & Davis, 1965; Kelley, 1967). Work on reactions to aid is no exception. Several studies have employed the theory of correspondent inferences to predict the conditions that precipitate attribution of prosocial or ulterior motivation for the donor's help (e.g., Gergen & Gergen, 1971, 1974). Other research has focused on how the locus of attribution made for needing help affects recipients' behavioral and evaluative responses. For example, individuals are less likely to seek help when the need for it is internalized (i.e., when needing aid is believed to reflect personal inadequacy) (Nadler & Porat, 1978).

Although rich in heuristic implications, predictions derived from equity, reactance, and attribution theories are lacking in two major respects. First, looking at the same behavioral phenomenon from different perspectives sometimes leads to conflicting predictions. For example, reactance theory suggests that since the recipient would be more compelled to reciprocate, aid given voluntarily and deliberately would restrict the recipient's freedom and elicit more negative reactions than aid given involuntarily or nondeliberately. However, attribution theories and related research (e.g., Gergen & Gergen, 1974) suggest that deliberate and voluntary help should elicit more favorable reactions from the recipient, since the donor's caring and concern are more apparent. Second, because of their different foci, each of the theoretical orientations has looked at only one "slice" of the phenomenon of reactions to aid. This leads to disjointed predictions of effects and has produced an incomplete set of data. For example, research anchored in equity theory has centered on reciprocity and related feelings and attitudes, while that employing attribution theories has stressed only the attributional consequences of receiving aid.

III. Threat to Recipient Self-Esteem and Perceived Control as Determinants of Reaction to Help

While the fact that help may have implications for recipient self-esteem was noted in earlier theoretical discussions (e.g., Blau, 1964; Ladieu et al., 1947), no formal statement of these effects was made. To amend this situation we proposed the threat to self-esteem model of reactions to aid (Fisher et al., 1982). In addition to considering explicitly the effect of help on recipient self-esteem, the model is unique in several major respects. First, it is the first conceptualization developed specifically to account for reactions to help. Because of this, it considers the effect of aid on a broad range of recipient responses: external perceptions (evaluations of the helper and the help), self-perceptions (self-esteem and affective state), and post-aid behavior (reciprocity, self-help, and help-seeking). Second, one could argue that other conceptualizations (equity, reactance, and attribution theories) can be subsumed by the threat to self-esteem model (cf. Fisher et al., 1982). While space limitations preclude a *full* exposition of our model (see Fisher et al., 1982, for such a discussion), we present it in some detail because it is the context within which further conceptual refinements and empirical data are discussed. Following our presentation of the original model, we suggest a conceptual development dealing with the effect of controllable and uncontrollable threat associated with a receipt of help. Section IV demonstrates how our research on donor-recipient similarity effects is interwoven with the model in a validational net.

A. THREAT TO SELF-ESTEEM AND THE RECEIPT OF HELP

The threat to self-esteem model suggests that receiving aid is a mixed blessing which includes negative, self-threatening *and* positive, self-supportive psychological elements. Dependency relations have potential for self-threat and - support due to (1) self-relevant messages contained in aid itself (e.g., cues of caring and concern; of inferiority and failure), (2) values instilled during socialization (e.g., that one should be independent and self-reliant; that one should excel in some area), and (3) inherent instrumental qualities (e.g., information, money).

Aid will be *supportive* to the extent that it transmits a positive self-relevant message (e.g., highlights the donor's caring for the recipient), conforms with important socialized values (e.g., is a reward for excellence—such as a fellowship—rather than, like welfare, an indication that one has failed to be independent and self-reliant), and contains instrumental qualities (e.g., information, money). Aid will be *threatening* to the extent that it transmits a negative self-relevant message to the recipient, conflicts with important socialized values (e.g., independence and self-reliance; fairness in social relations), and fails to contain instrumental benefits.

Situational conditions (qualities of the help and the helper) and recipient *personality characteristics* determine whether a particular receipt of help is supportive or threatening (i.e., contains a positive or negative self-relevant message, conforms or conflicts with socialized values, and includes instrumental qualities or not). To the extent that, overall, situational conditions and recipient personality characteristics highlight elements in help that elicit self-support (e.g., a positive self-relevant message) relative to aspects that elicit self-threat (e.g., inconsistency with socialized values), help is predominantly supportive. To the extent that situational conditions and recipient characteristics make more salient elements in help that elicit self-threat relative to self-support, it is predominantly threatening.

Help that is predominantly self-threatening elicits a cluster of negative/defensive reactions, whereas help that is predominantly supportive elicits a cluster of positive/nondefensive responses. The negative cluster of reactions that occur when help is threatening includes unfavorable *self-perceptions* (e.g., affect and self-evaluation), unfavorable *external perceptions* (e.g., of the helper and the help), and defensive *behavior* (e.g., increased self-help efforts to terminate the uneasy dependency; unwillingness to seek or receive further help). The positive cluster of responses that occur when help is supportive includes relatively favorable *self-perceptions,* favorable *external perceptions,* and nondefensive *behavior* (e.g., fewer self-help efforts; greater willingness to seek and receive help).

Regarding the long-term effectiveness of help in promoting recipient self-reliance and independence, the model predicts that self-threatening help can also be effective help. This is because self-threat in aid *motivates* one to end a threatening dependency relation by investing in self-help. While experimental data lend general support to the proposed relation between self-threat and self-help (Fisher & Nadler, 1976), more recent work on effective coping suggests an important moderator: the recipient's level of perceived control. In Section III,B we examine work on effective coping and its links to the threat to self-esteem model. Based on an integration of the two bodies of literature, we propose a fuller account of the role of self-threat in determining reactions to aid. Our refinement of the threat to self-esteem model results in more specific predictions concerning the short- and long-term consequences of help.

B. MODELS OF EFFECTIVE HELPING AND COPING: THE IMPORTANCE OF PERCEIVED CONTROL

As does the threat to self-esteem model, discussions on helping victims cope with undesirable life events (e.g., Brickman et al., 1982; Brickman, Kidder, Coates, Rabinowitz, Cohn, & Karuza, 1983; Cohn, 1983; Janoff-Bulman et al., 1983; Silver & Wortman, 1980) implicitly or explicitly address the effectiveness of help. A recurrent issue in these discussions is whether a particular coping strategy or helping encounter increases the probability that recipients will become self-reliant. Work on coping highlights the role of *cognitive–attributional* processes in affecting an individual's perceptions of control, and relates control to successful coping outcomes. Although this approach and the threat to self-esteem model share a common focus on self-help, they are based on different conceptual underpinnings. *Affective–motivational* processes are central to the threat of self-esteem approach, while the work on coping relies more heavily on cognitive concepts.

An influential model of coping was formulated by Brickman et al. (1982). Employing a cognitive–attributional approach, these researchers brought the issue of the effectiveness of help into the limelight. They stated that more self-help is likely when the helper believes that the recipient should exert efforts to control his or her future outcomes. Their model deals with moral attributions (perceptions of what one *should* do) rather than causal attributions (perceptions of what one *can* do). Its extension to the issue of reactions to help would imply that if recipients come to perceive that they should act to control their environment, they will be more likely to help themselves (e.g., Cohn, 1983).

A related emphasis on recipient perceptions of control as a prerequisite for effective helping is found in other discussions in the coping literature (e.g., Coates, Renzaglia, & Embree, 1983; Fisher & Farina, 1979). These are concerned with causal rather than moral attributions. Coates et al. note that help may often prompt the recipient to relinquish control over his or her fate, which in turn elicits helplessness. Similar consequences of helping have been reported in total care institutions such as hospitals (e.g., Taylor, 1979) and homes for the aged (e.g., Langer & Rodin, 1976), both of which limit recipient perceptions of control. Yet, helplessness is not a necessary product of professional helping relations. Research evidence (e.g., Fisher & Farina, 1979; Langer & Rodin, 1976; Rodin & Langer, 1977), and conceptual work (Coates *et al.*, 1983) suggest that if recipients come to believe they have control over their outcomes, passive reliance on external sources of help may be avoided.

Another conceptualization of the role of perceived control in self-help has been offered by research on coping among victims of negative life events. Janoff-Bulman and co-workers (Janoff-Bulman, 1979; Janoff-Bulman *et al.*, 1983) have found that attributing one's past victimization to behaviors that are under one's control (behavioral self-blame) leads to reduced feelings of vulnerability, to active coping efforts, and consequently to more effective coping (e.g., Bulman & Wortman, 1977; Janoff-Bulman, 1979). Whitcher-Alagna (1983) notes that medical treatment may be affected positively by enhancing patients' actual or perceived control. Similarly, Greenberg, Ruback, and Westcott (1983) discuss how crime victims can reduce anxieties about revictimization by doing specific things to reassert their control (e.g., putting extra locks on doors).

All the above conceptualizations stress the role of perceptions of control in effective helping and coping. Those who hold a degree of control help themselves more than those who do not. How can this emphasis on control be integrated with the threat to self-esteem model, which maintains that active self-help depends on the degree of threat in aid?

C. INTEGRATING THE COPING LITERATURE
    WITH THE THREAT TO SELF-ESTEEM MODEL

A closer examination of the two concepts (self-threat in aid and perceived control) suggests an integration between the threat to self-esteem model and most coping models. Each approach highlights a different aspect of control. The threat to self-esteem model centers on one's *motivation* to exert control through efforts to become independent. It specifies that self-threat is an important condition that motivates the recipient to terminate dependency. In contrast, most work on coping focuses on one's *perceived ability* to alter one's outcomes (cf. Bandura, 1977, 1982). These researchers maintain that self-help is a function of perceptions that one can or cannot control outcomes. We will refer to the type of control emphasized by the threat to self-esteem model as *motivation for control,* and to the type of control highlighted in the coping literature as *causal control.*[2]

[2]An implicit assumption in the coping literature is that there exists a constant (and high) degree of motivation for control (cf. Burger & Cooper, 1979, for a review). Nevertheless, this is not necessarily true for help recipients. Recipients may be comfortable with dependency, and have little desire to exert efforts to improve their situation (cf. also Brickman *et al.*, 1982). Other researchers

The distinction between the motivational and causal aspects of control is conceptually similar to that between causal and moral attributions made by others (cf. Brickman *et al.,* 1982; Heider, 1958). Motivation for control and causal control can be independent of each other: Recipients may perceive themselves as able to control their environment by investing in self-help, but may not be motivated to act. Conversely, they may be motivated to change current dependency, but may perceive themselves as unable to do so. In either instance, self-help is not likely to follow the receipt of aid. However, in the former case help is likely to be associated with a relatively favorable psychological state, while in the latter it is apt to elicit a negative, helplessness-like state (e.g., unfavorable affect and decreased self-esteem).

We would argue that for help to lead to subsequent self-help and independence, both causal control and motivation for control must be present. Thus, for help to be effective, two conditions must be met: (1) the recipient must perceive of him- or herself as *able* to change the situation necessitating help, and (2) in line with the threat to self-esteem approach, help should be self-threatening so the recipient is *motivated* to terminate dependency.

D. CONTROLLABLE AND UNCONTROLLABLE THREAT IN HELP: A FORMAL STATEMENT

Based on the above integration with cognitive–attributional work, help that is threatening (and therefore that elicits a high motivation to regain control) may be separated into two types. The distinction relies on whether or not the recipient expects to have control over the subsequent situation (i.e., whether he or she has high or low causal control). When threatening help is coupled with high expectations for control over future outcomes, *controllable self-threat* is experienced. In contrast, when threatening help is coupled with low expectations of control over the future, *uncontrollable self-threat* occurs. This leads to a refinement in the relation posited by the original formulation of our model (cf. Fisher *et al.,* 1982) between the threat to self-esteem in help and subsequent self-help. While the Fisher *et al.* (1982) model predicted that greater self-threat should lead to increased self-help, incorporating the notion of causal control leads to a refined prediction. Specifically, it is now posited that the initiation of self-help will depend on the interaction of self-threat and perceived control.

Our joint consideration of the motivational and causal aspects of control is not without parallels in the literature. For example, it is congruent with Wortman

---

(e.g., Burger & Cooper, 1979) have pointed out that motivation to exercise control can vary as a function of both the individual and the situation.

and Brehm's (1975) integration of learned helplessness and reactance theory. Regarding causal control, Wortman and Brehm predict that people who perceive high control over their outcomes initially respond to uncontrollable events by exerting efforts to regain control. In contrast, those without such expectations give up immediately and become depressed without an initial period of invigoration. Regarding motivation for control, Wortman and Brehm (1975) predict that one's efforts to reassert control via self-help depend on the importance of the outcome. More controlling efforts are expected when the value of the outcome is high rather than low. This emphasis on cognitive and motivational elements as determinants of invigoration or resignation corresponds to our view that self-help following aid will be influenced by both motivational and cognitive aspects of control.

In sum, the threat to self-esteem model maintains its initial distinction between self-threatening and self-supportive help, but now adds the concept of causal control. The refined model allows for the consideration of variables that will differentially affect immediate affective, evaluative, and behavioral reactions to help, as well as variables that will affect the motivation, or lack thereof, to end dependency. The integration of causal control with motivation for control allows one to delineate more specifically ways in which self-threat in aid can be harnessed to encourage future self-reliance.

Consistent with our initial formulation (cf. Fisher *et al.*, 1982, pages 49–50) and as summarized in Fig. 1, we propose the following.

1. Situational conditions (characteristics of the helper and of the help) and personality variables (recipient characteristics) determine the extent to which aid is self-supportive or self-threatening.

2. Aid that supports one's self-concept (i.e., is primarily self-supportive) elicits a cluster of positive, nondefensive reactions, including positive affect, favorable self- and other evaluations, and nondefensive behaviors (e.g., less self-help, high help-seeking).

Based on the posited interaction between self-threat and perceived control, we now propose that:

3. Aid which threatens one's self-concept (i.e., is primarily self-threatening) elicits one of two clusters of recipient responses, depending on whether or not the recipient expects to have control over subsequent outcomes (i.e., whether the self-threat is controllable or uncontrollable).

4. Self-threat following aid which is associated with control over subsequent outcomes (controllable self-threat) elicits short-term psychological distress (negative affect, unfavorable self- and other evaluations), and instrumental be-

Fig. 1. Schematic diagram of the threat × control model of reactions to help.

SELF-CONSEQUENCES

IMMEDIATE REACTIONS

LONG-TERM CONSEQUENCES

Conditions associated with a receipt of aid (characteristics of the help, characteristics of the helper, characteristics of the recipient).

Magnitude of self-threat or self-support in aid for the recipient

CONTINUUM OF EFFECTS ON SELF-ESTEEM

High self-support for the recipient's self-esteem

High self-threat to recipient's self-esteem

Conditions precipitating high perceived causal control

Conditions precipitating low perceived causal control

• positive affect
• positive evaluation of donor and aid
• high help seeking
• low motivation for improvement
• low degree of subsequent self-help

• negative affect
• negative evaluation of donor and aid
• low help seeking
• high motivation for future improvement
• high degree of subsequent self-help

• negative affect
• negative evaluation of donor and aid
• high help seeking
• high motivation for future improvement
• low degree of subsequent self-help

NO CHANGE

IMPROVEMENT
positive affect
positive evaluation donor and aid

Helplessness-like dependency

havioral responses (high self-help efforts, low help seeking).[3] After the self-threat has been diffused through self-help, a cluster of positive affective and evaluative responses related to newly gained independence are likely.

5. Self-threat following aid which is associated with lack of control over subsequent outcomes (uncontrollable self-threat) elicits a cluster of negative reactions (negative affect and unfavorable self- and other evaluations), and is not likely to lead to instrumental behavioral responses, but rather to continued reliance on external sources of help. This cluster of responses is likely to persist over time.

6. The degree of causal control experienced by aid recipients is determined by situational conditions and chronic beliefs about one's ability to end dependency through the investment of effort.

The stress literature suggests a number of situational conditions likely to be associated with high causal control in a helping context. For example, attributing current difficulties to unstable factors (e.g., lack of effort) is one such variable (cf. Dweck, 1975). In line with the drive-reduction hypothesis (Leventhal, 1970), knowledge of a specific behavioral route to deal with self-threat is likely to be associated with higher perceptions of control than if this were not the case. Perceived control is also related to recipient personality characteristics. For example, a study on the effects of peer tutoring suggests that high achievers, who tend to have stronger beliefs that they can control their environment through effort expenditure (e.g., Weiner, Frieze, Kukla, Reed, Rest, & Rosenbaum, 1972), are more likely than low achievers to respond to self-threatening help with self-help efforts (DePaulo, Webb, & Hoover, 1983).

IV. Research on the Effect
of Donor–Recipient Similarity

In this section we discuss a line of research bearing on the *validity* of the threat to self-esteem model—our work on the effect of donor–recipient similarity. We attend first to research testing the assertion of the model that situa-

---

[3]Recent discussions in the help-seeking literature have drawn a distinction between dependency-oriented and instrumental help seeking (e.g., Ames, 1983; Asser, 1978; LeGall, Gumerman, & Scott-Jones, 1983). Instrumental help seeking is "a proactive problem-solving strategy employed by persons who desire to achieve some goal" (Ames, p. 2). Dependency-oriented help seeking occurs when one abdicates control and seeks the full solution to a current problem. Operationally, instrumental help seeking is likely to take the form of partial requests (e.g., seeking a hint), while dependency-related help seeking results in requests for full solutions. Because our model centers on the avoidance of dependency under self-threatening conditions, our focus here is on dependency-oriented help seeking.

tional conditions and personality variables determine the extent to which help is self-threatening or self-supportive. Next, we discuss studies relevant to the proposed relation between the self-consequences of help and recipient behavior. Finally, we present data relating to the prediction that controllable and uncontrollable self-threat in aid elicit differential effects.

A. DONOR–RECIPIENT SIMILARITY: CONCEPTUAL LOGIC OF THE BASE RELATIONSHIP

The threat to self-esteem model states that situational conditions determine the self-threat or -support in aid. Our initial research on situational conditions focused on how similarity between the donor and the recipient affects the self-consequences of aid. Self-theorists have argued that one makes judgments about the self by comparing one's outcomes with those of relevant others. In addition, social comparison theory (Festinger, 1954), and related efforts (e.g., Brickman & Bulman, 1977; Mettee & Riskind, 1974; Nadler, Jazwinski, Lau, & Miller, 1980), indicate that the perceived *similarity* of two individuals determines the impact of one's fate on the second person's self-judgments. Only similar others' outcomes are psychologically relevant and lead to self-conclusions (e.g., Castore & DeNinno, 1977). So, when a similar other performs relatively better than another individual and offers to help that person, the recipient should experience a negative social comparison and resultant negative affect and self-evaluation (e.g., Nadler *et al.*, 1980; Tesser, 1980).

This suggests that receiving aid *may* be an interpersonal event which occasions an unfavorable social comparison, and which elicits self-threat and negative/defensive reactions. However, the negative aspects of aid may be psychologically relevant only when the helper is a similar (social comparison) other. When the donor is dissimilar, the positive, instrumental aspects of help are more psychologically salient, and help can elicit positive, nondefensive reactions. The above analysis is in line with our model, which suggests that both threatening elements (such as comparison stress) and supportive signs of donor caring and concern may be inherent in help. Further, situational conditions (in this case, donor–recipient similarity) determine the extent to which help is self-threatening or -supportive.

More specifically in terms of the model, a situational condition—similarity—affects both the *self-relevant message* in help, and whether the recipient can consider him- or herself to be conforming with *socialized values* of independence and self-reliance. Concerning the message, when similarity is high, cues of relative inferiority and dependency in aid are stronger, compared to the potential cues of caring and concern, than when similarity is low. How does donor–recipient similarity affect the recipient's perceived congruence with important socialized values? A similar donor highlights the inconsistency between societal norms of self-reliance and independence (exemplified by the social comparison other's position) and the recipient's own situation. In effect, the potential *comparison stress* in any interpersonal helping exchange is made salient by donor–recipient similarity.

1. Establishing the Base Relationship

To test this line of reasoning, we created an involving task (a stock market simulation) at which subjects failed. Participants needed resources (poker chips) to continue in the experiment. Each subject was paired with a partner. Some received help from their partner, who was manipulated to be similar or dissimilar to them, while others did not.[4] Donor–recipient similarity was operationalized by varying the degree of attitude similarity between the donor and the recipient. The experiment employed a 2 (attitudinally similar vs. dissimilar partner) × 2 (help vs. no help control) design. (For a thorough description of the experimental procedures, see Fisher & Nadler, 1974.)

As can be seen in Fig. 2, subjects receiving help from a similar other had lower self-perceptions (affect and ratings of self-confidence), than those in a similar partner, no-help control group. Aid from a dissimilar partner led to more favorable self-perceptions than the dissimilar partner, no-help control condition. Also, aid from a similar other was more self-threatening than help from a dissimilar one (Fisher & Nadler, 1974). This corroborates our prediction that help from a similar other is potentially threatening, whereas aid from a dissimilar other is potentially supportive.

2. Beyond Attitude Similarity

The results from the above experiment were somewhat limited in generalizability. Although attitudinally similar others serve for comparison purposes (Castore & DeNinno, 1977) and we draw more self-information from their fate than from that of dissimilar others (Novak & Lerner, 1968; Nadler *et al.*, 1980), the effects we observed could be unique to the case of donor–recipient attitude similarity and its associated consequences (e.g., liking; cf. Byrne, 1971). A stronger case for the argument that help from a similar other is self-threatening due to comparison stress would require a replication with similarity operationalized in some other way.

Fisher, Harrison, and Nadler (1978) addressed this issue. Here, the donor was said to have a similar or dissimilar level of task-relevant knowledge. Also, to

---

[4]Subjects in the no-help control group were not aware that anyone else received help.

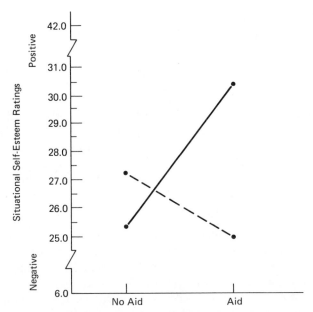

Fig. 2.   Effects of aid from a similar (– – –) or dissimilar (—) other on situational self-esteem. From Fisher, J. D., & Nadler, A., The effect of similarity between donor and recipient on recipient reactions to aid. *Journal of Applied Social Psychology,* 1974, **4,** 230–243. Reprinted by permission.

allow us to generalize beyond the type of financial aid used by Fisher and Nadler (1974), help consisted of advice on a pattern-recognition task. A 2 (help vs. no help) × 2 (similar vs. dissimilar task-relevant knowledge) between subjects design was run. As before, the focus was the effect of help on recipient self-evaluation. Results were in accord with the earlier study. Relative to an appropriate no-help control group, subjects receiving help from a donor with similar task-relevant knowledge had lower self-evaluations. When the donor had dissimilar (i.e., more) task-relevant knowledge, help led to more favorable self-evaluations than in an appropriate control group.[5]

Taken together, the data from both experiments suggest that donor–recipient similarity effects are not unique to attitude similarity manipulations. Support is accorded to the notion that the social comparison process, not some other correlate of attitude similarity (e.g., liking), is the most parsimonious explanation for the effect of similarity on recipient self-perception.

[5]Dissimilarity was operationalized as greater knowledge in this study; there was no dissimilar, lower knowledge condition. However, as will become quite clear in this discussion, the data in their entirety support the role of comparison stress as a mediator of self-threat in aid.

B. OTHER PERSON AND SITUATION DETERMINANTS
    OF THE SELF-CONSEQUENCES OF HELP

The first phase of our research demonstrated that help is a mixture of self-threatening and -supportive elements, and that donor–recipient similarity is a major situational determinant of the relative weight of each. The threat to self-esteem model states that situational and personality variables jointly determine the intensity of self-threat or -support in help (cf. Fisher *et al.*, 1982, pp. 49–50). Since we initially focused on donor–recipient similarity as a determinant of the self-consequences of help, the next stage of our research centered on the joint effects of other person and situation variables on this relationship.

1. The Effect of Persistent Self-Esteem

It would seem reasonable to assume that the recipient's persistent self-esteem could affect his or her sensitivity to the self-threatening and -supportive elements in help (cf. Underwood, 1975). If this were so, individuals with high and low self-esteem would be affected differentially by donor–recipient similarity. To test this possibility, Nadler *et al.* (1976) conducted an experiment in which subjects with high or low self-esteem (based on scores on the Cooper-smith, 1967, self-esteem inventory) received or did not receive help from an attitudinally similar or dissimilar other. The methods were very similar to those employed by Fisher and Nadler (1974).

The results (Fig. 3) indicate that, as hypothesized, people with high and low self-esteem respond differently to help from a similar other. For those with high self-esteem, help from a similar other elicited lower self-evaluations and less favorable affect than not receiving help from a similar partner. Subjects with low

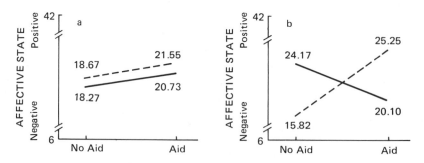

Fig. 3. Similarity by aid interaction for affective state (situational self-esteem) at each level of persistent self-esteem. —, Similar pair mate; – – –, dissimilar pair mate. (a) A × B at level C_1 (low self-esteem); $p < .90$. (b) A × B at level C_2 (high self-esteem); $p < .006$. From Nadler, A., Fisher, J. D., & Streufert, S., When helping hurts: Effects of donor–recipient similarity and recipient self-esteem on reactions to aid. *Journal of Personality*, 1976, **44**, 392–409. Reprinted by permission.

self-esteem were not threatened by aid from either partner. Thus, persistent self-esteem moderates the donor–recipient similarity effects we have observed.

These findings are congruent with a consistency approach to the effect of persistent self-esteem on responses to threatening events (Bramel, 1968). In terms of this approach, negative information about the self is disturbing to high self-esteem individuals because it is inconsistent with their positive self-cognitions. Such information is not disturbing to low self-esteem individuals, since it is consistent with their negative self-cognitions. In the present context, the threatening information about relative inferiority and dependency inherent in help from a similar other is inconsistent with high self-esteem individuals' view of self, so it precipitates negative affect and self-evaluation. For low self-esteem individuals, inferiority to and dependence on others are consistent with existing unfavorable self-conceptions. Therefore, help from a similar other does not pose a threat to self-esteem.

These findings, which are corroborated by related research (DePaulo et al., 1981; Nadler et al., 1979; Nadler, Sheinberg, & Jaffe, 1981; Nadler & Mayseless, 1983; Nadler, 1983; Tessler & Schwartz, 1972), have an important implication.[6] When interpreted in line with conceptual work by Underwood (1975) they corroborate a major assumption of the threat to self-esteem model: that elements of self-threat and -support in help mediate between the aid situation and the recipient's reactions (propositions 2 and 3, p. 94). Underwood (1975) suggested that the role of a presumed intervening construct can be validated if people who differ on a relevant personality dimension (persistent self-esteem in this case) respond (1) differentially, and (2) in a conceptually consistent manner to the manipulation in question. Since this occurred in the above study, the findings corroborate the threat to self-esteem assumption that self-related cues transmitted by help are a major determinant of recipient reaction.

2. The Effect of Task Centrality

Because similarity and friendship are empirically linked (e.g., Byrne, 1971), our donor–recipient similarity findings could have implications for understanding helping relations between friends. Since close others (such as friends) are often used for comparison purposes (e.g., Tesser, 1980), help from a friend could be more self-threatening than help from a stranger. However, this suggestion is at odds with commonsense notions about relations between friends and discussions of the positive effects of help from friends and relatives (e.g., Bar-Tal et al., 1977; Clark, 1983; Clark & Mills, 1979; DePaulo, 1982).

---

[6]There exist several studies which have found an opposite pattern: that help is more self-threatening for low self-esteem individuals (e.g., Morris & Rosen, 1973). However, closer scrutiny indicates that this empirical controversy is more apparent than real. The reader is referred to Nadler and Mayseless (1983) for a complete discussion.

How can our research on the threatening impact of donor–recipient similarity be reconciled with the apparently favorable effects of help from friends? First, our observations of comparison stress in help may be unique to laboratory settings where levels of similarity are carefully manipulated and other variables controlled. They may not apply to helping relations between friends. In that case, the external validity and overall implications of our earlier research would be diminished. Another possibility is that both our previous research and that of others is correct—under certain conditions. Help from a friend may be either more pleasant *or* more painful than help from a more socially distant other. An important situational variable that may moderate this effect is the ego relevance (or *centrality*) of the helping task (cf. also DePaulo, 1982).

The potential message of relative inferiority and dependency in help should be self-threatening only on tasks that are central to self-esteem (e.g., those perceived as related to intelligence). Thus, the comparison stress in help from a socially close (or a similar other) should be limited to help reflecting inferiority on a central dimension. If help reflects on a noncentral dimension (e.g., if it is precipitated by bad luck) no potential self-threat should be inherent, and its positive, supportive elements may be salient and meaningful, *especially* when the donor is a friend.

To test these assumptions, we ran an experiment in which subjects received help on a central or a noncentral task from a friend or a stranger (Nadler, Fisher, & Ben-Itzhak, 1983). The experimental task involved having subjects solve a mystery (see Nadler, Shapira, & Ben-Itzhak, 1982, for a detailed description of the procedures). Subjects could solve it only after receiving help from their partner. Half were helped twice (consecutively); the other half once. We will discuss only the responses of those helped twice—for a complete exposition of the data, see Nadler, Fisher, and Ben-Itzhak (1983).

As predicted, there was an interaction of social proximity × task centrality for the recipient's affect, $F(1, 43) = 3.93, p < .05$. Subjects receiving help from a friend on a central task had less positive affect than those who received such help from a stranger. Conversely, those receiving help from a friend on a noncentral task had more favorable affect than those receiving such help from a stranger. A parallel pattern was observed for the measure of self-evaluation (see Table 1).

Analyses of recipient external perceptions revealed similar patterns. As can be seen in Table I, liking toward the helper was lowest in the condition of maximal self-threat (help from a friend on a central task) and highest in the condition of maximal self-support (help from a friend on a noncentral task). Also, subjects expected the most negative future relations with a friend who helped on a central task. For both measures, the interaction of social proximity × centrality was highly significant, $F(1, 44) = 13.38, p < .001; F(1, 44) = 7.20, p < .01$, respectively.

TABLE I

EFFECTS OF AID FROM A STRANGER OR FRIEND ON RECIPIENT SELF-PERCEPTIONS AND EXTERNAL PERCEPTIONS[a]

Helper	Affect		Self-evaluations	
	Central	Noncentral	Central	Noncentral
Friend	3.98	5.63	5.08	6.33
Stranger	5.07	4.89	5.75	6.15

	Liking for helper		Expected relations	
	Central	Noncentral	Central	Noncentral
Friend	3.83	5.88	4.14	6.25
Stranger	5.25	4.50	5.36	5.36

[a]Adapted from Nadler, Fisher, and Ben-Itzhak (1983). *Journal of Personality and Social Psychology,* **44,** 310–321.

Regarding subjects' perceptions of the reasons for the helpers' benevolence, there were some interesting results. A social proximity × centrality interaction, $F(1, 44) = 8.81, p < .01$, indicates that subjects who had been helped twice by a friend were most likely to believe the helper's benevolence reflected a wish to show superiority (see Table II).

These findings portray a consistent pattern. They indicate that help from a socially close other may be especially pleasant *or* painful, and that the moderator of "pain" or "pleasure" in this context is task centrality. That help from a friend on a central task led subjects to believe their helper wanted to show relative superiority suggests that the self-threat in this condition is due to comparison stress. Overall, there is no *simple* answer regarding whether help from a friend elicits more or less favorable reactions than help from a stranger. One situational moderator is task centrality. This is consistent with our model's

TABLE II

MEAN AGREEMENT SCORES OF SUBJECTS WHO HAD BEEN HELPED TWICE WITH THE STATEMENT "MY PARTNER HELPED BECAUSE HE WANTS TO SHOW ME THAT HE IS MORE ABLE THAN MYSELF"

	Central help	Noncentral help
Friend	5.58	2.33
Stranger	2.92	2.82

assumption that situational conditions determine the relative weight of the threatening and supportive elements in help (e.g., comparison stress and signs of caring from a liked other, respectively).

These data show that comparison stress is not unique to *experimental* manipulations of interpersonal similarity. The potential for it is present in naturally occurring dyadic friendships. Given certain conditions, help may intensify comparison stress, cause a decrement in recipient affect, and self-evaluation, and introduce strain into otherwise harmonious interpersonal relations. Based on our findings, we can now state that help from a socially close other on a central task is threatening. Taken together with our earlier research on the effect of experimentally induced similarity, the most parsimonious explanation for the present findings is comparison stress inherent in the fate of a psychologically relevant other (cf. Tesser, 1980).

Overall, the second phase of our research is important at several levels. First, it suggests that the inconsistency between receiving help from a similar other and relevant self-cognitions is greater for high than low self-esteem individuals. Therefore, only the former are sensitive to the potential self-threat in such help. Second, it establishes that for help from a socially close other to be threatening it must reflect inferiority on an ego-relevant dimension. Finally, it extends beyond laboratory manipulations of interpersonal similarity to naturally occurring cases of social proximity.

Conceptually, the data thus far corroborate the basic assumptions of the threat to self-esteem model. Studies have validated the idea that help contains elements of self-threat and -support. Donor–recipient social proximity (as operationalized by interpersonal similarity and friendship) affects the message communicated by help and amplifies the inconsistency between dependency and internalized values, thereby determining the self-threat or -support in help. Social proximity has these effects because it determines the comparison stress in help. Also in line with our model, this relationship is moderated by situational and personality variables (e.g., task centrality and persistent self-esteem).

C. EXPLORING BEHAVIORAL RESPONSES

The studies described thus far center on how donor–recipient social proximity affects recipients' immediate affective and evaluative responses. The data show that the threat to self-esteem model predicts these quite nicely. Our model also states that the degree of self-threat in help determines recipient *behavior*. The third stage of our research relates donor–recipient similarity to this response dimension.

Our conceptualization predicts that when conditions associated with help elicit self-threat, recipients display a defensive behavior pattern. They may refrain from seeking help, and if it has been received, they are likely to engage in self-help efforts to terminate the uneasy dependency. If aid-related conditions cause help to be self-supportive, recipients display nondefensive behaviors. They seek help from others and help themselves less, since dependency is not aversive.

Applying this reasoning to the case of donor–recipient similarity suggests the following predictions. Since help from a similar other is relatively threatening, recipients should seek less help and engage in more self-help than when the donor is dissimilar. In line with the data in preceding sections, these effects should be apparent only when help reflects on a central dimension, and when the recipient has high self-esteem. In addition, when the self-threat in aid is controllable, reluctance to seek help and increased self-help following it should be greater than when self-threat is uncontrollable. However, the latter prediction is not addressed in this section since we examine only studies involving controllable self-threat.

To test some of the above propositions, Nadler, Fisher, and Kolker (1982) employed a 2 (attitudinally similar vs. dissimilar helper) $\times$ 2 (help on a central vs. noncentral task) $\times$ 2 (high vs. low self-esteem recipient) design. Subjects, who were 17- to 18-year old high school students, were asked to solve anagrams. Half were presented with an attitudinally similar partner, the other half with an attitudinally dissimilar one. Also, half (central task condition) were told performance was related to intelligence and creativity; the other half (noncentral task condition) that it depended on luck. Finally, subjects were divided into those with high and low persistent self-esteem.

Following our induction of need state, subjects were allowed to seek help from their partner. The amount of help each requested served as an index of help-seeking, and the results corroborated our predictions. A similarity $\times$ centrality interaction, $F(1, 120) = 3.94$, $p < .05$, indicated that the least help was sought by subjects with similar partners who believed they were performing a central task. When the help-seeking responses of high and low self-esteem individuals were compared, the similarity $\times$ centrality interaction was more salient for high than for low self-esteem subjects. The difference between the two groups was significant at the .05 level.

Thus, one is most reluctant to admit incompetence and inferiority by seeking help on a central task when donor–recipient similarity induces a high degree of comparison stress. Congruent with a consistency approach (cf. Nadler *et al.*, 1976, 1979; Nadler, Fisher, & Kolker, 1982; Tessler & Schwartz, 1972), high self-esteem individuals are most sensitive to this self-threat.

Our model also assumes that if the source of the threat is controllable, recipients will engage in efforts to end dependency. More self-help will occur if help is associated with controllable self-threat than when help is supportive. Thus, when the potential for control is present, greater self-help should occur when the donor is a socially close other and when help reflects inferiority on a central dimension, than when these conditions are absent.

We have obtained data that bear on this final prediction (Nadler, Goldberg, & Fisher, 1983). To examine differential self-help, we ran a 2 (attitudinally similar vs. dissimilar helper) × 2 (central vs. noncentral help) between-subjects design. Subjects participated in a quiz game and were presented with photographs and quotes of "famous people." The stimuli were presented by an attitudinally similar or dissimilar subject said to have been randomly chosen to be "quiz master." This person gave subjects a hint which helped them answer a question correctly and earn a monetary bonus. For half the subjects (noncentral aid conditions) the "quiz master" had the correct answers in front of him; for the other half (central aid conditions) help was supposedly based on personal knowledge.

Next, subjects were provided with a self-help opportunity. Participants were given a four-page document to read. They were told that the next part of the experiment assumed knowledge of the information in it, and that they could write down details for future reference. By including a specific behavioral route to future success in the experimental context, any self-threat generated by the experimental manipulations was rendered controllable. In effect, all subjects were given relatively high expectations for control over future outcomes. The number of units of information written down by subjects served as an index of self-help.

The results support our predictions. The two-way interaction of similarity × centrality, $F(1, 44) = 3.92, p < .05$, indicates that recipients of central aid from a similar other wrote down more information than recipients of noncentral aid from a similar other. No differences in self-help were observed in the other experimental conditions. Subjects' self-evaluations, measured immediately after the receipt of help, portray a consistent pattern. A marginal similarity × centrality interaction, $F(1, 44) = 2.61, p < .11$, suggests that recipients of central aid from a similar other had lower self-evaluations than recipients of noncentral aid from a similar other. Recipients of central aid from a dissimilar other tended to have higher self-evaluations than recipients of noncentral aid from a dissimilar other.

The study provides important support for the prediction of the threat to self-esteem model that threatening help precipitates motivation to restore self-esteem. Under controllable circumstances, this is manifested behaviorally by increased self-help.

Overall, the third phase of our research indicates that help-related conditions which contain a negative message for the recipient, and which amplify the inconsistency between values of self-reliance and the dependency in help, affect recipient *behavior*. To escape this negative message and inconsistency with socialized values, recipients avoid dependency by engaging in less help-seeking.

When they are dependent on threatening help and perceive themselves as able to change their lot, they try to terminate dependency and restore consistency through self-help.

D. RECIPIENT REACTION TO CONTROLLABLE AND UNCONTROLLABLE THREAT IN HELP

In the preceding sections, data were presented pertaining to the differential effects of self-supportive and -threatening help. Here we focus mostly on the differential effects of threatening help, when the threat is controllable or uncontrollable. The refinement of our model on which these studies are based, which was discussed in Section III,D, is a new conceptual development. It contains predictions that cover a wide range of recipient reactions; therefore much empirical work is needed to test all of its propositions. Here we present data which bear on the crux of the new conceptual assertion, i.e., that controllable and uncontrollable threat in help elicit differential self-help, affective, and evaluative responses. It is hoped that the heuristic value of the reconceptualization will stimulate additional research which more fully accounts for the hypothesized processes and effects.

Our refined model predicts more self-help under conditions of *controllable self-threat* (high motivation for control and high causal control) than under conditions of *uncontrollable self-threat* (high motivation for control and low causal control), or when help is supportive (low motivation for control). It also predicts that when controllable threat elicits self-help the threat is likely to be diffused, which occasions a positive shift in affective and evaluative reactions. We have completed an experiment that bears directly on these predictions (Nadler, Ben-Itzhak, & Fisher, 1983). Self-threat in help was manipulated via donor–recipient social proximity (cf. Nadler, Fisher, & Ben-Itzhak, 1983) and perceived control was experimentally induced by providing or not providing specific behavioral suggestions for approaching the problem of improving one's performance. It was assumed that the latter manipulation would result in increased causal control—the expectation that one would have control over future outcomes (see Thompson, 1981).

The study employed a 2 (help from a friend vs. help from a stranger) × 2 (suggestions vs. no suggestions for future improvement) design. The experimental task involved identifying the murderer in a detective story, and performance was linked to ego-central dimensions (i.e., intelligence) (see Nadler, Shapira, & Ben-Itzhak, 1982; Nadler, Fisher, & Ben-Itzhak, 1983, for a complete description of the procedures). After an initial failure to complete the task, all subjects received help from their partner enabling a correct solution of that particular task.

Subjects were then informed that in a subsequent part of the experiment they would work on an actual crime from police records.

First, however, participants were afforded a self-help opportunity. They were given a description of another murder, instructed to read it for as long as they wanted and to become familiar with it, and provided with a paper and pencil to write down details. Subjects were led to believe that these efforts would be instrumental later when they were presented with a list of questions about the crime. At this point, half were given specific behavioral suggestions on how to approach the problem of improving their performance. The other half were not. The time spent preparing for the impending task and the amount of information written down constituted self-help indices (Table III). Following the self-help measure, subjects responded to a questionnaire including attributions for task performance, indices of affect, and a measure of liking toward the donor (Table IV).

A main effect on the effort attribution item, $F(1, 44) = 88.24$, $p < .001$, indicates that subjects receiving specific suggestions attributed task performance more to effort than those not receiving them. This supports our contention that specific suggestions contribute to causal control—the expectation that one will have control over the subsequent situation. A two-way interaction, $F(1, 44) = 14.62$, $p < .001$, indicates that the most time was spent preparing for the next task by subjects receiving threatening help (from a friend) *and* specific behavioral suggestions for improvement. The analysis of the number of words written down by subjects preparing for the next task revealed a 2×2 interaction, $F(1, 44) = 13.81$, $p < .001$, due to the large number written by subjects who received help from a friend, along with specific suggestions. These results support our prediction that self-help is facilitated by controllable self-threat (i.e., high motivation for control and high causal control).

The findings for affect and liking also support our predictions. For affect, a 2×2 interaction, $F(1, 44) = 62.32$, $p < .001$, indicates that the lowest affect occurred in the uncontrollable threat (friend/no suggestions) cell. For subjects in the controllable threat (friend/suggestions) condition, self-help efforts diffused

TABLE III

MEAN SCORES ON INDICES OF SELF-HELP[a]

Helper	Time spent in preparation (min)		Number of words written	
	Instructions	No instructions	Instructions	No instructions
Friend	11.25	1.92	53.92	11.25
Stranger	5.58	2.17	26.75	9.67

[a]From Nadler, Ben-Itzhak, and Fisher (1983).

TABLE IV

MEAN SCORES ON AFFECT AND LIKING[a,b]

Helper	Affect		Liking toward donor	
	Instructions	No instructions	Instructions	No instructions
Friend	23.67	13.42	49.75	37.67
Stranger	24.92	24.00	49.83	48.42

[a]From Nadler, Ben-Itzhak, and Fisher (1983).
[b]Higher scores indicate more positive responses.

self-threat, and affect scores were no different than in the supportive help condition.

Similar patterns were evident for the measure of liking toward the donor. A 2×2 interaction, $F(1, 44) = 12.8$, $p < .001$ indicates that again the lowest liking occurred in the uncontrollable threat conditon. For subjects in the controllable threat condition, self-help efforts diffused the negative effects of self-threat, and liking scores were no different than in the supportive aid conditions.

Subjects' performance attributions are of particular interest in understanding the psychological processes operating. Of special conceptual importance are attributions to "ability" and "effort" of subjects in the various experimental cells (Table V). The analysis of variance (ANOVA) on ability attributions revealed a 2×2 interaction, $F(1, 44) = 81.81$, $p < .001$, due to the high degree to which subjects in the uncontrollable threat condition attributed their poor performance to lack of ability. Those in the other cells did not view this as a major cause of their performance. Regarding effort attributions, we noted earlier that subjects receiving specific suggestions attributed performance more to effort than those not receiving them. Also, although the two-way interaction did not reach

TABLE V

MEAN SCORES ON ATTRIBUTIONS FOR TASK PERFORMANCE[a,b]

	Ability attributions		Effort attributions	
	Instructions	No instructions	Instructions	No instructions
Friend	2.08	5.92	5.33	2.17
Stranger	2.08	2.00	5.00	1.83

[a]From Nadler, Ben-Itzhak, and Fisher (1983).
[b]For ability attributions, higher scores indicate less attribution to ability; for effort attributions, higher scores indicate greater attribution to ability.

significance, subjects in the controllable threat (friend/suggestions) condition agreed most with a statement that performance on similar tasks depends on effort.

Overall, the results importantly extend the data reported in previous sections. On the behavioral level, self-help is more likely when recipients believe they can *and* should regain independence by investing effort. Recipients of threatening help (aid from a friend) coped with threat by active self-help only when given a specific behavioral route. This supports our view that for threat in help to promote self-help and future independence, there must be high causal control. The attributional data corroborate this. Behavioral recommendations are associated with perceptions that effort is the route to achieve future success on similar tasks, and these perceptions are especially strong when behavioral recommendations are accompanied by high motivation for control. On the other hand, receiving threatening help in an uncontrollable environment elicits attributions of lack of ability for the failure necessitating help. Attributional analyses of learned helplessness (Abramson, Seligman, & Teasdale, 1978) state that such uncontrollable threat is apt to result in long-term dependency and passivity.

Our model predicts the short- and long-term consequences of receiving help. In the short run both controllable and uncontrollable threat elicit affective distress and unfavorable self- and external evaluations. In the long run, improvements in self- and external perceptions will occur following self-help efforts by recipients experiencing controllable threat. In the present study (Nadler, Ben-Itzhak, & Fisher, 1983), measures of affect and liking taken *after* self-help support this contention.

These data are also congruent with past research on the differential effects of self-threatening and -supportive help. Results of earlier studies show that central help from a socially close other elicits more negative reactions than such help from a stranger. In that work, the dependent measures were taken immediately after help and before any self-help opportunity. In the Nadler, Ben-Itzhak, and Fisher (1983) study, central help from a friend without specific behavioral recommendations (i.e., conditions of uncontrollable self-threat, which promote little self-help) similarly elicited lower affect and liking than help from a stranger (i.e., supportive help). Our studies that have found a *positive* relationship between self-threat and self-help (Fisher & Nadler, 1976; Nadler, Goldberg, & Fisher, 1983) measured self-help under controllable conditions in which subjects had a specific route through which they could improve.

Only a few other experiments have directly assessed postaid self-help and self-improvement. These too can be interpreted in line with our conceptualization. DePaulo *et al.* (1981) explored the link between the recipient's persistent self-esteem and subsequent improvement on an unrelated task. High and low self-esteem subjects received or did not receive help—some were given threatening help, others supportive help, and the remainder were in a control (no-help) condition. Subjects' performance on a set of unrelated tasks was assessed. High self-esteem subjects who received threatening help performed better than those in other conditions.

How do the DePaulo *et al.* findings relate to our prediction of an interaction between motivation for control and causal control determining self-help? Previous studies on help receiving (see Nadler & Mayseless, 1983, for a review) indicate that help containing negative elements is more threatening for high than for low self-esteem recipients. High self-esteem persons are *also* more likely to view themselves as able to control their fate, whereas low self-esteem is associated with feelings of personal helplessness (Abramson *et al.*, 1978). Therefore, help is likely to result in *controllable* self-threat and precipitate improved performance for high self-esteem individuals. This interpretation is congruent with Sigall and Gould's (1977) suggestion that when challenge to one's competence is coupled with the belief that efforts will be instrumental in meeting it, stressful events are met with active behavioral coping.

Finally, the finding that high but not low need achievers respond to threatening help from a same-age tutor with increased self-help (DePaulo, Webb, & Hoover, 1983) is worthy of note. Past research suggests that high achievers are more likely than low achievers to view outcomes as contingent on effort (e.g., Weiner *et al.*, 1972). Consequently, for them threat in help is apt to be perceived as controllable, leading to increased efforts to regain independence.

V. Applied Implications

This section is devoted to the applied implications of our research and theorizing. The practical significance of work on reactions to help is obvious: it is important for the effective operation of interpersonal and institutional helping relations. Here, we discuss two major domains of application. The first involves the implications of our research on donor–recipient social proximity effects for peer-tutoring programs. The second is more general, focusing on how controllable and uncontrollable threat in help relate to effective helping relations in "real world" settings.

A. PEER TUTORING

Research on donor–recipient social proximity effects applies to many interpersonal helping settings where the helper's identity constitutes a salient, immediately available source of information by which recipients draw self-conclusions. This may occur often in psychotherapy, social welfare, and counseling contexts, among others. Peer tutoring, which is becoming a popular educational technique (Allen, 1976, 1983), is another such setting. A major feature of peer tutoring is that the helper is more similar to the recipient than in the traditional student–teacher relationship, since both come from the same class or age group. In light of our findings regarding donor–recipient social proximity effects, this suggests that those in peer-tutoring programs could experience self-esteem distress. Such distress could be either controllable or uncontrollable. In the former case it could be "harnessed" to motivate self-help efforts and subsequent improvement, but in the latter it is likely to be destructive and to foster long-term dependence on external sources of help. We first examine the possibility that peer-tutoring harbors self-threat potential and then discuss data on differential reactions to controllable and uncontrollable self-threat in a peer-tutoring context.

To test whether peer-tutoring is relatively self-threatening for the tutee, a field experiment was conducted in an Israeli public school (Nadler, Fisher, & Klein, 1981). Fifth-grade children needing help in arithmetic were divided into two groups. One received help from a same-sex tutor from their class who had earned a very high grade in mathematics; the other was tutored by a same-sex tutor from the seventh grade. Both sets of tutors seemed to be quite competent to help the tutees with the work in question.[7] The children's affective and evaluative reactions to tutoring in the peer and nonpeer groups were assessed after the announcement of tutorial pairings, and following two consecutive tutoring sessions.

The findings indicate that children who received help from a peer had lower self-ratings of affect, $F(1, 22) = 11.48$, $p < .01$, than those tutored by a nonpeer. The former group also evaluated the tutor less favorably, $F(1, 22) = 5.02$, $p < .05$, and liked him or her less than the latter group, $F(1, 22) = 8.54$, $p < .01$. This general pattern of reactions was also evident after the initial announcement of tutorial pairings.

These data importantly extend the external validity of donor–recipient social proximity effects. In a "real world" setting, we observed that donor–recipient social proximity has consequences for the recipient's affect and evaluations of the donor. Until this point, comparison stress in help had been demonstrated only in the laboratory environment. More recently we have done research focusing on the effect, on subsequent self-help, of controllable and uncontrollable self-threat elicited by peer tutoring. The results of a pilot study (Nadler, Fisher, & Ben-Itzhak, 1984) are relevant.

[7]In some studies now in progress, degree of general, overall competence between the peer and nonpeer tutors is more closely controlled. However, existing data (Fisher & Nadler, 1976; Nadler & Fisher, 1979) suggest that the present confound between similarity and expertise does not posit a strong alternative interpretation.

The experiment employed a 2 (threatening help vs. no help) × 2 (specific behavioral suggestions vs. no suggestions) between subjects design. Israeli fourth graders received or did not receive threatening help—tutoring in multiplication—from a peer in the same class. One half were also given specific behavioral suggestions on how to approach the problem of improving its performance; the other half were not. We predicted that children in the controllable threat condition (tutored by a peer in the same class, and receiving specific behavioral suggestions) would be most likely to engage in self-help.

At the end of each tutoring session, children received a booklet containing self-help exercises, and were free to work on as many as they wanted. The average number each child performed served as the self-help measure. An analysis revealed a marginal interaction of help × specific behavioral suggestions, $F(1, 54)$, $= 2.59$, $p < .11$, indicating that children receiving threatening aid along with suggestions for improvement engaged in the most self-help. Although the results are only marginally significant and there are some inherent methodological difficulties, their applied implications and congruence with our earlier laboratory findings warrant their consideration.[8]

DePaulo, Webb, and Hoover (1983) also highlighted the role of controllable and uncontrollable threat in peer-tutoring. Their findings are unique and important for two reasons. Based on research regarding developmental aspects of social comparison concerns (e.g., Ruble, Boggiano, Feldman, & Loebl, 1980), DePaulo, Webb, and Hoover predicted that the threat in help from a peer will affect the behavior of older but not younger children (fourth but not second graders). Their results support this prediction, and further clarify the source of the threat in help from a socially close other. The fact that only children presumed to be old enough to experience comparison stress reacted to help in the predicted manner supports its role in the peer-tutoring context. Second, only high achievers responded to self-threat with increased self-help. This corroborates the notion that threat will lead to self-help only when it can be characterized as *controllable*. (As noted earlier, high achievers are more likely than low achievers to view effort expenditure as a coping strategy for current distress.)

The studies described above demonstrate the applied importance of the concepts and findings presented in this article. They suggest that careful attention be given to the conditions under which helping programs operate. If the ultimate purpose of helping is to enable recipients to regain self-reliance, help should induce a controllable self-threat. Yet, when the issue of effective helping relations in applied settings is considered in the context of the characteristics of people in need, an interesting paradox presents itself. This is the focus of the following discussion.

---

[8]Due to the insistence of school authorities, each experimental group represents a different fourth grade class in the same school.

B. THE HELP RECEIVING PARADOX

Most needy persons who receive help are at a physical, psychological, or financial low point in their lives at the onset of dependency. Thus, they may not view themselves as able to control their environment. Help under these conditions is apt to yield an unwanted result: helplessness-like passivity. This creates an inherent paradox: At points of greatest need, help may be ineffective.

How can this paradox be resolved? One route may be provided by our theorizing in the preceding sections. Helpers should first assess the recipient's perceived causal control. If it is low, causal perceptions should be modified. If *only* causal control is enhanced, self-help still may not occur. Unless comparable changes are introduced in motivation for control, recipients may be comfortable relying on assistance from others. The literature reviewed in this article suggests ways of modifying perceived causal control as well as motivation for control. For example, highlighting effort attributions for one's need state or giving recipients specific behavioral coping suggestions may affect perceived causal control, whereas building in a degree of comparison stress may affect motivation for control.

Our recommendations for increasing the effectiveness of helping relations should be viewed within the context of the environmental constraints operating in many applied settings. Conditions unrelated to the helping interaction often act to restrict the instrumentality of self-help so that it does not lead to future self-reliance. Welfare recipients may invest in self-help efforts and acquire new skills, only to discover that a gloomy economic situation prevents reaping the fruits of their new potential for independence. An ex-prisoner may invest in self-improvement efforts, but find that his or her criminal record crops up at every job interview. Klinger (1977) suggests that when efforts toward mastery are continuously unsuccessful, recipients may become increasingly frustrated and angry and end up in a ''depression phase'' characterized by pessimism and apathy.

VI. Summary and Concluding Remarks

In line with the threat to self-esteem model, our data lead to the following conclusions.

1. Conditions that cause help to deliver a negative self-related message and/or amplify the inconsistency between the recipient's state and important socialized values (e.g., of individual achievement and self-reliance), render help self-threatening. One such condition is donor–recipient social proximity, because it leads to comparison stress.

2. Situation and person variables moderate the relationship between donor–recipient social proximity and reaction to help. A necessary situational condition for comparison stress is that help reflect relative inadequacy on a psychologically *central* dimension. In accord with a consistency approach (Bramel, 1968; Nadler *et al.*, 1976, 1979; Nadler & Mayseless, 1983; Tessler & Schwartz, 1972), individuals with high self-esteem are relatively more sensitive to self-threat than those low in self-esteem.

3. In line with our model, self-threat and -support in help are reflected in recipient self-perceptions, external perceptions, and behaviors. These findings occur with different manipulations of self-threat and -support (donor–recipient attitude similarity; task-relevant knowledge; help from friends vs. strangers), with various experimental tasks, with different types of help (financial aid, advice, tutoring), and with different environments (laboratory and field settings).

4. An important moderator of these reactions is the recipient's level of perceived control. While relative to supportive help both controllable and uncontrollable self-threat lead to immediate affective distress and unfavorable evaluative reactions, controllable threat is associated with increased self-help efforts, which, in the long run, result in more favorable affective and evaluative responses. This demonstrates the importance of inducing high motivation for control as well as high causal control in order to achieve an effective helping encounter.

In addition to the above, one can view our work from a broader perspective. Our donor–recipient social proximity findings are congruent with the notion that both greater "pain" and "pleasure" are potentially inherent in close relations than in other types of interpersonal relations (e.g., Brickman & Bulman, 1977; Heider, 1958; Nadler *et al.*, 1980; Tesser, 1980; Tesser & Smith, 1980). In addition, our conceptualization and findings are relevant to the growing body of literature on effective coping with stress (e.g., Garber & Seligman, 1980). While such work has often centered on how active coping is moderated by perceived causal control (e.g., Garber & Seligman, 1980), our orientation highlights the value of considering motivation for control in this context. Active coping with stress is likely when one believes he or she *can* and *should* control the environment.

Regarding the social psychological investigation of helping, our approach represents a "missing link." An examination of textbooks in social psychology reveals that almost all devote a chapter to helping behavior. This reflects continuing interest in this area since the first studies were conducted almost two decades ago. Until recently, however, the topics explored have been confined to variables affecting *help-giving*. The focus previously centered on helping behavior rather than on helping relations. Our emphasis on the short- and long-term effects of receiving help presents a different and more dynamic orientation. It views helping as an interpersonal event that unfolds over time, and which includes a needy person who must decide whether or not to seek help, the reactions of that person to help under varying conditions, and the variables that determine the long-term effectiveness of help in promoting future independence. Such an approach shifts attention from the study of helping behavior to the dynamic exploration of helping relations.

Beyond the obvious conceptual importance of such a perspective, our orientation opens the door for a true link between social psychological research and theory on helping and the world of social problems. Taken together with discussions on the effectiveness of helping relations (Brickman *et al.*, 1982; Coates *et al.*, 1983; Cohn, 1983; DePaulo, Brown, & Greenberg, 1983) our conceptualization and empirical findings are relevant for the more effective operation of many interpersonal and institutional helping contexts. Knowing recipients' immediate and long-term responses to help is likely to result in an enhanced ability to create helping programs that will *truly* help the recipient and enable him or her to be self-reliant.

ACKNOWLEDGMENTS

Preparation of this article was supported by a United States–Israel Binational Science Foundation Grant to the two authors, who each contributed equally to its preparation. The authors thank Reuben M. Baron, Peggy Clark, Bella M. DePaulo, Nancy Eisenberg, Barry Goff, Martin Greenberg, Ronnie Janoff-Bulman, Louise Kidder, Sid Rosen, Roxane L. Silver, and Thomas Ashby Wills for their helpful comments on earlier drafts of the manuscript.

REFERENCES

Abramson, L. Y., Seligman, M. E. P., & Teasdale, J. (1978). Learned helplessness in humans: Critique and reformulation. *Journal of Abnormal Psychology, 87,* 49–74.
Adams, J. S. (1963). Toward an understanding of inequity. *Journal of Abnormal and Social Psychology, 67,* 422–436.
Allen, V. L. (Ed.) (1976). *Children as teachers: Theory and research on tutoring.* New York: Academic Press.
Allen, V. L. (1983). Reactions to help in peer tutoring: roles and social identities. In A. Nadler, J. D. Fisher, & B. M. DePaulo (Eds.), *New directions in helping* (Vol. 3, pp. 214–232). New York: Academic Press.
Ames, R. (1983). Help seeking and achievement motivation: Perspectives from attribution theory. In B. M. DePaulo, A. Nadler, & J. D. Fisher (Eds.), *New directions in helping* (Vol. 2, pp. 165–187). New York: Academic Press.
Anderson, O. W., & Anderson, R. M. (1972). Patterns of use of health services. In H. D. Freeman, S. Levine, & L. G. Keeder (Eds.), *Handbook of medical sociology* (2nd ed.). Englewood Cliffs, NJ: Prentice-Hall.
Asser, E. S. (1978). Social class and help-seeking behavior. *American Journal of Community Psychology, 6,* 465–475.
Bandura, A. (1977). Self-efficacy: Toward a unifying theory of behavioral change. *Psychological Review, 84,* 191–215.

Bandura, A. (1982). Self-efficacy mechanism in human agency. *American Psychologist*, **37**, 122–147.

Bar-Tal, D., Zohar, Y. B., Greenberg, M. S., & Hermon, M. (1977). Reciprocity in the relationship between donor and recipient and between harm-doer and victim. *Sociometry*, **40**, 293–298.

Benedict, R. (1967). *The chrysanthemum and the sword*. Cleveland & New York: World.

Berkowitz, L., & Friedman, P. (1967). Some social class differences in helping behavior. *Journal of Personality and Social Psychology*, **5**, 217–225.

Blau, P. M. (1964). *Exchange and power in social life*. New York: Wiley.

Bramel, D. (1968). Dissonance, expectation and the self. In R. Abelson, E. Aronson, T. M. Newcomb, W. J. McGuire, M. J. Rosenberg, & P. H. Tannenbaum (Eds.), *Sourcebook of cognitive consistency*. New York: Rand-McNally.

Brehm, J. W. (1966). *A theory of psychological reactance*. New York: Academic Press.

Brehm, S. S., & Brehm, J. W. (1981). *Psychological reactance: A theory of freedom and control*. New York: Academic Press.

Brehm, J. W., & Cole, A. H. (1966). Effect of a favor which reduces freedom. *Journal of Personality and Social Psychology*, **3**, 420–426.

Briar, S. (1966). Welfare from below: Recipients' view of the public welfare system. In J. Brock (Ed.), *The law of the poor*. San Francisco: Chandler.

Brickman, P., & Bulman, R. J. (1977). Pleasure and pain in social comparison. In J. M. Suls & R. L. Miller (Eds.), *Social comparison processes: Theoretical and empirical perspectives*. Washington, D.C.: Hemisphere Publ.

Brickman, P., Kidder, L. H., Coates, D., Rabinowitz, V., Cohn, E., & Karuza, J. (1983). The dilemmas of helping: Making aid fair and effective. In J. D. Fisher, A. Nadler, & B. M. DePaulo (Eds.), *New directions in helping* (Vol. 1, pp. 18–44). New York: Academic Press.

Brickman, P., Rabinowitz, V. C., Karuza, J., Jr., Coates, D., Cohn, E., & Kidder, L. (1982). Models of helping and coping, *American Psychologist*, **37**, 368–384.

Bulman, R. J., & Wortman, C. (1977). Attributions of blame and coping in the "real world": Severe accident victims react to their lot. *Journal of Personality and Social Psychology*, **35**, 351–363.

Burger, J. M., & Cooper, H. M. (1979). The desirability of control. *Motivation and Emotion*, **3**, 381–393.

Byrne, D. (1971). *The attraction paradigm*. New York: Academic Press.

Castore, C. H., & DeNinno, J. A. (1977). Investigations in the social comparison of attitudes. In J. M. Suls & R. L. Miller (Eds.), *Social comparison processes: Theoretical and empirical approaches*. Washington, D.C.: Halstead.

Castro, M. A. (1974). Reactions to receiving aid as a function of cost to the donor and opportunity to aid. *Journal of Applied Social Psychology*, **4**, 194–209.

Clark, M. S. (1983). Reactions to aid in communal and exchange relationships. In J. D. Fisher, A. Nadler, & B. M. DePaulo (Eds.), *New directions in helping* (Vol. 1, pp. 281–303). New York: Academic Press.

Clark, M. S., Gotay, C. C., & Mills, J. (1974). Acceptance of help as a function of similarity of the potential helper and opportunity to repay. *Journal of Applied Social Psychology*, **4**, 224–229.

Clark, M. S., & Mills, J. (1979). Interpersonal attraction in exchange and communal relationships. *Journal of Personality and Social Psychology*, **37**, 12–24.

Coates, D., Renzaglia, G., & Embree, M. C. (1983). When helping backfires: Help and helplessness. In J. D. Fisher, A. Nadler, & B. M. DePaulo (Eds.), *New directions in helping* (Vol. 1, pp. 253–276). New York: Academic Press.

Cohn, E. (1983). Effects of victims' and helpers' attributions for problem and solution on reactions to receiving help. In A. Nadler, J. D. Fisher, & B. M. DePaulo (Eds.), *New directions in helping* (Vol. 3, pp. 46–68). New York: Academic Press.

Coopersmith, S. (1967). *The antecedents of self-esteem*. San Francisco: Freeman.

DePaulo, B. M. (1978). Accepting help from teachers—when the teachers are children. *Human Relations, 31,* 459–474.

DePaulo, B. M. (1982). Social-psychological processes in informal help-seeking. In T. A. Wills (Ed.), *Basic processes in helping relationships.* New York: Academic Press.

DePaulo, B. M., Brittingham, G. C., & Kaiser, M. K. (1983). Receiving competence-relevant help: Effects on reciprocity, affect, and sensitivity to the helper's nonverbally expressed needs. *Journal of Personality and Social Psychology, 45,* 1045–1060.

DePaulo, B. M., Brown, P. L., & Greenberg, J. M. (1983). The effects of help on task performance in achievement contexts. In J. D. Fisher, A. Nadler, & B. M. DePaulo (Eds.), *New directions in helping* (Vol. 1, pp. 224–229). New York: Academic Press.

DePaulo, B. M., Brown, P., Ishii, S., & Fisher, J. D. (1981). Help that works: The effects of aid on subsequent task performance. *Journal of Personality and Social Psychology, 41,* 478–487.

DePaulo, B. M., Webb, W., & Hoover, C. (1983). *Reactions to help in a peer tutoring context.* Paper presented at the meeting of the American Education Research Association, Montreal, Canada, April, 1983.

Dweck, C. S. (1975). The role of expectations and attributions in alleviation of learned helplessness. *Journal of Personality and Social Psychology, 31,* 674–685.

Festinger, L. (1954). A theory of social comparison processes. *Human Relations, 1,* 117–140.

Fischer, E. H., & Turner, T. L. (1970). Orientations to seeking professional help: Development and research utility of an attitude scale. *Journal of Consulting and Clinical Psychology, 35,* 79–90.

Fischer, E. H., Winer, D., & Abramowitz, S. I. (1983). Seeking professional help for psychological problems. In A. Nadler, J. D. Fisher, & B. M. DePaulo (Eds.), *New directions in helping* (Vol. 3, pp. 163–185). New York: Academic Press.

Fisher, J. D., DePaulo, B. M., & Nadler, A. (1981). Extending altruism beyond the altruistic act: The mixed effects of aid on the help recipient. In J. P. Rushton & R. M. Sorrentino (Eds.), *Altruism and helping behavior.* Hillsdale, NJ: Erlbaum.

Fisher, J. D., & Farina, A. (1979). Consequences of beliefs about the nature of mental disorders. *Journal of Abnormal Psychology, 88,* 320–327.

Fisher, J. D., Harrison, C., & Nadler, A. (1978). Exploring the generalizability of donor–recipient similarity effects. *Personality and Social Psychology Bulletin, 4,* 626–630.

Fisher, J. D., & Nadler, A. (1974). The effect of similarity between donor and recipient on reactions to aid. *Journal of Applied Social Psychology, 4,* 230–243.

Fisher, J. D., & Nadler, A. (1976). Effect of donor resources on recipient self-esteem and self-help. *Journal of Experimental Social Psychology, 12,* 139–150.

Fisher, J. D., Nadler, A., & Whitcher-Alagna, S. (1982). Recipient reactions to aid. *Psychological Bulletin, 91,* 27–54.

Freeman, H. R. (1977). Reward vs. reciprocity as related to attraction. *Journal of Applied Social Psychology, 1,* 57–66.

Garber, J., & Seligman, M. E. P., (Eds.) (1980). *Human helplessness: Theory and applications.* New York: Academic Press.

Gergen, K. J., Ellsworth, P., Maslach, C., & Seipel, M. (1975). Obligation, donor resources, and reactions to aid in three nations. *Journal of Personality and Social Psychology, 3,* 390–400.

Gergen, K. J., & Gergen, M. (1971). International assistance from a psychological perspective. *1971 Yearbook of world affairs* (Vol. 25). London: Institute of World Affairs.

Gergen, K. J., & Gergen, M. (1974). Understanding foreign assistance through public opinion. *1974 Yearbook of world affairs* (Vol. 27). London: Institute of World Affairs.

Gergen, K. J., & Gergen, M. (1983). Interpretive Dimensions of International Aid. In A. Nadler, J. D. Fisher, & B. M. De Paulo (Eds.), *New directions in helping* (Vol. 3, pp. 329–348). New York: Academic Press.

Gergen, K. J., Morse, S. J., & Kristeller, J. L. (1973). The manner of giving: Cross-national continuities in reactions to aid. *Psychologia, 16,* 121–131.

Goldin, G. J., Perry, S. L., Margolin, R. J., & Stotsky, B. A. (1972). *Dependency and its implications for rehabilitation* (Rev. ed.). Lexington, MA: Heath.

Greenberg, M. S. (1980). A theory of indebtedness. In K. J. Gergen, M. S. Greenberg, & R. H. Willis (Eds.), *Social exchange: Advances in theory and research.* New York: Plenum.

Greenberg, M. S., & Bar-Tal, D. (1976). Indebtedness as a motive for acquisition of "helpful" information. *Representative Research in Social Psychology,* **1,** 19–27.

Greenberg, M. S., & Frisch, D. M. (1972). Effect of intentionality on willingness to reciprocate a favor. *Journal of Experimental Social Psychology,* **8,** 99–111.

Greenberg, M. S., Ruback, B., & Westcott, D. (1983). Seeking help from the police: The victims' perspective. In A. Nadler, J. D. Fisher, & B. M. DePaulo (Eds.) *New directions in helping* (Vol. 3, pp. 71–103). New York: Academic Press.

Greenberg, M. S., & Westcott, D. R. (1983). Indebtedness as a mediator of reactions to aid. In J. D. Fisher, A. Nadler, & B. M. DePaulo (Eds.), *New directions in helping* (Vol. 1, pp. 86–110). New York: Academic Press.

Gross, A. E., Wallston, B. S., & Piliavin, I. (1979). Reactance, attribution, equity, and the help recipient. *Journal of Applied Social Psychology,* **9,** 297–313.

Hatfield, E., & Sprecher, S. (1983). Equity theory and recipient reactions to aid. In J. D. Fisher, A. Nadler, & B. M. DePaulo (Eds.) *New directions in helping* (Vol. 1, pp. 113–135). New York: Academic Press.

Hatfield, E., Walster, G. W., & Piliavin, J. (1978). Equity theory and helping relationships. In L. Wispé (Ed.), *Altruism, sympathy and helping* (pp. 115–139). New York: Academic Press.

Heider, F. (1958). *The psychology of interpersonal relations.* New York: Wiley.

Janoff-Bulman, R. (1979). Characterological versus behavioral self-blame: Inquiries into depression and rape. *Journal of Personality and Social Psychology,* **37,** 1798–1809.

Janoff-Bulman, R., Madden, M., & Timko, C. (1983). Victim's reactions to aid: The role of perceived vulnerability. In A. Nadler, J. D. Fisher, & B. M. DePaulo (Eds.), *New directions in helping* (Vol. 3, pp. 21–42). New York: Academic Press.

Joffe, N. F. (1949). The dynamics of benefice among East-European Jews. *Social Forces,* **27,** 238–247.

Jones, E. E., & Davis, K. E. (1965). From acts to dispositions: The attribution process in person perception. In L. Berkowitz (Ed.), *Advances in experimental social psychology* (Vol. 2). New York: Academic Press.

Kahn, A., & Tice, T. E. (1973). Returning a favor and retaliating harm: The effects of stated intentions and actual behavior. *Journal of Experimental Social Psychology,* **9,** 43–56.

Kalish, R. A. (1967). Of children and grandfathers: A speculative essay on dependency. *The Gerontologist,* **7,** 65–69.

Kelley, H. H. (1967). Attribution theory in social psychology. In D. Levine (Ed.), *Nebraska symposium on motivation* (Vol. 15). Lincoln: University of Nebraska Press.

Klinger, E. (1977). *Meaning and void: Inner experience and the incentives in people's lives.* Minneapolis: University of Minnesota Press.

Kuppuswamy, B. (1978). Concept of begging in ancient thought. *Indian Journal of Social Work,* **39,** 187–192.

Ladieu, G., Hanfman, E., & Dembo, T. (1947). Studies in adjustment to visible injuries: Evaluation of help by the injured. *Journal of Abnormal and Social Psychology,* **42,** 169–192.

Langer, E. J., & Rodin, J. (1976). The effects of choice and enhanced personal responsibility for the aged: A field experiment in an institutional setting. *Journal of Personality and Social Psychology,* **34,** 191–198.

LeGall, S. N., Gumerman, R. A., & Scott-Jones, D. (1983). Instrumental help-seeking and everyday problem-solving: A developmental perspective. In B. M. DePaulo, A. Nadler, & J. D. Fisher (Eds.), *New directions in helping* (Vol. 2, pp. 265–283). New York: Academic Press.

Leventhal, H. (1970). Findings and theory in the study of fear communications. In L. Berkowitz (Ed.), *Advances in experimental social psychology* (Vol. 5). New York: Academic Press.

Lipman, A., & Sterne, R. (1962). Aging in the United States: Ascription of a terminal sick role. *Sociology and Social Research, 53,* 194–203.

McMullin, P. A., & Gross, A. E. (1983). Sex differences, sex roles, and health-related help-seeking. In B. M. DePaulo, A. Nadler, & J. D. Fisher (Eds.), *New directions in helping* (Vol. 2, pp. 233–263). New York: Academic Press.

Merton, R. K. (1968). Contributions to the theory of reference group behavior. In R. K. Merton (Ed.), *Social theory and group structure.* New York: Free Press.

Mettee, D. R., & Riskind, J. (1974). Size of defeat and liking of superior and inferior ability competitors. *Journal of Experimental Social Pychology, 10,* 333–351.

Morris, S. C. III, & Rosen, S. (1973). Effects of felt adequacy and opportunity to reciprocate on help-seeking. *Journal of Experimental Social Psychology, 9,* 265–276.

Nadler, A. (1983). Personal characteristics and help-seeking. In B. M. DePaulo, A. Nadler, & J. D. Fisher (Eds.), *New directions in helping* (Vol. 2, pp. 303–340). New York: Academic Press.

Nadler, A., Altman, A., & Fisher, J. D. (1979). Helping is not enough: Recipient's reactions to aid as a function of positive and negative self-regard. *Journal of Personality, 47,* 615–628.

Nadler, A., Ben-Itzhak, S. B., & Fisher, J. D. (1983). *Perceived control and threat to self-esteem as determinants of self-help.* Unpublished manuscript, Tel-Aviv University, Tel-Aviv, Israel.

Nadler, A., & Eshet, I. (1983). *Help-seeking for the self and the group by kibbutz and city adolescents in Israel.* Unpublished manuscript, Tel-Aviv University, Tel-Aviv, Israel.

Nadler, A., & Fisher, J. D. (1984). "With a little help from my friends": Effects of donor–recipient relationships on recipient's reactions to being helped. In E. Staub, J. Reykowski, J. Karylowski, & D. Bar-Tal (Eds.), *The development and maintenance of prosocial behavior.* New York: Plenum.

Nadler, A., & Fisher, J. D. (1979). *When giving does not pay: Reactions to aid as a function of donor expertise.* Unpublished manuscript, Tel-Aviv University, Tel-Aviv, Israel.

Nadler, A., Fisher, J. D., & Ben-Itzhak, S. (1983). With a little help from my friend: Effect of single or multiple act aid as a function of donor and task characteristics. *Journal of Personality and Social Psychology, 44,* 310–321.

Nadler, A., Fisher, J. D., & Ben-Itzhak, S. (1984). *Self-help following controllable and uncontrollable self-threat in a school environment.* Unpublished manuscript, Tel-Aviv University, Tel-Aviv, Israel.

Nadler, A., Fisher, J. D., & Klein, A. (1981). *Reactions to peer tutoring in a school environment.* Unpublished manuscript, Tel-Aviv University, Tel-Aviv, Israel.

Nadler, A., Fisher, J. D., & Kolker (1982). *Effects of similarity, task-centrality, and self-esteem on help-seeking behavior.* Unpublished manuscript, Tel Aviv University, Tel-Aviv, Israel.

Nadler, A., Fisher, J. D., & Streufert, S. (1974). The donor's dilemma: Recipient's reaction to aid from friend or foe. *Journal of Applied Social Psychology, 4,* 275–285.

Nadler, A., Fisher, J. D., & Streufert, S. (1976). When helping hurts: The effects of donor–recipient similarity and recipient self-esteem on reactions to aid. *Journal of Personality, 44,* 392–409.

Nadler, A., Goldberg, M., & Fisher, J. D. (1983). *Self-help as a function of donor–recipient attitude similarity and task centrality.* Unpublished manuscript, Tel-Aviv University, Tel-Aviv, Israel.

Nadler, A., Jazwinski, C., Lau, S., & Miller, C. (1980). The cold glow of success: Responses to social rejection as affected by attitude similarity between chosen and rejected individuals. *European Journal of Social Psychology, 10,* 279–289.

Nadler, A., Maler, S., & Friedman, A. (1984). Effects of helper's sex, subject's androgyny and self-evaluation on males' and females' willingness to seek and receive help. *Sex Roles, 10,* 327–339.

Nadler, A., & Mayseless, O. (1983). Recipient self-esteem and reactions to help. In J. D. Fisher, A. Nadler, & B. M. DePaulo (Eds.), *New directions in helping* (Vol. 1, pp. 167–186). New York: Academic Press.

Nadler, A., & Porat, I. (1978). Names do not help: Effects of anonymity and locus of need attribution on help-seeking behavior. *Personality and Social Psychology Bulletin,* **4,** 624–626.

Nadler, A., Shapira, R., & Ben-Itzhak, S. (1982). Good looks may help: Effects of helper's physical attractiveness and sex of helper on males' and females' help-seeking behavior. *Journal of Personality and Social Psychology,* **42,** 90–99.

Nadler, A., Sheinberg, O., & Jaffe, Y. (1981). Seeking help from the wheelchair. In C. Spielberger & I. Saranson (Eds.), *Stress and anxiety* (Vol. 8). Washington, D.C.: Hemisphere Publ.

Novak, D. W., & Lerner, M. J. (1968). Rejection as a consequence of perceived similarity. *Journal of Personality and Social Psychology,* **9,** 147–152.

Pettigrew, T. F. (1983). Seeking public assistance: A stigma analysis. In A. Nadler, J. D. Fisher, & B. M. DePaulo (Eds.), *New directions in helping* (Vol. 3, pp. 273–292). New York: Academic Press.

Rodin, J., & Langer, E. J. (1977). Long-term effects of a control relevant intervention with the institutionalized aged. *Journal of Personality and Social Psychology,* **35,** 897–902.

Rosen, B. (1971). Evaluation of help by a potential recipient. *Psychonomic Science,* **23,** 269–271.

Ruble, D. N., Boggiano, A. K., Feldman, N. S., & Loebl, J. H. (1980). Developmental analysis of the role of social comparison in self-evaluation. *Developmental Psychology,* **16,** 105–115.

Rushton, J. P., & Sorrentino, R. M. (Eds.) (1981). *Altruism and helping behavior: Social, personality, and developmental perspectives.* Hillsdale, NJ: Erlbaum.

Sigall, H., & Gould, R. (1977). The effects of self-esteem and evaluator demandingness on effort expenditure. *Journal of Personality and Social Psychology,* **35,** 12–20.

Silver, R. L., & Wortman, C. B. (1980). Coping with undesirable life events. In J. Garber & M. E. P. Seligman (Eds.), *Human helplessness.* New York: Academic Press.

Stapleton, R. E., Nacci, P., & Tedeschi, J. T. (1973). Interpersonal attraction and the reciprocation of benefits. *Journal of Personality and Social Psychology,* **28,** 199–205.

Taylor, S. E. (1979). Hospital patient behavior: Reactance, helplessness, or control? *Journal of Social Issues,* **35,** 156–184.

Tesser, A. (1980). Self-esteem maintenance in family dynamics. *Journal of Personality and Social Psychology,* **39,** 77–91.

Tesser, A., & Smith, J. (1980). Some effects of friendship and task relevance on helping: You don't always help the one you like. *Journal of Experimental Social Psychology,* **16,** 582–590.

Tessler, R. C., & Schwartz, S. H. (1972). Help-seeking, self-esteem, and achievement motivation: An attributional analysis. *Journal of Personality and Social Psychology,* **21,** 318–326.

Thompson, S. C. (1981). Will it hurt less if I can control it? A complex answer to a simple question. *Psychological Bulletin,* **90,** 89–101

Underwood, B. J. (1975). Individual differences as a crucible in theory construction. *American Psychologist,* **30,** 128–134.

Whitcher-Alagna, S. (1983). Receiving medical help: A psychosocial perspective on patient reactions. In A. Nadler, J. D. Fisher, & B. M. DePaulo (Eds.), *New directions in helping* (Vol. 3, pp. 131–161). New York: Academic Press.

Weiner, B., Frieze, I., Kukla, A., Reed, L., Rest, S., & Rosenbaum, R. M. (1972). Perceiving the causes of success and failure. In E. E. Jones, D. E. Kanouse, H. H. Kelley, R. E. Nisbett, S. Valins, & B. Weiner (Eds.), *Attribution: Perceiving the causes of behavior* (pp. 95–120). Morristown, NJ: General Learning Press.

Weitzman, L. J. (1979). *Sex role socialization.* Palo Alto, CA: Mayfield.

Wortman, C. B. (1983). Coping with victimization: Conclusions and implications for future research. *Journal of Social Issues, 39,* 195–221.

Wortman, C. B., & Brehm, J. W. (1975). Responses to uncontrollable outcomes: An integration of
reactance theory and the learned helplessness model. In L. Berkowitz (Ed.), *Advances in
experimental social psychology* (Vol. 8). New York: Academic Press.

THE ELABORATION LIKELIHOOD
MODEL OF PERSUASION

Richard E. Petty

DEPARTMENT OF PSYCHOLOGY
UNIVERSITY OF MISSOURI
COLUMBIA, MISSOURI

John T. Cacioppo

DEPARTMENT OF PSYCHOLOGY
UNIVERSITY OF IOWA
IOWA CITY, IOWA

123

ADVANCES IN EXPERIMENTAL
SOCIAL PSYCHOLOGY, VOL. 19

Copyright © 1986 by Academic Press, Inc.
All rights of reproduction in any form reserved.

I. Introduction

The study of attitudes and persuasion began as the central focus of social psychology (Allport, 1935; Ross, 1908). However, after a considerable flourishing of research and theory from the 1930s through the 1960s, interest in the topic began to wane. Two factors were largely responsible for this. First, the utility of the attitude construct itself was called into question as researchers wondered if attitudes were capable of predicting behavior. Because of this concern, some even concluded that it might be time to abandon the attitude concept (Abelson, 1972; Wicker, 1971). Second, so much conflicting research and theory had developed that it had become clear that "after several decades of research, there (were) few simple and direct empirical generalizations that (could) be made concerning how to change attitudes" (Himmelfarb & Eagly, 1974, p. 594). Reviewers of the attitudes literature during the early 1970s lamented this sorry state of affairs (e.g., Fishbein & Ajzen, 1972). For example, Kiesler and Munson (1975) concluded that "attitude change is not the thriving field it once was and will be again" (p. 443).

By the late 1970s considerable progress had been made in addressing important methodological and theoretical issues regarding the first substantive problem plaguing the field—the consistency between attitudes and behaviors. Conditions under which attitudes would and would not predict behavior were specified (e.g., Ajzen & Fishbein, 1977, 1980; Fazio & Zanna, 1981) and researchers began to explore the processes underlying attitude–behavior correspondence (Sherman & Fazio, 1983; Fazio, 1985). The attitude change problem was slower to be addressed, however. In 1977, Muzifer Sherif asked "What is the yield in the way of established principles in regard to attitude change?" He answered that there was a "reigning confusion in the area" and a "scanty yield in spite of (a) tremendously thriving output" (p. 370). In a review that generally heralded the arrival of a new optimism in the attitudes field, Eagly and Himmelfarb (1978) noted that "ambiguities and unknowns still abound" (p. 544; see Cialdini, Petty, & Cacioppo, 1981; Cooper & Croyle, 1984, for more recent reviews).

As we noted above, the major problem facing persuasion researchers was that after accumulating a vast quantity of data and an impressive number of theories—perhaps more data and theory than on any other single topic in the social sciences (see McGuire, 1985)—there was surprisingly little agreement concerning if, when, and how the traditional source, message, recipient, and channel variables (cf. Hovland, Janis, & Kelley, 1953; McGuire, 1969; Smith, Lasswell, & Casey, 1946) affected attitude change. Existing literature supported the view that nearly every independent variable studied increased persuasion in some situations, had no effect in others, and decreased persuasion in still other contexts. This diversity of results was apparent even for variables that on the surface, at least, would appear to be quite simple. For example, although it might seem reasonable to propose that by associating a message with an expert source agreement could be increased (e.g., see Aristotle's *Rhetoric*), the accumulated contemporary research literature suggested that expertise effects were considerably more complicated than this (Eagly & Himmelfarb, 1974; Hass, 1981). Sometimes expert sources had the expected effects (e.g., Kelman & Hovland, 1953), sometimes no effects were obtained (e.g., Rhine & Severance, 1970), and sometimes reverse effects were noted (e.g., Sternthal, Dholakia, & Leavitt, 1978). Unfortunately, the conditions under which each of these effects could be obtained and the processes involved in producing these effects were not at all apparent.

Our primary goal in this article is to outline a general theory of attitude change, called the Elaboration Likelihood Model (ELM; Petty & Cacioppo, 1981a), which we believe provides a fairly general framework for organizing, categorizing, and understanding the basic processes underlying the effectiveness of persuasive communications. Importantly, the ELM attempts to integrate the many seemingly conflicting research findings and theoretical orientations under one conceptual umbrella. The ELM began with our attempts to account for the differential persistence of communication-induced attitude change. After reviewing the literature on attitude persistence, we concluded that the many different empirical findings and theories in the field might profitably be viewed as emphasizing one of just two relatively distinct routes to persuasion (Petty, 1977; Petty & Cacioppo, 1978). The first type of persuasion was that which likely resulted from a person's careful and thoughtful consideration of the true merits of the information presented in support of an advocacy (central route). The other type of persuasion, however, was that which more likely occurred as a result of some simple cue in the persuasion context (e.g., an attractive source) that induced change without necessitating scrutiny of the true merits of the information presented (peripheral route). In the accumulated literature, the first kind of persuasion appeared to be more enduring than the latter (see Fig. 1; see Cook & Flay, 1978, and Petty, 1977, for reviews).

Following our initial speculation about the two routes to persuasion and the implications for attitudinal persistence (Petty, 1977; Petty & Cacioppo, 1978), we have developed, researched, and refined a more general theory of persuasion,

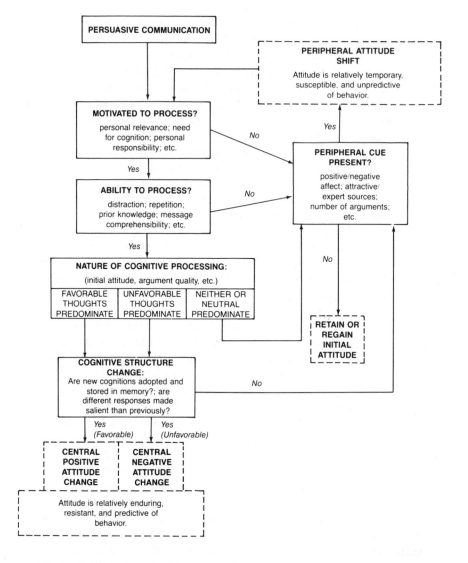

Fig. 1. Central and peripheral routes to persuasion. This figure depicts the two anchoring endpoints on the elaboration likelihood continuum (adapted from Petty, 1977; Petty & Cacioppo, 1978, 1981a).

the ELM, which is based on these two routes (Petty & Cacioppo, 1981a). In addition, we have addressed the various applications of this model to fields such as psychotherapy and counseling (Cacioppo, Petty, & Stoltenberg, 1985; Petty, Cacioppo, & Heesacker, 1984) and mass media advertising and selling (Cacioppo & Petty, 1985; Petty & Cacioppo, 1983a, 1984b; Petty, Cacioppo, & Schumann, 1984). In the remainder of this article we will outline the ELM as a series of postulates that make explicit the guiding assumptions and principles of the model. We will also provide a methodology for testing the major processes outlined by the ELM and we will review research which provides evidence relevant to the framework.

Before outlining our model of attitude change, however, it is important to define our use of the term *attitude*. Consistent with the positions of other attitude theorists (e.g., Thurstone, 1928), we regard attitudes as general evaluations people hold in regard to themselves, other people, objects, and issues. These general evaluations can be based on a variety of behavioral, affective, and cognitive experiences, and are capable of influencing or guiding behavioral, affective, and cognitive processes. Thus, a person may come to like a new political candidate because she just donated $100 to the campaign (behavior-initiated change), because the theme music in a recently heard commercial induced a general pleasantness (affect-initiated change), or because the person was impressed with the candidate's issue positions (cognitive initiated change). Similarly, if a person already likes a political candidate he may agree to donate money to the campaign (behavioral influence), may feel happiness upon meeting the candidate (affective influence), and may selectively encode the candidate's issue positions (cognitive influence).

II. Postulate 1: Seeking Correctness

Our first postulate and an important guiding principle in the ELM agrees with Festinger's (1950) statement that:

People are motivated to hold correct attitudes.

Incorrect attitudes are generally maladaptive and can have deleterious behavioral, affective, and cognitive consequences. If a person believes that certain objects, people, or issues are "good" when they are in fact "bad," a number of incorrect behavioral decisions and subsequent disappointments may follow. As Festinger (1954) noted, the implication of such a drive is that "we would expect to observe behavior on the part of persons which enables them to ascertain whether or not their opinions are correct" (p. 118). In his influential theory of social comparison processes, Festinger (1954) focused on how people evaluated the correctness of their opinions by comparing them to the opinions of others. In Section IX,B we address how the ELM accounts for attitude changes induced by exposure to the opinions of varying numbers of other people. But first we need to outline our other postulates.

III. Postulate 2: Variations in Elaboration

Postulate 2 states that:

> Although people want to hold correct attitudes, the amount and nature of issue-relevant elaboration in which people are willing or able to engage to evaluate a message vary with individual and situational factors.

By *elaboration* in a persuasion context, we mean the extent to which a person thinks about the issue-relevant arguments contained in a message. When conditions foster people's motivation and ability to engage in issue-relevant thinking, the "elaboration likelihood" is said to be high. This means that people are likely to attend to the appeal; attempt to access relevant associations, images, and experiences from memory; scrutinize and elaborate upon the externally provided message arguments in light of the associations available from memory; draw inferences about the merits of the arguments for a recommendation based upon their analyses; and consequently derive an overall evaluation of, or attitude toward, the recommendation. This conceptualization suggests that when the elaboration likelihood is high, there should be evidence for the allocation of considerable cognitive resources to the advocacy. Issue-relevant elaboration will typically result in the new arguments, or one's personal translations of them, being integrated into the underlying belief structure (schema) for the attitude object (Cacioppo & Petty, 1984a). As we will note shortly, sometimes this issue-relevant elaboration proceeds in a relatively objective manner and is governed mostly by the strength of the issue-relevant arguments presented, but at other times this elaboration is more biased and may be guided mostly by the person's initial attitude.

Of course, people are not motivated nor are they able to scrutinize carefully every message that they receive (cf. McGuire's, 1969, "lazy organism"), and it would not be adaptive for them to do so. As Miller, Maruyama, Beaber, and Valone (1976) noted, "It may be irrational to scrutinize the plethora of counterattitudinal messages received daily. To the extent that one possesses only a limited amount of information processing time and capacity, such scrutiny would disengage the thought processes from the exigencies of daily life" (p. 623). Current research in cognitive and social psychology provides strong support for the view that at times people engage in "controlled," "deep," "systematic," and/or "effortful" analyses of stimuli, and at other times the analyses are better characterized as "automatic," "shallow," "heuristic," and/or "mindless" (for further discussion, see Craik, 1979; Eagly & Chaiken, 1984; Kahneman, Slovic, & Tversky, 1982; Langer, 1978; and Schneider & Shiffrin, 1977).[1]

---

[1]See Petty and Cacioppo (1986) for discussion of the relationship between these distinctions and the central/peripheral distinction of the ELM.

A. THE ELABORATION CONTINUUM

One can view the extent of elaboration received by a message as a continuum going from no thought about the issue-relevant information presented to complete elaboration of every argument, and complete integration of these elaborations into the person's attitude schema. The likelihood of elaboration will be determined by a person's motivation and ability to evaluate the communication presented (see Fig. 1). In an earlier review of the attitude change literature (Petty & Cacioppo, 1981a), we suggested that the many theories of attitude change could be roughly placed along this elaboration continuum. At the high end of this continuum are theoretical orientations such as inoculation theory (McGuire, 1964), cognitive response theory (Greenwald, 1968; Petty, Ostrom, & Brock, 1981), information integration theory (Anderson, 1981), and the theory of reasoned action (Ajzen & Fishbein, 1980; Fishbein, 1980), which all assume that people typically attempt to carefully evaluate (though not always successfully) the information presented in a message, and integrate this information into a coherent position. Researchers within this tradition have emphasized the need to examine what kinds of arguments are persuasive and how variables affect the comprehension, elaboration, learning, integration, and retention of issue-relevant information (McGuire, 1985).

Other persuasion theories do not place much credence on the arguments in a message or issue-relevant thinking. Instead, they focus on how simple affective processes influence attitudes or on how people can employ various rules or inferences to judge their own attitudes or the acceptability of an attitudinal position. Although in most laboratory studies of attitude change subjects will have some motivation and/or ability to form at least a reasonable opinion either by scrutinizing arguments or making an inference about the acceptibility of the recommendation based on cues in the context, there are circumstances in which neither arguments nor acceptance cues are present. For example, when subjects are exposed to nonsense syllables (Staats & Staats, 1957) or polygons (Kunst-Wilson & Zajonc, 1980), no elaboration of arguments is possible because no arguments are presented, and validity cues may be irrelevant because there is no explicit ''advocacy'' to judge. Theories such as classical conditioning (Staats & Staats, 1958) and mere exposure (Zajonc, 1968, 1980), which describe evaluations of objects changing as a result of rather primitive affective and associational processes, are especially relevant under these circumstances. Although these theories have been tested and applied primarily in situations where no explicit ''advocacy'' is presented, they also should be applicable to situations in which an issue position is advocated, but people have virtually no ability and/or motivation to consider it. In these situations, attitudes may still be changed if the attitude object is associated with a relatively strong positive or negative affective cue, or a weaker cue is continually paired with the attitude object.

If no strong affective cues are presented, it is still possible for people to form a "reasonable" attitude without relying on scrutiny of the issue-relevant arguments presented by relying on various persuasion rules or inferences that may be either rather simple or relatively complex. For example, according to self-perception theory (Bem, 1972), people may come to like or dislike an object as a result of a simple inference based on their own behavior (e.g., if I bought it, I must like it). According to the heuristic model of persuasion (Chaiken, 1980; Eagly & Chaiken, 1984), people may evaluate messages by employing various rules that they have learned on the basis of past experience (e.g., people agree with people they like). Social judgment theory (Sherif & Sherif, 1967) proposes that people evaluate messages mostly on the basis of their perceived position— messages are contrasted and rejected if they appear too discrepant (fall in the latitude of rejection), but are assimilated and accepted if they appear closer to one's initial position (fall in the latitude of acceptance; Pallak, Mueller, Dollar, & Pallak, 1972).

In addition to the relatively simple acceptance/rejection rules proposed by the preceding models, attitude change may be affected by more complex reasoning processes, such as those based on balance theory (Heider, 1946; Insko, 1984) or certain attributional principles (e.g., Kelley, 1967; Eagly, Wood, & Chaiken, 1978). Importantly, even reliance on more complex inferences obviates the need for careful scrutiny of the issue-relevant arguments in a message. In other words, each of these processes (e.g., self-perception, assimilation, balance) is postulated to be sufficient to account for attitude change without requiring a personal evaluation of the issue-relevant arguments.[2] In sum, we have proposed that when either motivation or ability to process issue-relevant arguments is low, attitudes may be changed by associating an issue position with various affective cues, or people may attempt to form a reasonable opinion position by making an inference about the likely correctness or desirability of a particular attitude position based on cues such as message discrepancy, one's own behavior, and the characteristics of the message source.

B. DEVELOPMENTAL TRENDS IN ELABORATION

Interestingly, the attitude change processes that we have just described form an elaboration continuum which likely coincides with the manner in which attitude change processes develop through adulthood. Specifically, the very young child probably has relatively little motivation to think about the true merits of people, objects, and issues, and even less ability to do so. Thus, attitudes may

---

[2]Insko (1981) extended balance theory to include a person's consideration of issue-relevant arguments. This more general balance formulation therefore broadens the theory beyond peripheral processing.

be affected primarily by what feels good or bad. As children mature, they become more motivated to express correct opinions on certain issues, but their ability to scrutinize issue-relevant arguments may still be poor due to lack of knowledge. Therefore, they may be particularly reliant on certain cognitive rules based on personal experience such as, "My mother knows what's right," or "If I play with it, I must like it." Consistent with this reasoning, children have been shown to be more susceptible to appeals based on behavioral cues and self-perceptions than issue-relevant argumentation (e.g., Miller, Brickman, & Bolen, 1975).

Finally, as people move into adulthood, interests become more focused and the consequences of holding correct opinions on certain issues increase. In addition, as people's acquired knowledge and cognitive skills grow, this renders them more able to critically analyze issue-relevant information on certain topics and makes them less reliant than children on certain primitive heuristics (cf. Ross, 1981). As we noted earlier, of course, although people may have the requisite ability and motivation to scrutinize certain attitude issues, they will lack motivation and ability on others. Thus, simple inferences and affective cues may still produce attitude change in adults.

In sum, one's initial evaluations are likely to be largely hedonistic since, lacking the motivation and/or ability to consider issue-relevant arguments, attitudes will be based primarily on positive and negative affective cues associated with the attitude object. As development proceeds, some attitudes may be formed on the basis of simple inferences, decision rules, and social attachments. Finally, the formation and change of some attitudes become very thoughtful processes in which issue-relevant information is carefully scrutinized and evaluated in terms of existing knowledge. Importantly, our sequence of the developmental stages of influence is consistent with other developmental models of judgment. For example, in discussing the development of moral standards, Kohlberg (1963) identifies three developmental levels. At the first level (preconventional), moral evaluations are based primarily on the affective consequences of an act. At level 2 (conventional), evaluations of acts are based primarily on socially accepted rules and laws. Finally, at level 3 (postconventional), an evaluation of an act is based on a person's idiosyncratic but well-articulated moral code. The parallels to our stages of influence are obvious.

Although we have argued that there is a continuum of message elaboration ranging from none to complete, and that different attitude change processes may operate along the continuum, it is also important to note that these different theoretical processes can be viewed as specifying just two qualitatively distinct routes to persuasion. The first route, which we have called the "central route," occurs when motivation and ability to scrutinize issue-relevant arguments are relatively high. The second, or "peripheral route," occurs when motivation and/or ability are relatively low and attitudes are determined by positive or negative cues in the persuasion context which either become directly associated with the message position or permit a simple inference as to the validity of the message. In short, even though one can view message elaboration as a continuum, we can distinguish persuasion that is primarily a result of issue-relevant argumentation from persuasion that is primarily a result of some cue in the persuasion context that permits attitude change without argument scrutiny. In fact, we will find it useful elsewhere in this article to talk about the elaboration likelihood continuum by referring to the prototypical processes operative at each extreme.

IV.   Postulate 3: Arguments, Cues, and Elaboration

Much of our discussion so far is summarized in the next postulate.

> Variables can affect the amount and direction of attitude change by: (A) serving as persuasive arguments, (B) serving as peripheral cues, and/or (C) affecting the extent or direction of issue and argument elaboration.

In subsequent sections we discuss how many of the typical source, message, recipient, channel, and context variables manipulated in the accumulated persuasion research can be understood in terms of the three-part categorization above, but first we need to define and operationalize the constructs.

A.   ARGUMENT/MESSAGE QUALITY

One of the least researched and understood questions in the psychology of persuasion is "What makes an argument persuasive?" As we noted earlier, literally thousands of studies and scores of theories have addressed the question of how some extramessage factor (e.g., source credibility, repetition) affects the acceptance of a particular argument, but little is known about what makes a particular argument (or message) persuasive in isolation. In fact, the typical persuasion experiment employs only one message and examines how some extramessage factor affects acceptance of the message conclusion. Furthermore, studies that do include more than one message often do so for purposes of generalizability across topics, not because the messages are proposed to differ in some theoretically meaningful way (e.g., Hovland & Weiss, 1951). There are, of course, notable exceptions to our generalization. For example, a few studies have manipulated the comprehensibility or complexity of a message (e.g., Eagly, 1974; Eagly & Warren, 1976; Regan & Cheng, 1973), mostly to test McGuire's (1968) information processing model, but even these studies were not aimed at uncovering the underlying characteristics of persuasive arguments. Perhaps the most relevant research to date is that in which subjects are asked to rate arguments along various dimensions (e.g., validity, novelty) in order to determine what qualities make an argument persuasive (see Vinokur & Burnstein, 1974), but this kind of research is rare and in its infancy. After over 40 years of work on persuasion in experimental social psychology, Fishbein and Ajzen (1981) could accurately state that "the general neglect of the information contained in a message...is probably the most serious problem in communication and persuasion research" (p. 359).[3]

In the ELM, arguments are viewed as bits of information contained in a communication that are relevant to a person's subjective determination of the true merits of an advocated position. Because people hold attitudes for many different reasons (Katz, 1960), people will invariably differ in the kinds of information they feel are central to the merits of any position (Snyder & DeBono, 1985). Nevertheless, for purposes of testing the ELM, it is necessary to specify arguments that the vast majority of a specifiable population finds compelling rather than specious. In our research on the ELM, we have postponed the question of what specific qualities make arguments persuasive by defining argument quality in an empirical manner. In developing arguments for a topic, we begin by generating a large number of arguments, both intuitively compelling and specious ones, in favor of some issue (e.g., raising tuition). Then, members of the appropriate subject population are given these arguments to rate for persuasiveness. Based on these scores we select arguments with high and low ratings to comprise at least one "strong" and one "weak" message. Subsequently, other subjects are given one of these messages and are told to think about and evaluate it carefully. Following examination of the message, subjects complete a "thought-listing measure" (Brock, 1967; Greenwald, 1968), in which they are instructed to record the thoughts elicited by the message. These thoughts are then coded as to whether they are favorable, unfavorable, or neutral toward the position advocated (see Cacioppo & Petty, 1981c; Cacioppo, Harkins, & Petty, 1981, for further discussion of the thought-listing procedure). We define a "strong message" as one containing arguments (e.g., we should raise tuition so that more books can be purchased for the library) such that when subjects are *instructed* to think about the message, the thoughts that they generate are predominantly favorable. Importantly, for positive attitude change to occur, the thoughts should be more favorable than those available prior to message exposure. On the other hand, we define a "weak message" as one containing arguments (e.g., we should raise tuition so that more trees and shrubs can be planted on campus) such that when subjects are instructed to think about them, the thoughts that they generate are predominantly unfavorable. For negative change (boomerang) to occur, the thoughts should be more unfavorable than those available prior to message exposure.

---

[3]Notably, Fishbein and Ajzen (1975) and other expectancy value theorists (e.g., Rosenberg, 1956) have examined argument or attribute persuasiveness from a phenomenological perspective. However, the question of *why* a particular argument or attribute is seen as more positive or negative than others is still not addressed.

Once the messages meet the criterion of eliciting the appropriate profile of thoughts, they are checked for other characteristics. First, a panel of subjects rates the messages for overall believability. Our goal is to develop arguments that are strong and weak, but that do not strain credulity. (This is not to say that our arguments are necessarily veridical—just reasonably plausible to our subjects.) Next, people from the relevant subject pool rate the messages for comprehensibility, complexity, and familiarity. Again, our goal is to develop strong and weak messages that are roughly equivalent in their novelty and in our subjects' ability to understand them. The top panel of Fig. 2 depicts the results of a hypothetical study in which some extramessage "treatment" has no effect on persuasion. In this study, only the quality of the message arguments determined the extent of attitude change. We will compare this simple result with the other possibilities depicted in Fig. 2 in the remainder of this article.

B. PERIPHERAL CUES

According to the Elaboration Likelihood Model, one way to influence attitudes is by varying the quality of the arguments in a persuasive message. Another possibility, however, is that a simple cue in the persuasion context affects attitudes in the absence of argument processing. As we noted earlier, some cues will do this because they trigger relatively primative affective states that become associated with the attitude object. Various reinforcing (e.g., food; Janis, Kaye, & Kirschner, 1965) and punishing (e.g., electric shock; Zanna, Kiesler, & Pilkonis, 1970) stimuli have proved effective in this regard. Other cues work, however, because they invoke guiding rules (e.g., balance; Heider, 1946) or inferences (e.g., self-perception; Bem, 1972).

Since cues are postulated to affect attitude change without affecting argument processing, it is possible to test manipulations as potential cues by presenting them to subjects with the advocated position only (i.e., without accompanying persuasive arguments), as in prestige suggestion (see Asch, 1948). If the manipulation is a potential cue, it should have the ability to affect attitudes in the absence of any arguments. Alternatively, one could present an incomprehensible message (e.g., in a foreign language) on some topic along with the potential cue (e.g., speed of speech; Miller et al., 1976). Subjects could be asked to rate, for example, how likely it is that the speaker is convincing. Again, if the cue is operative, it should be capable of affecting judgments even if there are no arguments to process. Finally, a simple procedure might involve merely describing various potential cues to subjects (e.g., a message with 1 vs. 10 arguments; a message from an attractive vs. an unattractive source) and asking them which would more likely be acceptable and/or persuasive. These procedures would not, of course, indicate *why* a cue was effective (e.g., were the judgments due to affective association or the invocation of a simple decision rule?), nor would they eliminate the possibility that more thoughtful processes were involved (e.g., subjects might attempt to generate arguments consistent with the position; cf., Burnstein, Vinokur, & Trope, 1973). However, these procedures would indicate whether or not a manipulation has the *potential* to serve as a peripheral cue.

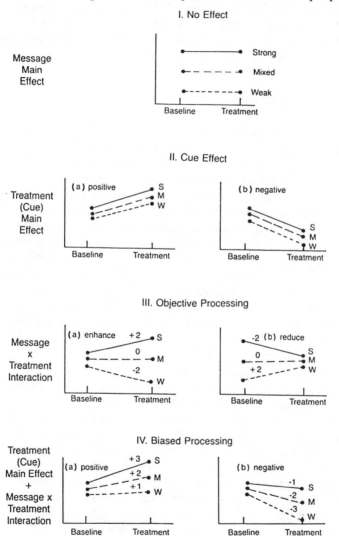

Fig. 2. Impact of variables on attitude change according to the ELM. Under conditions of high elaboration likelihood, attitudes are affected mostly by argument quality (I). Under conditions of low elaboration likelihood, attitudes are affected mostly by peripheral cues (II). Under conditions of moderate elaboration likelihood, varibles may enhance or reduce message processing in either a relatively objective (III) or relatively biased (IV) manner (adapted from Petty & Cacioppo, 1984c).

Panel II in Fig. 2 presents the results of a hypothetical study in which strong, weak, and mixed argument messages were presented along with a treatment that served as a peripheral cue. Note that in the pure case of cue processing, the cue affects all three kinds of messages equally. Since cues are most likely to operate when subjects are either unmotivated or unable to process issue-relevant arguments (as depicted in Fig. 1), the data show a strong effect for the cue treatment, but little effect for argument quality. In the left half of Panel 2 the cue is positive, and in the right half the cue is negative.

C. AFFECTING ELABORATION

We have now defined two of the key constructs in the Elaboration Likelihood Model: argument quality and peripheral cues. The third way in which a variable can affect persuasion is by determining the extent or direction of message processing. Variables can affect argument processing in a relatively objective or a relatively biased manner (Petty & Cacioppo, 1981a). In relatively *objective* processing, some treatment variable either motivates or enables subjects to see the strengths of cogent arguments and the flaws in specious ones, or inhibits them from doing so. In relatively *biased* processing some treatment variable either motivates or enables subjects to generate a particular kind of thought in response to a message, or inhibits a particular kind of thought. Relatively objective elaboration has much in common with "bottom-up" processing since the elaboration is relatively impartial and data driven. Relatively biased elaboration has more in common with "top-down" processing since the elaboration, for example, may be governed by a relevant attitude schema which guides processing in a manner leading to the maintenance or strengthening of the schema (cf. Bobrow & Norman, 1975; Landman & Manis, 1983). Postulate 4 deals further with the nature of relatively objective processing, and Postulate 6 deals further with the nature of relatively biased processing.

Of course, in order to test the ELM, it is important to assess how much message processing subjects are engaged in (i.e., how much cognitive activity or effort is devoted to issue-relevant thinking), and what variables affect elaboration. We have used four different procedures to assess the extent of thinking. The first procedure is the simplest and involves directly asking people how much effort they expended in processing the message, or how much thinking they were doing about the advocacy. Although we have found this method to prove sensitive in some studies (e.g., Cacioppo, Petty, & Morris, 1983; Petty, Harkins, & Williams, 1980), in others it has not produced differences even though there were other indications of differential processing (e.g., Harkins & Petty, 1981a, 1982). The problem, of course, is that although people may sometimes be aware of how much cognitive effort they are expending, people do not always have access to their cognitive processes (Nisbett & Wilson, 1977).

A second procedure involves using the thought-listing technique developed by Brock (1967) and Greenwald (1968). In this procedure, subjects list their thoughts either in anticipation of, during, or after message exposure, and the thoughts are subsequently categorized into theoretically meaningful units (e.g., counterarguments; source-related thoughts) by the subjects or independent judges. The thought-listing technique has proved to be an important supplemental tool in tracking the amount and type of cognitive activity involved in persuasion and resistance (see Cacioppo et al., 1981; Cacioppo & Petty, 1981c; for reviews of thought-listing methodology and results). Although statistical procedures have been used to show that cognitive activity mediates attitude effects in some instances (e.g., Cacioppo & Petty, 1979b; Insko, Turnbull, & Yandell, 1974; Petty & Cacioppo, 1977), thought listings do not provide definitive evidence for cognitive mediation because the evidence is basically correlational (cf. Miller & Colman, 1981).

A third procedure that we have used to assess the extent and affectivity of information processing activity involves the use of psychophysiological measures. For example, we have shown that facial electromyographic (EMG) activity is capable of distinguishing positive from negative reactions to stimuli (e.g., Cacioppo & Petty, 1979a) and that perioral (e.g., lip) EMG activity is capable of distinguishing cognitively effortful from less taxing mental work (e.g., Cacioppo & Petty, 1981b). The physiological procedures have several potential advantages over self-reports of cognitive activity and thought listings. For example, these measures can track psychological processes over time, and may be less susceptible to artifacts (e.g., demand characteristics) and subjects' inability to recall the process or content of their thoughts. Although work on psychophysiological assessments of attitudinal processes is in its early stages, these measures hold considerable promise for tracking and marking the underlying mediation of persuasion and resistance (see Cacioppo & Petty, 1981a, 1986; Petty & Cacioppo, 1983; for reviews).

The fourth procedure for assessing the extent of cognitive processing, and the one highlighted in this article, is based on our manipulation of message argument quality. This procedure is discussed in the next section.

V. Postulate 4: Objective Elaboration

Postulate 3 noted that variables could serve as arguments, cues, or affect processing. We further noted that processing could proceed in a relatively objective or biased manner. Postulate 4 deals with objective processing. Specifically:

Affecting motivation and/or ability to process a message in a relatively objective manner can do so by either enhancing or reducing argument scrutiny.

As we hinted above, our empirical method of defining argument quality allows us to assess the extent to which a variable affects argument processing and the extent to which this processing is relatively objective or biased. We shall consider first the expected consequences of variables affecting relatively objective processing.

Assume for the moment that we have created a control condition in which motivation or ability to process issue-relevant arguments is rather low. Subjects should show relatively little differentiation of strong from weak arguments in this condition. However, if a manipulation enhances argument processing in a relatively objective manner, then subjects should show greater differentiation of strong from weak arguments. More specifically, a message with strong arguments should produce more agreement when it is scrutinized carefully than when scrutiny is low, but a message with weak arguments should produce less overall agreement when scrutiny is high rather than low. This pattern of results is depicted in the left half of Panel III in Fig. 2. In a similar fashion, we can assess the extent to which a variable disrupts processing in a relatively objective manner. Consider a situation in which subjects are processing the message arguments quite diligently. These subjects should show considerable differentiation of strong from weak arguments. However, if argument processing is disrupted, due either to reduced motivation or ability, argument quality should be a less important determinant of persuasion. More specifically, a strong message should induce less agreement when processing is disrupted than when it is not, but a weak message should produce more agreement when processing is disrupted than when it is not. The right half of Panel III in Fig. 2 depicts this pattern. In addition to subjects' attitudes being more differentiated to weak and strong messages when argument processing is high rather than low, the profile of subjects' thoughts also should show greater differentiation of arguments when processing is high rather than low.

In sum, by manipulating argument quality along with some other variable, it is possible to tell whether that variable enhances or reduces argument processing in a relatively objective manner. If the variable enhances argument processing, subjects' thoughts and attitudes should be more polarized when the variable is present rather than absent, but if the variable reduces argument processing, subjects' thoughts and attitudes should be less polarized when the variable is present rather than absent. Before moving on to our postulates concerning peripheral cues and biased processing, we review some evidence that variables can affect persuasion by affecting the extent of argument processing in a relatively objective manner.

A. DISTRACTION

Research on distraction's effect on persuasion can be traced to an intriguing study by Allyn and Festinger (1961), in which high school students were presented with a speech which argued that teenage drivers are dangerous. The students were either forewarned of the opinion topic and told that their opinions would be assessed (opinion orientation) or were told simply that they were to assess the personality of the speaker (personality orientation). Although these two conditions did not differ in the average opinion change they induced, when analyses were conducted on the most involved subjects (those with extreme opinions or those who said the issue was important), a significant difference was found such that there was more persuasion in the personality than in the opinion orientation condition. Two possible explanations for this effect were offered. The initial explanation favored by Allyn and Festinger was that the "forewarning" in the opinion orientation condition stimulated the involved students to counterargue and/or derrogate the source (see also Freedman & Sears, 1965). A second explanation, proposed initially by Festinger and Maccoby (1964), was that the involved subjects in the personality orientation condition were distracted from the counterarguing and/or source derrogating in which they normally would have engaged.

In the years since the Allyn and Festinger experiment, a considerable number of studies have accumulated on both "forewarning" and "distraction," and it is now clear that both effects are viable. In this section we apply the ELM framework to "distraction" and discuss how this variable works by affecting information processing in a relatively *objective* manner. In section VII,B we apply the ELM to "forewarning" and address how this variable also works by affecting information processing, but in a relatively *biased* manner.

In 1973, Baron, Baron, & Miller reviewed the accumulated research on "distraction" and concluded that although many individual studies were susceptible to a wide variety of mediational interpretations, there were just two theoretical explanations that could account for the existing data parsimoniously. One explanation was the disruption of counterarguing interpretation favored by Festinger and Maccoby. Another interpretation offered by Baron *et al.*, however, was based, ironically, on Festinger's (1957) theory of cognitive dissonance. Baron *et al.* argued that distraction manipulations require subjects to exert more effort than usual in order to understand the message. Furthermore, "since choosing to hear a counterattitudinal message can be viewed as attitude-discrepant behavior, the effort required to comprehend a counterattitudinal message will directly determine the amount of dissonance created by the choice" (p. 317). One way for subjects to reduce this dissonance, of course, is for them to justify their effort by overvaluing the communication.

At the time of the review by Baron *et al.*, the available experiments did not allow a distinction between the two alternative theories because evidence that appeared to support either the counterargument or the dissonance position also could be seen as consistent with the other account. Importantly, even research using the thought-listing technique, which showed that with increasing distraction the number of counterarguments listed decreased (Keating & Brock, 1974; Osterhouse & Brock, 1970), was open to multiple interpretations. Was a reduction in negative thoughts obtained with distraction because distraction disrupted counterarguing, or was it because distraction induced attitude change via dissonance (or some other process) which was subsequently justified in the thought listings (Miller & Baron, 1973)?

Our initial use of the manipulation of strong and weak arguments (see section IV,A) came in an experiment that attempted to distinguish the dissonance from the counterargument disruption interpretations of distraction (Petty, Wells, & Brock, 1976, Experiment 1). A second aim of our experiment was to test a more general distraction formulation than "counterargument disruption." Specifically, we reasoned that if the predominant thoughts to a message without distraction were unfavorable, then distraction should disrupt these unfavorable thoughts and lead to increased agreement. However, if the predominant thoughts to a message without distraction were favorable, then distraction should disrupt these favorable thoughts resulting in decreased agreement. Our manipulation of argument quality provides a means of assessing this general "thought disruption" hypothesis as well as testing it against the predicted results from dissonance theory.

The thought disruption interpretation holds that distraction should enhance persuasion for a message containing weak arguments (since unfavorable thoughts should dominate under no distraction and would therefore be disrupted), but that distraction should *reduce* persuasion for a message containing strong arguments (since favorable thoughts should dominate under no distraction and would therefore be disrupted). The predictions from dissonance theory are quite different, however. Research on selective exposure and attention indicates that people prefer to hear weak rather than strong arguments against their own position (Kleinhesselink & Edwards, 1975; Lowin, 1967), suggesting that exerting effort to hear strong counterattitudinal arguments would induce more dissonance than exerting effort to hear weak ones. Because of this, dissonance theory predicts that for counterattitudinal messages, distraction should enhance persuasion more for strong arguments than for weak ones.

Two discrepant messages were prepared for our study. Both messages argued that tuition at the students' university should be increased by 20%, but the messages differed in the presentation of five key arguments. As explained previously, the strong arguments were selected so that they elicited primarily favorable thoughts when subjects were instructed to think about them, and the weak arguments were selected so that they elicited primarily negative thoughts. The distraction task required subjects to record on a monitoring sheet the quadrant in which Xs flashed on a screen in front of them. Subjects were either told that "no Xs would flash for now" (no distraction), or the Xs appeared on the screen at 15- (low distraction), 5- (medium distraction), or 3- (high distraction) sec intervals during the message. After hearing one of the messages over headphones, subjects completed attitude measures, were given 2.5 min to list their thoughts, and responded to ancillary questions. The attitude results are presented in Fig. 3, Box 1. Consistent with the general thought disruption hypothesis, a significant message quality × distraction interaction was obtained: increasing distraction was associated with more favorable attitudes when the message was weak, but increasing distraction was associated with less favorable attitudes when the message was strong. Analyses of the postmessage thoughts listed indicated that overall the messages differed in the number of counterarguments they elicited. In addition, high distraction reduced counterargument production for the weak, but not the strong message. Finally, high distraction tended to reduce the number of favorable thoughts elicited by the strong, but not the weak message.[4]

Several conceptual replications of our results have been reported. In one study, we exposed subjects to a strong or weak proattitudinal message under conditions of either low or medium distraction (Petty *et al.*, 1976, Experiment 2). As in our initial study, a significant message quality × distraction interaction was obtained: distraction was associated with increased agreement when the message was weak, but with decreased agreement when the message was strong (see Box 2, Fig. 3). In another study, Tsal (1984) prepared print ads containing strong or weak arguments for a variety of consumer products. As subjects were exposed to the ads via slides, they were either not distracted or were required to count the number of random "clicks" presented on tape. Again, distraction was associated with more favorable attitudes toward the products when the arguments were weak, but with less favorable attitudes when the arguments were strong (see also, Lammers & Becker, 1980).

In sum, the accumulated literature is very consistent with the view that distraction is one variable that affects a person's ability to process a message in a relatively objective manner. Specifically, distraction disrupts the thoughts that would normally be elicited by a message. Distraction should be especially important as a thought disrupter when people are highly motivated and able to process the message. If motivation and/or ability to process the message are low, distraction should have little effect (see Petty & Brock, 1981, for further discussion).

---

[4]Since the thought-listing data parallel the attitude data in nearly all of the studies that we report here, detailed results on this measure will not be described for the remaining studies that we review. Readers are referred to the original reports.

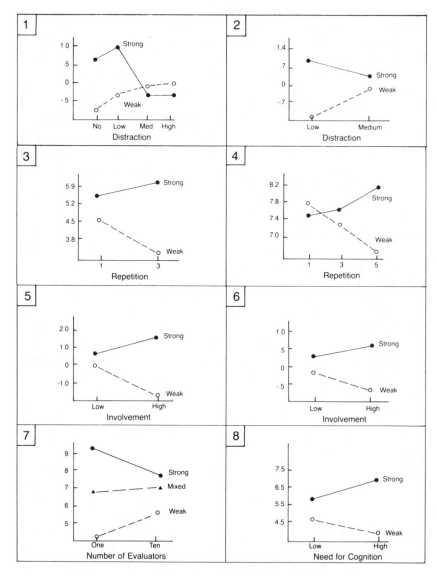

Fig. 3.   Variables that may enhance or reduce elaboration in a relatively objective manner. (1) Effects of distraction on attitudes following strong and weak counterattitudinal messages (data from Petty, Wells, & Brock, 1976; Experiment 1). (2) Effects of distraction on attitudes following strong and weak proattitudinal messages (data from Petty, Wells, & Brock, 1976; Experiment 2). (3) Effects of message repetition on initial attitudes following strong and weak messages (data from Cacioppo & Petty, 1985). (4) Effects of message repetition on delayed attitudes following strong and weak messages (data from Cacioppo & Petty, 1980a, Experiment 2). (5) Effects of personal relevance on

B. REPETITION

Repetition of stimuli has been shown to increase liking (e.g., Zajonc, 1968), decrease liking (e.g., Cantor, 1968) and have no effect on attitudes (e.g., Belch, 1982). The most common finding in the persuasion literature, however, is that repeating a persuasive communication tends to first increase and then decrease agreement (e.g., Cacioppo & Petty, 1979b; Calder & Sternthal, 1980; Gorn & Goldberg, 1980). A variety of theoretical accounts has been proposed for the effects of repeated exposure, including message learning, response competition, and others (see reviews by Harrison, 1977; Sawyer, 1981).

Based on the accumulated research, we proposed that message repetition guides a sequence of psychological reactions to a persuasive communication best conceptualized as a two-stage attitude-modification process (Cacioppo & Petty, 1979b). In the first stage, repeated presentations of a message provide recipients with a greater opportunity to consider the implications of the content of the message in a relatively objective manner. Thus, just as distraction can disrupt information processing, repetition can enhance a person's ability to process the message arguments. The benefit of repetition should be most apparent when additional opportunities are needed to process a message, such as when ability to process the full implications of the message with only one exposure is low (e.g., the message is complex), or when motivation to process with one exposure is low. Once a person has considered the implications of the message, however, the second stage of information processing commences. In this second stage, the relatively objective processing of the first stage ceases as tedium and/or reactance are elicited by the excessive exposures. Both tedium and reactance will tend to result in decreased message acceptance either by serving as simple negative affective cues or by biasing the nature of information processing in a negative direction (see Section VII,C). In this section we explore the consequences of the first (objective) stage of information processing.

In order to provide a test of our view that moderate repetition can affect persuasion by increasing the opportunity to scrutinize arguments in a relatively objective manner, we conducted a study in which students were exposed to a message advocating that seniors at their university be required to take a comprehensive exam in their major area as a requirement for graduation (see Cacioppo

---

attitudes following pro- (strong) and counterattitudinal (weak) messages (data from Petty & Cacioppo, 1979b; Experiment 1). (6) Effects of personal relevance on attitudes following strong and weak counterattitudinal messages (data from Petty & Cacioppo, 1979b; Experiment 2). (7) Effects of personal responsibility on attitudes following strong, weak, and mixed messages (data from Petty, Harkins, & Williams, 1980; Experiment 2). (8) Effects of need for cognition on attitudes following strong and weak messages (data from Cacioppo, Petty, & Morris, 1983; Experiment 2).

& Petty, 1985, for details). As in our work on distraction, half of the subjects heard a message containing strong arguments and half heard a message containing weak arguments. In addition, half of the subjects heard the message once, and half heard the message three times in succession. An analysis of subjects' postmessage attitudes toward the senior comprehensive exam issue revealed a message quality × repetition interaction (see Box 3, Fig. 3). Subjects showed greater attitudinal differentiation of strong from weak arguments when the message was presented three times rather than just once.

In another study (Cacioppo & Petty, 1980a, Experiment 2), we provided a conceptual replication and in addition examined the delayed impact of message repetition. In this study, students were exposed to a strong or weak message in favor of raising the price of their local newspaper. The message was presented to subjects as an audiotape of a telephone interview with a local resident. The strong message emphasized the benefits subscribers would receive from the price increase, whereas the weak message emphasized the benefits to management. Subjects were instructed to evaluate the sound quality of the tapes, and the message was played either one, three, or five times in succession. Immediately following exposure, subjects listed their thoughts about the tapes and rated the sound quality. From 8 to 14 days later, individuals were contacted by an interviewer who appeared unrelated to the initial experimenter. The second experimenter, who was blind to the respondents' initial experimental conditions, inquired about a number of community issues including attitudes toward increasing the price of the local paper. Consistent with the previous study, a message quality × repetition interaction was obtained (see Box 4, Fig. 3). Again, subjects showed greater attitudinal differentiation of strong from weak arguments as repetition increased.[5]

C.   PERSONAL RELEVANCE/INVOLVEMENT

We have now discussed two of the major variables that can affect a person's *ability* to scrutinize issue-relevant arguments in a relatively objective manner. Motivational variables are also important in affecting the likelihood of message elaboration. Perhaps the most important variable in this regard is the personal relevance of the message. Previous social psychological analyses of personal

[5]For exploratory purposes, a third group of subjects received a message containing novel arguments that were weak but "subtly contradictory." Subjects exposed to this message showed an inverted-U attitude pattern with repetition. It is also important to note in considering the effects of repetition that the number of repetitions required to enhance argument processing but not induce tedium or reactance will depend on a number of factors. For example, the more complex, the more lengthy, or the more rapidly presented is the message, the more repetitions that may be necessary for the full implications of the arguments to be realized. Thus, what is "moderate" and what is "excessive" repetition will depend on a number of factors (see Cacioppo & Petty, 1985).

relevance have labeled this construct (or variations of it) "ego-involvement" (Rhine & Severance, 1970; Sherif, Sherif, & Nebergall, 1965), "issue involvement" (Kiesler, Collins, & Miller, 1969), "personal involvement" (e.g., Apsler & Sears, 1968; Sherif, Kelly, Rodgers, Sarup, & Tittler, 1973), "vested interest" (Sivacek & Crano, 1982), and others. In brief, consistent with prevailing definitions, we regard personal relevance as the extent to which an advocacy has "intrinsic importance" (Sherif & Hovland, 1961) or "personal meaning" (Sherif et al., 1973). Personal relevance occurs when people expect the issue "to have significant consequences for their own lives" (Apsler & Sears, 1968) . Of course, relevance can be judged in terms of a variety of dimensions, such as the number of personal consequences of an issue, the magnitude of the consequences, and the duration of the consequences. For example, some advocacies may remain high in personal relevance for many people over a long period of time (e.g., changing the United States income tax structure), other advocacies may have personal relevance for a more circumscribed period and/or audience (e.g., raising college tuition), and still other advocacies may have personal relevance only under certain very transient conditions (e.g., refrigerator ads have higher relevance when a person is in the market for this appliance).[6]

Most of the early research on the personal relevance of an issue indicated that increasing personal involvement was associated with resistance to persuasion (Miller, 1965; Sherif & Hovland, 1961), and the most prominently mentioned explanation for this finding was derived from social judgment theory (Sherif et al., 1965). Involvement was believed to be associated with a greater probability of message rejection because people were postulated to hold expanded "latitudes of rejection" as personal involvement increased, and incoming messages would therefore be more likely to fall within the unacceptable range of a person's implicit attitude continuum (Eagly & Manis, 1966). To account for the fact that increasing relevance was associated with increased resistance mostly for counterattitudinal and not proattitudinal issues (e.g., Eagly, 1967), Pallak et al. (1972) proposed that increasing involvement (or commitment) increased the probability of rejecting counterattitudinal messages because these messages were *contrasted* (seen as further away from one's own position

---

[6]This kind of "issue relevance" can be contrasted with another kind of self-relevance referred to as "response involvement" (Zimbardo, 1960) or "task involvement" (Sherif & Hovland, 1961). In this second kind of involvement, the attitudinal issue per se is not particularly important or relevant to the person, but adopting a position that will maximize the immediate situational rewards is (cf. Zanna & Pack, 1975). For example, the issue of raising taxes in the United States has personal implications for most United States taxpayers (high issue involvement) whereas the issue of raising taxes in England does not. However, one's expressed attitude on the latter topic may become important while entertaining one's British boss for dinner (high response involvement). In some cases, response involvement should lead to increased influence (Zimbardo, 1960) and in other cases to decreased influence (e.g., Freedman, 1964), depending upon which enhances self-presentation.

than they really were and therefore more objectionable), but proattitudinal messages were *assimilated* (seen as closer to one's own position and therefore more acceptable).

Importantly, explanations of involvement based on social judgment theory did not consider the nature of the issue-relevant arguments presented in the communication. Instead, as involvement increased, a message was thought to induce increased assimilation (and acceptance) or increased contrast (and rejection) based on the particular position that it was judged to espouse. The ELM suggests an alternative analysis of the effects of personal involvement or relevance (Petty & Cacioppo, 1979b). Specifically, we suggested that as personal relevance increases, people become more motivated to process the issue-relevant arguments presented. As the personal consequences of an advocacy increase, it becomes more important for people to form a veridical opinion because the consequences of being incorrect are greater. Because of the greater personal implications people should be more motivated to engage in the cognitive work necessary to evaluate the true merits of the proposal.

Much of the early work on issue involvement was conducted by finding existing groups that differed in the extent to which an issue was important (as assessed by membership in issue-relevant groups), and thus was correlational in nature (e.g., Hovland, Harvey, & Sherif, 1957). More recent investigators have chosen to study issue relevance by varying the issue and message between subjects (e.g., Lastovicka & Gardner, 1979). For example, some undergraduate students would receive a message on a highly involving issue (e.g., increasing tuition), whereas others would receive a message on an issue of low relevance (e.g., increasing park acreage in a distant city; Rhine & Severance, 1970). Although this research is interesting in that these involvement classifications probably capture the personal relevance concept as it often occurs in the "real world," several interpretive problems are introduced. Specifically, distinctions based on different kinds of people or different issues may confound personal relevance with other factors (see discussion by Kiesler *et al.*, 1969). One particularly likely confound is that people in the high relevance groups or who receive the high relevance issues may be more familiar with the issue and may have more topic-relevant knowledge. Thus, in addition to possessing greater motivation to process the messages, it is likely that these subjects also have greater ability to do so. Thus, when a message contains information that is inconsistent with subjects' initial opinions, high relevance subjects should be more motivated and generally more able to generate counterarguments to the arguments presented. However, when a message contains information that is consistent with the subjects' initial attitudes, high relevance subjects should be more motivated and generally more able to elaborate the strengths of the arguments. In sum, it is possible that differences in message-relevant elaboration between high and low relevance subjects (rather than assimilation/contrast effects) may account for the different effects obtained for pro- and counterattitudinal issues in previous research on personal involvement.

In order to test our formulation, we first sought to replicate previous research using a manipulation of personal relevance that did not include differences in familiarity with the issue and arguments as a component. Employing a procedure introduced by Apsler and Sears (1968), we had subjects in both high and low relevance groups receive the same message on the same topic, but high involvement subjects were led to believe that the advocacy would affect them personally, whereas low involvement subjects were led to believe that the advocacy would have no personally relevant implications.

In our initial experiment (Petty & Cacioppo, 1979b, Experiment 1), undergraduate students received either a proattitudinal message extolling the virtues of more lenient coed visitation hours on college campuses, or a counterattitudinal message contending that colleges should be more strict in their coed visitation policies. The message arguments were pretested so that the counterattitudinal message arguments were weak and elicited predominantly unfavorable thoughts, and the proattitudinal message arguments were strong and elicited predominantly favorable thoughts when subjects were instructed to think about them. To manipulate personal relevance, half of the subjects was told that the speaker was advocating that the change in visitation hours be implemented at their own university (Notre Dame), whereas the other half was told that the speaker advocated the change for a distant college (Juanita Junior College). As depicted in Box 5 of Fig. 3, a message direction/quality × relevance interaction was obtained on the measure of subjects' attitudes toward the change in visitation policy. When the message was counterattitudinal (and weak), increased relevance was associated with decreased acceptance, but when the message was proattitudinal (and strong), increased relevance was associated with greater acceptance.

Although this study provides evidence consistent with our view that increasing personal relevance enhances motivation to scrutinize message content, it is still possible that attitude change was mediated by assimilation/contrast effects since the strong arguments advocated a proattitudinal position and the weak arguments advocated a counterattitudinal one. To provide a stricter test of the Elaboration Likelihood Model, we conducted a second experiment (Petty & Cacioppo, 1979b, Experiment 2) in which all subjects were exposed to a counterattitudinal message advocating that college seniors should be required to pass a comprehensive exam in their major area as a requirement for graduation. For half of the subjects, the arguments in the message were strong and compelling, and for the other half, the arguments were weak and specious. Finally, for half of the subjects the speaker advocated that the exam policy be instituted at their own university (University of Missouri), and for half the speaker advocated implementation at a distant school (North Carolina State). The results were identical to those in the preceding study (see Box 6, Fig. 3). A message quality × relevance interaction indicated that as relevance increased, subjects' attitudes and thoughts showed greater discrimination of strong from weak arguments. More specifical- ly, when the message was strong, increasing relevance produced a significant increase in attitudes, but when the message was weak, increasing relevance produced a significant decrease in attitudes.

In the context of examining the effects of other variables, we have repli- cated the interaction of personal relevance and argument quality several times (e.g., Petty, Cacioppo, & Heesacker, 1981; Petty & Cacioppo, 1984a). Subse- quent studies have also supported the view that as personal relevance increases, information processing increases in intensity and/or complexity (e.g., Harkness, DeBono, & Borgida, 1985; see Burnkrant & Sawyer, 1983). Although this research is consistent with the idea that people become more likely to undertake the cognitive work of evaluating issue-relevant arguments as personal relevance increases, several caveats are in order concerning possible limitations on this effect. First, we suspect that there are some circumstances where personal in- terests are so intense, as when an issue is intimately associated with central values (e.g., Ostrom & Brock, 1968), that processing will either terminate in the interest of self-protection or will become biased in the service of one's own ego (e.g., Greenwald, 1980, 1981).

A second factor to consider, however, is that, as we noted above, in the "real world" there is likely to be a natural confounding between the personal relevance of an issue and the amount of prior thinking a person has done about the pool of issue-relevant arguments. There are at least two potentially important consequences of this prior thinking. First, because of the prior consideration, people may have a greater ability or may be more practiced in defending their beliefs. This would reduce susceptibility to counterattitudinal appeals. Second, if a person has considered an issue many times in the past, it may be more difficult to motivate the person to think about another message on the same topic because the person may feel that all arguments have been evaluated (and rejected) al- ready. This would make it less likely that new compelling arguments would be processed.

A final factor to consider is the empirically derived nature of the strong and weak arguments used in our research. This empirical derivation is an important methodological tool in that it allows us to test the extent of argument processing induced by different variables. However, in the "real world," where persuaders are often confined to posing arguments that are veridical (rather than plausible), it may generally be difficult to generate arguments on some issues that elicit primarily favorable thoughts when people scrutinize them. Importantly, even if all of these factors combine to make it generally more difficult to obtain in- creased persuasion with increased personal relevance in the real world, the ELM accounts for this resistance by tracking the extent to which enhancing relevance affects the elaboration of the issue-relevant arguments presented.

D. PERSONAL RESPONSIBILITY

We have argued and provided evidence for the view that personal relevance enhances motivation to process issue-relevant arguments. There is also reason to believe that personal responsibility produces similar effects. Ever since Ringelmann, a German researcher, found that group productivity on a rope-pulling task failed to reach the levels predicted based on individual performance (see Steiner, 1972), several contemporary social psychologists have replicated this effect and pursued its underlying cause. Recent research has documented that at least part of the reduced performance in groups (called "social loafing" by Latané, Williams, & Harkins, 1979) results from loss of motivation rather than ability (Ingham, Levinger, Graves, & Peckham, 1974; Latané et al., 1979).

Although most of the research following Ringelmann has focused on tasks requiring physical exertion (e.g., Harkins, Latané, & Williams, 1980; Kerr & Bruun, 1981), in an exploratory study we examined the possibility that people who shared responsibility for a *cognitive* task would exert less *mental* effort than people who were individually responsible. In this study (Petty, Harkins, Williams, & Latané, 1977) we asked undergraduates to judge a poem and an editorial ostensibly written by fellow students. Our subjects were led to believe that they were the only one, 1 of 4, or 1 of 16 evaluators. All of them actually read the same two communications, and after exposure to each stimulus they were asked three questions designed to measure their perceived cognitive involvement in the task (e.g., to what extent were you trying hard to evaluate the communication?). Students who were solely responsible for the evaluation reported putting more effort into their evaluations than those who shared responsibility. Although no measures of actual cognitive effort or work were obtained in our initial study, subsequent research has obtained relevant evidence. For example, Harkins and Petty (1982) employed a brainstorming task in which students were asked to generate uses for objects. The students were either told that "you alone are responsible for listing uses" or that "you share the responsibility for listing uses for this object with nine other persons whose uses will be combined with yours." When confronted with objects for which it was relatively easy to generate uses (i.e., knife, box), solely responsible subjects generated significantly more uses than subjects who shared the responsibility (when the task was more difficult and challenging, no loafing was obtained).

In three studies, Brickner, Harkins, and Ostrom (1985) asked subjects to list their thoughts about the implementation of senior comprehensive exams (no messages were presented). Subjects were either told that they were the only person listing thoughts or that they shared the responsibility with a partner. In addition, the personal relevance of the exam proposal was varied by telling subjects either that the exam proposal was being considered for next year at their own university or that it was being considered either for a future date or for another university. When the issue was low in personal relevance, subjects who shared responsibility generated significantly fewer thoughts than those who were individually responsible. As might be expected if personal relevance motivates issue-relevant thinking (Petty & Cacioppo, 1979b), less loafing occurred in groups when the issue had high personal relevance.

The implications of this research for persuasion are straightforward: the greater the personal responsibility for evaluating an issue, the more people should be willing to exert the cognitive effort necessary to evaluate the issue-relevant arguments presented. To test this hypothesis, we asked undergraduates to provide peer feedback on editorial messages ostensibly written by journalism students (Petty, Harkins, & Williams, 1980, Experiment 2). Subjects were led to believe that they were either the only person responsible for evaluating an editorial or 1 of 10 people who shared the responsibility. Subjects received one of three versions of a message arguing that seniors should be required to pass a comprehensive exam in their major as a requirement for graduation. One message contained strong arguments, another contained weak arguments, and a third contained a mixture of arguments (and elicited a mixture of favorable and unfavorable thoughts). After reading the appropriate message, subjects provided an evaluation and listed their thoughts. The attitude results, graphed in Box 7 of Fig. 3, revealed a message quality × responsibility interaction. As personal responsibility for evaluation decreased, the quality of the arguments in the message became a less important determinant of the evaluations. More specifically, group evaluators were significantly more favorable toward the weak message, but were significantly less favorable toward the strong message than individual evaluators. As expected, evaluations of the mixed message were unaffected by the extent of responsibility.

E. NEED FOR COGNITION

Just as there are situational factors that influence the likelihood that individuals will think about and elaborate upon the arguments provided in a message, so too must there be individual factors governing message processing, and, indirectly, persuasion. Cohen, Stotland, and Wolfe (1955) introduced an individual difference called the "need for cognition," which they described as "a need to structure relevant situations in meaningful, integrated ways. It is a need to understand and make reasonable the experiential world" (p. 291). Early research on this construct suggested that people high in need for cognition made more discriminating judgments and were more motivated to think about persuasive communications (e.g., Cohen, 1957). Unfortunately, the objective tests used to gauge individual differences in need for cognition were never described in detail or published, and are apparently no longer available. Because of the great relevance of individual differences in motivation to think to the ELM and to cognitive social psychology more generally, we developed and validated a new assessment instrument (Cacioppo & Petty, 1982; Cacioppo, Petty, & Kao, 1984). Specifically, in an initial study, we generated a pool of statements concerning a person's reactions to engaging in effortful thinking in a variety of situations (e.g., "I really enjoy a task that involves coming up with new solutions to problems") and tested them on two groups of people presumed to differ substantially in their tendencies to engage in and enjoy effortful cognitive endeavors (i.e., university faculty vs. assembly line workers). Thus, the need for cognition scale (NCS) was designed to distinguish individuals who dispositionally tend to engage in and enjoy effortful analytic activity from those who do not (see Cacioppo & Petty, 1982, 1984b, for further information about scale construction and validation).

The results of several studies indicate that individuals high in need for cognition do indeed enjoy relatively effortful cognitive tasks, even in the absence of feedback about performance. For example, in one study (Cacioppo & Petty, 1982; Experiment 4), subjects were given either simple or complex rules to use in performing a boring number circling task. Afterward, subjects were asked to express their attitudes about the task. Results revealed that subjects generally disliked the task, but a significant interaction revealed that individuals high in need for cognition tended to prefer the complex to the simple task whereas individuals low in need for cognition tended to prefer the simple to the complex task. In another study, subjects who were low in need for cognition "loafed" on a brainstorming task when they were part of a group that was responsible for generating uses for an object, but subjects who were high in need for cognition did not loaf on this cognitive task (i.e., they generated the same high number of uses whether they were solely or jointly responsible; Petty, Cacioppo, & Kasmer, 1985).

Again, the implications for responses to persuasive communications are straightforward. If people high in need for cognition tend to engage in and enjoy effortful cognitive activity, they should be particularly likely to evaluate a message by scrutinizing and elaborating the issue-relevant arguments presented. In order to test this hypothesis, we exposed high and low need for cognition subjects to a set of strong or weak arguments for a counterattitudinal position (raising tuition at their university; Cacioppo et al., 1983, Experiment 2). After message exposure, subjects were asked to provide an overall evaluation of the message arguments and their personal opinion about the issue. Both measures indicated that subjects high in need for cognition scrutinized the message more carefully than subjects low in need for cognition. Specifically, the strong and weak messages induced more polarized evaluations and attitudes for high than low need for cognition subjects (attitude results are graphed in Box 8, Fig. 3). In addition, we reasoned that if subjects high in need for cognition were more likely to derive their attitudes through a considered evaluation of the arguments central to the recommendation, then there should be a stronger association between message evaluations and attitudes for subjects high than low in need for cognition. Separate correlations within each group provided support for this hypothesis. As expected, the correlation between argument evaluation and personal opinion was significantly larger in the high ($r = .70$) than the low ($r = .22$) need for cognition group.

VI.   Postulate 5: Elaboration versus Cues

It is now clear that a wide variety of variables can affect a person's motivation and/or ability to consider issue-relevant arguments in a relatively objective manner. The implications of this are that when the arguments in a message are "strong," persuasion can be increased by enhancing message scrutiny but reduced by inhibiting scrutiny. However, when the arguments are weak, persuasion can be increased by reducing scrutiny, but can be decreased by enhancing scrutiny. In detailing these processes (depicted in Panel III, Fig. 2), Postulate 4 brings under one conceptual umbrella the operation of a seemingly diverse list of variables such as distraction, repetition, personal relevance, and others, whose effects had been explained previously with a variety of different theories (e.g., dissonance, social judgment). In Section IX we discuss additional variables that affect objective processing.

Although it is now apparent that argument quality will be an important determinant of persuasion when motivation and ability to process message arguments are high, what happens when motivation and/or ability are low? Postulate 5 addresses this issue:

> As motivation and/or ability to process arguments is decreased, peripheral cues become relatively more important determinants of persuasion. Conversely, as argument scrutiny is increased, peripheral cues become relatively less important determinants of persuasion.

In the remainder of this section we examine this postulate in regard to variables affecting processing in a relatively objective manner (e.g., personal relevance). In Section VII, we apply this same postulate to variables affecting processing in a relatively biased manner.

A.   PERSONAL RELEVANCE/INVOLVEMENT AND THE
OPERATION OF CUES

Testing Postulate 5 requires establishing two kinds of persuasion contexts: one in which the likelihood of message-relevant elaboration is high, and one in which the elaboration likelihood is low. In discussing Postulate 4 we noted several candidates for varying the elaboration likelihood (e.g., distraction, repetition), but most research pertaining to this postulate has varied the personal relevance of the communication. In this section we discuss our own work and other studies in which peripheral cues were tested under different personal relevance conditions. We focus first on source cues, and then on message cues.

1. Source Cue Studies

In our initial investigation of source cues, we asked college students to listen to a message over headphones that advocated that seniors be required to pass a comprehensive exam in their major as a requirement for graduation (Petty, Cacioppo, & Goldman, 1981). Three variables were manipulated in the study: personal relevance, argument quality, and source expertise. In the high relevance conditions, the speaker advocated that the exam policy be instituted at the students' own university next year, thereby affecting all current students. In the low relevance conditions, the speaker advocated that the policy begin in 10 years, thereby affecting no current students. Half of the students heard eight cogent arguments in favor of the recommendation and half heard eight weak arguments. Finally, half of the students were told that the tape they would hear was based on a report prepared by a local high school class, and half were told that the tape was based on a report prepared by the Carnegie Commission on Higher Education, which was chaired by a Princeton University Professor. The expertise of the message source, of course, provides a peripheral cue that permits an assessment of the advocacy without any need to think about the issue-relevant arguments.

Following message exposure, subjects rated their attitudes concerning comprehensive exams. In addition to significant main effects for source and arguments (more favorable evaluations with strong than weak arguments, and expert than inexpert source), two significant interactions provided support for Postulate 5. First, a relevance × message quality interaction replicated our previous finding that argument quality was a more important determinant of persuasion for high than low relevance subjects (Petty & Cacioppo, 1979b). In addition, however, a relevance × source expertise interaction indicated that the source cue was a more important determinant of attitudes for low than high relevance subjects. The results for all cells of this study are graphed in the left half of Fig. 4. In the top panel it can be seen that under low relevance conditions, increasing source expertise enhanced attitudes regardless of message quality (a cue effect as depicted in the left side of Panel II in Fig. 2). However, in the bottom left panel of Fig. 4, it can be seen that under high relevance conditions, source expertise had no impact on attitudes; only argument quality was important.

In a conceptual replication of this study we employed a different manipulation of relevance, a different issue and arguments, a different cue, and a different

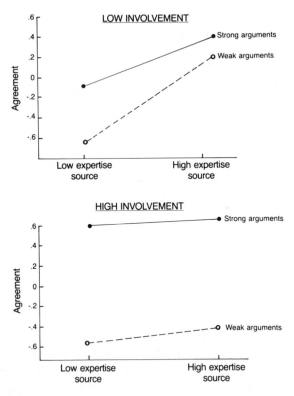

Fig. 4. Source factors under high and low relevance. (Left) Source expertise serves as a peripheral cue under low relevance conditions (top), but only argument quality affects attitudes under high relevance (bottom) (data from Petty, Cacioppo, & Goldman, 1981). (Right) Famous product endorsers serve as a peripheral cue under low relevance conditions (top), but only product quality information affects attitudes under high relevance (bottom) (data from Petty, Cacioppo, & Schumann, 1983).

method of message presentation. In this study (Petty, Cacioppo, & Schumann, 1983), undergraduates were asked to examine a booklet containing 12 magazine advertisements. Each of the ads was preceded by a brief description of the purpose of the ad. A variety of both familiar and unfamiliar ads appeared in the booklet, but the crucial ad was for a fictitious new product, "Edge disposable razors." Two things were done to either enhance or reduce the personal relevance of the ad for this product. In the high relevance groups, the ad was preceded by a description indicating that the product would be test marketed soon in the subjects' community. In the low relevance groups, the crucial ad was preceded by a description indicating that the product would be test marketed soon in several distant cities. In addition, all subjects were told before examining any

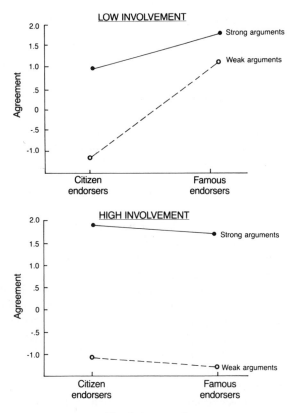

Fig. 4. (*continued*).

ads that at the end of the experiment they would be given a free gift for their participation. In the high relevance groups, they were told that they would be allowed to choose among several brands of disposable razors. In the low relevance groups, they were told that they would be selecting among brands of toothpaste (an ad for toothpaste appeared in the ad booklet). In sum, the high relevance subjects were not only led to believe that the crucial product would be available in their local area soon, but they also believed that they would make a decision about the product class. In contrast, the low relevance subjects believed that the product would not be available in their local area in the forseeable future and did not expect to make a decision about that product class.

Four different versions of the razor ad were constructed. Two featured photographs of two well-known and -liked sports celebrities, and two featured middle-aged citizens described as Californians. The product endorsers served as the manipulation of the peripheral cue. Finally, two of the ads contained six persuasive statements about the product (e.g., handle is tapered and ribbed to prevent slipping) and two ads contained six specious or vague statements (e.g., designed with the bathroom in mind).

Following examination of the ad booklet, subjects indicated their attitudes about the products depicted, including of course, Edge razors. In addition to main effects for argument quality and relevance (more favorable attitudes with strong than weak arguments and low than high relevance), two significant interactions paralleled the results of our previous study (Petty, Cacioppo, & Goldman, 1981). A relevance × message quality interaction revealed that the arguments in the ad were a more important determinant of product attitudes for high than low relevance subjects, but a relevance × endorser interaction revealed that the status of the product endorsers was a more important determinant of attitudes for low than high relevance subjects. The results of this study are graphed in the right half of Fig. 4. In the top panel it can be seen that the endorsers served as a simple cue under low relevance conditions (enhancing the effectiveness of both messages). The bottom panel indicates that only argument quality affected attitudes in the high relevance conditions.

Other studies have also provided support for Postulate 5 by showing that simple source cues are more important determinants of persuasion when personal relevance is low rather than high. For example, in one of the earliest experimental studies on source expertise, Hovland and Weiss (1951) had subjects read a message and then told them about the source. The source was either highly credible or lacked credibility. Four different topics (with appropriate sources) were used in the experiment. Although Hovland and Weiss in collapsing their data across the four topics concluded that the high credibility sources produced more change than the sources of low credibility, an analysis of the credibility effect for individual topics indicates that the credibility effect was reasonably strong for the two topics with the lowest direct relevance and prior knowledge (e.g., "Can a practical atomic powered submarine be built in the present time?"), but was weak and insignificant for the two most relevant topics (e.g., "As a result of TV, will there be a decrease in the number of movie theaters in operation by 1955?").

In a more recent study, Chaiken (1980; Experiment 2) manipulated the personal relevance of an issue by telling students that their university was considering switching from a semester to a trimester system either next year or after they graduated. Subjects either read a message from a likable source who presented one strong argument or from a dislikable source who presented five strong arguments. When the issue was of little relevance, the likable source was significantly more persuasive than the dislikable source (i.e., the source cue was effective). When the issue was of high relevance, however, subjects tended to be more persuaded by the message with five strong arguments than one even though the source was dislikable (see also Rhine & Severance, 1970).

2. *Message Cue Studies*

Distinctions between attitude changes based on source factors versus changes based on message factors have a long history in social psychology (e.g., Kelman & Hovland, 1953). In fact, the studies of source cues just described may appear to provide evidence consistent with the distinctions others have made between source and message orientations (e.g., Kelman & Eagly, 1965; McDavid, 1959; Harvey, Hunt, & Schroder, 1961). However, the central/peripheral distinction of the ELM is not equivalent to a source/message dichotomy. Importantly, the ELM holds that both source and message factors may serve as peripheral cues (and both source and message factors may affect information processing; see Section IX,B). Consider a person who is not motivated or able to think about the actual merits of the arguments in a message. For this person, it might be reasonable to assume that the more arguments contained in the message, the more meritorious it is. Although the literature on persuasion clearly indicates that increasing the number of arguments in a message is often an effective way to increase persuasion (e.g., Eagly & Warren, 1976; Insko, Lind, & LaTour, 1976; Maddux & Rogers, 1980), most have argued that this is because with more arguments, people generate and/or integrate more favorable issue-relevant beliefs (e.g., Calder, Insko, & Yandell, 1974; Chaiken, 1980). According to the ELM, it would be possible for the number of arguments in a message to affect issue-relevant thinking in some circumstances, but to affect persuasion by serving as a simple cue in other situations.

To test this hypothesis we conducted two studies (Petty & Cacioppo, 1984a). In one experiment, undergraduates received a written message on the topic of instituting senior comprehensive exams. For some subjects, the message had high personal relevance (it advocated that the exam policy begin at their university next year), and for others the relevance was very low (it advocated that the exam policy be instituted in 10 years). Subjects received one of four messages in favor of the exam proposal. One message contained nine strong arguments, one contained three strong arguments (randomly selected from the nine), one contained nine weak arguments, and one contained three weak ones (randomly selected from the nine). Following exposure, subjects gave their attitudes on the exam proposal. A main effect for message quality was obtained as were two significant interactions. A relevance × message length interaction revealed that the number of arguments in the message was a more important determinant of persuasion under low than high relevance. However, a relevance × message quality interaction revealed that the cogency of the arguments presented was a more important determinant of persuasion under high than low relevance conditions. The top half of Fig. 5 graphs the results. In the left panel it can be seen that under low relevance, the number of arguments serves as a simple cue, increasing agreement regardless of argument quality. In the right panel, it can be seen that under high relevance, the number of arguments acts to enhance argument pro-

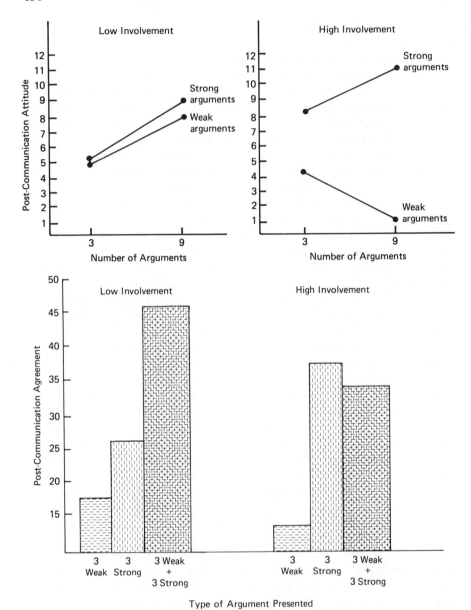

Fig. 5. Message factors under high and low relevance. (Top) Number of message arguments serves as a peripheral cue under low relevance conditions (left) but affects information processing under high relevance (right) (data from Petty & Cacioppo, 1984a; Experiment 2). (Bottom) Number of message arguments serves as a peripheral cue under low relevance (left) but affects information processing under high relevance (right) (data from Petty & Cacioppo, 1984a; Experiment 1).

cessing: when the arguments are strong increasing their number enhances persuasion, but when their quality is weak, increasing their number reduces persuasion.

In our second study, undergraduates were asked to read one of three messages. All of the messages concerned a faculty proposal to increase tuition, but in the high relevance conditions the proposal was for the students' own university, whereas in the low relevance conditions the proposal was for a distant but comparable university. The message that subjects read contained either three cogent arguments, three weak arguments or six arguments (three strong and three weak). After reading the assigned message, subjects indicated their attitudes toward the idea of raising tuition. Statistical comparison of the messages processed under high and low relevance conditions revealed the following (see bottom half of Fig. 5). When the issue was of low relevance, three strong arguments did not elicit more agreement than three weak arguments, but the message with six arguments (three strong and weak) elicited more agreement than either of the three-argument messages. When the message was highly relevant, however, three strong arguments did elicit more agreement than three weak arguments, but the six-argument message did not enhance persuasion over presenting three strong arguments. Again, argument quantity served as a cue under low relevance, but argument quality was more important under high relevance.

Langer, Blank, and Chanowitz (1978) explored the importance of the perception of arguments in a field study of compliance. All subjects in this study were standing in line to make copies when a confederate approached them with a request to make either 5 (low personal consequences) or 20 (high consequences) copies. The request was accompanied by either a valid reason ("I'm in a rush"), a "placebic" reason ("I have to make copies"), or no reason. Both kinds of reasons were more successful than no reason when the personal consequences were low (i.e., argument quality was unimportant), but the valid reason was significantly more potent than the placebic reason when the personal consequences were high. Folkes (1985) provided a partial replication of this effect. In two field studies using the inconsequential request (making five copies), respondents were equally willing to comply whether the request contained the valid or the placebic reason. In a third study, however, subjects were asked to guess how they would respond to the requests and to "think carefully before answering." When instructed to think before responding, the valid reason produced significantly more anticipation of compliance than the placebic reason.[7] In sum,

---

[7]Although providing a partial replication of Langer *et al.* (1978), Folkes takes issue with Langer's assertion that the placebic information is processed "mindlessly." Folkes argues that if the reasons are processed automatically under low consequences conditions, then a poor reason should be as effective as a valid one. However, she found that a poor reason (e.g., "because I don't want to wait") was significantly less effective than a valid or placebic one under low consequences conditions. The ELM would predict that the validity of a reason would become even *more* important when the personal consequences are high. This was untested in Folkes' study.

as personal relevance or thoughtfulness increases, the quality of issue-relevant arguments becomes more important than the quantity of arguments provided.

3. Additional Cue Studies

In addition to the research on source and message cues noted above, other studies have provided support for Postulate 5 by showing that simple cues are more important determinants of evaluations when personal relevance is low rather than high. For example, in one study, Gorn (1982) manipulated the personal relevance of a product (pen) and exposed subjects to ads for two different brands. One ad was attribute oriented and provided product-relevant information (e.g., "never smudges"), whereas the other ad featured pleasant music rather than information. Of the subjects in the high relevance condition, 71% chose the pen advertised with information, but in the low relevance condition, 63% chose the pen advertised with the pleasant music ($p < .001$; see Batra & Ray, 1984, 1985, for further discussion on how affectively oriented ads have greater impact under conditions of low than high involvement).

In two pertinent studies, Borgida and Howard-Pitney (1983) varied the visual prominence of discussants in a videotaped two-person conversation along with the personal relevance of the discussion topic. Previous research had shown that observers' evaluative judgments and attributions of causality tended to be more extreme for visually salient than nonsalient actors, a phenomenon called "top of the head" processing by Taylor and Fiske (1978). Based on the research we reviewed previously showing that personal relevance enhances message processing and reduces cue potency, Borgida and Howard-Pitney reasoned that perceivers' judgments of the discussion should become less influenced by the seemingly trivial visual salience cue (and presumably more by the content of the discussion) as the topic increased in personal importance. Their results supported this reasoning.

In sum, the accumulated research on personal relevance has provided strong support for Postulate 5 (see also, Taylor, 1975). Some studies have shown that various simple cues in the situation (i.e., source credibility/likability, mere number of arguments, pleasant music, visual salience) exert a more powerful effect on judgments when personal relevance is low rather than high. Other studies have shown that the quality of issue-relevant arguments exerts a more powerful effect on judgments when personal relevance is high rather than low. Still other studies have demonstrated both of these effects within the same experiment (e.g., Petty, Cacioppo, & Goldman, 1981).[8]

[8]Chaiken (1980) argued that just as issue relevance can determine the route to persuasion (Petty & Cacioppo, 1979b), so too can manipulations of response involvement, such as varying whether or not a person expects to be interviewed on an issue (see footnote 5). We suspect that this is true mostly when issue relevance is also reasonably high (as it was in Chaiken's study; Experiment 1). If issue

B. OTHER MODERATORS OF CUE EFFECTIVENESS

The research that we have just reviewed clearly indicates that the personal relevance of a message is an important determinant of the route to persuasion. According to the Elaboration Likelihood Model, however, other variables should also determine the route to persuasion by affecting a person's motivation and/or ability to process the arguments in a message. In discussing Postulate 4, we identified five variables that affect motivation and/or ability to process a message in a relatively objective manner. Each of these variables should be capable of moderating the route to persuasion.

For example, in an early study we showed how distraction disrupted argument processing resulting in more agreement when the arguments were weak but less agreement when the arguments were strong (Petty *et al.*, 1976). Just as arguments become less important determinants of persuasion as distraction is increased, simple cues should become *more* important determinants of persuasion as distraction is increased. Although this hypothesis has not been tested directly, available research is consistent with this idea. In one study, Kiesler and Mathog (1968) exposed undergraduates to a variety of relatively involving messages (e.g., requiring dormitory bed checks) under conditions of either distraction (copying lists of two-digit numbers) or no distraction. In addition, the credibility of the message advocacy was manipulated. The study resulted in a distraction × credibility interaction showing that distraction enhanced persuasion only when the source was highly credible. Consistent with previous theories of distraction (see Section V,A), this interaction has been accounted for by arguing that distraction enhances persuasion only when the source is credible because more credible sources induce more dissonance, or because more credible sources induce more counterarguing (Baron *et al.*, 1973; Kiesler & Mathog, 1968; Petty & Brock, 1981). The ELM provides a different yet equally plausible account for this effect. Rather than emphasizing the finding that distraction enhances persuasion when source credibility is high, the ELM views the interaction as showing that credibility enhances persuasion when distraction is high (Petty & Cacioppo, 1984c). In other words, when people are disrupted from processing the issue-relevant arguments by distraction, simple cues in the persuasion context become more powerful determinants of influence.

---

relevance is low, but response involvement is high, impression management motives (rather than concerns about adopting a veridical position based on examination of issue-relevant arguments) may determine the attitude expressed (see Cialdini, Levy, Herman, Kozlowski, & Petty, 1976). Although it is possible for impression management concerns to lead to extensive issue-relevant cognitive activity in some situations (e.g., a student assigned to argue in a public debate may carefully research the position in order to make a favorable impression), more typically, impression management concerns may not necessitate a careful evaluation of issue-relevant arguments (Cialdini & Petty, 1981; Moscovici, 1980).

In addition to personal relevance and distraction, the other variables discussed under Postulate 4 should also be moderators of the route to persuasion. For example, we have already noted that argument quality becomes a more important determinant of persuasion as people feel more personal responsibility for message evaluation (Petty *et al.*, 1980), and for individuals high rather than low in need for cognition (Cacioppo *et al.*, 1983). Although it has not yet been tested, the ELM expects that peripheral cues in the persuasion context should generally be more important for group than individually responsible message evaluators, and for individuals low rather than high in need for cognition. Before concluding this section, we note two additional variables that appear to moderate the route to persuasion.

One previously unmentioned variable that appears to affect the extent of issue-relevant thinking is the modality of message presentation. In general, audio and video presentations compared to print give people less opportunity to process issue-relevant arguments because exposure is forced rather than self-paced. Thus, presenting messages in written form should be especially important when the arguments are complex and difficult to process rapidly (Chaiken & Eagly, 1976). On the other hand, if it is generally more difficult to process issue-relevant arguments when exposure is forced rather than self-paced, simple cues in the persuasion context should be more powerful determinants of persuasion in the former than in the latter modality. Studies which have manipulated medium of presentation and source cues have supported this proposition. Thus, both source credibility (Andreoli & Worchel, 1978) and likability (Chaiken & Eagly, 1983) have had a greater impact on attitudes when a message was presented on video or audio tape rather than in written form.

Interestingly, the nature of the message itself has also been implicated as a determinant of whether a person processes mostly issue-relevant arguments, or searches for simple cues to determine message acceptability. For example, research suggests that messages that are either overly vague (Pallak *et al.*, 1983), or overly quantified (Yalch & Elmore-Yalch, 1984), may induce reliance on peripheral cues. The ELM would expect this to occur to the extent that these messages reduce either subjects' ability (vague message) or motivation (overly quantified message) to process issue-relevant arguments (Witt, 1976).

VII.   Postulate 6: Biased Elaboration

We have now seen that a wide variety of variables can moderate the route to persuasion by increasing or decreasing the extent to which a person is motivated or able to process the issue-relevant arguments in a relatively objective manner. As we noted in discussing Postulate 3, however, variables can also affect persuasion by affecting motivation and/or ability to process message arguments in a more biased fashion. Specifically, Postulate 6 states:

> Variables affecting message processing in a relatively biased manner can produce either a positive (favorable) or negative (unfavorable) motivational and/or ability bias to the issue-relevant thoughts attempted.

As we will see, there are a number of ways to induce biased processing, but often the bias results from a person's initial attitude becoming a more important schema in guiding processing (e.g., Tesser, 1978). Panel IV in Fig. 2 graphs the expected results for a variable that biases information processing activity. In the left half of the panel, the effects of a variable that produces a positive cognitive bias (enhancing favorable thoughts and/or reducing negative thoughts) is depicted. It is instructive to compare this pattern with the pattern of data in the two panels above it. First note that *unlike* a variable operating as a simple positive cue (left half of panel II), a variable producing a positive processing bias is not expected to affect all messages equally. Since the pure cue processor is not elaborating message arguments at all, the effectiveness of the cue is not constrained by the arguments presented. The biased processor, however, is attempting to process the arguments and in this regard is similar to the objective processor. Nevertheless, an important difference between objective and biased processing exists. The objective processor is motivated or is able to discover the "true validity" of the message, and thus strong arguments induce more persuasion and weak arguments induce less persuasion with more processing. In stark contrast, the biased processor is either particularly motivated or able to generate a particular kind of thought, often in defense of an initial attitude. However, even though the person is biased in processing a communication, the arguments in the message pose some limitation on this bias. For example, consider a person who is truly motivated to *counterargue* (and not simply discount) an advocacy. This person's task is simpler to the extent that the message provides weak rather than strong arguments in support of its position (see right half of Panel IV, Fig. 2).

Figure 2 summarizes the ways in which a treatment can affect attitude change according to the ELM, and it shows how these different processes can be tested by varying argument quality. First, a treatment can have no effect on persuasion for either strong or weak arguments (such as a peripheral cue under conditions of high elaboration likelihood; Panel I). Second, a treatment may produce only a main effect (Panel II). If so, it suggests that the treatment is operating as a simple positive or negative cue (low elaboration likelihood conditions). However, if a treatment interacts with message quality, it suggests that the treatment is affecting the elaboration likelihood. If the interaction follows the form depicted in Panel III of Fig. 2, it suggests that the processing is relatively objective. If a treatment main effect and an interaction as depicted in Panel IV of Fig. 2 is obtained, it suggests that the treatment is biasing information processing.

As Panel IV indicates, a treatment which biases thinking in a positive direction should generally have a greater impact on a strong than a weak message because it will be more difficult for a person to generate favorable thoughts to weak than strong message arguments. On the other hand, a variable which biases thinking in a negative direction should generally have a greater impact on a weak than a strong message because it will be more difficult for a person to generate counterarguments to strong than weak arguments.

Importantly, these predictions (and the depictions in Panel IV of Fig. 2) assume that in the baseline (control) condition, relatively little issue-relevant thinking is occurring. However, consider a control (comparison) condition in which subjects are maximally processing strong and weak arguments. If the experimental treatment includes a variable that biases thinking in a positive direction, it will be difficult to observe more favorable attitudes to the strong arguments in the experimental than the control condition since the arguments are already being processed maximally in the control condition (i.e., a ceiling effect is operating). However, the positive bias may result in more favorable attitudes toward the weak message than observed in the control condition (since no ceiling effect is operating). Thus, it may appear that the positive bias is working better for the weak than the strong message.

Similarly, if the experimental treatment includes a variable that biases thinking in a negative direction, it will be difficult to observe more negative attitudes toward the weak arguments than in the control condition if control subjects are highly motivated and able to process the message objectively (without bias). Thus, it may appear that the negative bias is working better for the strong than the weak message (because of a floor effect for the weak arguments). The caveat here is to include an appropriate control or baseline condition so that ceiling and floor effects are not problems. In general, when testing variables hypothesized to enhance processing, it is better to include control conditions in which processing is minimal. When testing variables hypothesized to reduce processing, the opposite holds.

In the remainder of this section we review evidence consistent with the view that some variables affect information processing in a relatively biased rather than a relatively objective manner. Importantly, a consideration of Postulates 5 and 6 together indicates that just as there is a tradeoff between a person's motivation and ability to process a message in a relatively objective manner and the effectiveness of peripheral cues, so too is there a tradeoff between biased processing and the operation of cues. As argument scrutiny is reduced, whether objective or biased, peripheral cues become more important determinants of persuasion. As argument scrutiny is increased, whether objective or biased, peripheral cues become less important. We now turn to some of the major variables affecting information processing in a relatively biased manner, and consider both message processing effects and the operation of peripheral cues.

A. PRIOR KNOWLEDGE

One of the most important variables affecting information processing activity is the extent to which a person has an organized structure of knowledge (schema) concerning an issue (Britton & Tesser, 1982; Higgins, Herman, & Zanna, 1981; Wyer & Srull, 1984). Although it is possible for prior knowledge to enable more objective information processing in some instances (Bobrow & Norman, 1975), since stored knowledge tends to be biased in favor of an initial opinion, more often than not this prior knowledge will enable biased scrutiny of externally provided communications (Craik, 1979; Taylor & Fiske, 1984). Specifically, schema-driven processing tends to be biased such that external information is processed in a manner that contributes to the perseverance of the guiding schema (e.g., Ross, Lepper, & Hubbard, 1975). Thus, the more issue-relevant knowledge people have, the more they tend to be able to counterargue communications opposing their initial positions and to cognitively bolster (pro-argue) congruent messages (e.g., Lord, Ross, & Lepper, 1979).

1. *Message Processing Effects*

The impact of knowledge structures on attitude-relevant processing is shown clearly in Tesser's program of research on the effects of "mere thought" (e.g., Sadler & Tesser, 1973; Tesser & Conlee, 1975; Tesser, 1976). In a series of studies, Tesser has shown that when instructed to think about an issue or object, attitudes tend to become more polarized in the direction of their initial tendency (i.e, they become more schema consistent; see Tesser, 1978, for a review). Importantly, this polarization effect requires that subjects have an organized store of issue-relevant information to guide processing, and that they are motivated to employ this issue-relevant knowledge in defense of their initial opinions. In the absence of these conditions, mere thought may not lead to polarization (Linville, 1982; Millar & Tesser, 1984; Tesser & Leone, 1977).

Although Tesser's research has focused on situations in which no message is provided to subjects, similar schema-driven processing can be observed when people evaluate persuasive messages. For example, in one study we exposed subjects to a proattitudinal message that was either relevant or irrelevant to a self-schema (Cacioppo, Petty, & Sidera, 1982). Our hypothesis was that schema-relevant messages would be more likely to invoke schematic processing than irrelevant messages (e.g., Cantor & Mischel, 1979), and that schema activation would enhance a person's ability to cognitively bolster the congruent message. Employing a procedure adapted from Markus (1977), we identified two groups of students who were attending a major Catholic university. Some of the students were categorized as possessing a "religious" self-schema whereas others were categorized as possesing a "legalistic" schema. Subjects received a generally weak message that supported their own opinions on an issue (e.g., against government support of abortion), and the message either employed a religious or a legalistic perspective in the arguments presented. An analysis of subjects' ratings of message persuasiveness revealed a schema type × message type interaction: the legalistic message was seen as more persuasive by the legalistic than the religious subjects, and the religious message was seen as more persuasive by the religious than the legalistic subjects. In addition, recipients generated more topic-relevant thoughts when the message was reflective than when it was unreflective of their self-schema. Further analyses revealed that this effect was accounted for mostly by the increased generation of favorable thoughts to schema-reflective messages.

If a message is inconsistent with a person's initial opinion, however, it would be expected that prior knowledge would enhance the person's ability to counterargue the message. In a test of this hypothesis, Wood (1982; Experiment 1) assessed the prior knowledge and experience people had on the issue of environmental preservation by asking them to list their beliefs and previous behaviors concerning environmental preservation. Subjects were divided into high and low belief and behavior retrieval groups based on a median split on the number of beliefs and behaviors listed. Consistent with the view that this assessment technique taps prior knowledge, subjects who generated more behaviors indicated that they had thought more about preservation, knew more about the topic, and were more involved than subjects who generated fewer behaviors (no effects were found for belief retrieval, however). One to two weeks later, subjects returned and read a counterattitudinal message providing four arguments against environmental preservation. After message exposure, subjects reported their attitudes and gave their thoughts. Subjects who had high prior knowledge changed less in the direction of the message than subjects with low prior knowledge. In addition, subjects with high prior knowledge (as assessed by behavior retrieval) generated more counterarguments and fewer favorable thoughts in response to the message. In sum, the available research is generally consistent with the view that prior knowledge enables counterarguing of incongruent messages (Wood, 1982) and bolstering of proattitudinal ones (Cacioppo *et al.*, 1982).

2. Cue Effects

Research is also generally consistent with the view that simple cues or decision rules are more likely to affect susceptibility to influence when prior knowledge is low rather than high. One cue that has been studied in the context of previous issue-relevant knowledge is gender. Previous studies of sex differences in persuasion have provided some support for the view that females are more susceptible to influence than males in some contexts (see reviews by

Cooper, 1979; Eagly & Carli, 1983), and one explanation for this effect is based on the idea that females may have been socialized to be more agreeable (i.e., concerned with social harmony) than males (e.g., Eagly, 1978). To the extent that females have learned to be more agreeable and less dominant than males, the invocation of this socialized female gender role or category (cf. Deaux, 1984) could lead to a sex difference in influenceability. However, according to the ELM, attitude expression based on the female gender role should be more likely when women have little ability to process the issue-relevant information presented than when ability is high.

In a test of this hypothesis, we exposed male and female undergraduates to photographs relevant to domains for which men and women had rated their knowledge differently (Cacioppo & Petty, 1980b). Half of the photos depicted football tackles (high male knowledge) and half depicted current fashions (high female knowledge). Each photograph was accompanied by a set of comments attributed to another subject. The comments were either completely factual and descriptive (e.g., the dress is blue, the runner's feet are off the ground) or included an evaluation (e.g., that's a great tackle) that was either accurate or inaccurate. Subjects were asked to rate the extent to which they agreed with the comments made by the other subject. The ELM suggests that to the extent that gender roles provide simple rules as to how one should behave (e.g., "As a woman, I should maintain harmony"), such rules should operate mostly when ability (and/or motivation) to evaluate the stimuli are low. In our study, when the comments were completely factual and easily verifiable, both males and females should be equally able to evaluate the comments whether they concerned fashions or football; thus, there should be no sex differences in extent of agreement. When the comments were evaluative rather than descriptive, however, knowledge is required to confidently evaluate the statements. For football tackles, then, the invocation of the female gender role should lead to women showing more agreement than men whether the evaluations were accurate *or* inaccurate. Actual accuracy should make little difference because in both cases women would have little confidence (due to low knowledge) in their judgments. When the judgments concerned fashions, however, women do have the requisite knowledge and confidence to make judgments. Thus, they should be more accepting of the accurate evaluations, but less accepting of the inaccurate evaluations than men. The data from our study generally conformed to this pattern. Other research has also supported the view that prior knowledge is an important determinant of sex differences in influenceability (e.g., Karabenick, 1983; Sistrunk & McDavid, 1971).

Another simple rule that people sometimes use is based on observation of their own behavior and the situational constraints imposed upon it (i.e., the self-perception principle; Bem, 1967, 1972). For example, if an initially agreeable behavior is overjustified, people may reason that their behavior is governed more by the reward than their attitude and come to evaluate the behavior less positively (e.g., Lepper, Greene, & Nisbett, 1973; see Deci & Ryan, 1980). Wood (1982; Experiment 2) reasoned that this relatively simple inference process based on a behavioral cue should be a more potent determinant of attitudes for people who have relatively little knowledge on a topic. In a test of this hypothesis, she found that low knowledge subjects used a monetary incentive to make an inference about their attitudes (as self-perception theory would expect), but high knowledge subjects were unaffected by this simple external cue (see Chaiken & Baldwin, 1981; and Fiske, Kinder, & Larter, 1983; for additional evidence).

Finally, we note that simple affective cues may be a more important determinant of attitudes when prior knowledge is low rather than high. For example, Srull (1983) had subjects rate their general knowledge about automobiles (cf. Bettman & Park, 1980; Johnson & Russo, 1981). Following a mood-induction procedure in which subjects were placed in a positive, negative, or neutral mood, they were exposed to an attribute-oriented ad for a new car and then asked to evaluate it. The attitudes of low knowledge subjects (as determined by a median split) were significantly affected by the mood manipulation, but attitudes of high knowledge subjects were not influenced by this simple affective cue.

3. Testing the ELM

In general, research on prior knowledge has provided support for the ELM view that when prior knowledge is low, simple cues in the persuasion context affect influence, but when prior knowledge is high, message processing is biased because previous knowledge enables the counterarguing of incongruent messages and the bolstering of congruent ones. However, more definitive support for the ELM analysis of prior knowledge requires a study in which knowledge is varied along with argument strength and a peripheral cue.

Fortunately, Wood, Kallgren, and Priesler (1985) reported such a study. In this study, Wood and colleagues asked undergraduates to list their beliefs and behaviors relevant to environmental preservation. Subjects were divided into three groups based on a combination of the total number of beliefs and behaviors listed (creating high, medium, and low knowledge groups). Subjects returned 1 to 2 weeks later and were exposed to one of four persuasive messages. The messages differed in both the strength and length of the arguments presented. Two of the messages contained three strong arguments favoring an antipreservation view and two messages contained three weak arguments. Two versions of each argument were developed, however. One version contained short concise statements of the arguments, and the other contained longer more wordy versions of essentially the same information. The long and short versions were equated in terms of strength and ease of comprehension.

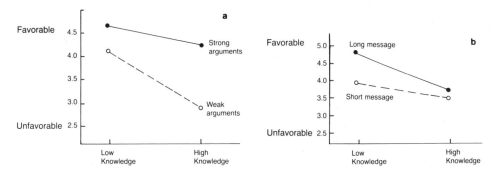

Fig. 6.   Prior knowledge biases message processing. (a) Increased knowledge makes it easier to counterargue weak than strong message arguments. (b) Length of arguments serves as a peripheral cue for low but not high knowledge subjects (data adapted from Wood, Kallgren, & Priesler, 1985; see Footnote 9).

After exposure to one of the versions of the message, subjects indicated their attitudes on the topic of environmental preservation. Overall, a main effect for knowledge was obtained indicating that as knowledge increased, subjects were more resistant to the counterattitudinal appeal. In addition, individual cell comparisons revealed that the attitudes of high knowledge subjects were affected by argument quality, but the attitudes of low knowledge subjects were not. A closer inspection of this interaction pattern (graphed in Fig. 6a) indicates that although high knowledge subjects were generally more resistant to all messages than low knowledge subjects, this was especially true for the message containing weak arguments. As noted previously, this particular interaction pattern suggests that high knowledge subjects were better able (and perhaps more motivated) to counterargue the incongruent message, but that it was more difficult to counterargue the strong than the weak version of it (cf. Panel IV, Fig. 2). In addition, planned comparisons indicated that the attitudes of low knowledge subjects were affected by argument length, but the attitudes of high knowledge subjects were not (see Fig. 6b). In sum, low knowledge subjects' attitudes were affected by the simple cue of message length, but high knowledge subjects used their prior knowledge in an attempt to defend their attitudes. They were more successful in doing this when the arguments in the message were weak rather than strong.[9]

[9]For ease of exposition we have graphed the data based on a median split on knowledge (W. Wood, personal communication, October 18, 1984) rather than the three-way split reported in the published article. As might be expected, the three-way split only enhances the differences between high and low knowledge groups, though the median split is based on a larger sample size.

B. FOREWARNINGS

Just as some variables generally enhance a person's ability to engage in biased processing of a persuasive message, such as prior knowledge, so too can variables enhance a person's *motivation* to process a message in a biased fashion, even if ability is held constant. For example, McGuire (1964) argued that inoculation treatments enhance resistance to persuasion mostly by increasing peoples' motivation to defend their beliefs. The persuasion literature has identified other variables that increase motivation to defend beliefs, and the most researched category of variables is "forewarning" (see Smith, 1982).

Papageorgis (1968) noted that two conceptually distinct kinds of warnings have been studied by persuasion researchers. One kind of treatment forewarns message recipients of the upcoming topic and/or position of the persuasive message (warning of message content). A second kind of treatment suggests to subjects that they are the targets of an influence attempt (forewarning of persuasive intent). Although some studies have explored the effects of combining the two kinds of forewarnings (e.g., Allyn & Festinger, 1961; Brock, 1967), it is possible to study their effects separately. Also, although many studies have shown that forewarnings can reduce the persuasive impact of a message, other studies have shown that forewarnings can enhance persuasion (e.g., Cooper & Jones, 1970; Mills, 1966). Importantly, which effect is obtained appears to depend largely on a person's motivation and ability to think about the issue. With low motivation and/or ability, forewarnings have tended to either have no effect or to enhance change in the direction of the advocacy. With high motivation and ability, however, resistance to persuasion has generally resulted (e.g., Apsler & Sears, 1968; Freedman, Sears, & O'Conner, 1964; Petty & Cacioppo, 1979a). According to the ELM, when motivation (e.g., personal relevance) and/or ability (e.g., prior knowledge) to think about an issue are low, forewarnings should enhance the salience of various cues (e.g., attractive sources; e.g., Mills & Aronson, 1965) or motives (e.g., impression management; e.g., Cialdini, Levy, Herman, & Evenbeck, 1973) in the situation that are capable of producing attitude change without issue-relevant thinking. When motivation and ability are high, however, forewarnings should modify attitudes by affecting issue-relevant thinking.

1. Warning of Message Content

A forewarning of message content gives message recipients advance indication of what the message is about. McGuire and Papageorgis (1962) hypothesized that the advance warning would motivate recipients to begin considering information that would support their beliefs and counterargue opposing arguments (i.e., biased processing). Consistent with this view, a content forewarning is most effective when there is a sufficient time delay between the warning and message to allow thinking (Freedman & Sears, 1965; Hass & Grady, 1975; Petty & Cacioppo, 1977). In addition, studies employing the thought-listing procedure (e.g., Brock, 1967; Petty & Cacioppo, 1977) and psychophysiological assessments (Cacioppo & Petty, 1979a) have supported the view that when confronted with an impending counterattitudinal message on an involving issue, people use the period between the forewarning and the message to bolster their initial opinions. This "biased scanning" of arguments on the issue (cf. Janis & Gilmore, 1965) enables greater resistance to the subsequent message.

If accessing one's issue-relevant information prior to a persuasive attack assists in resisting the subsequent message, then a forewarning of the impending

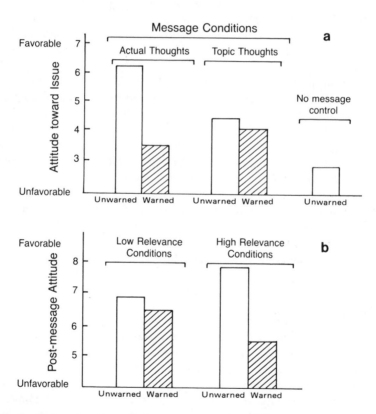

Fig. 7. Forewarnings bias message processing. (a) Forewarning of an involving counterattitudinal message topic and anticipatory topic-relevant thinking produce resistance to a message with strong arguments (data from Petty & Cacioppo, 1977; Experiment 2). (b) Forewarning of persuasive intent produces resistance to a message with strong arguments on a counterattitudinal topic when the issue is of high relevance (data from Petty & Cacioppo, 1979a).

message topic is not really necessary for resistance, but rather it is necessary for people to access their issue-relevant knowledge in preparation for the message. In a study testing this hypothesis (Petty & Cacioppo, 1977, Experiment 2), we told students in an introductory psychology class that they soon would be hearing a guest lecture from a counseling psychologist. Half of the students were warned several minutes in advance of the lecture that the speaker would advocate that all freshmen and sophomores be required to live in campus dorms (an involving counterattitudinal issue). The remaining subjects were unaware of the topic of the speech. After 3 min of sitting quietly, the students were given either three additional minutes to list the thoughts that occurred to them during the preceding minutes (actual thoughts) or they were instructed to list their thoughts on the topic of requiring freshmen and sophomores to live in dorms (topic-relevant thoughts). Following this procedure, the guest speaker presented a five-min advocacy on the topic, and the students' attitudes were measured. A control group of subjects responded to the attitude measure prior to the warning and advocacy.

The results of the study are depicted in Fig. 7a. The data for subjects in the "actual thoughts" groups were in accord with previous research employing involving counterattitudinal issues (e.g., Freedman & Sears, 1965). Specifically, the unwarned subjects were influenced by the message, but the warned subjects did not differ from controls. More interestingly, however, is that when subjects listed their thoughts about the message topic prior to receiving it, the warning had no unique effect. Subjects resisted the message whether they were warned or not. The resistance of the unwarned group that accessed issue-relevant cognitions prior to message exposure indicates that it is not the forewarning per se that induces resistance. Rather, the accessing of attitude-supportive beliefs prior to message exposure (which can be triggered by a warning) biases message processing and thereby facilitates resistance (cf. Miller, 1965).

2. Warning of Persuasive Intent

A forewarning of persuasive intent must work differently than a warning of message content because a warning of intent does not indicate the topic of the message. Thus, this kind of warning cannot enable a potential recipient to access the relevant store of issue-relevant cognitions prior to message exposure. As might be expected, then, unlike a warning of message content, a warning of persuasive intent is equally effective in inducing resistance whether it immediately precedes or comes several minutes before message exposure (Hass & Grady, 1975). What then is the psychological process responsible for the resistance conveyed by making the persuasive intent of a message salient? Brehm (1966, 1972) has argued that restricting a person's perceived freedom to think or act in a particular way arouses a psychological state of "reactance" that motivates people to restore their freedom. When a speaker announces an intention to persuade a recipient, this may be perceived as a direct threat to the person's freedom to hold a particular attitude (Hass & Grady, 1975). One way to demonstrate or reassert freedom, of course, is to resist the persuasive message.

According to the ELM, a warning of persuasive intent may induce resistance in one of three ways. First, the warning may serve as a simple rejection cue leading the person to discount the message without considering it (cue effect). Second, the warning may lead the person to more carefully scrutinize the message arguments leading to resistance when the arguments are weak but not when they are strong (objective processing). Finally, the warning may motivate the recipient to actively counterargue the message drawing upon previous knowledge in order to attack the message to the best of one's ability (biased processing). The results of several studies suggest that the latter process is responsible for the resistance conveyed by a warning of persuasive intent.

For example, in one study, Kiesler and Kiesler (1964) varied whether the information about persuasive intent preceded or came after the message. Persuasive intent only reduced persuasion when it came before the message. If the statement of intent served as a simple rejection cue, it should have produced resistance regardless of its position. In another study (Watts & Holt, 1979), a warning of persuasive intent given before the message reduced persuasion only when the message was not accompanied by distraction. The fact that distraction during the message eliminated the effect of the forewarning is consistent with the view that a warning works by affecting ongoing message processing. When this processing is disrupted by distraction, the warning is ineffective.

Although these studies are consistent with the idea that a forewarning of intent affects message processing rather than serving as a simple cue, they do not indicate whether the processing is relatively objective or biased. In a study designed to explore this issue (Petty & Cacioppo, 1979a), we told students that they would be evaluating radio editorials. Some were further told that the tape that they would hear "was designed specifically to try to persuade you and other college students of the desirability of changing certain college regulations." Others were simply told that the tape was prepared as part of a journalism class project. In addition to the warning manipulation, the personal relevance of the advocacy was manipulated. Some subjects were led to believe that the advocated change would affect them personally because the change would be implemented next year (high relevance), whereas others were led to believe that it would not affect them either because the change would not take effect for 10 years (low relevance-date) or because it was proposed for next year but for a different university (low relevance-place). All subjects received a message containing five strong arguments in favor of requiring seniors to take a comprehensive exam as a requirement for graduation.

The results of this study revealed a main effect for warning and a warning $\times$

relevance interaction on the postmessage attitude measure (see Fig. 7b). Although the warning decreased agreement overall, the effect was only significant under the high relevance conditions. The fact that the warning worked better under high than low relevance again suggests that the warning is not operating as a simple rejection cue. As we detailed in Section VI,A, cues tend to work better under low than high relevance conditions. Also, since the warning reduced persuasion even though the arguments were strong, this suggests that the warning induced biased rather than objective processing. When subjects were not warned, increasing involvement enhanced persuasion as would be expected if the arguments were strong and relevance increased subjects' motivation to process the arguments in a relatively objective manner (Petty & Cacioppo, 1979b). It appears that when a forewarning of persuasive intent was introduced under high involvement, the nature of the information processing changed as subjects became less objective, and more intent on finding fault with the message arguments in order to reassert their attitudinal freedom. Consistent with this reasoning, under high involvement, subjects who were warned generated significantly more counterarguments and fewer favorable thoughts than unwarned subjects in a postmessage thought listing.

C. OTHER BIASING TREATMENTS

Although we have focused on two highly researched variables that appear to enable or motivate biased information processing (prior knowledge and forewarning), other treatments may also bias the nature of message processing. We have already noted that McGuire's (1964) discussion of inoculation treatments provides a cogent example.

In our own research we have suggested several procedures for biasing the processing of a persuasive message. For example, in one study (Petty & Brock, 1979) we embedded a bogus personality assessment within an overall Barnum personality description (e.g., Forer, 1949). Subjects who in one experiment were led to believe that they had "closed-minded" personalities, subsequently generated a more one-sided profile of thoughts than subjects who were led to believe that they were "open-minded." In another study (Wells & Petty, 1980), we attempted to bias thought production by instructing subjects to make vertical or horizontal head movements while they processed a persuasive message. Whether the message was pro or counterattitudinal, subjects who engaged in vertical (yes) movements agreed with the message more than subjects who engaged in horizontal head movements. In other studies we have found that excessive message repetition (Cacioppo & Petty, 1979b) and the presence of hecklers (Petty & Brock, 1976) led to reduced agreement even though the arguments presented were strong.

The research on each of these independent variables (e.g., heckling, excessive repetition) clearly indicates that they are unlikely to enhance objective information processing. However, although there is some correlational evidence (e.g., from thought listings) to suggest that some of these treatments bias the nature of information processing, the studies may also be interpreted as indicating that the treatments serve as simple acceptance or rejection cues. For example, horizontal head movements, hecklers, or excessive repetition may not facilitate the production of counterarguments, but may instead induce negative affect that becomes associated with the advocacy (see Zajonc & Markus, 1982). Alternatively, the negative affect may bias information processing by increasing access to other information linked to negative states (Bower, 1981; Clark & Isen, 1982). Research that includes these treatments along with message quality and other motivational and ability variables should allow more definitive distinction of these possibilities (see also Section IX,B).

VIII. Postulate 7: Consequences of Elaboration

In the preceding sections of this article we have outlined how the ELM accounts for the initial attitude changes induced by persuasive messages. Postulate 7 deals with the different consequences of attitude changes induced via the central and the peripheral routes. Specifically:

> Attitude changes that result mostly from processing issue-relevant arguments (central route) will show greater temporal persistence, greater prediction of behavior, and greater resistance to counterpersuasion than attitude changes that result mostly from peripheral cues.

There are several reasons why these differential consequences would be expected. Recall that under the central route, attitude changes are based on a thoughtful consideration of issue-relevant information and an integration of that information into an overall position. Under the peripheral route, however, an attitude is based on a simple cue that provides some affective association or allows some relatively simple inference as to the acceptability of the message. Thus, attitude changes induced via the central route involve considerably more cognitive work than attitude changes induced under the peripheral route. The process of elaborating issue-relevant arguments involves accessing the schema for the attitude object in order to evaluate each new argument (e.g., by comparing it to information previously stored in memory). Under the peripheral route, however, the schema may be accessed only once to incorporate the affect or inference elicited by a salient cue. Or, a peripheral schema unrelated to the issue schema may be invoked in order to evaluate the cue (i.e., is the source credible?). Under the central route, then, the issue-relevant attitude schema may be accessed, rehearsed, and manipulated more times strengthening the interconnections among the components and rendering the schema more internally consistent, accessible, enduring, and resistant than under the peripheral route (cf. Crocker, Fiske, & Taylor, 1984; McGuire, 1981).[10]

The greater the accessibility of the information supporting an attitude, the greater the likelihood that the same attitude will be reported over time if people consider their prior knowledge before reporting their attitudes. Even if people do not scan their store of attitude-relevant information before reporting their attitudes in some circumstances (Lingle & Ostrom, 1981), the greater accessibility and endurance of the attitude itself would enhance the likelihood that the same attitude would be reported at two points in time. Also, the greater the accessibility of the information supporting an attitude and the more well organized it is, the greater the likelihood that this attitude-relevant knowledge can be used to defend the attitude from subsequent attack. Finally, the greater the accessibility of the attitude itself, the greater the likelihood that it can guide behavior (Fazio, Chen, McDonel, & Sherman, 1982).

In sum, the greater memory trace and accessibility of attitudes and attitude-relevant information for influence occurring via the central versus the peripheral route renders people more *able* to report the same attitude over time, to defend their beliefs, and to act on them. A motivational factor may also be relevant, however. Specifically, the process of scrutinizing issue-relevant arguments may generally be more deliberate than the processes of affective association and the invocation of well-rehearsed (even automatic) decision rules (Cialdini, 1984). Thus, changes induced under the central route may be accompanied by a subjective perception that considerable thought accompanied opinion formation. This perception may induce more confidence in the attitude, and attitudes held with more confidence may be more likely to be reported over time, slower to be abandoned in the face of counterpropaganda, and more likely to be acted upon.

A. PERSISTENCE OF PERSUASION

If extended issue-relevant thinking increases the temporal persistence of opinion change, then conditions that foster issue-relevant elaboration should be accompanied by greater attitudinal persistence than conditions that minimize elaboration. Among all the ways to change attitudes, *role playing* may be the influence paradigm that requires the most issue-relevant thinking in order to

---

[10]Of course, if a peripheral cue is *repeatedly* associated with an attitude object, relative persistence of influence may result (e.g., Weber, 1972).

produce persuasion. In role playing research people are required to generate or improvise their own arguments for a message (e.g., King & Janis, 1956). Importantly, research indicates that to the extent that people have sufficient knowledge and skill to generate their own messages, the attitude changes induced by these messages are especially persistent (e.g., Elms, 1966; Watts, 1967).

In role playing studies subjects are instructed to think about an issue position, whereas in other research the experimental conditions elicit issue-relevant thought spontaneously. For example, in research on anticipatory attitude shifts, subjects are induced to expect to discuss an issue or receive a message on some topic, and attitudes are measured prior to the discussion or message presentation (Cialdini & Petty, 1981). In one anticipatory change study relevant to persistence (Cialdini et al., 1976), we led college students to believe that they would discuss a campus issue with another student who held a position opposite to their own. Subjects were told that the discussion would take place either immediately or 1 week later, and the issue to be discussed was either one that was personally important to the students or unimportant. While waiting for the discussion to begin, subjects listed their thoughts on the issue and then reported their attitudes. Although subjects in all conditions showed some anticipatory shifting of their positions, only one group of subjects maintained their new issue positions after they had been informed that the discussion was cancelled. This group, subjects who expected to immediately discuss a personally important issue, were presumably the most motivated to undertake the cognitive work necessary to prepare for the discussion. Consistent with this analysis, these subjects listed significantly more thoughts that supported their own positions in anticipation of the discussion than subjects in the other cells.

In both the role playing research and the research on anticipatory shifts, attitude changes that were accompanied by considerable issue-relevant cognitive activity led to more persisting shifts than changes induced with less issue-relevant thinking. However, in both of these paradigms, no persuasive messages were presented. According to the ELM, the same result should hold if the attitude changes resulted from exposure to a persuasive communication. Specifically, the greater the elaboration of the message arguments, the more persistent the resulting attitude change should be. In a direct empirical test of this hypothesis (Petty, Cacioppo, & Heesacker, 1985), we had students listen to three persuasive messages. Each message began with a description of the origin of the message and provided a brief biography of the message source. The first two messages served as filler material and were identical for all subjects. The third message contained the experimental manipulations. Half of the subjects were led to believe that the advocacy concerned an imminent change in policy at their own university (high relevance) and half were led to believe that the advocacy concerned a proposed change in policy at a distant university (low relevance). Half of the students received a message from a very prestigious and credible source;

this message contained six strong arguments in support of senior comprehensive exams. The other half of the students received a message from a low prestige, inexpert source; this message contained six weak arguments in support of senior comprehensive exams.

Based on our previous research (Petty & Cacioppo, 1979b; Petty, Cacioppo, & Goldman, 1981; see Section VI,A), and pilot testing of the sources and messages under high and low relevance conditions, we expected both the high and low involvement groups who received the positive source–strong arguments message to show equivalent amounts of initial persuasion. However, the change in the high relevance group should be based mostly on a careful evaluation and elaboration of the strong issue-relevant arguments, whereas the change in the low relevance group should be based mostly on the positive source cue. Similarly, the rejection of the advocacy in the high and low relevance groups exposed to the negative source–weak arguments message should be equivalent initially, but in the high involvement group the rejection should be based mostly on scrutiny of the weak arguments, whereas in the low relevance group the rejection should be based mostly on the negative source.

An analysis of subjects' immediate postmessage attitudes concerning senior comprehensive exams provided support. Both high and low relevance groups of subjects exposed to the strong message/source were more favorable than controls, and both groups of subjects exposed to the weak message/source were less favorable than controls. More interestingly, however, the degree of personal relevance had an impact on whether or not these initial attitudes persisted. From 10 to 14 days following message exposure, subjects were called by phone and were asked their opinions concerning a number of campus issues including the general idea of senior comprehensive exams. An analysis of variance (ANOVA) on the initial and delayed attitudes of high relevance subjects revealed only a main effect for type of communication. The positive source–strong arguments message was more effective than the negative source–weak arguments message both initially and at the delayed testing. An analysis on the attitudes of low relevance subjects, however, revealed a communication × time of measurement interaction. For these subjects, the initial difference between the two message conditions was no longer appparent at the delayed testing. In short, those subjects who formed their initial attitudes based on a careful consideration of issue-relevant arguments (high relevance) showed greater persistence of attitude change than those subjects whose initial attitudes were based primarily on the source cue (low relevance).

Other persuasion studies also support the view that conditions that foster people's ability or motivation to engage in issue-relevant cognitive activity enhance the persistence of persuasion. Thus, using more interesting or involving issues about which subjects have more knowledge (e.g., Ronis, Baumgardner, Leippe, Cacioppo, & Greenwald, 1977), providing more time to think about the message (Mitnick & McGinnies, 1958), leading people to believe that they will be interviewed on the attitude issue (Chaiken, 1980), increasing message repetition (Johnson & Watkins, 1971), and reducing distraction (Watts & Holt, 1979) have all been associated with increased temporal persistence of attitude change (see Cook & Flay, 1978; Petty, 1977; for reviews, and Petty & Cacioppo, 1986, for a discussion of how the ELM differs from alternative models of attitude persistence, such as Kelman, 1961).

B. ATTITUDE–BEHAVIOR LINK

The previous section provided support for the view that attitude changes based primarily on thoughtful consideration (or self-generation) of issue-relevant arguments produced more enduring persuasion than changes based primarily on simple cues in the persuasion context. Research is also consistent with the view that attitude changes induced via the central route are more predictive of behavior than changes induced via the peripheral route.

As we noted earlier, perhaps the most effortful form of processing occurs when attitude change results from the self-generation of arguments. These changes, then, should be especially predictive of behavior. In a relevant program of research, Fazio and Zanna (1981) explored the consequences of attitudes formed via direct rather than indirect experience. When an attitude is formed via direct personal experience, the attitude is necessarily based on self-generated information. When an attitude is based on indirect experience (i.e., a message from others), less effortful processing may be involved. In some sense then, the distinction between direct and indirect experience is analogous to the distinction between attitudes based on role-playing (i.e., self-generation of arguments) versus passive exposure. Importantly, the research on direct versus indirect experience clearly indicates that the former attitudes are better predictors of behavior than the latter (see Fazio, 1985). The ELM suggests that one reason for this is that attitude formation based on direct experience may typically require more effortful elaboration of the merits of the object (e.g., puzzle; Regan & Fazio, 1977) than attitude formation based on passive exposure.

In our own research, we have also found that conditions that foster a high elaboration likelihood produce higher attitude–behavior correlations than conditions in which the elaboration likelihood is low. For example, in one study (described previously in Section VI,A,1), we exposed subjects to mock magazine advertisements for a disposable razor under conditions of either high or low personal relevance (Petty, Cacioppo, & Schumann, 1983). The ads that subjects saw contained either strong or weak arguments for the product and featured either a famous (likable) or an ordinary endorser. In addition to assessing product attitudes in this study, we also asked subjects to rate how likely they were to purchase the product (behavioral intentions). Under high relevance, both attitudes and intentions were affected significantly by the manipulation of argument quality. Under low relevance, however, attitudes were affected by the manipulation of endorser attractiveness, but behavioral intentions were not. The peripheral cue of endorser attractiveness was sufficient to enhance liking for the product when motivation to scrutinize product arguments was low, but was not sufficient to produce a change in behavioral intentions. Overall, the attitude–intention correlation under high relevance was .59, whereas under low relevance it was .36.

Just as increasing motivation to process issue-relevant arguments should enhance the utility of attitudes in predicting behavior, so too should enhancing ability to process the message. In a relevant study, Schumann, Petty, and Cacioppo (1985) exposed subjects to advertisements containing strong arguments for a new pen either one, four, or eight times in the context of a simulated television program. Each repetition of the message, of course, gives subjects an additional opportunity to consider the product-relevant information. After message exposure, subjects rated their attitudes toward the advertised pen, their likelihood of purchasing this brand in the near future, and the amount of time they spent thinking about the product during the program. Subjects reported engaging in more thought about the product as repetition increased, and the attitude–intention correlation also improved significantly with repetition.

Finally, we have obtained evidence that people who differ dispositionally in their tendency to engage in and enjoy thinking also differ in the extent to which their attitudes predict behavior (Cacioppo, Petty, Kao, & Rodriguez, 1985). Specifically, we found that the attitudes toward the candidates in the 1984 presidential election predicted voting intentions and reported behavior better for people who were high rather than low in their "need for cognition" (Cacioppo & Petty, 1982; see Section V,E). In sum, when the experimental conditions or dispositional factors enhanced peoples' motivation or ability to elaborate issue-relevant information, attitude–behavior correlations were higher than when elaboration was low (Cialdini et al., 1981; see also Pallak, Murroni, & Koch, 1983; Sandelands & Larson, 1985; Sivacek & Crano, 1982).[11]

---

[11]Our argument that the more issue relevant elaboration involved in attitude change the greater the attitude–behavior correlation should be, may appear to conflict with a claim by Wilson, Dunn, Bybee, Hyman, and Rotondo (1984) that analyzing reasons for one's attitudes *reduces* attitude–behavior consistency. However, in the research supporting the Wilson et al. contention, one effect of having subjects think about the reasons behind their attitudes was to produce a change in attitudes. Thus, Wilson et al. compared the ability of an *initial* attitude to predict behavior with the ability of a *changed* attitude. The new attitude was less predictive than the old one. Importantly, the ELM addresses a comparison between two initial attitudes (one formed via the central and one formed via the peripheral route) *or* two newly changed attitudes (one changed via the central and one changed via the peripheral route). The ELM predicts that the central attitudes will predict behavior better than comparable attitudes formed or changed via the peripheral route.

C. RESISTANCE TO COUNTERPERSUASION

The final consequence of the route to persuasion is that attitudes formed via the central route should be more resistant to counterpropaganda than attitudes formed via the peripheral route. Importantly, the *resistance* of an attitude to attack is conceptually distinct from the temporal *persistence* of an attitude. Thus, some attitudes may be highly persistent, but only if they are not attacked. Other attitudes may be very transient even in a vacuum. Likewise, it is possible for some attitudes to be very resistant to change, but only in the short term. Despite the conceptual independence of persistence and resistance, we have already outlined the reasons why the ELM holds that usually these two qualities will go together. Attitudes based on extensive issue-relevant thinking will tend to be both persistent and resistant, whereas attitudes based on peripheral cues will tend to be transient and susceptible to counterpersuasion.

Attitudes for which persistence and resistance do *not* go together provide an intriguing target of study. Perhaps the most dramatic example of the possible independence of persistence and resistance is found in cultural truisms. Truisms such as "you should brush your teeth after every meal" tend to be highly persistent in a vacuum, but very susceptible to influence if attacked. As McGuire (1964) noted, people have very little practice in defending these beliefs because they have never been challenged. Furthermore, the ELM would contend that these beliefs are highly susceptible to persuasion because they were probably *formed* with very little issue-relevant thinking. It is likely that people come to accept many cultural truisms sometime during childhood. The truisms are continually presented by powerful, likable, and expert sources (e.g., parents, teachers, television characters) with little or no justification. The continual pairing of the belief with a positive cue results in a relatively persistent attitude, but one that cannot be defended when subsequently attacked.

Most research on attitudinal resistance has focused on how various treatments can help bolster an attitude that a person already has. For example, in an important program of research, McGuire (1964) has provided impressive evidence for the view that attitudes can be made more resistant by providing people with the requisite motivation and/or ability to counterargue opposing messages. The underlying logic of McGuire's inoculation theory is that a threat to a previously unassailed belief motivates the person to defend that belief when it is attacked in the future. An initial attack on a person's belief also provides practice in defending the belief. In another relevant program of research, Burgoon and his colleagues (e.g., Burgoon, Cohen, Miller, & Montgomery, 1978) investigated how the manner in which an initial message is processed can affect susceptibility to a subsequent message on the same topic (see review by Smith, 1982).

The work of McGuire and Burgoon has focused on how an initial belief held by a person can be made more resistant or susceptible by providing some treat-

182 RICHARD E. PETTY AND JOHN T. CACIOPPO

ment that enhances or reduces the person's motivation and/or ability to counterargue a subsequent opposing communication. This work is consistent with the ELM in that it demonstrates that attitudes can be made more resistant by motivating or enabling people to engage in additional thought about the reasons or arguments supporting their attitudes. To date, however, no research has explicitly tested the ELM prediction that the manner in which an attitude is formed or changed has important implications for the resistance of the attitude. Specifically, the ELM predicts that people who come to accept an issue position because of a peripheral cue (e.g., source expertise) should be more susceptible to an attacking message than people who adopt the same issue position based on a careful scrutiny and elaboration of the message arguments.

IX. Complicating Factors

We have now presented the major postulates of the Elaboration Likelihood Model and some research relevant to these postulates. In reviewing the evidence for the ELM we have focused deliberately on variables and instances that were straightforward and relatively unambiguous in interpretation. Although it would be nice if we could provide an exhaustive list of variables that serve as peripheral cues and variables that affect message processing in either an objective or a biased manner, we have already seen that this is not possible. For example, we have argued that the effects on information processing of some variables may shift from relatively objective to relatively biased as the variable reaches very high levels. For example, although increasing personal relevance and message repetition may generally enhance subjects' motivation and/or ability to see the merits of strong arguments and the flaws in weak ones, we have suggested that when personal relevance or message repetition reaches very high levels, the initially objective processing may become biased as the person becomes motivated to reject the advocacy (Cacioppo & Petty, 1979b; Petty & Cacioppo, 1979b). In short, some variables have multiple effects on information processing. In addition, we have seen that some variables may affect information processing under certain conditions, but serve as peripheral cues in other contexts. For example, we reviewed evidence in Section VI,A that manipulation of the number of arguments in a message could serve as a peripheral cue when the personal relevance of the message was low, but that increasing the number of arguments in a message could increase the amount of information processing activity when the personal relevance of the message was high (Petty & Cacioppo, 1984a). In this section we will comment briefly on these and other intricacies of the ELM.

A. VARIABLES WITH MULTIPLE EFFECTS ON ELABORATION

In most of the research that we have discussed so far, we have examined the isolated effects of different source, message, recipient, and channel factors on information processing. However, in most natural persuasion situations, many variables combine to create the overall persuasion context. For example, consider a high need for cognition person who is part of a jury whose members share responsibility for evaluating an expert witness who presents weak arguments in a corporate tax case in a courtroom with noisy distractions. All of the many variables present in this situation must be considered jointly to determine the probable persuasive impact of the testimony. Normally, sharing cognitive responsibility with a group reduces information processing activity (Petty, Cacioppo, & Harkins, 1983), but our message recipient dispositionally tends to like to think (Cacioppo, Petty, & Morris, 1983) and is therefore less susceptible to motivation loss in groups (Petty, Cacioppo, & Kasmer, 1985). Therefore, *motivation* to process the message is likely to be high despite the group responsibility. However, due to a lack of prior knowledge about corporate taxes and the distractions inherent in the situation, our message recipient may have little *ability* to process the weak message arguments (Petty, Wells, & Brock, 1976; Wood, Kallgren, & Priesler, 1985). Thus, the perceived expertise of the witness may serve as a potent influence cue (Kiesler & Mathog, 1968).

Our example assumes that each of the features of the persuasion situation (e.g., distraction, group responsibility) can be considered separately and independently regardless of the levels of the other variables with which it is combined. If so, one can roughly add (subtract) the effects of each variable to determine the overall elaboration likelihood. Although this is often possible, as we discuss next, it is also possible for one variable to have very different effects on information processing depending on the level of other variables.

For example, some variables may increase information processing at one level of another factor, but may actually decrease processing at a different level of that factor. In one study exploring this possibility, we varied the personal relevance of a message, whether concluding summaries of the message arguments were framed as statements or as rhetorical questions (cf. Zillmann, 1972), and whether the arguments presented were strong or weak. In this study (Petty, Cacioppo, & Heesacker, 1981), all subjects heard over headphones a message advocating that seniors take a comprehensive exam in their major as a requirement for graduation. The study was designed to test our view that summarizing arguments as rhetorical questions (e.g., "Wouldn't instituting a comprehensive exam be an aid to those who seek admission to graduate and professional schools?") rather than as declarative statements, would motivate more thinking about the arguments. If rhetoricals enhance relatively objective processing, then their use should lead to more agreement if the message arguments are strong, but less agreement if the arguments are weak. However, this enhanced elaboration with rhetoricals should be evident mostly when people are not naturally devoting much effort to processing the message arguments, such as when the personal

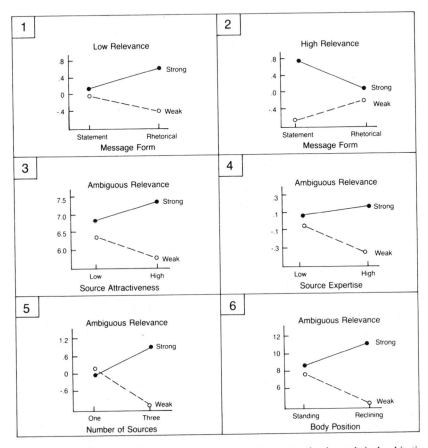

Fig. 8. Additional variables that may affect information processing in a relatively objective manner. (1) Effects of rhetorical questions on attitudes following strong and weak messages of low relevance (data from Petty, Cacioppo, & Heesacker, 1981). (2) Effects of rhetorical questions on attitudes following strong and weak messages of high relevance (data from Petty, Cacioppo, & Heesacker, 1981). (3) Effects of social attractiveness on attitudes following strong and weak messages of uncertain relevance (data from Puckett et al., 1983). (4) Effects of expertise on attitudes of field-dependent subjects following strong and weak messages of uncertain relevance (data from Heesacker et al., 1983). (5) Effects of multiple sources on attitudes following strong and weak messages of uncertain relevance (data from Harkins & Petty, 1981a; Experiment 4). (6) Effects of recipient posture on attitudes following strong and weak messages of uncertain relevance (data from Petty, Wells, Heesacker, Brock, & Cacioppo, 1983).

relevance of the message is low. When people are already naturally motivated to process the message, such as when personal relevance is high, we expected that the use of rhetoricals would either have no further effect on elaboration, or might even be disruptive of ongoing information processing. The results of our study supported these expectations. When personal relevance was low, the use of rhetorical questions increased elaboration (see Box 1, Fig. 8), but when personal relevance was high, subjects reported that the rhetorical questions were distracting and argument scrutiny was reduced (see Box 2, Fig. 8).

Burnkrant and Howard (1984) replicated our rhetoricals study making a few key changes. Again, subjects were presented with the strong or weak version of our senior comprehensive exam message that was made either high or low in personal relevance. Instead of hearing the message over headphones, however, subjects were presented with the message as a written communication. In addition, instead of summarizing each message argument as a rhetorical question after the argument was presented, all rhetorical questions *preceded* the presentation of the message arguments. Burnkrant and Howard argued that these changes should eliminate the distraction effect that we observed under high involvement. First, presenting the message in print rather than orally gives subjects time to stop the message to consider arguments fully (see Section VI,B). Thus, the rhetoricals need not disrupt processing even if subjects are highly involved. Second, placing the rhetorical questions at the beginning rather than at the end of the arguments has the advantage of generating interest and curiosity while avoiding the disadvantage of interrupting the train of thought concerning the argument just presented. Their results were consistent with this reasoning. The use of introductory rhetorical questions in print enhanced argument elaboration regardless of the personal relevance of the issue. When paired with the strong arguments, rhetorical questions increased agreement, but when paired with the weak arguments, rhetorical questions decreased agreement. The studies on rhetorical questions provide cogent examples of how an independent variable can have different but predictable effects on elaboration depending on the level of other variables, such as personal relevance and modality of message presentation.

A second way in which the impact of one variable may depend on the level of another factor is in whether the variable induces relatively objective or relatively biased information processing. For example, we have demonstrated that increasing the degree of personal relevance of a message can enhance a person's motivation to process the message in a relatively objective manner (Petty & Cacioppo, 1979b). However, we have also seen that this processing may become biased if personal relevance is combined with a threat, such as that induced by a forewarning of persuasive intent (Petty & Cacioppo, 1979a). In short, personal relevance per se may motivate increased processing, but when combined with some threat, the processing may be directed in the defense of one's initial position.

B. VARIABLES THAT AFFECT ELABORATION AND SERVE AS CUES

In Section IX,A we argued that whether or not a particular variable enhances or diminishes processing, or motivates relatively objective or relatively biased processing, may depend on the level of other variables in the persuasion context. Similarly, whether a variable affects information processing or serves as a peripheral cue may depend on the level of other elements in the persuasion situation. We discuss this feature of the ELM below.

1. Source Expertise/Attractiveness

In Section I, we noted that one aspect of persuasion research that has disappointed reviewers of the field is that even variables that were expected to be quite simple in their effects on attitude change have instead proved to be quite complex. We also noted that perhaps the most dramatic example of this was the conflicting results of research on features of the message source (Eagly & Himmelfarb, 1974). Postulate 3 (Section IV) of the ELM outlines the several different ways in which source (and other) factors can affect persuasion: they can serve as arguments, they can serve as cues, or they can affect argument processing. In the research that we have reviewed so far, we have focused on how source factors operate when the elaboration likelihood is either very high or very low. We have seen that when people are unmotivated and/or unable to process a message, they rely on simple cues in the persuasion context, such as the expertise or attractiveness of the message source, although other cues may be used if they are more salient. Importantly, since subjects are either unmotivated or unable to evaluate message arguments, a positive source tends to enhance persuasion and a negative source tends to reduce persuasion, regardless of message quality (e.g., see top panels in Fig. 4).

On the other hand, when people are highly motivated and able to process message arguments, strong arguments are more effective than weak ones despite the presence of peripheral cues such as source credibility and attractiveness (e.g., see bottom panels in Fig. 4). When motivation and ability to process are high, people are concerned with evaluating the true merits of the advocacy. In order to do this, they will scrutinize all available and inferred information in the immediate persuasion context, and attempt to relate it to information stored previously in memory. Interestingly, a consideration of source factors may be part of a person's attempt to evaluate issue-relevant information when the elaboration likelihood is high. For example, under some circumstances a source feature may itself serve as a persuasive argument by providing information central to the merits of the attitude object (e.g., a physically attractive source, without saying anything, may provide persuasive visual testimony as to the effectiveness of a beauty product; Kahle & Homer, 1985; Petty & Cacioppo, 1981b). Additionally, a consideration of source information might help a person in evaluating the true merits of any given argument (e.g., is the expert source biased or does the source have a vested interest?).

It may now appear that the cases of high and low elaboration likelihood are quite clear. Source factors affect agreement with a message by serving as simple acceptance or rejection cues when the elaboration likelihood is low, but do not serve as simple cues when the elaboration likelihood is high. Instead, they are considered along with the message arguments in an attempt to evaluate the true merits of the advocacy. These conclusions, however, are only part of the story of how source factors impact on persuasion. As we noted in Section III,A, we view elaboration likelihood as a continuum anchored at one end by the peripheral route to persuasion, and at the other end by the central route. In all of our research described in the previous sections, we have attempted to create and describe relatively clear instances of central and peripheral routes to persuasion. Thus, for example, in our research on motivation to process, subjects were either highly involved with the topic (e.g., students were confronted with an advocacy that had implications for their own graduation; Petty, Cacioppo, & Goldman, 1981), or very uninvolved (e.g., the students were certain that there were no personal implications of the advocacy). The extreme high and low elaboration likelihood conditions have been quite useful for theory testing purposes and in explicating the two routes to persuasion. However, these conditions represent only part of the elaboration likelihood continuum.

Specifically, many day to day persuasion contexts are unlikely to be as high or as low in elaboration likelihood as the conditions we have deliberately created in our initial research. For example, people are sometimes uncertain as to the personal relevance of an issue, or have moderate rather than very high or very low knowledge on a topic. We have proposed that under more moderate conditions, people use source characteristics to determine how much to think about the message (Petty & Cacioppo, 1981a, 1984c). When the personal consequences or prior knowledge on an issue are moderate or unclear, people may not be sure if the message is worth thinking about or if they are able to do so. Under these circumstances, characteristics of the message source can help a person decide if the message warrants (or needs) careful scrutiny. In our own research on moderate levels of motivation to process, undergraduate students have been led to believe that a change in policy was being advocated for their university, but they were not told when or if this policy ever would be implemented. Thus, unlike our studies on high and low personal relevance (see Section VI,A), subjects could not be certain whether or not the change in policy would affect them.

In one study (Puckett, Petty, Cacioppo, & Fisher, 1983), for example, we told subjects that students in an evening undergraduate continuing education course had written essays on the issue of whether comprehensive exams should be given in a student's major area of study as a prerequisite for obtaining a bachelor's degree. Each subject was given a folder containing a typed essay along with a card containing a picture and a brief description of the author of the essay. Two major variables were manipulated in the study: (1) the social attractiveness of the author (socially attractive authors were more physically attractive and had better family backgrounds and more prestigious hobbies than the socially unattractive authors), and (2) the quality of the arguments in the editorial (either strong or weak). A third variable, age of the essay author, was also manipulated but this factor had no effect on persuasion. After looking through the appropriate folder, subjects were asked to rate their own opinions about the senior comprehensive exam issue. The major result indicated that the arguments were more carefully processed when they were associated with a socially attractive than a socially unattractive source. More specifically, the significant message quality × source attractiveness interaction was due to the joint tendencies for attractiveness to enhance agreement with the proposal when the arguments presented were strong, but for attractiveness to reduce agreement when the arguments presented were weak (see Box 3, in Fig. 8). The latter effect (an attractive source reducing agreement), of course, is opposite to what one normally would expect the effect of attractive sources to be (see review by Chaiken, 1985).

In a study conceptually similar to the Puckett *et al.* (1983) study, we again left the degree of personal relevance ambiguous and manipulated the quality of the arguments presented in favor of senior comprehensive exams. This time, however, subjects heard rather than read the message, and we varied source expertise rather than social attractiveness (Heesacker, Petty, & Cacioppo, 1983). Some subjects were led to believe that the source of the message was a professor of education at Princeton University (high expertise), and others were led to believe that the source was a local high school student (low expertise). The subjects in this study were divided into those who were relatively field dependent or independent as assessed by the embedded figures test (Ekstrom, French, & Harmon, 1962). The data for field-dependent subjects showed a message quality × source expertise interaction (see Box 4, Fig. 8). Similar to the effect observed for social attractiveness, the arguments were more carefully processed when they were presented by the expert than by the inexpert source. Again, the interaction was due to the joint tendencies for strong arguments to be more persuasive when presented by an expert, but for weak arguments to be less persuasive when presented by an expert, and again the latter effect is opposite to what one normally would expect the effect of expertise to be.[12]

---

[12]Field-independent subjects showed only a main effect for argument quality, probably because these subjects were generally more motivated and/or able to extract meaning from stimuli (Witkin, Goodenough, & Oltman, 1979). If field-independent subjects generally have a higher elaboration likelihood, then they would be more likely to process message arguments regardless of the source.

In sum, although the operation of source factors may seem quite simple on the surface, the ELM indicates that their operation, although orderly and predictable, is quite complex. In separate experiments, we have seen that when personal relevance is high, source factors can serve as persuasive arguments or assist in the evaluation of arguments; when personal relevance is low, source factors can serve as simple cues; and when personal relevance is moderate or ambiguous, source factors can affect the extent of message processing. Since all of these effects are obtained under different conditions, however, it is not surprising that a great diversity of results has been observed in the literature.

2. Other Variables with Multiple Functions

We have now seen how some source variables can serve as arguments in some contexts, cues in other contexts, and affect argument processing in still other situations. This general principle, which is stated explicitly in Postulate 3 (Section IV), was applied mostly to separate variables as we explicated the various postulates of the ELM. However, it should now be clear that any *one* variable can serve in all of these roles. A few more examples should help to elucidate how one variable can serve in multiple roles depending on the specific features of the persuasion context.

First, consider the impact of the number of other people who endorse a particular attitudinal position. Traditional analyses of the number of message sources have assumed that the more people who are perceived to advocate a position (up to some limit), the more conformity pressure that is induced, and the more agreement that results (e.g., Asch, 1951; White, 1975). One popular explanation for this conformity effect is that people shift toward the majority view out of a desire to hold a correct opinion (Festinger, 1954). An alternative point of view is that the more people who are associated with a particular position, the more recipients may think about the position advocated (Burnstein & Sentis, 1981; Burnstein & Vinokur, 1977) or about the specific arguments presented (Harkins & Petty, 1981a,b). This enhanced thinking might lead to more or less agreement depending on the nature of the thinking. For example, Harkins & Petty (1981a) found that when the personal relevance of a proposal was left ambiguous, increasing the number of sources who presented strong arguments enhanced persuasion, but that increasing the number of sources who presented weak arguments reduced persuasion (see Box 5, Fig. 8).

Importantly, we do not mean to suggest that expert/attractive sources invariably enhance information processing when involvement is moderate. Under some conditions, for example, it may be more adaptive and/or necessary to engage in more scrutiny of a moderate or low than a clearly credible source (Petty & Cacioppo, 1981a, 1984c).

The initial (conformity) explanation of multiple source effects is consistent with the view that the mere number of other people advocating a position serves as a simple peripheral cue as to the validity of the advocacy. The second (information processing) interpretation, however, is more consistent with the view that the attitude changes induced by multiple sources follow the central route to persuasion (Harkins & Petty, 1983). The ELM, of course, suggests that both of these processes may operate in different situations. When the elaboration likelihood is very low (such as when personal relevance is low or distraction is high), people will be unmotivated to evaluate the issue-relevant information presented and may use the number of people who support the issue as a simple cue as to the worth of the proposal. When the elaboration likelihood is moderate, people may use the number of sources advocating a position as an indication of whether the message is worth considering. Finally, when the elaboration likelihood is very high, message recipients will undertake a deliberate assessment of the message arguments and the number of endorsers will have little further value as a motivator of thought or as a simple acceptance cue. No experiment to date, however, has examined the impact of the number of sources across the full elaboration likelihood continuum.[13]

Factors associated with the message source, of course, are not the only variables that can both serve as cues and affect message processing. Message variables can likewise serve in both roles. We have already discussed how the number of arguments could serve as a simple cue when personal relevance was low, but affect information processing when personal relevance was high (Petty & Cacioppo, 1984a). Similarly, recipient and context variables may serve in multiple roles. For example, we have shown that the physical posture of a message recipient can affect the extent of elaboration under moderate involvement conditions. In one study (Petty, Wells, Heesacker, Brock, & Cacioppo, 1983), people who were reclining comfortably during message exposure showed greater attitudinal differentiation of strong from weak message arguments than people who were standing (see Box 6, Fig. 8). If subjects were presented with a message they were unmotivated or unable to elaborate, however, then posture (or other factors related to comfort during message exposure) might serve as simple positive or negative affective cues (e.g., Griffit & Veitch, 1971).

Importantly, even though the ELM holds open the possibility that variables can affect agreement either by having an impact on information processing or by serving as simple cues, the ELM specifies, in a general manner at least, the conditions under which each process is likely to operate. Thus, a whole list of source (e.g., credibility, attractiveness, number of sources), message (e.g.,

---

[13]Our analysis of multiple sources assumes that all sources are advocating the same position. When conflicting positions are advocated by different numbers of people (as in minority influence), the situation becomes more complex (see Maass & Clark, 1984).

number of arguments, use of rhetoricals, discrepancy), audience (e.g., recipient posture, presence of hecklers, false physiological feedback), and other variables may affect attitudes by modifying information processing under certain conditions (e.g., ambiguous personal relevance), but affect attitudes by serving as simple cues in other contexts (e.g., low prior knowledge).

X. Summary and Conclusions

At the most general level, we have outlined two basic routes to persuasion. One route is based on the thoughtful (though sometimes biased) consideration of arguments central to the issue, whereas the other is based on affective associations or simple inferences tied to peripheral cues in the persuasion context. When variables in the persuasion situation render the elaboration likelihood high, the first kind of persuasion occurs (central route). When variables in the persuasion situation render the elaboration likelihood low, the second kind of persuasion occurs (peripheral route). Importantly, there are different consequences of the two routes to persuasion. Attitude changes via the central route appear to be more persistent, resistant, and predictive of behavior than changes induced via the peripheral route.

In the body of this article we have discussed a wide variety of variables that proved instrumental in affecting the elaboration likelihood, and thus the route to persuasion. In fact, one of the basic postulates of the Elaboration Likelihood Model, that variables may affect persuasion by increasing or decreasing scrutiny of message arguments, was highly useful in accounting for the effects of a seemingly diverse list of variables (see Figs. 3 and 8). The effects of these variables had been explained with many different theoretical accounts in the accumulated persuasion literature. The ELM was successful in tying the effects of these variables to one underlying process. We have also seen that many different variables could serve as peripheral cues, affecting persuasion without issue-relevant thinking. Finally, we saw that some variables were capable of serving in multiple roles, enhancing or reducing thinking in some contexts, and serving as simple acceptance or rejection cues in others.

We began this article by noting that reviewers of the attitude change literature have been disappointed with the many conflicting effects observed, even for ostensibly simple variables. For example, manipulations of source expertise have sometimes increased persuasion, sometimes have had no effect, and have sometimes decreased persuasion. Similarly, studies testing different theories have sometimes found the theory to be useful in predicting attitude change, and at other times have found the theory to be unpredictive. For example, self-perception processes appear to operate under some conditions, but not others.

The Elaboration Likelihood Model attempts to place these many conflicting results and theories under one conceptual umbrella by specifying the major processes underlying persuasion and indicating how many of the traditionally studied variables and theories relate to these basic processes. Thus, we have seen that a seemingly simple variable like source credibility actually is capable of affecting persuasion in rather complex ways. The ELM, however, elucidates the conditions under which these different effects are likely to operate. Similarly, we have seen that a theoretical process such as self-perception, which emphasizes a simple inference based on behavioral cues, is likely to operate when the elaboration likelihood is relatively low but not when the elaboration likelihood is very high.

We believe that perhaps the greatest strength of the Elaboration Likelihood Model is that it specifies the major ways in which variables can have an impact on persuasion, and it points to the major consequences of these different mediational processes. In one sense, the ELM is rather simple. It indicates that variables can affect persuasion in a limited number of ways: A variable can serve as a persuasive argument, serve as a peripheral cue, or affect argument scrutiny in either a relatively objective or a relatively biased manner. In confining the mediational processes of persuasion to just these possibilities, the ELM provides a simplifying and organizing framework that may be applied to many of the traditionally studied source, message, recipient, and context variables. The postulates of the ELM do *not* ultimately indicate *why* certain arguments are strong or weak, why certain variables serve as cues, or why certain variables affect information processing. Instead, the ELM limits the mediational processes of persuasion to a finite set, and specifies, in a general way at least, the conditions under which each mediational process is likely to occur and the consequences of these processes. In doing this, the ELM may prove useful in providing a guiding set of postulates from which to interpret previous work, and in suggesting new hypotheses to be explored in future research.

ACKNOWLEDGMENTS

Research described in this article and preparation of the article were supported by grants BNS 7913753, 8217096, 8414853, 8418038, and 8444909 from the National Science Foundation. We are grateful to Icek Ajzen, Robert Cialdini, Chester Insko, and Abraham Tesser for their helpful comments on an earlier draft of this article.

REFERENCES

Abelson, R. (1972). Are attitudes necessary. In B. T. King & E. McGinnies (Eds.), *Attitudes, conflict, and social change*. New York: Academic Press.
Ajzen, I., & Fishbein, M. (1977). Attitude–behavior relations: A theoretical analysis and review of empirical research. *Psychological Bulletin, 84*, 888–918.

Ajzen, I., & Fishbein, M. (1980). *Understanding attitudes and predicting social behavior.* Englewood Cliffs, NJ: Prentice-Hall.

Allport, G. W. (1935). Attitudes. In C. Murchison (Ed.), *Handbook of social psychology* (Vol. 2). Worchester, MA: Clark University Press.

Allyn, J., & Festinger, L. (1961). The effectiveness of unanticipated persuasive communications. *Journal of Abnormal and Social Psychology,* **62,** 35–40.

Anderson, N. (1981). Integration theory applied to cognitive responses and attitudes. In R. Petty, T. Ostrom, & T. Brock (Eds.), *Cognitive responses in persuasion.* Hillsdale, NJ: Erlbaum.

Andreoli, V., & Worchel, S. (1978). Effects of media, communicator, and message position on attitude change. *Public Opinion Quarterly,* **42,** 59–70.

Apsler, R., & Sears, D. O. (1968). Warning, personal involvement, and attitude change. *Journal of Personality and Social Psychology,* **9,** 162–166.

Asch, S. (1948). The doctrine of suggestion, prestige, and imitation in social psychology. *Psychological Review,* **55,** 250–276.

Asch, S. (1951). Effects of group pressure upon the modification and distortion of judgment. In H. Guetzkow (Ed.), *Groups, leadership, and men.* Pittsburgh: Carnegie.

Baron, R. S., Baron, P., & Miller, N. (1973). The relation between distraction and persuasion. *Psychological Bulletin,* **80,** 310–323.

Batra, R., & Ray, M. (1984). Advertising situations: The implications of differential involvement and accompanying affective responses. In R. J. Harris (Ed.), *Information processing research in advertising.* Hillsdale, NJ: Erlbaum.

Batra, R., & Ray, M. (1985). How advertising works at contact. In L. Alwitt & A. Mitchell (Eds.), *Psychological processes and advertising effects: Theory, research and application.* Hillsdale, NJ: Erlbaum.

Belch, G. E. (1982). The effects of television commercial repetition on cognitive responses and message acceptance. *Journal of Consumer Research,* **9,** 56–65.

Bem, D. J. (1967). Self-perception: An alternative interpretation of cognitive dissonance phenomena. *Psychological Review,* **74,** 183–200.

Bem, D. J. (1972). Self-perception theory. In L. Berkowitz (Ed.), *Advances in experimental social psychology* (Vol. 6). New York: Academic Press.

Bettman, J. R., & Park, C. W. (1980). Effects of prior knowledge and experience and phase of the choice process on consumer decision processes: A protocol analysis. *Journal of Consumer Research,* **7,** 234–248.

Bobrow, D. G., & Norman, D. A. (1975). Some principles of memory schemata. In D. G. Bobrow & A. Collins (Eds.), *Representation and understanding: Studies in cognitive science.* New York: Academic Press.

Borgida, E., & Howard-Pitney, B. (1983). Personal involvement and the robustness of perceptual salience effects. *Journal of Personality and Social Psychology,* **45,** 560–570.

Bower, G. H. (1981). Mood and memory. *American Psychologist,* **11,** 11–13.

Brehm, J. W. (1966). *A theory of psychological reactance.* New York: Academic Press.

Brehm, J. W. (1972). *Responses to loss of freedom: A theory of psychological reactance.* Morristown, NJ: General Learning Press.

Brickner, M. A., Harkins, S. G., & Ostrom, T. M. (1985). The effects of personal involvement: Thought provoking implications for social loafing. *Journal of Personality and Social Psychology,* in press.

Britton, B. K., & Tesser, A. (1982). Effects of prior knowledge on use of cognitive capacity in three complex cognitive tasks. *Journal of Verbal Learning and Verbal Behavior,* **21,** 421–436.

Brock, T. C. (1967). Communication discrepancy and intent to persuade as determinants of counterargument production. *Journal of Experimental Social Psychology,* **3,** 269–309.

Burgoon, M., Cohen, M., Miller, M., & Montgomery, C. (1978). An empirical test of a model of resistance to persuasion. *Human Communications Research*, **5**, 27–39.

Burnkrant, R. E., & Howard, D. J. (1984). Effects of the use of introductory rhetorical questions versus statements on information processing. *Journal of Personality and Social Psychology*, **47**, 1218–1230.

Burnkrant, R. E., & Sawyer, A. (1983). Effects of involvement on information processing intensity. In R. J. Harris (Ed.), *Information processing research in advertising*. Hillsdale, NJ: Erlbaum.

Burnstein, E., & Sentis, K. (1981). Attitude polarization in groups. In R. Petty, T. Ostrom, & T. Brock (Eds.), *Cognitive responses in persuasion* (pp. 197–216). Hillsdale, NJ: Erlbaum.

Burnstein, E., & Vinokur, A., (1977). Persuasive argumentation and social comparison as determinants of attitude polarization. *Journal of Experimental Social Psychology*, **13**, 315–332.

Burnstein, E., Vinokur, A., & Trope, Y. (1973). Interpersonal comparison versus persuasive argumentation: A more direct test of alternative explanations for group induced shifts in individual choice. *Journal of Experimental Social Psychology*, **9** 236–245.

Cacioppo, J. T., Harkins, S. G., & Petty, R. E. (1981). The nature of attitudes and cognitive responses and their relationships to behavior. In R. Petty, T. Ostrom, & T. Brock (Eds.), *Cognitive responses in persuasion*. Hillsdale, NJ: Erlbaum.

Cacioppo, J. T., & Petty, R. E. (1979a). Attitudes and cognitive response: An electrophysiological approach. *Journal of Personality and Social Psychology*, **37**, 2181–2199.

Cacioppo, J. T., & Petty, R. E. (1979b). Effects of message repetition and position on cognitive responses, recall, and persuasion. *Journal of Personality and Social Psychology*, **37**, 97–109.

Cacioppo, J. T., & Petty, R. E. (1980a). Persuasiveness of communications is affected by exposure frequency and message quality: A theoretical and empicial analysis of persisting attitude change. In J. H. Leigh & C. R. Martin (Eds.), *Current issues and research in advertising*. Ann Arbor: University of Michigan Graduate School of Business Administration.

Cacioppo, J. T., & Petty, R. E. (1980b). Sex differences in influenceability: Toward specifying the underlying processes. *Personality and Social Psychology Bulletin*, **6**, 651–656.

Cacioppo, J. T., & Petty, R. E. (1981a). Electromyograms as measures of extent and affectivity of information processing. *American Psychologist*, **36**, 441–456.

Cacioppo, J. T., & Petty, R. E. (1981b). Electromyographic specificity during covert information processing. *Psychophysiology*, **18**, 518–523.

Cacioppo, J. T., & Petty, R. E. (1981c). Social psychological procedures for cognitive response assessment: The thought listing technique. In T. Merluzzi, C. Glass, & M. Genest (Eds.), *Cognitive assessment*. New York: Guilford.

Cacioppo, J. T., & Petty, R. E. (1982). The need for cognition. *Journal of Personality and Social Psychology*, **42**, 116–131.

Cacioppo, J. T., & Petty, R. E. (1984a). The Elaboration Likelihood Model. *Advances in Consumer Research*, **11**, 673–675.

Cacioppo, J. T., & Petty, R. E. (1984b). The need for cognition: Relationship to attitudinal processes. In R. McGlynn, J. Maddux, C. Stoltenberg, & J. Harvey (Eds.), *Social perception in clinical and counseling psychology*. Lubbock: Texas Tech University Press.

Cacioppo, J. T., & Petty, R. E. (1985). Central and peripheral routes to persuasion: The role of message repetition. In A. Mitchell & L. Alwitt (Eds.), *Psychological processes and advertising effects*. Hillsdale, NJ: Erlbaum.

Cacioppo, J. T., & Petty, R. E. (1986). Stalking rudimentary processes of social influence: A psychophysiological approach. In M. P. Zanna, J. M. Olson, & C. P. Herman (Eds.). *Social influence: The Ontario symposium* (Vol. 5). Hillsdale, NJ: Erlbaum, in press.

Cacioppo, J. T., Petty, R. E., & Kao, C. (1984). The efficient assessment of need for cognition. *Journal of Personality Assessment*, **48**, 306–307.

Cacioppo, J. T., Petty, R. E., Kao, C., & Rodriguez, R. (1985). *Central and peripheral routes to persuasion: An individual difference perspective.* Unpublished manuscript, University of Iowa, Iowa City.

Cacioppo, J. T., Petty, R. E., & Morris, K. (1983). Effects of need for cognition on message evaluation, recall, and persuasion. *Journal of Personality and Social Psychology, 45,* 805–818.

Cacioppo, J. T., Petty, R. E., & Sidera, J. (1982). The effects of a salient self-schema on the evaluation of proattitudinal editorials: Top-down versus bottom-up message processing. *Journal of Experimental Social Psychology, 18,* 324–338.

Cacioppo, J. T., Petty, R. E., & Stoltenberg, C. (1985). Processes of social influence: The elaboration likelihood model of persuasion. In P. Kendall (Ed.), *Advances in cognitive behavioral research and therapy* (Vol.4). New York: Academic Press.

Calder, B. J., Insko, C., & Yandell, B. (1974). The relation of cognitive and memorial processes to persuasion in a simulated jury trial. *Journal of Applied Social Psychology, 4,* 62–93.

Calder, B. J., & Sternthal, B. (1980). Television commercial wearout: An information processing view. *Journal of Marketing Research, 17,* 173–186.

Cantor, G. N. (1968). Children's "like–dislike" ratings of familiarized and nonfamiliarized visual stimuli. *Journal of Experimental Child Psychology, 6,* 651–657.

Cantor, N., & Mischel, W. (1979). Prototypes in person perception. In L. Berkowitz (Ed.), *Advances in experimental social psychology* (Vol. 12). New York: Academic Press.

Chaiken, S. (1980). Heuristic versus systematic information processing and the use of source versus message cues in persuasion. *Journal of Personality and Social Psychology, 39,* 752–756.

Chaiken, S. (1985). Physical appearance and social influence. In C. P. Herman, M. P. Zanna, & E. T. Higgins (Eds.), *Physical appearance, stigma and social behavior: The Ontario symposium* (Vol. 4). Hillsdale, NJ: Erlbaum, in press.

Chaiken, S., & Baldwin, M. W. (1981). Affective–cognitive consistency and the effect of salient behavioral information on the self-perception of attitudes. *Journal of Personality and Social Psychology, 41,* 1–12.

Chaiken, S., & Eagly, A. H. (1976). Communication modality as a determinant of message persuasiveness and message comprehensibility. *Journal of Personality and Social Psychology, 34,* 605–614.

Chaiken, S., & Eagly, A. H. (1983). Communication modality as a determinant of persuasion: The role of communicator salience. *Journal of Personality and Social Psychology, 45,* 241–256.

Cialdini, R. B. (1984). Principles of automatic influence. In J. Jacoby & C. S. Craig (Eds.), *Personal selling: Theory, research, and practice.* Lexington, MA: Heath.

Cialdini, R. B., Levy, A., Herman, P., & Evenbeck, S. (1973). Attitudinal politics: The strategy of moderation. *Journal of Personality and Social Psychology, 25,* 100–108.

Cialdini, R. B., Levy, A., Herman, P., Kozlowski, L., & Petty, R. E. (1976). Elastic shifts of opinion: Determinants of direction and durability. *Journal of Personality and Social Psychology, 34,* 663–672.

Cialdini, R. B., & Petty, R. E. (1981). Anticipatory opinion effects. In R. Petty, T. Ostrom, & T. Brock (Eds.), *Cognitive responses in persuasion* (pp. 217–235). Hillsdale, NJ: Erlbaum.

Cialdini, R. B., Petty, R. E., & Cacioppo, J. T. (1981). Attitude and attitude change. *Annual Review of Psychology, 32,* 357–404.

Clark, M. S., & Isen, A. M. (1982). Toward understanding the relationship between feeling states and social behavior. In A. Hastorf & A. Isen (Eds.), *Cognitive social psychology.* New York: Elsevier-North Holland.

Cohen, A. (1957). Need for cognition and order of communication as determinants of opinion change. In C. Hovland *et al.* (Eds.), *The order of presentation in persuasion.* New Haven, CT: Yale University Press.

Cohen, A., Stotland, E., & Wolfe, D. (1955). An experimental investigation of need for cognition. *Journal of Abnormal and Social Psychology,* **51,** 291–294.

Cook, T. D., & Flay, B. (1978). The temporal persistence of experimentally induced attitude change: An evaluative review. In L. Berkowitz (Ed.), *Advances in experimental social psychology* (Vol.11). New York: Academic Press.

Cooper, H. M. (1979). Statistically combining independent studies: meta-analysis of sex differences in conformity research. *Journal of Personality and Social Psychology,* **37,** 131–146.

Cooper, J., & Croyle, R. T. (1984). Attitudes and attitude change. *Annual Review of Psychology,* **35,** 395–426.

Cooper, J., & Jones, R. A. (1970). Self-esteem and consistency as determinants of anticipatory opinion change. *Journal of Personality and Social Psychology,* **14,** 312–320.

Craik, F. I. M. (1979). Human Memory. *Annual Review of Psychology,* **30,** 63–102.

Crocker, J., Fiske, S. T., & Taylor, S. E. (1984). Schematic bases of belief change. In R. Eiser (Ed.), *Attitudinal judgment.* New York: Springer-Verlag.

Deaux, K. (1984). From individual differences to social categories: Analysis of a decade's research on gender. *American Psychologist,* **39,** 105–116.

Deci, E. L., & Ryan, R. M. (1980). The empirical exploration of intrinsic motivational processes. In L. Berkowitz (Ed.), *Advances in experimental social psychology* (Vol.13). New York: Academic Press.

Eagly, A. H. (1967). Involvement as a determinant of response to favorable and unfavorable information. *Journal of Personality and Social Psychology Monograph,* **7**(3 Pt. 2).

Eagly, A. H. (1974). Comprehensibility of persuasive arguments as a determinant of opinion change. *Journal of Personality and Social Psychology,* **29,** 758–773.

Eagly, A. H. (1978). Sex differences in influenceability. *Psychological Bulletin,* **85,** 86–116.

Eagly, A. H., & Carli, L. (1983). Sex of researchers and sex-typed communications as determinants of sex differences in influenceability. *Psychological Bulletin,* **90,** 1–20.

Eagly, A. H., & Chaiken, S. (1984). Cognitive theories of persuasion. In L. Berkowitz (Ed.), *Advances in experimental social psychology* (Vol. 17). New York: Academic Press.

Eagly, A. H., & Himmelfarb, S. (1974). Current trends in attitude theory and research. In S. Himmelfarb & A. Eagly (Eds.), *Readings in attitude change.* New York: Wiley.

Eagly, A. H., & Himmelfarb, S. (1978). Attitudes and opinions. *Annual Review of Psychology,* **29,** 517–554.

Eagly, A. H., & Manis, M. (1966). Evaluation of message and communication as a function of involvement. *Journal of Personality and Social Psychology,* **3,** 483–485.

Eagly, A. H., & Warren, R. (1976). Intelligence, comprehension, and opinion change. *Journal of Personality,* **44,** 226–242.

Eagly, A. H., Wood, W., & Chaiken, S. (1978). Causal inferences about communicators and their effect on opinion change. *Journal of Personality and Social Psychology,* **36,** 424–435.

Ekstrom, R. B., French, J. W., & Harmon, H. H. (1962). *Kit of factor referenced cognitive tests.* Princeton, NJ: Educational Testing Service.

Elms, A. C. (1966). Influence of fantasy ability on attitude change through role-playing. *Journal of Personality and Social Psychology,* **4,** 36–43.

Fazio, R. H. (1985). How do attitudes guide behavior? In R. M. Sorrentino & E. T. Higgins (Eds.), *The handbook of motivation and cognition: Foundations of social behavior.* New York: Guilford.

Fazio, R. H., Chen, J., McDonel, E., & Sherman, S. J. (1982). Attitude accessibility, attitude–behavior consistency, and the strength of the object–evaluation association. *Journal of Experimental Social Psychology,* **18,** 339–357.

Fazio, R. H., & Zanna, M. P. (1981). Direct experience and attitude behavior consistency. In L. Berkowitz (Ed.), *Advances in experimental social psychology,* (Vol.14, pp. 161–202). New York: Academic Press.

Festinger, L. (1950). Informal social communication. *Psychological Review,* **57,** 271–282.

Festinger, L. (1954). A theory of social comparison processes. *Human Relations,* **7,** 117–140.

Festinger, L. (1957). *A theory of cognitive dissonance.* Stanford, CA: Stanford University Press.

Festinger, L., & Maccoby, N. (1964). On resistance to persuasive communications. *Journal of Abnormal and Social Psychology,* **68,** 359–366.

Fishbein, M. (1980). A theory of reasoned action: Some applications and implications. In H. Howe & M. Page (Eds.), *Nebraska symposium on motivation, 1979.* Lincoln: University of Nebraska Press.

Fishbein, M., & Ajzen, I. (1972). Attitudes and opinions. *Annual Review of Psychology,* **23,** 487–544.

Fishbein, M., & Ajzen, I. (1975). *Belief, attitude, intention, and behavior: An introduction to theory and research.* Reading, MA: Addison-Wesley.

Fishbein, M., & Ajzen, I. (1981). Acceptance, yielding and impact: Cognitive processes in persuasion. In R. Petty, T. Ostrom, & T. Brock (Eds.), *Cognitive responses in persuasion.* Hillsdale, NJ: Erlbaum.

Fiske, S. T., Kinder, D. R., & Larter, W. M. (1983). The novice and the expert: Knowledge-based strategies in political cognition. *Journal of Experimental Social Psychology,* **19,** 381–400.

Folkes, V. (1985). Mindlessness or mindfulness: A partial replication and extension of Langer, Blank and Chanowitz. *Journal of Personality and Social Psychology,* **48,** 600–604.

Forer, B. (1949). The fallacy of personal vlaidation. *Journal of Abnormal and Social Psychology,* **44,** 118–123.

Freedman, J. L. (1964). Involvement, discrepancy, and change. *Journal of Abnormal and Social Psychology,* **69,** 290–295.

Freedman, J. L., & Sears, D. O. (1965). Warning, distraction and resistance to influence. *Journal of Personality and Social Psychology,* **1,** 262–266.

Freedman, J. L., Sears, D. O., & O'Conner, E. F. (1964). The effects of anticipated debate and commitment on the polarization of audience opinion. *Public Opinion Quarterly,* **28,** 615–627.

Gorn, G. (1982). The effects of music in advertising on choice behavior: A classical conditioning approach. *Journal of Marketing Research,* **46,** 94–101.

Gorn, G., & Goldberg, M. (1980). Children's responses to repetitive TV commercials. *Journal of Consumer Research,* **6,** 421–425.

Greenwald, A. G. (1968). Cognitive learning, cognitive response to persuasion, and attitude change. In A. Greenwald, T. Brock, & T. Ostrom (Eds.), *Psychological foundations of attitudes* (pp. 148–170). New York: Academic Press.

Greenwald, A. G. (1980). The totalitarian ego: Fabrication and revision of personal history. *American Psychologist,* **35,** 603–618.

Greenwald, A. G. (1981). Ego task analysis: An integration of research on ego-involvement. In A. Hastorf & A. Isen (Eds.), *Cognitive social psychology.* Amsterdam: Elsevier.

Griffit, W., & Veitch, R. (1971). Hot and crowded: Influences of population density and temperature on interpersonal affective behavior. *Journal of Personality and Social Psychology,* **17,** 92–98.

Harkins, S. G., Latané, B., & Williams, K. D. (1980). Social loafing: Allocaing effort or taking it easy. *Journal of Experimental Social Psychology,* **16,** 457–465.

Harkins, S. G., & Petty, R. E. (1981a). The effects of source magnification of cognitive effort on attitudes: An information processing view. *Journal of Personality and Social Psychology,* **40,** 401–413.

Harkins, S. G., & Petty, R. E. (1981b). The multiple source effect in persuasion: The effects of distraction. *Personality and Social Psychology Bulletin, 7,* 627–635.

Harkins, S. G., & Petty, R. E. (1982). Effects of task difficulty and task uniqueness on social loafing. *Journal of Personality and Social Psychology, 43,* 1214–1229.

Harkins, S. G., & Petty, R. E. (1983). Social context effects in persuasion: The effects of multiple sources and multiple targets. In P. Paulus (Ed.), *Basic group processes.* New York: Springer-Verlag.

Harkness, A. R., DeBono, K. G., & Borgida, E. (1985). Personal involvement and strategies for making contingency judgments: A stake in the dating game makes a difference. *Journal of Personality and Social Psychology, 49,* 22–32.

Harrison, A. A. (1977). Mere exposure. In L. Berkowitz (Ed.), *Advances in experimental social psychology* (Vol. 10). New York: Academic Press.

Harvey, O. J., Hunt, D. E., & Schroder, H. M. (1961). *Conceptual systems and personality organization.* New York: Wiley.

Hass, R. G. (1981). Effects of source characteristics on cognitive responses and persuasion. In R. Petty, T. Ostrom, & T. Brock (Eds.), *Cognitive responses in persuasion.* Hillsdale, NJ: Erlbaum.

Hass, R. G., & Grady, K. (1975). Temporal delay, type of forewarning, and resistance to influence. *Journal of Experimental Social Psychology, 11,* 459–469.

Heesacker, M., Petty, R. E., & Cacioppo, J. T. (1983). Field dependence and attitude change: Source credibility can alter persuasion by affecting message-relevant thinking. *Journal of Personality, 51,* 653–666.

Heider, F. (1946). Attitudes and cognitive organization. *Journal of Psychology, 21,* 107–112.

Higgins, T., Herman, C. P., & Zanna, M. P. (Eds.). (1981). *Social cognition: The Ontario symposium* (Vol. 1). Hillsdale, NJ: Erlbaum.

Himmelfarb, S., & Eagly, A. H. (1974). Orientations to the study of attitudes and their change. In S. Himmelfarb & A. Eagly (Eds.), *Readings in attitude change.* New York: Wiley.

Hovland, C. I., Harvey, O. J., & Sherif, M. (1957). Assimilation and contrast effects in reactions to communications and attitude change. *Journal of Abnormal and Social Psychology, 55,* 244–252.

Hovland, C. I., Janis, I., & Kelley, H. H. (1953). *Communication and persuasion.* New Haven, CT: Yale University Press.

Hovland, C. I., & Weiss, W. (1951). The influence of source credibility on communication effectiveness. *Public Opinion Quarterly, 15,* 635–650.

Ingham, A., Levinger, G., Graves, J., & Peckham, V. (1974). The Ringelmann effect: Studies of group size and group performance. *Journal of Experimental Social Psychology, 10,* 371–384.

Insko, C. A. (1981). Balance theory and phenomenology. In R. Petty, T. Ostrom, & T. Brock (Eds.), *Cognitive responses in persuasion.* Hillsdale, NJ: Erlbaum.

Insko, C. A. (1984). Balance theory, the Jordan paradigm, and the Wiest tetrahedron. In L. Berkowitz (Ed.), *Advances in experimental social psychology* (Vol.18). New York: Academic Press.

Insko, C. A., Lind, E. A., & LaTour, S. (1976). Persuasion, recall, and thoughts. *Representative Research in Social Psychology, 7,* 66–78.

Insko, C. A., Turnbull, W., & Yandell, B. (1974). Facilitating and inhibiting effects of distraction on attitude change. *Sociometry, 37,* 508–528.

Janis, I. L., & Gilmore, J. B. (1965). The influence of incentive conditions on the success of role playing in modifying attitudes. *Journal of Personality and Social Psychology, 1,* 17–27.

Janis, I. L., Kaye, D., & Kirschner, P. (1965). Facilitating effects of "eating while reading" on responsiveness to persuasive communications. *Journal of Personality and Social Psychology, 1,* 181–186.

Johnson, E. J., & Russo, J. E. (1981). Product familiarity and learning new information. *Advances in Consumer Research,* **8,** 151–155.

Johnson, H. H., & Watkins, T. A. (1971). The effects of message repetitions on immediate and delayed attitude change. *Psychonomic Science,* **22,** 101–103.

Kahle, L. R., & Homer, P. M. (1985). Physical attractiveness of the celebrity endorser: A social adaptation perspective. *Journal of Consumer Research,* **11,** 954–961.

Kahneman, D., Slovic, P., & Tversky, A. (Eds.) (1982). *Judgment under uncertainty: Heuristics and biases.* London and New York: Cambridge University Press.

Karabenick, S. A. (1983). Sex-relevance of content and influenceability: Sistrunk and McDavid revisited. *Personality and Social Psychology Bulletin,* **9,** 243–252.

Katz, D. (1960). The functional approach to the study of attitudes. *Public Opinion Quarterly* **24,** 163–204.

Keating, J. P., & Brock, T. C. (1974). Acceptance of persuasion and the inhibition of counterargumentation under various distraction tasks. *Journal of Experimental Social Psychology,* **10,** 301–309.

Kelley, H. H. (1967). Attribution theory in social psychology. In D. Levine (Ed.), *Nebraska symposium on motivation* (Vol. 15). Lincoln: University of Nebraska Press.

Kelman, H. C. (1961). Processes of opinion change. *Public Opinion Quarterly,* **25,** 57–78.

Kelman, H. C., & Eagly, A. H. (1965). Attitude toward the communicator, perception of communication content, and attitude change. *Journal of Personality and Social Psychology,* **1,** 63–78.

Kelman, H. C., & Hovland, C. I. (1953). Reinstatement of the communicator in delayed measurement of opinion change. *Journal of Abnormal and Social Psychology,* **48,** 327–335.

Kerr, N., & Bruun, S. (1981). Ringelmann revisited: Alternative explanations for the social loafing effect. *Personality and Social Psychology Bulletin,* **7,** 224–231.

Kiesler, C. A., Collins, B., & Miller, N. (1969). *Attitude change: A critical analysis of theoretical approaches.* New York: Wiley.

Kiesler, C. A., & Kiesler, S. (1964). Role of forewarning in persuasive communications. *Journal of Abnormal and Social Psychology,* **68,** 547–549.

Kiesler, S. B., & Mathog, R. (1968). The distraction hypothesis in attitude change. *Psychological Reports,* **23,** 1123–1133.

Kiesler, C. A., & Munson, P. A. (1975). Attitudes and opinions. *Annual Review of Psychology,* **26,** 415–456.

King, B. T., & Janis, I. L. (1956). Comparison of the effectiveness of improvised versus non-improvised role-playing in producing opinion change. *Human Relations,* **9,** 177–186.

Kleinhesselink, R. R., & Edwards, R. E. (1975). Seeking and avoiding belief-discrepant information as a function of its perceived refutability. *Journal of Personality and Social Psychology,* **31,** 787–790.

Kohlberg, L. (1963). The development of children's orientations toward a moral order. I. Sequence in the development of moral thought. *Vita Humana,* **6,** 11–33.

Kunst-Wilson, W. R., & Zajonc, R. B. (1980). Affective discrimination of stimuli that cannot be recognized. *Science,* **207,** 557–558.

Lammers, H. B., & Becker, L. A. (1980). Distraction: Effects on the perceived extremity of a communication and on cognitive responses. *Personality and Social Psychology Bulletin,* **6,** 261–266.

Landman, J., & Manis, M. (1983). Social cognition: Some historical and theoretical perspectives. In L. Berkowitz (Ed.), *Advances in experimental social psychology* (Vol. 16). New York: Academic Press.

Langer, E. (1978). Rethinking the role of thought in social interaction. In J. Harvey, W. Ickes, & R. Kidd (Eds.), *New directions in attribution research* (Vol. 2). Hillsdale, NJ: Erlbaum.

Langer, E., Blank, A., & Chanowitz, B. (1978). The mindlessness of ostensibly thoughtful action. *Journal of Personality and Social Psychology, 36*, 635–642.

Lastovicka, J., & Gardner, D. (1979). Components of involvement. In J. Maloney & B. Silverman (Eds.), *Attitude research plays for high stakes*. Chicago: American Marketing Association.

Latané, B., Williams, K., & Harkins, S. G. (1979). Many hands make light the work: The causes and consequences of social loafing. *Journal of Personality and Social Psychology, 37*, 822–832.

Lepper, M. R., Greene, D., & Nisbett, R. E. (1973). Undermining children's intrinsic interest with extrinsic reward: A test of the "overjustification" hypothesis. *Journal of Personality and Social Psychology, 28*, 129–137.

Lingle, J. H., & Ostrom, T. M. (1981). Principles of memory and cognition in attitude formation. In R. E. Petty, T. Ostrom, & T. Brock (Eds.), *Cognitive responses in persuasion*. Hillsdale, NJ: Erlbaum.

Linville, P. (1982). The complexity–extremity effect and age based stereotyping. *Journal of Personality and Social Psychology, 42*, 193–210.

Lord, C. G., Ross, L., & Lepper, M. R. (1979). Biased assimilation and attitude polarization: The effects of prior theories on subsequently considered evidence. *Journal of Personality and Social Psychology, 37*, 2098–2109.

Lowin, A. (1967). Approach and avoidance as alternate modes of selective exposure to information. *Journal of Personality and Social Psychology, 6*, 1–9.

Maass, A., & Clark, R. D. (1984). Hidden impact of minorities. Fifteen years of minority influence research. *Psychological Bulletin, 95*, 428–450.

Maddux, J. E., & Rogers, R. W. (1980). Effects of source expertness, physical attractiveness, and supporting arguments on persuasion: A case of brains over beauty. *Journal of Personality and Social Psychology, 38*, 235–244.

Markus, H. (1977). Self-schemata and processing information about the self. *Journal of Personality and Social Psychology, 35*, 63–78.

McDavid, J. (1959). Personality and situational determinants of conformity. *Journal of Abnormal and Social Psychology, 58*, 241–246.

McGuire, W. J. (1964). Inducing resistance to persuasion: Some contemporary approaches. In L. Berkowitz (Ed.), *Advances in experimental social psychology* (Vol. 1). New York: Academic Press.

McGuire, W. J. (1968). Personality and attitude change: An information-processing theory. In A. Greenwald, T. Brock, & T. Ostrom (Eds.), *Psychological foundations of attitudes*. New York: Academic Press.

McGuire, W. J. (1969). The nature of attitudes and attitude change. In G. Lindzey & E. Aronson (Eds.), *The handbook of social psychology* (2nd ed., Vol. 3). Reading, MA: Addison-Wesley.

McGuire, W. J. (1981). The probabilogical model of cognitive structure and attitude change. In R. E. Petty, T. M. Ostrom, & T. C. Brock (Eds.), *Cognitive responses in persuasion*. Hillsdale, NJ: Erlbaum.

McGuire, W. J. (1985). Attitudes and attitude change. In G. Lindzey & E. Aronson (Eds.), *Handbook of social psychology* (3rd ed., Vol. 2.). New York: Random House.

McGuire, W. J., & Papageorgis, D. (1962). Effectiveness of forewarning in developing resistance to persuasion. *Public Opinion Quarterly, 26*, 24–34.

Millar, M. G., & Tesser, A. (1984). *Thought-induced attitude change: The effects of schema structure and commitment*. Unpublished manuscript. University of Georgia, Athens.

Miller, N. (1965). Involvement and dogmatism as inhibitors of attitude change. *Journal of Experimental Social Psychology, 1*, 121–132.

Miller, N., & Baron, R. S. (1973). On measuring counterarguing. *Journal for the Theory of Social Behavior*, **3**, 101–118.

Miller, N., & Colman, D. (1981). Methodological issues in analyzing the cognitive mediation of persuasion. In R. E. Petty, T. M. Ostrom, & T. C. Brock (Eds.), *Cognitive responses in persuasion*. Hillsdale, NJ: Erlbaum.

Miller, N., Maruyama, G., Beaber, R., & Valone, K. (1976). Speed of speech and persuasion. *Journal of Personality and Social Psychology*, **34**, 615–625.

Miller, R. L., Brickman, P., & Bolen, D. (1975). Attribution versus persuasion as a means for modifying behavior. *Journal of Personality and Social Psychology*, **31**, 430–441.

Mills, J. (1966). Opinion change as a function of the communicator's desire to influence and liking for the audience. *Journal of Experimental Social Psychology*, **2**, 152–159.

Mills, J., & Aronson, E. (1965). Opinion change as a function of the communicator's attractiveness and desire to influence. *Journal of Personality and Social Psychology*, **1**, 173–177.

Mitnick, L., & McGinnies, E. (1958). Influencing ethnocentrism in small discussion groups through a film communication. *Journal of Abnormal and Social Psychology*, **56**, 82–92.

Moscovici, S. (1980). Toward a theory of conversion behavior. In L. Berkowitz (Ed.), *Advances in experimental social psychology* (Vol. 13). New York: Academic Press.

Nisbett, R. E., & Wilson, T. D. (1977). Telling more than we can know: Verbal reports on mental processes. *Psychological Review*, **84**, 231–259.

Osterhouse, R. A., & Brock, T. C. (1970). Distraction increases yielding to propaganda by inhibiting counterarguing. *Journal of Personality and Social Psychology*, **15**, 344–358.

Ostrom, T. M., & Brock, T. C. (1968). A cognitive model of attitudinal involvment. In R. Abelson et al. (Eds.), *Theories of cognitive consistency: A sourcebook*. Chicago: Rand McNally.

Pallak, M. S., Mueller, M., Dollar, K., & Pallak, J. (1972). Effect of commitment on responsiveness to an extreme consonant communication. *Journal of Personality and Social Psychology*, **23**, 429–436.

Pallak, S. S., Murroni, E., & Koch, J. (1983). Communicator attractiveness and expertise, emotional versus rational appeals, and persuasion. *Social Cognition*, **2**, 122–141.

Papageorgis, D. (1968). Warning and persuasion. *Psychological Bulletin*, **70**, 271–282.

Petty, R. E. (1977). *A cognitive response analysis of the temporal persistence of attitude changes induced by persuasive communications*. Unpublished doctoral dissertation. Ohio State University, Columbus.

Petty, R. E., & Brock, T. C. (1976). Effects of responding or not responding to hecklers on audience agreement with a speaker. *Journal of Applied Social Psychology*, **6**, 1–17.

Petty, R. E., & Brock, T. C. (1979). Effects of "Barnum" personality assessments on cognitive behavior. *Journal of Consulting and Clinical Psychology*, **47**, 201–203.

Petty, R. E., & Brock, T. C. (1981). Thought disruption and persuasion: Assessing the validity of attitude change experiments. In R. Petty, T. Ostrom, & T. Brock (Eds.), *Cognitive responses in persuasion* (pp. 55–79). Hillsdale, NJ: Erlbaum.

Petty, R. E., & Cacioppo, J. T. (1977). Forewarning, cognitive responding, and resistance to persuasion. *Journal of Personality and Social Psychology*, **35**, 645–655.

Petty, R. E., & Cacioppo, J. T. (1978). *A cognitive response approach to attitudinal persistence*. Paper presented at the annual meeting of the American Psychological Association, Toronto, Canada.

Petty, R. E., & Cacioppo, J. T. (1979a). Effects of forewarning of persuasive intent and involvement on cognitive responses and persuasion. *Personality and Social Psychology Bulletin*, **5**, 173–176.

Petty, R. E., & Cacioppo, J. T. (1979b). Issue-involvement can increase or decrease persuasion by enhancing message-relevant cognitive responses. *Journal of Personality and Social Psychology*, **37**, 1915–1926.

Petty, R. E., & Cacioppo, J. T. (1981a). *Attitudes and persuasion: Classic and contemporary approaches.* Dubuque, IA: Wm. C. Brown.

Petty, R. E., & Cacioppo, J. T. (1981b). Issue involvement as a moderator of the effects on attitude of advertising content and context. *Advances in Consumer Research,* **8,** 20–24.

Petty, R. E., & Cacioppo, J. T. (1983a). Central and peripheral routes to persuasion: Application to advertising. In L. Percy & A. Woodside (Eds.), *Advertising and consumer psychology* (pp. 3–23). Lexington, MA: Heath.

Petty, R. E., & Cacioppo, J. T. (1983b). The role of bodily responses in attitude measurement and change. In J. T. Cacioppo & R. E. Petty (Eds.), *Social psychophysiology: A sourcebook.* New York: Guilford.

Petty, R. E., & Cacioppo, J. T. (1984a). The effects of involvement on responses to argument quantity and quality: Central and peripheral routes to persuasion. *Journal of Personality and Social Psychology,* **46,** 69–81.

Petty, R. E., & Cacioppo, J. T. (1984b). Motivational factors in consumer response to advertisements. In R. Geen, W. Beatty, & R. Arkin, *Human motivation: Physiological, behavioral, and social approaches* (pp. 418–454). Boston: Allyn & Bacon.

Petty, R. E., & Cacioppo, J. T. (1984c). Source factors and the elaboration likelihood model of persuasion. *Advances in Consumer Research,* **11,** 668–672.

Petty, R. E., & Cacioppo, J. T. (1986). *Communication and persuasion: Central and peripheral routes to attitude change.* New York: Springer-Verlag, in press.

Petty, R. E., Cacioppo, J. T., & Goldman, R. (1981). Personal involvement as a determinant of argument-based persuasion. *Journal of Personality and Social Psychology,* **41,** 847–855.

Petty, R. E., Cacioppo, J. T., & Harkins, S. G. (1983). Group size effects on cognitive effort and attitude change. In H. Blumberg, A. Hare, V. Kent, & M. Davies (Eds.), *Small groups and social interaction* (Vol. 1, pp. 165–181). London: Wiley.

Petty, R. E., Cacioppo, J. T., & Heesacker, M. (1981). The use of rhetorical questions in persuasion: A cognitive response analysis. *Journal of Personality and Social Psychology,* **40,** 432–440.

Petty, R. E., Cacioppo, J. T., & Heesacker, M. (1984). Central and peripheral routes to persuasion: Application to counseling. In R. McGlynn, J. Maddux, C. Stoltenberg, & J. Harvey (Eds.), *Social perception in clinical and counseling psychology* (pp. 59–89). Lubbock: Texas Tech University Press.

Petty, R. E., Cacioppo, J. T., & Heesacker, M. (1985). *Persistence of persuasion: A test of the Elaboration Likelihood Model.* Unpublished manuscript. University of Missouri, Columbia.

Petty, R. E., Cacioppo, J. T., & Kasmer, J. (1985). *Effects of need for cognition on social loafing.* Paper presented at the Midwestern Psychological Association Meeting, Chicago.

Petty, R. E., Cacioppo, J. T., & Schumann, D. (1983). Central and peripheral routes to advertising effectiveness: The moderating role of involvement. *Journal of Consumer Research,* **10,** 134–148.

Petty, R. E., Cacioppo, J. T., & Schumann, D. (1984). Attitude change and personal selling. In J. Jacoby & S. Craig (Eds.), *Personal selling: Theory, research, and practice* (pp. 29–55). Lexington, MA: Heath.

Petty, R. E., Harkins, S. G., & Williams, K. D. (1980). The effects of group diffusion of cognitive effort on attitudes: An information processing view. *Journal of Personality and Social Psychology,* **38,** 81–92.

Petty, R. E., Harkins, S. G., Williams, K. D., & Latané, B. (1977). The effects of group size on cognitive effort and evaluation. *Personality and Social Psychology Bulletin,* **3,** 579–582.

Petty, R. E., Ostrom, T. M., & Brock, T. C. (Eds.) (1981). *Cognitive responses in persuasion,* HIllsdale, NJ: Erlbaum.

Petty, R. E., Wells, G. L., & Brock, T. C. (1976). Distraction can enhance or reduce yielding to propaganda: Thought disruption versus effort justification. *Journal of Personality and Social Psychology, 34,* 874–884.

Petty, R. E., Wells, G. L., Heesacker, M., Brock, T., & Cacioppo, J. T. (1983). The effects of recipient posture on persuasion: A cognitive response analysis. *Personality and Social Psychology Bulletin, 9,* 209–222.

Puckett, J., Petty, R. E., Cacioppo, J. T., & Fisher, D. (1983). The relative impact of age and attractiveness stereotypes on persuasion. *Journal of Gerontology, 38,* 340–343.

Regan, D. T., & Cheng, J. B. (1973). Distraction and attitude change: A resolution. *Journal of Experimental Social Psychology, 9,* 138–147.

Regan, D. T., & Fazio, R. (1977). On the consistency between attitude and behavior: Look to the method of attitude formation. *Journal of Experimental Social Psychology, 13,* 28–45.

Rhine, R., & Severance, L. (1970). Ego-involvement, discrepancy, source credibility, and attitude change. *Journal of Personality and Social Psychology, 16,* 175–190.

Ronis, D. L., Baumgardner, M., Leippe, M., Cacioppo, J. T., & Greenwald, A. G. (1977). In search of reliable persuasion effects: I. A single session procedure for studying persistence of persuasion. *Journal of Personality and Social Psychology, 35,* 548–569.

Rosenberg, M. (1956). Cognitive structure and attitudinal affect. *Journal of Abnormal and Social Psychology, 53,* 367–372.

Ross, E. A. (1908). *Social psychology: An outline and a sourcebook.* New York: Macmillan.

Ross, L. (1981). The "intuitive scientist" formulation and its developmental implications. In J. H. Flavell & L. Ross (Eds.), *Social cognitive development: Frontiers and possible futures.* London and New York: Cambridge University Press.

Ross, L., Lepper, M., & Hubbard, M. (1975). Perseverance in self-perception and social perception: Biased attributional processes in the debriefing paradigm. *Journal of Personality and Social Psychology, 32,* 880–892.

Sadler, O., & Tesser, A. (1973). Some effects of salience and time upon interpersonal hostility and attraction during social isolation. *Sociometry, 36,* 99–112.

Sandelands, L. E., & Larson, J. R. (1985). When measurement causes task attitudes: A note from the laboratory. *Journal of Applied Psychology, 70,* 116–121.

Sawyer, A. G. (1981). Repetition, cognitive responses and persuasion. In R. Petty, T. Ostrom, & T. Brock (Eds.), *Cognitive responses in persuasion* (pp. 237–261). Hillsdale, NJ: Erlbaum.

Schneider, W., & Shiffrin, R. M. (1977). Controlled and automatic human information processing: I. Detection, search, and attention. *Psychological Review, 84,* 1–66.

Schumann, D., Petty, R. E., & Cacioppo, J. T. (1985). *Effects of involvement, repetition, and variation on responses to advertisements.* Unpublished manuscript. University of Missouri, Columbia.

Sherif, C. W., Kelly, M., Rodgers, H. L., Sarup, G., & Tittler, B. (1973). Personal involvement, social judgment, and action. *Journal of Personality and Social Psychology, 27,* 311–327.

Sherif, C. W., Sherif, M., & Nebergall, R. E. (1965). *Attitude and attitude change: The social judgment–involvement approach.* Philadelphia: Saunders.

Sherif, M. (1977). Crisis in social psychology: Some remarks towards breaking through the crisis. *Personality and Social Psychology Bulletin, 3,* 368–382.

Sherif, M., & Hovland, C. I. (1961). *Social judgment: Assimilation and contrast effects in communication and attitude change.* New Haven, CT: Yale University Press.

Sherif, M., & Sherif, C. W. (1967). Attitude as the individual's own categories: The social judgment–involvement approach to attitude and attitude change. In C. W. Sherif & M. Sherif (Eds.), *Attitude, ego-involvement, and change.* New York: Wiley.

Sherman, S. J., & Fazio, R. H. (1983). Parallels between attitudes and traits as predictors of behavior. *Journal of Personality, 51,* 308–345.

Sistrunk, F., & McDavid, J. W. (1971). Sex variable in conforming behavior. *Journal of Personality and Social Psychology*, **17**, 200–207.

Sivacek, J., & Crano, W. D. (1982). Vested interest as a moderator of attitude–behavior consistency. *Journal of Personality and Social Psychology*, **43**, 210–221.

Smith, B. L., Lasswell, H. D., & Casey, R. D. (1946). *Propaganda, communication, and public opinion*. Princeton, NJ: Princeton University Press.

Smith, M. J. (1982). *Persuasion and human action*. Belmont, CA: Wadsworth.

Snyder, M., & DeBono, K. G. (1985). Appeals to image and claims about quality: Understanding the psychology of advertising. *Journal of Personality and Social Psychology*, **49**, 586–597.

Srull, T. K. (1983). The role of prior knowledge in the acquisition, retention, and use of new information. *Advances in Consumer Research*, **10**, 572–576.

Staats, A. W., & Staats, C. K. (1958). Attitudes established by classical conditioning. *Journal of Abnormal and Social Psychology*, **57**, 37–40.

Staats, C. K., & Staats, A. W. (1957). Meaning established by classical conditioning. *Journal of Experimental Psychology*, **54**, 74–80.

Steiner, I. (1972). *Group process and productivity*. New York: Academic Press.

Sternthal, B., Dholakia, R., & Leavitt, C. (1978). The persuasive effect of source credibility: A test of cognitive response analysis. *Journal of Consumer Research*, **4**, 252–260.

Taylor, S. E. (1975). On inferring one's attitude from one's behavior: Some delimiting conditions. *Journal of Personality and Social Psychology*, **31**, 126–131.

Taylor, S. E., & Fiske, S. (1978). Salience, attention, and attributions: Top of the head phenomena. In L. Berkowitz (Ed.), *Advances in experimental social psychology* (Vol.11). New York: Academic Press.

Taylor, S. E., & Fiske, S. (1984). *Social cognition*. Reading, MA: Addison-Wesley.

Tesser, A. (1976). Thought and reality constraints as determinants of attitude polarization. *Journal of Research in Personality*, **10**, 183–194.

Tesser, A. (1978). Self-generated attitude change. In L. Berkowitz (Ed.), *Advances in experimental social psychology* (Vol.11). New York: Academic Press.

Tesser, A., & Conlee, M. C. (1975). Some effect of time and thought on attitude polarization. *Journal of Personality and Social Psychology*, **31**, 262–270.

Tesser, A., & Leone, C. (1977). Cognitive schemas and thought as determinants of attitude change. *Journal of Experimental Social Psychology*, **13**, 340–356.

Thurstone, L. L. (1928). Attitudes can be measured. *American Journal of Sociology*, **33**, 529–544.

Tsal, Y. (1984). *The role of attention in processing information from advertisements*. Unpublished manuscript. Cornell University, Ithaca, New York.

Vinokur, A., & Burnstein, E. (1974). The effects of partially shared persuasive arguments on group-induced shifts: A group problem solving approach. *Journal of Personality and Social Psychology*, **29**, 305–315.

Watts, W. A. (1967). Relative persistence of opinion change induced by active compared to passive participation. *Journal of Personality and Social Psychology*, **5**, 4–15.

Watts, W. A., & Holt, L. E. (1979). Persistence of opinion change induced under conditions of forewarning and distraction. *Journal of Personality and Social Psychology*, **37**, 778–789.

Weber, S. J. (1972). *Opinion change is a function of the associative learning of content and source factors*. Unpublished doctoral dissertation. Northwestern University, Evanston, Illinois.

Wells, G. L., & Petty, R. E. (1980). The effects of overt head-movements on persuasion: Compatibility and incompatibility of responses. *Basic and Applied Social Psychology*, **1**, 219–230.

White, G. L. (1975). Contextual determinants of opinion judgments: Field experimental probes of judgmental relativity boundary conditions. *Journal of Personality and Social Psychology*, **32**, 1047–1054.

Wicker, A. (1971). An examination of the "other variable" explanation of attitude–behavior inconsistency. *Journal of Personality and Social Psychology, 19,* 18–30.

Wilson, T. D., Dunn, D., Bybee, J., Hyman, D., & Rotondo, J. (1984). Effects of analyzing reasons on attitude–behavior consistency. *Journal of Personality and Social Psychology, 47,* 5–16.

Witkin, H. A., Goodenough, D. R., & Oltman, P. K. (1979). Psychological differentiation: Current status. *Journal of Personality and Social Psychology, 37,* 1127–1145.

Witt, W. (1976). Effects of quantification in scientific writing. *Journal of Communication, 26,* 67–69.

Wood, W. (1982). Retrieval of attitude-relevant information from memory: Effects on susceptibility to persuasion and on intrinsic motivation. *Journal of Personality and Social Psychology, 42,* 798–810.

Wood, W., Kallgren, C., & Priesler, R. (1985). Access to attitude relevant information in memory as a determinant of persuasion. *Journal of Experimental Social Psychology, 21,* 73–85.

Wyer, R. S., & Srull, T. (1984). *The handbook of social cognition.* Hillsdale, NJ: Erlbaum.

Yalch, R. F., & Elmore-Yalch, R. (1984). The effect of numbers on the route to persuasion. *Journal of Consumer Research, 11,* 522–527.

Zajonc, R. B. (1968). Attitudinal effects of mere exposure. *Journal of Personality and Social Psychology Monograph Supplement, 9,* 1–27.

Zajonc, R. B. (1980). Feeling and thinking: Preferences need no inferences. *American Psychologist, 35,* 151–175.

Zajonc, R. B., & Markus, H. (1982). Affective and cognitive factors in preferences. *Journal of Consumer Research, 9,* 123–131.

Zanna, M. P., Kiesler, C. A., & Pilkonis, P. A. (1970). Positive and negative attitudinal affect established by classical conditioning. *Journal of Personality and Social Psychology, 14,* 321–328.

Zanna, M. P., & Pack, S. J. (1975). On the self-fulfilling nature of apparent sex differences in behavior. *Journal of Experimental Social Psychology, 11,* 583–591.

Zillmann, D. (1972). Rhetorical elicitation of agreement in persuasion. *Journal of Personality and Social Psychology, 21,* 159–165.

Zimbardo, P. G. (1960). Involvement and communication discrepancy as determinants of opinion conformity. *Journal of Abnormal and Social Psychology, 60,* 86–94.

NATURAL EXPERIMENTS ON THE EFFECTS OF MASS MEDIA VIOLENCE ON FATAL AGGRESSION: STRENGTHS AND WEAKNESSES OF A NEW APPROACH

David P. Phillips

DEPARTMENT OF SOCIOLOGY
UNIVERSITY OF CALIFORNIA, SAN DIEGO
LA JOLLA, CALIFORNIA

I. Introduction

The laboratory experiment provides the social psychologist with an exceptionally powerful tool for testing causal hypotheses. In contrast to some other approaches (like sociological surveys or anthropological field studies), the experiment allows the investigator to assess hypotheses quickly, cheaply, and rigorously. Unfortunately, these advantages are counterbalanced by a well-known limitation—it is difficult to generalize confidently from the behavior studied in the laboratory to everyday behavior in the real world.

ADVANCES IN EXPERIMENTAL
SOCIAL PSYCHOLOGY, VOL. 19

Copyright © 1986 by Academic Press, Inc.
All rights of reproduction in any form reserved.

For most research problems, the investigator should not beg the question of generalizability but attempt to answer it. This is particularly true when the researcher is studying topics that have great significance for public policy, e.g., when studying the effects of mass media violence. Since the early 1960s this topic was almost always investigated in the laboratory. Although there is consensus that mass media violence can elicit aggression in this setting (Comstock, 1975; Murray & Kippax, 1979; Roberts & Bachen, 1981; Phillips, 1982a; Pearl, Bouthilet, & Lazar, 1982), researchers disagree on whether one can extrapolate these results from the laboratory to the world beyond (for interesting reviews of this issue, see Comstock, 1975, pp. 30–40; Berkowitz & Donnerstein, 1982).

The problem of external validity that plagues the laboratory experiment can be avoided to a considerable degree through the use of natural experiments with demographic data. In this article, I will describe natural experiments and their findings. In contrast to their laboratory counterparts, these natural experiments permit us to estimate the *real-world* impact of *naturally varied* media diets on *serious, adult* aggression.

II. Natural Experiments on Effects of Mass Media Violence on Fatal Aggression

Like the laboratory study, the natural experiment compares aggressive behavior under experimental and control conditions. However, in the natural experiment these conditions are created by nature rather than by the experimenter. This point can be illustrated with the following paradigmatic investigation: Homicides in the United States are examined before and after a highly publicized homicide story, with the prestory period serving as a natural control condition and the poststory period as an experimental condition. After correcting for trends and seasonal factors, the researcher then seeks to determine the following.

1. Are publicized homicide stories followed by an increase in United States homicide rates? This conclusion would be expected if homicide stories trigger additional homicides.

2. Do United States homicide rates rise most after the most heavily publicized homicide stories?

3. Does the rise in homicide rates occur mainly in those geographic areas where the homicide stories are publicized?

If the researcher finds the results just listed, he will then have some evidence suggesting that mass media violence elicits serious adult aggression in the real world.

Studies with this design have been employed to assess the impact of media violence on other-directed aggression (as in homicide) and on self-directed aggression (as in suicide). Traditional approaches to media effects have restricted attention to other-directed aggression. However, there are several reasons why it is important to study self-directed aggression as well. First, suicides outnumber homicides in all industrialized societies, with suicides generally occurring 10 to 30 times more frequently (Phillips, 1982a). Even in the United States, which has one of the highest homicide rates in the world, suicides still outnumber homicides (United States National Center for Health Statistics, 1946–1980). Second, it is easier to study the impact of suicide stories than the impact of homicide reports. Although suicides are very frequent in the United States, publicized suicide *stories* are quite rare. Because of this, it is relatively easy to assess the separate impact of each suicide report. In contrast, homicide stories are very much more frequent, and thus it is harder to separate the effect of one homicide story from another.

This section reviews natural experiments on the impact of mass media stories on (1) suicides (Section II,A), (2) suicidal accidents (Sections II,B and C), and (3) homicides (Sections II,D and E).

A. STUDIES ON THE IMPACT OF PUBLICIZED SUICIDE
STORIES ON SUICIDES

Before we examine the most widely cited study in this area it will be helpful to consider its precursors. As Lester (1972) noted, early work on imitative suicide was inconclusive (Motto, 1967) or contradictory (Crawford & Willis, 1966; Seiden, 1968), or could be explained by processes other than imitation (Weiss, 1958; Kreitman, Smith, & Tan, 1969). Motto approached the research problem rather indirectly by hypothesizing that suicide rates should fall during newspaper strikes, because during these periods potential suicides would find no publicized suicides to imitate. Motto examined the suicide rates in seven cities undergoing newspaper strikes and found no evidence to support his hypothesis. In a later study, Motto (1970) examined an eighth city experiencing a newspaper strike. He found that male suicide rates rose during the strike, while female rates fell. He concluded from this that newspaper strikes produce a drop in suicides, at least among females. One could equally well conclude, however, that newspaper strikes produce a rise in suicides, at least among males. Even if one supposes, with Motto, that the newspaper strike did indeed produce the drop in female suicides, this need not imply that the drop occurred because suicides were not publicized during the period. First, some stories may have been publicized despite the newspaper strike, because television and radio news was still broadcast. Second, a city changes in many ways during a strike and some of these

changes (rather than the presumed absence of suicide stories) might have produced the drop in female suicides.

Other, early research on imitative suicide is based on very small samples.
Crawford and Willis (1966) studied six pairs of suicides and found evidence of
imitation in three pairs and no evidence in the remaining three. Seiden (1968)
looked at five suicides which occurred in close spatial and temporal proximity
and concluded that imitation was not involved. Weiss (1958) noted that sometimes a person commits suicide on the anniversary of his spouse's death. This
phenomenon might indeed be produced by imitation or, alternatively, grief.
Kreitman et al. (1969) noted that persons who attempted suicide had an unusually large number of suicidal friends. This phenomenon could be caused by
imitation or by the tendency for suicide-prone persons to choose each other as
friends.

After reviewing these early studies, Lester concluded ''On the whole, therefore, contagion and suggestibility effects are equally difficult both to document
and to rule out. . . Clearly, the analysis of this topic is at too early a stage for
reliable conclusions to be drawn'' (1972, pp 188–189).

Subsequent to Lester's review, Phillips (1974) conducted an investigation
which was designed to overcome the methodological difficulties described
above. Phillips gathered a systematic list of suicide stories covered by *Facts on
File* (a national index of the news) and appearing on the front page of the *New
York Times* from 1947 to 1968. This newspaper was chosen because it was the
only large-circulation paper with an index that covered the entire postwar period.
Later in this investigation, additional newspapers were also examined. Using
official statistics (United States National Center for Health Statistics, 1946–
1969), Phillips (1974) then examined the monthly fluctuation of United States
suicides before and after the publicized suicide stories. Before assessing the
impact of the stories he first corrected for the effect of trends and seasons on
suicides. The way in which this was accomplished can be illustrated by the case
of Daniel Burros, one of the front-page suicide stories that was studied. Burros
was a leader of the Ku Klux Klan who committed suicide on November 1, 1965,
after newspapers revealed that he was Jewish. In that month, 1710 suicides were
recorded in the United States. One can determine whether the number of deaths
in this experimental period is unusually high by comparing it with two control
periods: November 1964 (with 1639 suicides) and November 1966 (with 1665
suicides). The average, $(1639 + 1665)/2 = 1652$, can be taken as an estimate of
the number of suicides expected in November 1965 under the null hypothesis that
Burros's suicide story had no effect on national suicides. It is evident that this
method of estimating the expected number of suicides corrects for the effects of
seasons on suicides and for the impact of linear trends in the level of suicide.
Because the observed number of suicides during the experimental period (1710)
was greater than the number expected (1652), there was a rise in United States
suicides just after Burros committed suicide.

This procedure was used to assess the impact of each of the front-page suicide stories listed in Table I,[1] which displays the number of United States suicides observed after a front-page suicide and the number expected under the null hypothesis that front-page suicide stories have no effect. It is evident that United States suicides increased after 26 publicized suicide stories and decreased after 7 of them. Given the null hypothesis, the probability of finding 26 or more suicide peaks out of 33 is .00066 (binomial test, $p = .5$, $n = 33$, $r \geq 26$).[2] Hence, there is a statistically significant tendency for United States suicides to rise just after front-page suicide stories. Phillips (1974) named this rise "the Werther effect" after Goethe's fictional hero, whose portrayed suicide is thought to have spurred many readers to take their own lives.

The evidence just presented is merely suggestive; it does not prove the hypothesis that publicized suicide stories trigger a rise in United States suicides. In order to increase confidence in such a hypothesis, it is necessary to (1) generate and test additional predictions that should hold if suicide stories trigger imitative behavior, and (2) assess competing hypotheses that may also be capable of explaining the observed findings.

1. Testing Additional Predictions

a. First Prediction: Timing of the Peak in Suicides. If the peak in suicides is caused by the publicizing of suicide stories, then this peak should occur only *after* the publicized story. Monthly suicide statistics do not allow us to test this prediction as precisely as is desirable. Nevertheless, a rough test is possible and reveals no peak in suicides before the publicized story. This is evident from Fig. 1, which displays the rise in suicides in the United States for the month before the story, the month of the story, and in the months thereafter. It is evident that suicide levels are slightly lower than expected in the month before the story and substantially higher than expected in the month of the story and in the month thereafter. In these two months, the number of excess suicides is 2034 (1275 +

---

[1]Minor modifications to this procedure were sometimes necessary. For example, if Burros' suicide had been discussed on November 30, 1965, instead of November 1, it would be inappropriate to seek the effects of Burros' death in November; December would be a more appropriate choice. In general, if the *Times* discussed a front-page suicide late in the month (after the 23rd) the month after the suicide story was examined. This cut-off date was chosen because it was arbitrarily assumed that the effect of a front-page story would last only 2 weeks. This implies that a front-page story will have its major effect in the month of the story if the story appears on or before the 23rd. Although this procedure seems plausible, it is also somewhat arbitrary. Hence, it is reassuring to learn that the peak in suicides after publicized stories still appears when different procedures are followed, e.g., if the 15th is used as a cut-off date. For a fuller discussion of this topic, see Phillips (1974, p. 342).

[2]The stories of Burros and Morrison occur very close together and are treated as one to avoid problems of statistical dependency. Similarly, the Graham and Ward suicide stories are treated as one story only. Thus, although there are 35 stories listed in Table I, they are treated as 33 to ensure that the statistical significance of the results in Table I is not artificially high.

TABLE I

Rise in the Number of Suicides in the United States after Suicide Stories Publicized on Page 1 of the New York Times[a]

Name of publicized suicide	Date of suicide story	Observed number of suicides in month after suicide story[b]	Expected number of suicides in month after suicide story	Rise in U.S. suicides after suicide story: observed − expected number of suicides
Lockridge, author	March 8, 1948	1510	1521.5	−11.5
Landis, filmstar	July 6, 1948	1482	1457.5	24.5
Brooks, financier	August 28, 1948	1250	1350	−100.0
Holt, betrayed husband	March 10, 1949	1583	1521.5	61.5
Forrestal, ex-Secretary of Defense	May 22, 1949	1549	1493.5	55.5
Baker, professor	April 26, 1950	1600	1493.5	106.5
Lang, police witness	April 20, 1951	1423	1519.5	−96.5
Soule, professor	August 4, 1951	1321	1342	−21.0
Adamic, writer	September 5, 1951	1276	1258.5	17.5
Stengel, New Jersey police chief	October 7, 1951	1407	1296.5	110.5
Feller, United Nations official	November 14, 1952	1207	1229	−22.0

LaFollette, Senator	February 25, 1953[c]	1435	1412	23.0
Armstrong, inventor of F.M. Radio	February 2, 1954	1240	1227	13.0
Hunt, Senator	June 20, 1954	1458	1368.5	89.5
Vargas, Brazilian president	August 25, 1954	1357	1321.5	35.5
Norman, Canadian ambassador	April 5, 1957	1511	1649.5	-138.5
Young, financier	January 26, 1958	1361	1352	9.0
Schupler, New York City Councilman	May 3, 1958	1672	1587	85.0
Quiggle, admiral	July 25, 1958	1519	1451	68.0
Zwillman, underworld leader	February 27, 1959	1707	1609	98.0
Bang-Jensen, United Nations diplomat	November 27, 1959	1477	1423	54.0
Smith, police chief	March 20, 1960	1669	1609	60.0
Gedik, Turkish minister	May 31, 1960	1568	1628.5	-60.5
Monroe, filmstar	August 6, 1962	1838	1640.5	197.5
Graham, publisher, Ward involved in Profumo Affair	August 4, 1963	1801	1640.5	160.5
Heyde and Tillman,[d] Nazi officials	February 14, 1964	1647	1584.5	62.5
Lord, New Jersey party chief	June 17, 1965	1801	1743	58.0

(continued)

TABLE I (*continued*)

Name of publicized suicide	Date of suicide story	Observed number of suicides in month after suicide story[b]	Expected number of suicides in month after suicide story	Rise in U.S. suicides after suicide story: observed − expected number of suicides
Burros, KKK leader Morrison, war critic	November 1, 1965 November 3, 1965	1710	1652	58.0
Mott, American in Russian jail	January 22, 1966	1757	1717	40.0
Pike, son of Bishop Pike	February 5, 1966	1620	1567.5	52.5
Kravchenko, Russian defector	February 26, 1966	1921	1853	68.0
LoJui-Ching, Chinese army leader	January 21, 1967	1821	1717	104.0
Amer, Egyptian field marshall	September 16, 1967	1770	1733.5	36.5
Total				1298.5

[a]Source of suicide statistics: United States Department of Health, Education, and Welfare, Public Health Service, *Vital Statistics of the U.S.*, Yearly Volumes, 1947–1968. (Reprinted from Phillips, 1974; used by permission.)

[b]For rules determining the month to be examined, see text.

[c]All February statistics have been normed for a month of 28 days.

[d]The suicides of Heyde and Tillman were discussed in the same story.

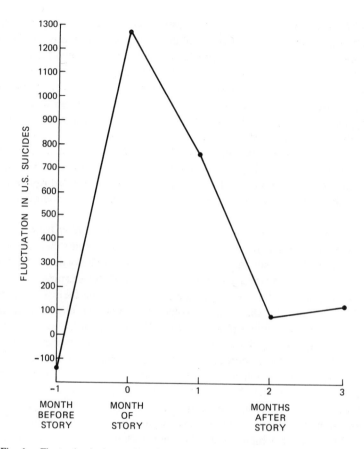

Fig. 1.   Fluctuation in the number of suicides in the United States before, during, and after the month of the suicide story. (After Phillips, 1974; used by permission.)

759). This is an average of 58.1 excess suicides for each of the suicide stories in Table I.[3]

Of course, it is possible that some of the excess suicides in the month of a story occur *before* the appearance of that story. However, the following evidence renders this possibility unlikely. If suicides rise only after a story appears, then stories appearing late in the month should elicit a relatively small rise in suicides in the month of the story, and a relatively larger rise in suicides in the month after

---

[3]The total number of excess suicides in the month of the suicide story (1275) is not equal to the sum of the excess suicides listed in Table I (1298.5). This is because (as noted in footnote 1) the number of excess suicides in Table I was calculated sometimes for the month after the suicide story and sometimes for the month of the story, depending on whether the story appeared late or early in the month.

the story. Conversely, stories appearing early in the month should elicit a relatively large rise in suicides in the month of the story, and a relatively smaller rise in the month after the story. These predictions are consistent with the available data: Stories appearing on or before the 15th of the month are associated with a total rise of 636 suicides in the month of the story and in the month thereafter; 98% of this rise (624/636) occurs in the month of the story. In contrast, for stories appearing after the 15th of the month, only 47% of the rise (651/1398) occurs in the month of the story.

This monthly evidence is supplemented by a study of *daily* suicide statistics (Bollen & Phillips, 1982). This study, to be reviewed later, found no evidence of a rise in suicides before publicized stories. However, the study did replicate the original finding of the Werther effect—a peak in suicides just after suicide stories.

    b.   Second Prediction: Variation in Size of Werther Effect by Amount of Publicity Given to Each Story.   If the Werther effect occurs because some people imitate publicized suicide stories, then the more publicity devoted to these stories, the larger the Werther effect should be. Thus, for example, the more days a story appears on the front page, the greater should be the rise in suicides thereafter. Unfortunately, the *Times* devoted more than one day of front page coverage to only three suicides (those of Ward, Forrestal, and Schupler). On the average, United States suicides increased by 100.3 in the month after these three stories, and by a smaller amount, 33.2, after the remaining stories in Table I. These data suggest a relationship between the number of days a story is publicized and the size of the Werther effect. The evidence is not compelling, however, because of the small number of stories receiving multiday coverage in the *Times*. A more effective analysis can be performed with a more "sensationalistic" newspaper, which may tend to carry suicide stories for two, three, or even four days on its front page. An analysis of the *New York Daily News*, the most popular daily newspaper during the period under study, produces more compelling evidence ($p = .0083$) linking days of coverage with size of effect: After "one-day" stories, United States monthly suicides increased by an average of 28.54; after "two-day" stories, 35.25; after "three-day" stories, 82.63; after "four-day" stories, 197.5.

    c.   Third Prediction: Relationship between Location of the Werther Effect and Location of the Publicity Devoted to Each Suicide Story.   If the Werther effect is caused by publicized suicide stories, then suicides should increase primarily in the geographic area where the suicide story is publicized. This expectation is consistent with available data: Phillips (1974) found that stories primarily publicized in New York City were followed by larger increases in New York City than in the rest of the country. In parallel fashion, he found that suicide stories publicized in the United States but not in Britain were followed by larger rises in American suicides than in British ones.

In sum, the evidence above is consistent with the hypothesis that publicized suicide stories elicit a rise in self-directed aggression. Nonetheless, one might prefer a more traditional explanation for these findings if it were consistent with the available data. Four such explanations will be briefly assessed here. (For more information on these assessments and for evaluations of additional, minor alternative explanations, see Phillips, 1974).

2. Assessing Competing Explanations

a. Possible Coroner Effect. Perhaps the publicized suicide does not elicit any imitative behavior whatever but merely prompts the coroner to classify some ambiguous deaths as suicides. Thus, the news of Marilyn Monroe's death may have influenced a suggestible coroner to classify an unusually large proportion of poisonings as "suicide" rather than as "accident," "murder," or "undetermined."[4] If this type of misclassification does in fact occur, then the increase in suicidal poisonings after Monroe's death should be counterbalanced by an equally large *decrease* in the competing categories of accidental poisoning, homicidal poisoning, and undetermined poisoning. However, there is no empirical evidence for such decreases. More generally, for all publicized suicide stories, there is no evidence that increases in suicides of a given type are counterbalanced by equivalent decreases in accidents, murders, or undetermined deaths of the same type.

b. Precipitation Rather Than Causation. As another possibility, the publicized suicide might serve merely to precipitate some suicides that would have occurred soon anyway, even in the absence of the suicide story. If this were so, the increase in suicides just after a suicide story should be counterbalanced by an equally large *decrease* in suicides a little later. However, no such decrease has been found.

c. Grief. It might also be that the front page stories elicit grief rather than imitation, and it is this grief that triggers a rise in United States suicides. This explanation is not plausible for two reasons. First, very few of the front-page suicides were well-known and well-loved individuals. On the contrary, many were in trouble with the law, Nazi officials, leaders of the Ku Klux Klan, or underworld leaders. Others were relatively obscure foreigners or Americans whose suicides were covered, not because of their fame, but because of the bizarre nature of their deaths. It does not seem likely that such people could elicit sufficient grief to elicit a rise in the national suicide rate. The "grief explanation" can also be evaluated more empirically by examining the monthly suicide rate after the death of persons who are much better known and better loved than

---

[4]Here, the phrase "undetermined" is an abbreviation for "undetermined whether purposefully or accidentally inflicted." Undetermined deaths are coded E980–E989 in the *Eighth Revision of the International Classification of Diseases* (United States National Center for Health Statistics, 1968).

the majority of the suicides in Table I, i.e., after the death of Presidents. When this analysis is performed for the period 1900–1968, one finds no evidence of a significant increase in suicides that would be expected if the "grief explanation" were correct.

   d. Prior Conditions. Perhaps prior conditions (like a downturn in the economy) produce both the publicized suicide and the subsequent peak in suicides that we have labeled "the Werther effect." This explanation is not plausible for several reasons. It cannot account for the fact that the size of the Werther effect is related to the amount of publicity devoted to the suicide story. Nor can it account for the fact that the location of the publicity devoted to the story is related to the location of the increase in suicides. Finally, the "prior conditions" explanation cannot account for the fact that the publicized suicide always seems to occur *before* the wave of increased suicides, and not in the middle of this wave, as would be expected if this explanation were correct.

   e. Conclusion. All in all, none of the assessed alternative explanations appears to be consistent with the data. The best available explanation for the findings at present is that publicized suicide stories prompt some imitative behavior. The study just reviewed appears to provide the first systematic, quantitative evidence suggesting that some mass media stories prompt a rise in fatal, self-directed aggression among United States adults.

   Subsequent studies have replicated and elaborated these findings. Bollen and Phillips (1982) examined daily United States suicides for a time period (1972–1976) not covered in Phillips's (1974) original study. They also extended the original study by examining the effect of suicide stories covered by network television news shows and by using two methods for controlling on extraneous variables—quasi-experimental analysis (as in the original study) and regression analysis. They found that United States suicides increase significantly just after television news stories about suicides, with the rise disappearing after about 10 days.

   Wasserman (1984) extended the data in Table I to cover an additional period, stretching from 1948 to 1977 (rather than 1948–1968 as in Phillips's original study). Repeating the quasi-experimental approach used by Phillips, he again found a significant increase in monthly United States suicides. Wasserman also reexamined the data with regression analysis, controlling for the influence of unemployment and the celebrity status of the front-page suicides. His analysis revealed that United States suicides rise significantly after publicized suicides of celebrities, while publicized noncelebrity suicides do not appear to elicit imitative behavior.

   The data used in all these investigations suggest that publicized suicides trigger additional, imitative suicides, but the precise nature of this imitative process cannot be elucidated with the demographic data under study. The studies reviewed in Section II,B provide further clues to the imitative processes that may be involved.

B. STUDIES ON THE IMPACT OF PUBLICIZED SUICIDE
   STORIES ON MOTOR VEHICLE ACCIDENTS
   WITH A SUICIDAL COMPONENT

Motor vehicle accidents are the fifth leading cause of death in our society (United States National Center for Health Statistics, 1960–1980). Although the evidence is far from conclusive, several studies suggest that some of these accidents have a suicidal component (for a review of these studies, see Phillips, 1979). If this is so, motor vehicle accidents should behave like suicides and increase markedly just after publicized suicide stories. In addition, the greater the publicity given to the suicide story, the greater should be the rise in motor vehicle accidents thereafter. If motor vehicle accidents do indeed behave in this way, then we will have evidence that mass media effects are more extensive than was previously supposed.

Phillips (1977, 1979) examined this possibility using California daily auto accident fatalities provided by the California Highway Patrol for the period 1966–1973 (California Highway Patrol, 1966–1973). He generated an exhaustive list of front-page suicide stories from the reference libraries of the *Los Angeles Times* and the *San Francisco Chronicle,* the most popular newspapers in the two largest Standard Metropolitan Statistical Areas in the state. Later in the study he examined three additional California newspapers with large circulations.

If front-page suicide stories elicit a rise in motor vehicle accident fatalities, then this rise can be detected by a technique adapted from Phillips (1974). The use of this technique can be illustrated with the suicide of Yukio Mishima, a famous author whose death was heavily publicized in California. Mishima killed himself on Tuesday, November 24, 1970. In the "experimental period" consisting of the week after Mishima's death (November 24–30) there were 117 motor vehicle accident fatalities (MVAF) in California. One can determine whether this is an abnormally large number of MVAF by comparing this number with the number of MVAF in "control periods" in other years.[5] These control periods are matched with the experimental period in several, important ways.

1. *Month of year.* The control periods are chosen to fall in November, so as to match the experimental period. This procedure controls for seasonal fluctuations in MVAF.

[5]At the time of this study, only four states published tabulations of daily motor vehicle fatalities: California, Texas, Michigan, and South Carolina. California was chosen for analysis because it had the largest population; at the midpoint of the study period this state accounted for 9.81% of all United States motor vehicle fatalities. For the week after the publicized suicide, one might wish to examine fatality rates rather than the number of fatalities. Unfortunately, it was not possible to do so because the weekly population counts needed for this analysis do not exist. One might also wish to expand the analysis from newspaper publicity to include local radio and television publicity as well. Unfortunately, this type of expanded analysis would be very difficult because local stations do not generally keep indexes of the stories they have covered through the years.

TABLE II

RISE IN MOTOR VEHICLE FATALITIES AFTER PUBLICIZED SUICIDES, CALIFORNIA 1966–1973[a]

Identity of publicized suicide	Date of publicized suicide	Observed number of motor vehicle deaths in the week after the suicide	Expected number of motor vehicle deaths in the week after the suicide[b]	% Rise in motor vehicle deaths: 100 × ([observed − expected]/expected)
A. Korbel, winemaker	4-21-1966	96	89.67	7.06
S. Youngren, union leader	5-17-1966	79	80.40	−1.74
Lo Jui-Ching, army leader	1-19-1967	81	80.92	.10
J. Hughes, businessman[c]	2-23-1967			
E. Joe, student[c]	2-23-1967	102	78.90	29.28
S. Abshear, student[c]	2-23-1967			
A. Amer, Egyptian general	9-14-1967	99	101.20	−2.17
M. Berg, L. A. policeman	9-23-1967	105	100.70	4.27
V. Janko, Czech general	3-14-1968	88	84.25	4.45
F. Chegwin, mass murderer	8-8-1968	100	89.40	11.86

H. Luedke, NATO admiral[c]	11-10-1968 ⎫	120	89.14	34.62
V. Latham, housewife[c]	11-10-1968 ⎭			
J. Palach, Czech student	1-16-1969	102	78.08	30.64
Y. Mishima, author	11-24-1970	117	98.88	18.33
J. Mattison, prisoner	2-25-1971	90	85.61	5.13
B. Pollack, orchestra leader	6-7-1971	82	102.70	-20.16
G. Giffe, hijacker	10-4-1971	104	97.50	6.67
G. Logan, mass murderer	11-26-1971	89	82.57	7.79
J. Van Praag, psychologist	3-7-1972	103	75.67	36.12
M. Oufkir, defense minister	8-17-1972	101	83.89	20.40
M. Brody, millionaire	1-26-1973	65	81.00	-19.75
E. Brudno, ex-P.O.W.	6-3-1973	98	102.14	-4.05
W. Inge, playwright	6-10-1973	100	88.03	13.60

[a]From Phillips (1979; p. 1155).
[b]See text for data sources and for methods of calculating expected number of deaths.
[c]Suicides occurring within 1 week of each other and therefore treated as one story.

2. *Day of week.* The control periods are chosen so as to run from Tuesday through Monday, matching the days in the experimental period.

3. *Holiday periods.* If the experimental period includes a holiday, the control periods are similarly constituted. If the experimental period does not include a holiday, the control periods don't either. This procedure controls for the effect of holiday weekends on MVAF.

For the period under analysis, four control periods containing no publicized suicides and matching the experimental period in the ways described above were identified. The number of MVAF in each of these four control periods was calculated and a regression line was fitted to these data. On the basis of this regression line Phillips (1979) calculated that 98.88 MVAF should occur in the experimental period under the null hypothesis that publicized suicides do not trigger additional deaths. As is evident, the observed number of MVAF in the experimental period (117) is substantially greater than the number expected under the null hypothesis (98.88; $p < .05$, one-tailed t test).

The control procedure just described for the case of Mishima was used to analyze all of the publicized suicides in Table II. (For more details on this procedure and evidence that alternative statistical procedures also yield significant results, see Phillips, 1979, notes 11 and 12). It is evident from this table that California MVAF rose by 9.12% ($p = .011$, t test, one-tail) in the week after publicized suicides. Summing the columns in this table, we see that there were a total of 1921 MVAF observed in the week after the publicized suicides, and only 1770.65 expected under the null hypothesis. This implies that MVAF rose by 150.35 (1921 − 1770.65) just after the suicide stories, for an average of 7.5 "extra" MVAF per story.

If the rise in MVAF is somehow triggered by the publicized suicides, then it should not appear before these suicides occur. Table III displays the day-by-day fluctuation of MVAF before and after the publicized suicides under examination. In this table the techniques used for calculating the expected number of MVAF per day are parallel to those described earlier for calculating the expected number per week. (For more details, see Phillips, 1979, note 13.) Two striking findings are evident in this table. First, MVAF do not rise just before publicized suicides, only afterward. Second, the poststory rise in MVAF is concentrated on the third day after the publicized suicide, when MVAF rise by 31.29%. This three-day lag, which is at present unexplained, seems to be a relatively stable phenomenon—as we will see below, it appears in a replicative study by Bollen and Phillips (1981), and in several other studies to be reviewed (Phillips, 1978, 1980a, 1983).

If MVAF increase because of publicized suicides, then the more publicity devoted to the suicide, the more MVAF should rise thereafter. Unfortunately, it is difficult to measure accurately the local radio and television publicity in

TABLE III

DAILY FLUCTUATION IN MOTOR VEHICLE FATALITIES FOR A 2-WEEK PERIOD BEFORE, DURING, AND AFTER PUBLICIZED SUICIDES[a]

Number of days before or after publicized suicides	Number of deaths observed	Number of deaths expected[b]	Percentage fluctuation: $100 \times$ ([observed − expected]/expected)
2 days before	237	247.038	−4.06
1 day before	264	268.714	−1.75
Day of publicized suicide	260	247.716	+4.96
1 day after	269	254.037	+5.89
2 days after	313	300.624	+4.12
3 days after	338	257.440	+31.29
4 days after	264	244.205	+8.11
5 days after	244	236.771	+3.05
6 days after	233	225.477	+3.34
7 days after	226	236.694	−4.52
8 days after	304	278.341	+9.22
9 days after	329	315.091	+4.41
10 days after	288	291.293	−1.13
11 days after	240	236.073	+1.66

[a]From Phillips (1979; p. 1156) by permission.
[b]For the method of calculating the number of deaths expected, see text.

California because there are many local stations and they do not index their news coverage. However, newspaper coverage can be easily and accurately determined, and Phillips (1979) was able to examine the front-page coverage of the top five California newspapers, which together accounted for 41% of all daily newspaper circulation in California for the period under study. For each publicized suicide, he determined (1) the number of days a story was carried on the front page of each newspaper, and (2) the average daily circulation of each newspaper (from Ayer Press, *Directory of Publications,* 1966–1973). Using this information, he calculated a weighted index of the publicity devoted to each story: $\Sigma x_i y_i$. Here, x_i is the circulation of newspaper i at the the time of the story, and y_i is the number of days that newspaper i carried the story on page 1. This five-newspaper index correlated positively ($r = .59, p < .005$) with the change in MVAF after each story (Table IV, column 3). On the average, MVAF increased by 18.84% after stories receiving more than the median amount of publicity and decreased by a statistically insignificant amount, 0.60%, after stories receiving less than the median amount of publicity.

These findings raise several interesting questions. For example, did suicide stories tend to result in more single-car rather than multiple-car accidents? Was the driver who died after a suicide story similar to the person described in that

TABLE IV

Relationship between the Amount of Publicity Devoted by the Five Biggest California Newspapers to Each Suicide Story and the Rise in Motor Vehicle Fatalities after Each Story[a]

Name of publicized suicide[b]	Total circulation of newspapers covering the story	Rise in motor vehicle fatalities in the week after the story (%)
Palach	2,627,084	+30.64
Logan	1,858,095	+7.79
Lo Jui-Ching	1,799,279	+.10
Van Praag	1,673,972	+36.12
Mishima	1,641,766	+18.33
Luedke and Latham	1,578,018	+34.62
Hughes, Joe, and Abshear	1,414,326	+29.28
Giffe	1,376,928	+6.67
Janko	1,348,430	+4.45
Oufkir	1,022,359	+20.40
Inge	1,004,908	+13.60
Pollack	966,293	−20.16
Brudno	951,263	−4.05
Chegwin	856,621	+11.86
Amer	847,869	−2.17
Berg	847,869	+4.27
Korbel	750,000	+7.06
Youngren	750,000	−1.74
Mattison	478,704	+5.13
Brody	458,163	−19.75

[a]From Phillips (1979; p. 1158) by permission.

[b]To facilitate analysis, suicide stories have been listed in the order of the amount of publicity received by each story.

story? Did stories about suicide combined with murder trigger multiple-car accidents (this being a method by which a driver can commit murder and suicide simultaneously)? None of these questions could be answered with the California Highway Patrol (1966–1973) tabluations used by Phillips (1979) because these tabulations were not subclassified by sex, race, type of accident, or location of crash. However, these questions can be answered with computerized death certificates provided by the California Bureau of Vital Statistics (1969–1973). Unfortunately, detailed information of this sort was not available for the full period under study (1966–1973) but only for 1969–1973; thus, it should be stressed that the MVAF findings described below are based on a subset of the years examined previously.

Phillips (1979) first isolated a set of MVAF that were most likely to contain a high proportion of suicidal crashes. These were adult MVAF that occurred 3 days after the publicized suicide, when fatalities peak at 31% above normal. The MVAF in this "experimental period" were then compared with the MVAF in two control periods: the first of these fell one week before the experimental period, and the second, one week after.[6] This procedure ensures that the control period always falls on the same day of the week as the experimental period and, in general, control periods and experimental periods are matched with respect to month and year. This method of matching experimental and control periods corrects for the effects of day of the week, season, and year on MVAF.

Using computerized death certificates and the procedure just described, Phillips (1979) then systematically compared the characteristics of MVAF in the experimental period (i.e., 3 days after the story) with those in the control groups.

Researchers have often supposed that suicidal accidents are more likely to involve single-car crashes than other types. If this is so, the ratio of single-vehicle MVAF to other MVAF should be much higher in the experimental period than in the control periods. This prediction was supported by the data, which revealed a ratio of .88 for the experimental period and one of .43 for the control period. The difference between these two ratios was significant at .0213 (hypergeometric; one-tailed test; for more information on this finding and on this use of the hypergeometric, see Phillips, 1979, p. 1162 and note 18).

Proceeding with the present argument, if the persons dying in the experimental period have identified with the person in the suicide story, one might expect to find them to be similar to the person described in the story. This similarity should be particularly evident when we focus on *drivers* rather than passengers, and when we focus on *single*-vehicle rather than multiple-vehicle crashes.

It was difficult to provide a systematic test of these predictions, because the death certificates provide only a limited range of information on each decedent; thus, many types of similarities (e.g., psychological characteristics) could not be studied with the data under analysis. Phillips was restricted to a study of demographic similarities between the publicized suicides and persons dying in the experimental period. He was further restricted by the fact that nearly all of the publicized suicides concerned white males—hence it was not useful to study similarities with respect to race or sex. Instead, he confined his analysis to age and produced the following findings.

---

[6]The method of choosing control periods in the first part of this study could not be used in the second part, because this method is feasible when a relatively large time period is examined (1966–1973) but not for the shorter period covered in the second part of the paper (1969–1973).

1. There was a positive correlation between the age of the publicized suicide and the age of drivers in single-vehicle MVAF in the experimental period ($r = .4634$, $p = .023$; Spearman $\rho = .444$, corrected for ties, $p < .05$).

2. In contrast, drivers dying in *multiple*-car crashes in the experimental period were not similar in age to the publicized suicide ($r = .0655$, $p = .416$).

3. *Passengers* dying in the experimental period were not similar in age to the person described in the suicide story ($r = .21$, $p = .146$).

4. Finally, drivers in single-vehicle crashes occurring in the *control periods* were also not significantly similar in age to the person described in the suicide story.

In sum, it was only *drivers* in *single*-vehicle crashes who died just *after* the suicide story who were significantly similar to the person described in that story. It is very difficult to account for these findings without proposing some causal link between the publicized suicide story and the rise in MVAF just afterward.

This link was further strengthened by an additional finding: the location of the publicity accorded to the suicide story was associated with the location of the MVAF in the experimental period. Thus, MVAF rose in Los Angeles (but not in San Francisco) after a story publicized in Los Angeles but not in San Francisco. Conversely, MVAF rose in San Francisco (but not in Los Angeles) after a story publicized in San Francisco but not in Los Angeles. Finally, MVAF rose in both places after stories publicized in both places. In short, after a suicide story MVAF were abnormally frequent mainly in the area where the suicide story is publicized.

Phillips (1979) uncovered an interesting finding that further supported the hypothesis that publicized suicides lead to a rise in suicidal car crashes. In a crash of this sort, the driver is consciously or unconsciously trying to die; hence, just before the crash, he may well have his foot on the accelerator rather than the brake, and he may be steering to hit rather than avoid an approaching obstacle. The victims of such a suicidal crash should die very soon after the crash occurs because the driver means the crash to be lethal. On the other hand, the victims of a conventional crash may well take much longer to die because the driver in this type of crash has his foot on the brake, not the accelerator, and is steering to avoid rather than hit an approaching obstacle. These considerations suggest that the average time between crash and death should be very short in the experimental period and markedly longer in the control periods. The evidence supported this prediction—the average time between crash and death was 1.016 days in the experimental period, but much greater, 4.131 days, in the control periods ($p = .0324$; one-tailed t test for difference between means). Thus, MVAF victims dying just after a publicized suicide story typically died much more rapidly than persons crashing at other times.

It seems plausible that the type of crashes elicited by a suicide story will depend in part on the nature of that story. Two major types of story can be distinguished: (1) the pure suicide story, in which a person kills himself alone, and (2) the murder–suicide story, in which a person kills others as well as himself. One might expect that pure suicide stories should elicit single-car crashes in which the driver dies, while murder–suicide stories should induce multiple-car crashes in which passengers die as well. These expectations were supported by the data. Multiple-vehicle accidents involving passenger deaths were much more frequent after murder–suicide stories than after pure suicide stories. Conversely, single-vehicle crashes involving driver deaths were more common after pure suicide stories than after murder–suicide stories. These findings suggest that pure suicide stories tend to prompt some people to commit suicide but not murder, while murder–suicide stories prompt others to commit both murder and suicide. Further support for this notion appears in Phillips (1978, 1980a; reviewed in Section II,C).

In sum, Phillips (1977, 1979) uncovered the following findings for California, from 1966 through 1973.

1. MVAF increased significantly by 9.12% in the week after publicized suicides, with most of the increase being concentrated on the third day, when a 31% increase was observed.

2. The more publicity given to the suicide story, the greater was the increase in MVAF thereafter.

3. This increase was particularly marked in those geographic areas where the story was most heavily publicized.

4. Single-vehicle MVAF increased more than multiple-vehicle MVAF just after a publicized suicide.

5. The drivers in these single-vehicle MVAF were unusually similar in age to the publicized suicide, but passengers dying in the same crashes were not. Furthermore, drivers in multiple-vehicle crashes were not similar in age to the publicized suicide, nor were drivers who died just before the publicized story.

6. Persons crashing just after a publicized suicide died much more quickly than did MVAF victims during control periods.

7. Pure suicide stories were followed by particularly large increases in single-vehicle driver deaths, while murder–suicide stories were followed by particularly large increases in multiple-vehicle passenger deaths.

The most striking of all these findings—the 31% peak 3 days after a publicized suicide—has been replicated with MVAF data for Detroit for the period 1972–1976 (Bollen and Phillips, 1981). For this city, MVAF rose by 35% 3 days after a publicized suicide. All of the findings described above are consistent with the hypothesis that publicized suicide stories elicit imitative suicides, some of which are disguised as motor vehicle fatalities. At present, no alternative hypotheses have been offered to explain these data.

C. STUDIES OF THE IMPACT OF MURDER–SUICIDE STORIES ON NONCOMMERCIAL AIRPLANE CRASHES

A small part of the California MVAF study was concerned with the impact of murder–suicide stories. The results suggested that a more systematic study should be devoted exclusively to the impact of this type of story. It would be desirable to investigate this topic by counting the number of overt murder–suicides before and after publicized murder–suicide stories. Unfortunately, this straightforward approach is not feasible with death certificate data because these do not indicate whether a given death is part of a murder–suicide. Lacking information of this sort,[7] one is forced to approach the problem more circuitously.

Some murderers may disguise a murder–suicide as an accident in order to protect their families from notoriety and insurance problems. If this is so, then some accidents may have a murder–suicide component and the frequency of these accidents may be expected to increase after publicized murder–suicides. Prompted by these considerations, Phillips (1978, 1980a) examined official daily statistics on fatal, noncommercial plane crashes (United States National Transportation Safety Board, 1968–1973) for the entire United States. (For a review of studies on purposive airplane crashes, see Phillips, 1980a.)

Phillips then gathered an exhaustive list of murder–suicide stories that appeared on the front page of the *New York Times* or the *Los Angeles Times* or appeared on the ABC, CBS, or NBC network evening television news programs. In order to ensure that such stories would be maximally likely to interest American pilots, the following criteria were used for selecting them: (1) The story must concern deaths occurring in the United States. (2) The story must concern one murderer acting alone. This criterion was established because a pilot bent on murder–suicide is more likely to identify with a single murderer than with several murderers acting together. (3) The story must concern a murderer and victim who died within a short space of time—arbitrarily defined as 48 hours. This type of story is most likely to affect a pilot bent on murder–suicide, because a person who deliberately crashes his plane is likely to kill himself and his passengers nearly simultaneously. (4) The story must concern a murderer who kills two or more victims; such a story is maximally likely to receive attention from the mass media.

Figure 2 displays the fluctuation of noncommercial airplane crashes before and after murder–suicide stories. It is instructive to compare this graph with the

---

[7]However, such an investigation would be feasible with police records.

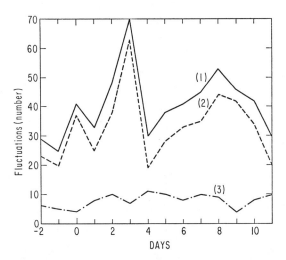

Fig. 2. Daily fluctuation of noncommercial plane fatalities in the United States for a two-week period before, during (day 0), and after publicized murder–suicides (1968–1973). Line (1) indicates the fluctuation of fatalities for all noncommercial plane crashes; line (2) indicates the fluctuation of fatalities for multifatality noncommercial plane crashes; line (3) indicates the fluctuation of fatalities for single-fatality noncommercial plane crashes. For sources of data, see text. Reprinted from Phillips (1980a; p. 1005).

daily fluctuation of motor vehicle fatalities after suicide stories (displayed in Table III, and graphed in Fig. 3). Juxtaposing the graph for motor vehicle fatalities with the graph for airplane accidents, we notice a pronounced family resemblance. In both figures, the effect seems to last about 8 or 9 days; both graphs rise to a primary peak on the third day and a secondary peak on the eighth day. As we will see later, this third day peak also appears in a study of homicides (Phillips, 1983). The processes underlying these patterns are at present unknown, but they seem to be sufficiently stable to deserve further investigation.

Figure 2 shows the separate fluctuation of multiple-death and single-death crashes. Multiple-death crashes increased significantly ($p = .016$) after the murder–suicide stories, but single-death crashes did not. This finding would be expected if the murder–suicide story prompts someone to commit both murder and suicide. (For information on the significance tests used, see Phillips, 1980a, note 6.)

If murder–suicide stories prompt an increase in noncommercial plane crashes, then the more publicity devoted to each story, the more plane crashes should increase thereafter. In the midpoint of the period under study, there were 1838 daily newspapers in the United States and thus it is not easy to measure the total amount of newspaper publicity devoted nationwide to a murder–suicide story. Instead of attempting to examine all of these newspapers, Phillips (1980a)

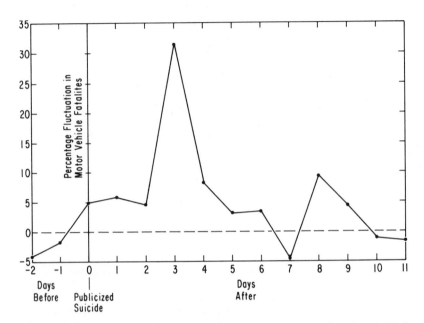

Fig. 3.   Daily fluctuation in motor vehicle accident fatalities for a 2-week period before, during, and after publicized suicides. Reprinted from Phillips (1979; p. 1157).

picked a subset of newspapers that were most likely to catch the attention of airplane pilots. Almost half of all the operative civilian aircraft in the United States are concentrated in only nine states. The largest newspaper from each of these states was examined to determine whether a story was carried on the front page. The publicity devoted to a story by these newspapers was then measured by the same index, $\Sigma\; x_i y_i$, that was used in the earlier study of MVAF (Section II,B; Phillips, 1979). As predicted, the amount of newspaper publicity devoted to a story was strongly correlated with the number of multifatality plane crashes occurring just afterward ($r = .637$; $p = .003$, one-tailed test).

Surprisingly, the amount of network *television* coverage was not significantly correlated with the increase in plane crashes. This may have been because television publicity was indexed very crudely as the number of networks carrying a story (rather than the total number of seconds of airtime devoted to the story).

If newspaper stories about murder–suicide elicit a rise in airplane accidents, then this rise should occur mainly in the states that are known to publicize the story. This expectation was supported by the data—there was a significant association ($p = .023$, hypergeometric test, one-tailed) between the location of publicity accorded to a story and the location of multifatality plane crashes that occur just afterward. At present, the only explanation that seems to fit all the findings is that publicized murder–suicide stories elicit additional murder–suicides, some of which are disguised as plane crashes (and some as automobile crashes).

The results just reviewed all pertain to 266 *non*commercial plane crashes whose behavior was summarized in Fig. 2. Surprisingly, Phillips (1980a) found that *commercial* plane crashes also displayed a statistically significant peak just after murder–suicide stories; in addition, the more publicity devoted to a story, the greater the chance of a commercial crash just afterward. However, because there were only 16 commercial airplane crashes in the period under study, it seems advisable to regard these findings as preliminary and suggestive, despite their statistical significance. As in all scientific work, confidence increases with replication and with sample size, and future research should attempt to determine whether other United States and foreign commercial plane crashes also increase significantly just after murder–suicide stories.

D. STUDIES ON THE IMPACT OF VIOLENT MEDIA STORIES
    ON HOMICIDES IN THE UNITED STATES—THE CASE
    OF REWARDED VIOLENCE

Up to now, we have been concerned with the impact of mass media violence on self-directed aggression (Phillips, 1974; Bollen & Phillips, 1982) or on a mixture of self-directed and other-directed aggression (Phillips, 1977, 1978, 1979, 1980a). We now turn to the impact of violent stories on "pure" other-directed aggression, i.e., homicides.

Berkowitz and Macaulay (1971) conducted the first modern study of this topic. They analyzed monthly Federal Bureau of Investigation (F.B.I.) statistics for 40 United States cities to determine whether homicides increased significantly after two heavily publicized murder stories: (1) The John Kennedy assassination, and (2) the murders by Speck and Whitman (which were treated as one story because they occurred so close together). Berkowtiz and Macaulay found no significant increase in homicides after these stories, although they did find a significant rise in other violent crimes, notably aggressive assaults and robberies (which, by definition, involve the use of threat). Property crimes, on the other hand, were unaffected. The failure to see a significant increment in homicides could have occurred because (1) homicide stories do not elicit imitative murders or (2) the research techniques used were not sufficiently sensitive to detect an effect. The second alternative seems plausible because Berkowitz and Macaulay examined the effect of only *two* stories on *monthly* homicide data for 40 cities rather than for the entire country.

At first glance, it would seem quite easy to increase the sensitivity of the Berkowitz and Macaulay analysis by examining the impact of many homicide stories on daily data for the United States. Unfortunately, this apparently straightforward approach to the problem must contend with a severe and perhaps intractable problem. There are so many fictional and nonfictional homicide stories in the mass media that it is very difficult to estimate the separate effects of each story.

Although it is hard to overcome this problem directly, it is possible to circumvent it. Rather than attempt to assess the impact of frequent, violent homicide stories, one can evaluate the effects of other violent stories which occur less frequently. These stories can be selected on the basis of criteria listed by Comstock (1977) in a review of the research literature. According to Comstock, violent stories are most likely to be imitated when the violence is presented as (1) real, (2) exciting, (3) uncriticized, and, indeed, (4) justified and (5) rewarded. Finally, violence is most likely to elicit imitation when (6) the perpetrator of the violence is presented as intending to injure his victim.

Very few mass media stories meet all of the criteria listed above and, in addition, are rare and heavily publicized. However, stories about heavyweight championship prizefights fit all of these requirements. These fights occur relatively seldom and are heavily publicized; furthermore, the violence in these fights is presented as real, exciting, uncriticized, justified, and rewarded. Finally, it is obvious that the boxers intend to injure each other. In a classic series of experiments, Berkowitz and associates (e.g., Berkowitz & Rawlings, 1963; Berkowitz & Geen, 1966, 1967) showed that prizefights do indeed elicit aggressive behavior in laboratory subjects who are exposed to them. In sum, Comstock's review and Berkowitz's studies both suggest that it would be fruitful to determine whether prizefights elicit aggression, not only in the laboratory, but in the real world as well.

Phillips (1983) gathered an exhaustive list of heavyweight championship prizefights and examined the fluctuation of United States daily homicides (United States National Center for Health Statistics, 1973–1978) before and after these prizefights occurred. Using multivariate time-series regression analysis, Phillips corrected for the influence of seasons, day of the week, holidays, and secular trends. The results of his analysis are displayed in Table V, which indicates that United States homicides rose significantly on the third day after the prizefight (by 7.47 per fight) and less markedly but still significantly on the fourth day (by 4.15 per fight). Thus, homicides increased by a total of 11.62 just after each heavyweight championship prizefight under study. As in the earlier studies of auto accidents and plane crashes, the effect peaked on the third day, when homicides were 12.46% above the normal level. This rise in homicides was not "canceled out" by a subsequent drop below normal. Thus, the prizefight does not serve merely to "move up" some homicides that would have occurred very soon anyway, even in the absence of the fight.

Demographic data reveal that the type of person killed just after the prizefight was significantly similar to the type of person beaten in the prizefight.

TABLE V

UNITES STATES HOMICIDES REGRESSED ON HEAVYWEIGHT
PRIZE FIGHT, CONTROLLING FOR DAILY, MONTHLY, YEARLY,
AND HOLIDAY EFFECTS, 1973–1978[a]

Regressand HOMICIDES[b]	R^2 .671	$\bar{R}^2$ .665	D.F. 2148	N 2190

Regressor	Regression coefficient	t Statistic
Intercept	55.34*	30.16
HOMICIDE(1)	.12*	5.64
PFIGHT(−1)	1.97	.94
PFIGHT(0)	1.95	.93
PFIGHT(1)	−.26	−.13
PFIGHT(2)	1.32	.63
PFIGHT(3)	7.47***	3.54
PFIGHT(4)	4.15†	1.97
PFIGHT(5)	−.60	−.29
PFIGHT(6)	3.28	1.57
PFIGHT(7)	.35	.17
PFIGHT(8)	.99	.47
PFIGHT(9)	3.10	1.48
PFIGHT(10)	2.28	1.09
Monday	−16.46*	−21.74
Tuesday	−16.71*	−17.97
Wednesday	−18.42*	−19.13
Thursday	−15.81*	−15.88
Friday	−8.02*	−8.41
Saturday	14.54*	16.95
February	1.88**	1.99
March	1.13	1.23
April	.43	.46
May	−.69	−.73
June	1.61	1.74
July	4.16*	4.46
August	4.46*	4.83
September	3.91*	4.16
October	2.79*	3.02
November	3.04*	3.25
December	5.86*	6.30
1973	−1.11	−1.70
1974	1.71*	2.62
1975	1.28	1.96
1976	−3.01*	−4.60
1977	−1.73*	−2.65
New Year's Day	41.08*	10.29
Memorial Day	−1.05	−.28
Independence Day	21.61*	5.89
Labor Day	16.92*	4.56
Thanksgiving	18.34*	4.98
Christmas	10.25*	2.79

[a]From Phillips (1983; p. 562) by permission.

[b]The variable HOMICIDE(1) indicates homicides lagged one
day. Two-tailed t tests are used for all seasonal variables; one-tailed
t tests for prizefight variables.

  *Significant at .01 or better.

 **Significant at .05 or better.

***Significant at .0002.

 †Significant at .025.

Thus, after a young, white male was beaten in the fight, the murders of young white males increased significantly, but not the murders of young, black males. Conversely, after a young, black male was beaten, the murders of young black males increased significantly, but not the murders of young, white males. This type of effect, in which the aggression target is similar to the media-portrayed victim, has also been found in laboratory studies of prizefights (e.g., Berkowitz & Rawlings, 1963; Berkowitz & Geen, 1966, 1977).[8]

If prizefights trigger an increase in homicides, then the most heavily publicized fights should trigger the largest increases. It is difficult to assess this hypothesis carefully, because the typical heavyweight prizefight is publicized over many months in many media—on closed circuit television, in advertising, and in sports stories in newspapers, magazines, and radio, and the network evening news. Instead of performing an exhaustive analysis of publicity, Phillips (1983) merely assigned prizefights to two broad categories—those discussed on the network evening news, and those that were not. He found that homicides increased by an average of 11.127 after stories in the first category, and by 2.833 for stories in the second. The difference between these two figures was statistically significant ($p = .0286$; two-sample t test, one-tailed), and thus we have some evidence suggesting that the publicity accorded to a fight affects the rise in homicides thereafter. In this connection, it is perhaps worth noting that the most touted of all the prizefights in this period, the so-called "Thrilla in Manila" between Mohammed Ali and Joe Frazier, displayed the largest third-day peak in homicides.

It might be supposed that the prizefight does not elicit imitative violence but merely triggers an increase in gambling and violent arguments, some of which result in death. If this were so, then one should also find a peak in homicides after the Superbowl because this event elicits even more gambling than prizefights do. However, homicides do not peak significantly just after the Superbowl, and thus the evidence does not support the "gambling hypothesis."

Perhaps the prizefight does trigger violent behavior, but only in audience members who are *physically present* at the fight. If this argument is correct, one could not claim that Phillips's findings indicate that *mass media* violence triggers a rise in homicides. Given the "physical presence" argument, United States homicides should not increase after prizefights that are held overseas because the enormous majority of Americans who follow these fights do so through the media and not in person. The data do not support the "physical presence"

---

[8]It would also be desirable to study "aggressor modeling," i.e., to determine whether there is a relationship between the characteristics of the *winning* boxer and the characteristics of those who commit murder just after the prizefight. Unfortunately, this type of analysis is not possible with the death certificate data used by Phillips, because these do not describe the characteristics of the murderer, only of his victim. However, this analysis would be quite feasible (and valuable) if one were to analyze police records rather than death certificates.

hypothesis: United States homicides increase after foreign prizefights at least as much as they do after fights held within United States borders. This suggests that the effect of the prizefight must be facilitated through publicity generated by the mass media.

Baron and Reiss (1985) presented an initially plausible alternative explanation for the findings in the prizefight paper. They claimed that the third-day increase in homicides is an artifact of heteroscedasticity associated with the timing of the prizefights. They tested this claim by examining the fluctuation of homicides after BOGUS prizefights, which occurred 1 year ahead of the real ones and were constrained to fall on the same day of the week as the real one did. If homicides rise on the third day after real fights because of the timing of these fights, then homicides should rise on the third day after BOGUS fights, too, since the BOGUS fights exhibit the same timing as the real ones. Reexamining the 1973–1978 data analyzed in Phillips (1983), Baron and Reiss found a small third-day peak after BOGUS fights ($t = 1.75$), which compared with a larger, more significant ($t = 3.55$) peak after the real fights. They found no peak on the *fourth* day after BOGUS prizefights to match the significant peak on the fourth day after real fights. They concluded from this evidence that the peak in homicides after real fights was an artifact of the timing of these fights.

In response, Phillips and Bollen (1985) presented the following evidence: (1) When the prizefight study is extended from 1973–1978 to 1973–1979, the third-day peak after BOGUS prizefights becomes insignificant ($t = 1.20$). In contrast, the third-day peak after the *real* fights *increases* in significance (from $t = 3.55$ to $t = 3.70$). (2) Baron and Reiss restricted their attention to BOGUS AHEAD fights, which occurred 1 year ahead of the real ones. Their argument implies that a third-day peak should also be found after BOGUS BEHIND fights (which occur 1 year behind the real fights) because these fights also exhibit the same timing as the real fights. However, far from observing a third-day *peak,* one actually finds a *drop* in homicides after BOGUS BEHIND fights (in both the 1973–1978 and 1973–1979 samples). (3) As noted earlier, Phillips (1983) found that publicized prizefights were followed by unusually large increases in homicides. If Baron and Reiss are right, these large increases do not occur because of publicity but because of the timing of the publicized prizefights. If so, similarly large rises should also be found after the BOGUS "publicized" prizefights which are associated with the real ones, because they exhibit the same timing as the real ones. Phillips and Bollen (1985) found no tendency for BOGUS AHEAD or BOGUS BEHIND "publicized" prizefights to be followed by unusually large rises in homicides. In short, the publicity "accorded" to a BOGUS prizefight was not associated with the rise in homicides thereafter; in contrast, *real* prizefights did show an association between publicity and size of effect. (4) Similarly, *real* prizefights showed an association between race of losing boxer and race of men murdered just afterward, but BOGUS prizefights did not. (5) If the rise in homicides after real prizefights is an artifact of timing associated with hetero-scedasticity, then this rise should disappear after correction for hetero-scedasticity. Phillips and Bollen (1985) found that the third-day peak remained significant after correcting for heteroscedasticity. They also showed that the third-day peak is not an artifact of holiday effects. Very few stories fall near holidays, and when these are omitted from the analysis, the mortality peak remains strongly significant. The above evidence shows that Baron and Reiss's (1985) artifact hypothesis is an extremely implausible explanation of the prizefight findings in Phillips (1983).[9]

At the moment, the only hypothesis that fits the data is that heavyweight championship prizefights trigger an increase in aggressive behavior, some of which eventuate in homicide.[10] The study just presented provided the first, systematic evidence suggesting that one form of mass media violence tends to elicit a significant increase in fatal, other-directed aggression.

[9]Baron and Reiss claimed that the suicide findings in Bollen and Phillips (1982) were also an artifact of timing and heteroscedasticity. In response, Phillips and Bollen (1985) expanded the data set (from 1972–1976 to 1972–1979) and reanalyzed the data in a fashion parallel to that described above. They showed that BOGUS AHEAD and BOGUS BEHIND suicide stories, 1972–1979, were not followed by significant increases in suicides (though real stories were). They also showed that the significant peak in suicides after real stories persisted after correcting for heteroscedasticity and holiday effects.

[10]It was not meaningful to test this hypothesis further by determining whether the location of the prizefight publicity was related to the location of the increase in homicides, because heavyweight championship prizefights are heavily publicized in all parts of the United States.

Freedman (1984) criticized almost all field and correlational studies of mass media effects, including the prizefight study summarized here. Freedman's critique of these findings is both in-complete and inaccurate. For example, he failed to indicate that the prizefight study presents a set of three major interconnected findings: (1) an increase in homicides after prizefights, (2) a correlation between the size of this increase and the amount of publicity devoted to the prizefight story, and (3) a correlation between the characteristics of the losing boxer and those murdered just after the prizefight. When Freedman did choose to summarize a finding, he often described it inaccurately. For instance, he noted that the "analysis indicated that the increase [in homicides] occurred only if the fight took place outside the United States, if it was covered on network news, and if the expected number of homicides on Day 3 was relatively high" (1984, p. 233). Here, Freedman's summary is incorrect on every point. Freedman also wonders "what kind of process would cause the effect to reappear on Days 6 and 9?" (1984, p. 233). In fact, the prizefight paper presented no evidence of a statistically significant peak in homicides on Days 6 and 9. Despite these flaws in Freedman's discussion, one of his questions does bear further consideration: why should homicides peak at a slightly different time after white-loser fights than after black-loser fights? The following considera-tions might help to resolve this question. There is a lag between the date of the homicidal *attack* and the actual date of *death* from homicide. The length of this lag varies by race, by type of homicide (gunshot, knife, etc.) and by other factors, like age. Hence, it is possible that prizefights trigger simultaneous homicidal attacks on both blacks and whites, but because of the nature of these attacks, the lag between attack and death is a little longer for one race than for the other. Future research should explore this question.

E. STUDIES ON THE IMPACT OF VIOLENT MEDIA STORIES ON
    HOMICIDES IN THE UNITED STATES—THE CASE
    OF PUNISHED VIOLENCE

Up to now we have considered what happens when violence is publicly
rewarded, as in prizefights. It is alsointeresting to consider the converse situation, in which violence is publicly *punished,* as in "guilty verdict" murder trials.
We know that United States homicides *increase* markedly just after violence is
rewarded in the prizefight. Do homicides *decrease* significantly just after violence is punished in the courtroom?

The effect of punishing a model has been studied both in the laboratory and
in the real world. These two types of research provide contradictory findings. In
the laboratory, Bandura and associates (1963, 1965) found that after children see
a violent model punished they behave less aggressively than their counterparts in
the control groups. On the other hand, "real world" studies of capital punishment have almost never found a deterrent effect (Blumstein, Cohen, & Nagin,
1978; Great Britain Royal Commission on Capital Punishment, 1953; Canada
Department of the Solicitor General, 1972; United Nations Economic and Social
Council, 1973).[11]

Failure to see a deterrent effect of capital punishment may have occurred for
two reasons: (1) there is no effect, or (2) the research techniques used are too
insensitive to detect it. It is worth noting that almost all studies of capital
punishment examine *yearly* rather than daily or weekly homicide statistics. A
small, short-term deterrent effect may not be detectable with yearly data. In
addition, almost all investigations in this area have examined the impact of
changes in capital punishment *legislation* rather than the impact of publicized
executions or death sentences. It is conceivable that the potential murderer may
be powerfully affected by a publicized execution, while remaining unaffected by
an abstract change in legislation.

In addition to Phillips (1980) and Phillips and Hensley (1984), there are
only three other published studies which have examined *daily* or weekly homicides after executions or death sentences (Dann, 1935; Graves, 1956; Savitz,
1968). Phillips's research will be reviewed shortly; the other three investigations
found no deterrent effect. This may have occurred because each of these three
studies suffered from at least one of the following problems: (1) The study failed
to focus on *publicized* punishments; (2) the study examined only a very few
executions; or (3) the study examined a small geographic area or a brief time

[11]However, some evidence for deterrence was presented in two papers by Phillips (1980b,
1982b; to be reviewed later) and in Ehrlich's (1975) study of contemporary American yearly homicide data. Ehrlich's study, however, has been extensively criticized (see, e.g., Beyleveld, 1982;
Bowers & Pierce, 1975; Klein, Forst, & Filatov, 1978; Passell, 1975).

TABLE VI

WEEKLY HOMICIDES BEFORE, DURING, AND AFTER PUBLICIZED EXECUTIONS (LONDON, 1858–1921)[a]

Name of person executed and date of execution story in the *Times* (1)	Number of column inches devoted to the story in the *Times* (2)	Number of homicides in week of execution story (3)	Control period			Difference between observed number of deaths in execution week (col. 3) and number expected (col. 6) (7)
			Number of homicides in week before experimental period (4)	Number of homicides in week after experimental period (5)	Average number of weekly homicides in control period (6)	
Wainwright (12/22/1875)	1694.5	0	1	0	.5	−.5
Crippen (11/24/1910)	1570.0	0	1	0	.5	−.5
Muller (11/15/1864)	1362.4	1	1	2	1.5	−.5
Webster (7/30/1879)	972.9	0	2	5	3.5	−3.5
Mapleton (11/28/1881)	828.8	2	6	2	4.0	−2.0
Lamson (4/29/1882)	790.0	0	0	2	1.0	−1.0
Seddon (4/19/1912)	614.3	1	2	1	1.5	−.5
Cream (11/16/1892)	558.1	0	1	0	.5	−.5

Field and Gray (2/5/1921)	553.8	0	0	0	.0	.0
Chapman (4/8/1903)	389.5	0	1	2	1.5	−1.5
Peace (2/26/1879)	363.9	0	1	2	1.5	−1.5
Read (12/5/1894)	349.4	2	1	3	2.0	.0
Milsom and Fowler (6/10/1896)	294.6	0	2	0	1.0	−1.0
Owen (8/9/1870)	224.6	0	1	1	1.0	−1.0
Devereux (8/16/1905)	215.1	1	3	0	1.5	−.5
Mackay (1/30/1913)	208.4	0	1	0	.5	−.5
Sheward (4/21/1869)	199.6	6	2	1	1.5	+4.5
Dougal (7/15/1903)	154.3	1	2	0	1.0	.0
Brinkley (8/14/1907)	129.6	2	1	0	.5	+1.5
Taylor (1/3/1883)	111.3	2	0	0	.0	+2.0
Dickman (8/10/1910)	101.1	0	1	0	.5	−.5
Stratton brothers (5/24/1905)	91.0	1	0	0	.0	+1.0

[a]From Phillips (1980b; p. 148) by permission.

period and hence only a small number of homicides were analyzed. In short, prior to the research to be reviewed there were no published studies which examined the fluctuation of *daily or weekly* homicides after *many heavily publicized* punishment stories.

Phillips (1980b) attempted to solve these methodological problems. He searched the document sections in the Library of Congress, the National Library of Medicine, and the British Museum for a geographic area that simultaneously practiced capital punishment and published daily or weekly homicide statistics. He found only one place that met these requirements—London, for the period 1858–1921. (After this time, the British continued to practice capital punishment but stopped publishing weekly homicide statistics.) He then used a standard casebook of notorious murderers (Wilson & Pitman, 1962) to generate a list of heavily publicized English executions from 1858 to 1921. Table VI lists these executions (ranked by the amount of publicity each received) and the number of homicides before, during, and after the week of each execution. The week of the execution was termed the experimental period, and the 2 weeks straddling this time were termed the control period. This method of choosing controls corrects for the effect of seasons and time trends. In addition, because the experimental and control periods contain the same days of the week, the procedure also corrects for the effects of day of the week. Under the null hypothesis, the number of homicides in the experimental period should have no tendency to fall below the average weekly number in the control period. In contrast, under the alternative hypothesis, the number of homicides in the experimental period should generally fall below the average weekly number in the control period.

Table IV, column 7 indicates whether the number of homicides in the experimental period is less than the weekly average in the control period (indicated by a " $-$ "), or more than the average (indicated by a " $+$ "). In three cases the number in the experimental period equaled the weekly average in the control period. In the remaining 19 cases, there were 15 " $-$ " signs and 4 " $+$ " signs. Given the null hypothesis, the probability of 15 " $-$ " and 4 " $+$ " signs is .0096 (binomial distribution, $p = .5$, $n = 19$). Hence, there was a statistically significant tendency for London homicides to fall below the number expected during the week of a highly publicized execution.

The definition of the control period cited above (the 2 weeks straddling the experimental period) is plausible but arbitrary. Phillips (1980b) showed that when other plausible definitions were used (e.g., the 4 weeks straddling the experimental period) the results remained statistically significant.

If a publicized execution deters some homicides, then the greater the publicity devoted to that execution, the greater should be the drop in homicides associated with it. Newspaper publicity devoted to an execution story can be measured systematically and exhaustively only for those newspapers whose contents are exhaustively indexed. The *London Times* was the only London news-

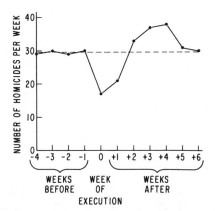

Fig. 4.   The frequency of weekly homicides before, during, and after 22 publicized executions, London, 1858–1921. Reprinted from Phillips (1980b; p. 145).

paper indexed for the period 1858–1921. This newspaper was not ideal for the purposes of the study because it had a smaller circulation than many other newspapers and because it appealed mainly to middle and upper class audiences. Nonetheless, this paper did devote a great deal of space to the executions under study, and the number of column inches accorded by *The Times* to an execution story (Table VI, column 2) was used as a rough indicator of the total amount of publicity devoted to each story. The Spearman rank correlation between publicity devoted to the story (Table VI, column 2) and the drop in homicides in the week of the execution (column 6) was .546 ($p = .0035$; calculations corrected for ties). Hence, the greater the publicity accorded to the execution, the greater was the drop in homicides associated with it.

It is important to discover whether the deterrent effect of the execution is canceled out by a subsequent rise in homicides above the normal level. Figure 4 graphs the weekly fluctuation of homicides before and after the publicized executions in TableVI. It is evident from visual inspection and from calculations that the drop in homicides immediately after the execution nearly matches the subsequent rise. The most plausible interpretation of this finding is that London homicides were temporarily deterred for a 2-week period following publicized executions; then the temporarily deterred homicides reappeared after the publicized execution had faded from memory. This evidence suggests that "the lesson of the scaffold" is real, but only short-lived.

The pattern observed in Fig. 4 helps to explain why previous studies of capital punishment uncovered no deterrent effect. As noted earlier, nearly all these studies used yearly homicide data; such data could not reveal a brief deterrent effect of the type implied in Fig. 4. Evidently, future research on the deterrent effects of capital punishment should examine daily or weekly data, not yearly statistics.

The study of London homicides suffered from a number of limitations.

1. It used weekly rather than daily statistics. Consequently, one cannot tell exactly when homicides decline in relation to the execution; perhaps part of the decline occurs in anticipation of the approaching execution.

2. Although the study examined a very long time period (1858–1921), it analyzed a relatively small number of homicides in a relatively small area.

3. The study may not have analyzed the data as powerfully as possible because it employed nonparametric techniques rather than time series regression analyses.

4. The study examined historical data for London, whereas most researchers in the United States would prefer to consider deterrence effects for contemporary America. In nineteenth century London, executions were often public, in contrast to current United States practices. In addition, television and radio did not exist in the nineteenth century, whereas they are a prominent feature of the American culture today. Because of these considerations, it would be risky to infer that capital punishment in the United States affects homicides in the same way that it apparently did in London many years ago.

5. Finally, and most importantly, the London study did not compare the deterrent effect of capital punishment with the deterrent effect of life sentences. This comparison is obviously important to the debate on the desirability of capital punishment.

A study by Phillips and Hensley (1984) was designed to overcome the problems listed above. These researchers were able to examine daily statistics for all known United States homicides between 1973 and 1979, comprising more than 140,000 deaths. Information on these homicides was recorded on magnetic tape by the National Center for Health Statistics and was distributed by the InterUniversity Consortium for Political Science Research. Applying time series analysis (Johnston, 1972; Ostrom, 1978) to these data, Phillips and Hensley then examined the fluctuation of United States daily homicides after publicized death sentences, executions, life sentences, and acquittals as well as heavyweight championship prizefights, which were included for purposes of comparison. All of these events may be conceptualized as lying along a continuum. At one end is the prizefight, which *rewards* physical violence; at the other end is the death sentence, execution, and life sentence, which *punish* it. Somewhere in the middle is the acquittal; here the accused is neither punished nor rewarded in a clear and unambiguous fashion. As Phillips and Hensley (1984) noted, "Some witnesses [to the trial] may believe that the accused is truly guilty and is in effect being rewarded by being allowed to 'get away with murder.' Others may believe that the accused is truly innocent and has been unfairly punished by having to endure a lengthy and nervewracking trial. Still a third segment of the audience may regard the 'not guilty' verdict as neither a reward nor a punishment." The study by Phillips and Hensley presented the first systematic analysis of daily homicides after mass media stories in which violence is *rewarded, punished,* or treated *neutrally.*

Table VII (taken from this study) focuses on white homicides, because nearly all the publicized trials and executions involved white murderers and white victims. If modeling plays an important role in deterrent effects, these judicial events should have their primary impact on *white* murderers and white victims.[12]

The variables REWARD(0), $\cdots$, REWARD(4) estimate the effect of prizefights 0 to 4 days after the fight. (Note that the values of these regression coefficients in Table VII differ from the values of the prizefight coefficients in Table V because the earlier table pertains to *all* homicides, not just the homicides of white victims. Furthermore, each table covers a slightly different time period.)

The variables PUNISH(0), $\cdots$, PUNISH(4) estimate the effects of publicized executions, death sentences, and life sentences, considered as a single group of events. (Later, their separate effects will also be described.) Finally, the variables NEUTRAL(0), $\cdots$, NEUTRAL(4) estimate the effects of publicized acquittals. The table also corrects for the influence of day of the week, month, year, and holidays, and estimates the magnitude of these influences.

It is evident from this table that homicides were markedly affected by day of the week (with Friday and Saturday displaying very high levels) and by certain holidays (particularly New Year). In contrast, homicides fluctuated very little by month and by year. Finally, we can see that white homicides *rose* significantly after violence was rewarded in the prizefight by an average of 3.54 after each prizefight. In strong contrast, white homicides *fell* significantly after violence punished by execution, death sentence, and life sentence, by an average of 3.32 after each punishment story. Finally, homicides did not go up or down significantly just after publicized acquittals.

Table VII examines homicide fluctuations for only a very brief period—0–4 days after the publicized events. When longer time periods were examined, Phillips and Hensley (1984) found that the drop in homicides following the publicized punishments was not canceled out by a subsequent rise in homicides above normal. Thus, in marked contrast to the London study, the current investigation of United States data provided no evidence that temporarily deterred homicides reappear after the "lesson of the scaffold" has faded from memory.

Up to now we have focused on the impact of heavily publicized punishment stories—those appearing on the television network evening news broadcasts (Vanderbilt University, 1973–1979). When we turn to stories which were not on

---

[12]In general, there is a very strong tendency for murderers to kill victims of their own race (United States Department of Justice, 1983), and thus Table VII, which focuses explicitly on white murder victims, is also implicitly focusing on white murderers, as well.

TABLE VII

United States White Homicides Regressed on Publicized Judicial
Actions, Controlling for Daily, Monthly, Yearly, and Holiday
Effects, 1973–1979[a]

Regressand HOMICIDES	R^2 .438	$\bar{R}^2$ .428	D.F. 2509	N 2556
Regressor	Regression coefficient		t Statistic	
Intercept	39.06		37.14*	
HOMICIDE(1)	0.03		1.52	
Monday	−7.23		−15.82*	
Tuesday	−7.52		−14.94*	
Wednesday	−8.38		−16.56*	
Thursday	−7.04		−13.68*	
Friday	−4.35		−8.63*	
Saturday	4.12		8.55*	
January	−3.40		−5.75*	
February	−2.80		−4.64*	
March	−4.11		−6.92*	
April	−4.08		−6.83*	
May	−4.31		−7.05*	
June	−3.12		−5.24*	
July	−0.80		−1.35*	
August	−1.20		−2.02	
September	−1.78		−2.93*	
October	−1.95		−3.30*	
November	−0.94		−1.52	
1973	−6.55		−14.05*	
1974	−4.55		−9.96*	
1975	−3.75		−8.28*	
1976	−6.03		−13.04*	
1977	−4.34		−9.53*	
1978	−3.08		−6.83*	
New Year's	12.96		6.97*	
Memorial Day	−0.45		−.33	
Independence Day	2.91		1.68	
Labor Day	2.68		1.94	
Thanksgiving	−1.05		−.86	
Christmas	5.32		3.06*	
REWARD(0)	1.08		.83	
REWARD(1)	0.91		.70	
REWARD(2)	0.59		.45	
REWARD(3)	3.54		2.72*	
REWARD(4)	0.71		.55	
NEUTRAL(0)	−3.45		−1.71	

(continued)

TABLE VII (continued)

Regressand	R^2	$\bar{R}^2$	D.F.	N
HOMICIDES	.438	.428	2509	2556

Regressor	Regression coefficient	t Statistic
NEUTRAL(1)	0.79	.39
NEUTRAL(2)	1.88	.93
NEUTRAL(3)	0.30	.15
NEUTRAL(4)	−0.34	−.17
PUNISH(0)	0.24	.17
PUNISH(1)	0.85	.62
PUNISH(2)	−0.58	−.42
PUNISH(3)	−1.54	−1.12
PUNISH(4)	−3.32	−2.43[†]

[a]The variable HOMICIDE(1) indicates homicides lagged 1 day. Two-tailed t tests are used for all seasonal variables; one-tailed t tests for REWARD and PUNISH variables (because the direction of the effect can be predicted) and two-tailed tests for NEUTRAL variables (where the direction of the effect cannot be predicted).

*Significant at .01 or better.

†Significant at .0076.

these broadcasts, and thus received much less publicity, we find no evidence of a deterrent effect. Of course this finding would be expected if publicity plays an important role in the impact of mass media stories. (Incidentally, because the publicized stories received a great deal of attention in all parts of the United States, it was not sensible to seek a relationship between the location of the publicity accorded each story and the location of the drop in homicides thereafter.)

Thus far we have not assessed the separate effects of executions, death sentences, and life sentences. It is important to do so, however, because such an assessment can throw some light on the debate on capital punishment. If one found life sentences to have a significantly smaller effect than death sentences or executions, this would provide some support for proponents of capital punishment. On the other hand, if there is no significant difference between the effects of life sentences and harsher forms of punishment, then this would remove one of the arguments in favor of capital punishment.

Phillips and Hensley (1984) could not investigate this question as thoroughly as was desirable because only seven death sentences and executions were widely publicized during the period under study (1973–1979). Phillips and Hensley found that homicides declined by an average of 2.73 after each life sentence and by a little more, 3.39, after each death sentence and execution. However, the difference between these two figures is not statistically significant.

Thus, the data in the present study do not support proponents of capital punishment, but it is possible that different conclusions will be reached when additional capital punishments become available for study.

The study just presented provided the first evidence suggesting that some homicides in the United States are deterred by publicized life sentences, death sentences, and executions. In general, the effects of these punishments are small and brief; thus it is not surprising that studies using small populations or yearly homicide data failed to uncover a deterrent effect. Future investigations of this topic should examine *daily* homicides for a *large area* after *many publicized* punishments.

III. Conclusion

This article has reviewed nonlaboratory experiments linking mass media violence with subsequent fluctuations in suicide, homicide, and accidents. Taken together, these natural experiments provide the first systematic body of evidence suggesting that some types of mass media violence tend to elicit fatal aggression among United States adults. This evidence provides a valuable supplement to laboratory and field experiments and suggests that mass media violence exerts serious effects, not only in the laboratory, but in the real world as well.

The studies under review examine only a small range of mass media stories (about suicide, murder–suicide, prizefights, and punishments) and a small range of fatal activities (suicides, homicides, and accidents in automobiles and airplanes). Future research should seek to broaden this range and determine whether many types of mass media stories affect a wide variety of activities. Efforts to generalize the findings will not always be easy, because some of the data that will be needed may be inaccurate or inaccessible. Some lines of possible research, together with anticipated difficulties, are briefly sketched below.

1. Fictional versus Nonfictional Stories

Thus far we have focused only on nonfictional stories because accurate, accessible indexes are available only for such stories. The situation is quite different for fictional stories: there is no systematic, exhaustive index of television stories about suicide, prizefights, death sentences, and so on. The one attempt to estimate the impact of *fictional* suicide stories failed because an inaccurate, nonexhaustive index was inadvertently used. Phillips (1982b) generated a list of soap opera suicide stories in 1977 from weekly newspaper summaries of soap opera plots. He found some evidence suggesting that United States suicides and fatal and nonfatal auto accidents increased after the appearance of these stories. However, Kessler and Stipp (1984) showed that the newspaper summaries were inaccurate and that many of the effects found in this study became insignificant when more accurate soap opera summaries were used. Thus, at present, we do not know whether fictional mass media stories trigger fatal aggression, as their nonfictional counterparts seem to do.

Although a systematic index of fictional television stories does not seem to exist, such an index could be created with the cooperation of the television networks, which maintain scripts of past programs. The creation of such an index, although laborious and fraught with political difficulties, would surely be of great scientific interest since most television stories are fictional and it is important to assess the putative effects of these events.

2. Fatal versus Nonfatal Behavior

Up to now, we have focused only on the *fatal* consequences of mass media stories—suicides, homicides, and so on. It is also important to examine nonfatal behavior. For example, it is important to learn whether prizefights trigger a rise not only in fatal assaults but in nonfatal assaults as well. In addition, researchers should attempt to answer questions like the following: Do publicized rape stories trigger additional, imitative rapes? When a rapist is given a long jail sentence does the frequency of rapes decline? Are arson stories followed by an abrupt rise in arson? Investigations like these will not be easy because accurate daily counts of rape, arson, and assault do not seem to be available for large geographic areas. It may be possible to circumvent this problem by limiting attention to one police jurisdiction (say New York or Los Angeles) in order to get daily data that are more accessible and perhaps more accurate.

One could easily cite additional examples of desirable research, but it is unnecessary to do so. Instead what is needed is a systematic program of exploration which makes fuller use of an underutilized research technique: the natural experiment. At present, very little is known about the effect of media violence on serious, adult aggression in the real world. Future research is urgently needed to resolve issues that have great importance not only for science but for public policy as well.

REFERENCES

Ayer Press. (1966–1973). *Ayer directory of publications.* Philadelphia: Ayer Press.
Bandura, A. (1965). Influences of models' reinforcement contingencies on the acquisition of imitative responses. *Journal of Personality and Social Psychology,* **1,** 589–595.
Bandura, A., Ross, D., and Ross, S. A. (1963) Vicarious reinforcement and imitative learning. *Journal of Abnormal and Social Psychology,* **67,** 601–607.
Baron, J. N., & Reiss, P. C. (1985). Same time next year: Aggregate analyses of the mass media and violent behavior. *American Sociological Review,* **50,** 347–363.
Berkowitz, L., & Donnerstein, E. (1982). External validity is more than skin deep. *American Psychologist,* **37,** 245–257.

Berkowitz, L., & Geen, R. (1966). Film violence and the cue properties of available targets. *Journal of Personality & Social Psychology*, **3**, 525–530.

Berkowitz, L., & Geen, R. (1967). Stimulus qualities of the target of aggression: a further study. *Journal of Personality and Social Psychology*, **5**, 364–368.

Berkowitz, L., & Macaulay, J. (1971). The contagion of criminal violence. *Sociometry*, **34**, 238–260.

Berkowitz, L., & Rawlings, E. (1963). Effects of film violence on inhibitions against subsequent aggression. *Journal of Abnormal and Social Psychology*, **66**, 405–412.

Beyleveld, D. (1982). Ehrlich's analysis of deterrence: methodological strategy and ethics in Isaac Ehrlich's research and writing on the death penalty as a deterrent. *British Journal of Criminology*, **22**, 101–123.

Blumstein, P., Cohen, D., & Nagin, D. (Eds.) (1978). *Deterrence and incapacitation: Estimating the effects of criminal sanctions on crime rates*. Washington, D.C.: U.S. Government Printing Office.

Bollen, K. A., & Phillips, D. P. (1981). Suicidal motor vehicle fatalities in Detroit: a replication. *American Journal of Sociology*, **87**, 404–412.

Bollen, K. A., & Phillips, D. P. (1982). Imitative suicides: a national study of the effects of television news stories. *American Sociological Review*, **47**, 802–809.

Bowers, W. J., & Pierce, G. L. (1975). The illusion of deterrence in Isaac Ehrlich's research on capital punishment. *Yale Law Journal*, **85**, 187–208.

California Bureau of Vital Statistics (1969–1973). *Computerized list of death certificates* (yearly issues). Sacramento: California Bureau of Vital Statistics.

California Highway Patrol (1966–1973). *Annual report of fatal and injury motor vehicle traffic accidents* (yearly volumes). Sacramento: California Highway Patrol.

Canada Department of the Solicitor General (1972). *A study of the deterrent effect of capital punishment*. Ottawa: Queen's Printer.

Comstock, G. (1975). *Television and human behavior: The key studies*. Santa Monica, CA: Rand.

Comstock, G. (1977). Types of portrayal and aggressive behavior. *Journal of Communication*, **27**, 189–198.

Crawford, J. P., & Willis, J. H. (1966). Double suicide in psychiatric hospital patients. *British Journal of Psychiatry*, **112**, 1231–1235.

Dann, R. H. (1935). The deterrent effect of capital punishment. *Friends Social Service Series*, Bulletin 29.

Ehrlich, I. (1975). The deterrent effect of capital punishment: a question of life and death. *American Economic Review*, **65**, 397–417.

Freedman, J. L. (1984). Effect of television violence on aggressiveness. *Psychological Bulletin*, **96**, 227–246.

Graves, W. F. (1956). A doctor looks at capital punishment. *Journal of the Loma Linda University School of Medicine*, **10**, 137–142.

Great Britain Royal Commission on Capital Punishment. (1953).*Report*. London: H.M. Stationery Office.

Johnston, J. (1972). *Econometric methods*. New York: McGraw-Hill.

Kessler, R. C., & Stipp, H. (1984). The impact of fictionaltelevision suicide stories on U.S. fatalities: A replication. American Journal of Sociology, **90**, 151–167.

Klein, L., Forst, B., & Filatov, V. (1978). The deterrenteffect of capital punishment: an assessment of the estimates. In A. Blumstein, D. Cohen, & D. Nagin (Eds.), *Deterrence and incapacitation*. Washington, D.C.: U.S. Government Printing Office.

Kreitman, N., Smith, P., & Tan, E. (1969). Attempted suicide in social networks. *British Journal of Preventive and Social Medicine*, **23**, 116–123.

Lester, D. (1972). *Why people kill themselves*. Springfield, IL: Charles C. Thomas.

Motto, J. A. (1967). Suicide and suggestibility. *American Journal of Psychiatry,* **124,** 252–256.

Motto, J. A. (1970). Newspaper influence on suicide. *Archives of General Psychiatry,* **23,** 143–148.

Murray, J., & Kippax, S. (1979). From the early window to the late night show: international trends in the study of television's impact on children and adults. In L. Berkowitz (Ed.), *Advances in experimental social psychology* (Vol. 12, pp. 253–320). New York: Academic Press.

Ostrom, C. W. (1978). *Time series analysis: Regression techniques.* Beverly Hills, CA: Sage.

Passell, P. (1975). The deterrent effect of the death penalty: a statistical test. *Stanford Law Review,* **28,** 61–80.

Pearl, D., Bouthilet, L., & Lazar, J. (Eds.) (1982). *Television and behavior: Ten years of scientific evidence and implications for the eighties. Vol. 1: Summary report.* Washington, D.C.: U.S. Government Printing Office.

Phillips, D. P. (1974). The influence of suggestion on suicide: substantive and theoretical implications of the Werther effect. *American Sociological Review,* **39,** 340–354.

Phillips, D. P. (1977). Motor vehicle fatalities increase just after publicized suicide stories. *Science,* **196,** 1464–1465.

Phillips, D. P. (1978). Airplane accident fatalities increase just after stories about murder and suicide. *Science,* **201,** 148–150.

Phillips, D. P. (1979). Suicide, motor vehicle fatalities, and the mass media: evidence toward a theory of suggestion. *American Journal of Sociology,* **84,** 1150–1174.

Phillips, D. P. (1980a). Airplane accidents, murder, and the mass media: towards a theory of imitation and suggestion. *Social Forces,* **58,** 1001–1024.

Phillips, D. P. (1980b). The deterrent effect of capital punishment: new evidence on an old controversy. *American Journal of Sociology,* **86,** 139–148.

Phillips, D. P. (1982a). The behavioral impact of violence in the mass media: a review of the evidence from laboratory and nonlaboratory investigations. *Sociology and Social Research,* **66,** 387–398.

Phillips, D. P. (1982b). The impact of fictional television stories on U.S. adult fatalities: New evidence on the effect of the mass media on violence. *American Journal of Sociology,* **87,** 1340–1359.

Phillips, D. P. (1983). The impact of mass media violence on U.S. homicides. *American Sociological Review,* **48,** 560–568.

Phillips, D. P., & Bollen, K. A. (1985). Same time last year: Selective data dredging for negative findings. *American Sociological Review,* **50,** 364–371.

Phillips, D. P., & Hensley, J. (1984). When violence is rewarded or punished: the impact of mass media stories on homicide. *Journal of Communication,* **34,** 101–116.

Roberts, D. F., & Bachen, C. M. (1981). Mass communication effects. In M. R. Rosenzweig & L. W. Parker (Eds.), *Annual review of psychology.* Palo Alto, CA: Annual Reviews.

Savitz, L. (1968). A study in capital punishment. *Journal of Criminal Law, Criminology, and Police Science,* **49,** 338–341.

Seiden, R. H. (1968). Suicide behavior contagion on a college campus. In N. L. Farberow (Ed.), *Proceedings of the fourth international conference on suicide prevention.* Los Angeles: Delmaro.

United Nations Economic and Social Council. (1973). *Capital punishment.* New York: United Nations.

United States Department of Justice. (1983). *Uniform crime reports. Crime in the United States.* Washington, D.C.: U.S. Government Printing Office.

United States National Center for Health Statistics (1968). *International classification of diseases for use in the United States* (8th revision). Washington, D.C.: U.S. Government Printing Office.

United States National Center for Health Statistics (1946–1980). *Vital statistics of the United States* (yearly volumes). Washington, D.C.: U.S. Government Printing Office.

United States National Transportation Safety Board (1968–1973). *Briefs of accidents U.S. civil aviation* (yearly volumes). Washington, D.C.: U.S. Government Printing Office.

Vanderbilt University (1973–1979). *Vanderbilt television news archives* (yearly volumes). Nashville: Joint University Libraries.

Wasserman, I. (1984). Imitation and suicide: A reexamination of the Werther effect. *American Sociological Review, 49,* 427–436.

Weiss, E. (1958). The clinical significance of the anniversary reaction. *General Practicioner, 17,* 117–119.

Wilson, C., & Putnam, P. (1962). *The encyclopedia of murder.* New York: Putnam's.

PARADIGMS AND GROUPS

Ivan D. Steiner

DEPARTMENT OF PSYCHOLOGY
UNIVERSITY OF MASSACHUSETTS
AMHERST, MASSACHUSETTS

I. Introduction

In 1973, my colleague, Seymour Berger, and I were recruited to participate in a hastily arranged symposium at a meeting of the New England Social Psychological Association. The topic under discussion was the future of social psychology, and I expressed the same optimistic prediction I had voiced a year or two earlier in a Katz–Newcomb lecture (Steiner, 1974): by the late 1970s social psychology would rediscover the group and regain its health. The gist of Berger's comments was that by the 1990s social psychology would be hard to find anywhere; it would have been assimilated into other areas of psychology, such as learning, motivation, and cognition. I had never before known Berger to say such things, and was more than a little dismayed to hear him express such wrongheaded and even traitorous views. But it now seems that he was more nearly correct than I, for social psychology seems scarcely more visible than the group, and neither is manifesting the vigor I predicted. The major aim of this

251

ADVANCES IN EXPERIMENTAL
SOCIAL PSYCHOLOGY, VOL. 19

Copyright © 1986 by Academic Press, Inc.
All rights of reproduction in any form reserved.

article is to apply the wisdom of hindsight to events that were not very clearly revealed by foresight.

During the early 1970s it was comparatively easy to believe that the declining popularity of group dynamics was a temporary phenomenon. The enthusiasm of the 1950s had waned, but the Vietnam War had seemed to create a new Zeitgeist in which collective action was replacing the self-reliant individualism of the 1960s. If social psychologists were at least somewhat responsive to the temper of the times the widespread occurrence of meetings, demonstrations, political crusades, boycotts, and picketing should have favored a more "groupy" brand of social psychology. And if social psychologists were at least as opportunistic as other mortals, one might expect them to be attracted to intellectual provinces that were not already overpopulated. The dynamics of the single individual had long been the favorite hunting ground of traditional psychologists, while sociologists, anthropologists, and political scientists had established themselves as investigators of institutions, societies, and large-scale organizations. But no discipline had systematically examined the behaviors of committees, work crews, and athletic teams. Surely social psychologists could be counted upon to heed Lewin's (1947b) call for research into group dynamics.

In retrospect, it appears that neither of my two major reasons for predicting a resurgence of the group was well founded. The turmoil of the 1960s and early 1970s had not created a Zeitgeist that identified groups rather than individuals as the crucial actors on the world's stage. Perhaps, as Sampson (1977) has argued, the theme that best describes our ethos is self-contained individualism, and this orientation was so profoundly stamped upon us that it was unlikely to be very greatly altered by a decade of conflict and dissillusionment. In any event, social psychology's focus on the individual seems not to have been greatly altered. To be sure, a few scholars (Altman, 1976; Pepitone, 1976; Proshansky, 1976; Sampson, 1977; Secord, 1976; Stokols, 1976) have deplored the tendency to treat individuals in isolation from the situations in which they operate. But these critics have proposed something more ambitious than a return to the group as the unit for study. Instead, they have suggested that the unit for analysis should include norms and institutional arrangements, the physical setting in which action occurs, and (in the case of some writers) pertinent historical, economic, and ideological aspects of the larger society. So, although the events of the 1960s and early 1970s induced an occasional doubt concerning the proper "object" of social psychological inquiry, those doubts did not lead to a revival of the group. Indeed, a survey of 229 "prominent" social psychologists (Lewicki, 1982) found that only 14% of all respondents named group dynamics topics as ones that were likely to be popular during the next decade. By contrast, 73% anticipated the continued popularity of cognitive social psychology.

Nature may abhor a vacuum but social psychologists apparently do not. My assumption that expediency would lead us away from the crowded areas of personality, attitudes, and cognition, and into the comparatively uncultivated province of group dynamics, has not been confirmed. It is possible, of course, that such a shift was not actually as expedient or opportunistic as I had thought. Group research is generally more difficult and often more risky than is investigation of the single individual. Funding agencies are not always highly supportive of the relatively large-scale projects that are needed when one studies groups, and researchers who have been trained as investigators of the individual's behavior may feel unprepared to undertake work of a different kind. It is also possible that academicians are especially inclined to cling to the tried and tested concerns of their disciplines when jobs and financial support are scarce—as they have been since the early 1970s. House (1977) noted that following the affluent 1950s both psychologically and sociologically trained social psychologists tended to retreat to their parent disciplines. Insecure times may discourage the kind of risk taking that is involved when one explores untried paths.

It now seems likely to me that there was an even more compelling reason for social psychologists' continuing aversion to the group. In many cases their indoctrination into intellectual affairs had created an allegiance to conceptual schemes and methodological principles that were inimcal to the study of groups.

II. Paradigms

All scientific inquiry is guided by assumptions, some of which are shared by many disciplines. Thus all branches of science posit the existence of a real world "out there"—a world that is presumed to be mirrored with some degree of accuracy by one's senses and by the inferences one draws from the data the senses provide. To be sure, these inferences may sometimes be seriously flawed, but they are nevertheless believed to be inferences about events that are occurring outside the imagination of the scholar. Solopism is not popular among scientists.

Regardless of which sector of the "real world" a scientist wishes to explore, he confronts a problem that was highlighted by Sir Francis Bacon: the subtlety of nature greatly exceeds the subtlety of the human senses. What registers in our direct experience is generally less than the whole truth, and is often capable of being construed in many different ways. Moreover, the realm of potentially observable events is so large that the scientist, like the man on the street, can sample only a small portion of what is available. Specialized disciplines have evolved to cope with such complexities, each to some degree choosing its own domain of observable events and developing its own code of written or unwritten rules concerning the manner in which observations should be made and how they should be interpreted. Thus individual scientists are not entirely free to do as they please; chemists, astronomers, and psychologists are enjoined by their colleagues to observe specific classes of phenomena, to make observations in consensually validated ways, and to employ approved patterns of thought when interpreting observations. Each discipline, or each "school" within a discipline, has its own set of rules about what is good or acceptable practice, its own priorities, and its own list of rarely questioned assumptions. Such an agenda for action is sometimes (e.g., Kuhn, 1962) called a *paradigm,* a term we will employ without attempting to be completely loyal to anyone else's use of the word.

It is possible to argue (Elms, 1975) that social psychology never developed a common core of rules, priorities, and assumptions that were unique to the field and accepted by all, or almost all, of its practitioners. Instead, it remained a loosely bound confederation of factions held together by a shared conviction that one or more parent discipline (usually psychology or sociology) was not properly pursuing certain kinds of knowledge. But agreement concerning parental inadequacies did not produce a consensus concerning what should be studied and how investigation should go forth. Nevertheless, as time passed, certain paradigmatic preferences became increasingly evident. It is our contention that this set of dominant, though never universally accepted, paradigmatic preferences inhibited a resurgence of interest in groups since the 1960s.

III.   Dominant Paradigmatic Preferences
of Social Psychology

Observation became the bedrock of science when men like Galileo and Newton challenged the word of authority as the ultimate source of understanding. But assigning the fundamental role to observation left important questions unanswered. Who should observe what, and under what circumstances? Is understanding promoted by positing the occurrence of unobserved events that are presumed to operate in conjunction with those that are observed? Each scientific discipline tended to provide its own answers to questions such as these, and when social psychology emerged upon the scene during the early part of this century, its advocates generally adopted the answers provided by one or another of those previously established disciplines.

Although the philosophical roots of social psychology can be linked to antiquity (Allport, 1954), our present purposes are adequately served by looking back no further than a hundred years. The first textbooks in social psychology were not published until 1908, and the discipline did not become an organized, empirical investigative enterprise for another dozen or so years. In Germany,

Moede began his research on coacting groups in 1913, and 5 years later the American sociologist Thomas and Znaniecki (1918) published the first volume of their intensive inquiry into the adjustment of the Polish peasant in this country. By 1924 F. H. Allport had performed his pioneering research on social facilitation (Allport, 1924b) and had produced a social psychology textbook (Allport, 1924a) which, by comparison with its predecessors, still retains a distinctly modern flavor. Of course, much of importance had been written previous to these critical years, and many "social psychological" experiments had been performed well before Moede and Allport reported their results. But empirical social psychological research, performed by persons who considered themselves to be social psychologists, first flourished during the second and third decades of this century. This section of the article reviews the way questions of paradigmatic import were answered during the formative period of the history of social psychology and during later stages of its development.

A.   WHOSE ACTIONS SHALL BE STUDIED?

From the beginning, social psychologists have told one another whether human social behavior could best be understood by conceiving the individual person *or* some variously defined collection of persons as the "actor" whose conduct is to be observed, understood, predicted, and perhaps controlled. There have been enthusiastic proponents on all sides of this issue, as well as occasional compromisers. Because the identity of the actor has a bearing on several other paradigmatic concerns, we will survey the history of this issue a little more thoroughly than others.

*1.   Early F. H. Allport versus É. Durkheim versus
       Later F. H. Allport*

F. H. Allport (1924a,b) maintained that scientific concepts must have unambiguously denotable referents. And in Allport's judgment, the single individual met that criterion very well; we experience each individual as a separate entity, the parts of which function as an organized whole. By contrast, according to Allport, a group cannot be seen, felt, heard, or smelled as something distinctively different from the individuals who are its members. We cannot touch or point to a group without touching or pointing to its component parts, and the actions of the group inevitably turn out to be the behaviors of its individual members. No matter how closely we look, it is always the individuals who convene, discuss, decide, and depart. In short, the group is an illusion; it is the individuals whose actions *can* and should be observed.

Allport's rejection of any unit larger than the single individual was in sharp opposition to a sociological perspective endorsed by Durkheim in 1895. According to Durkheim, a society, organization or group " . . . is not identical to a sum of its parts, it is something else with different properties than those present-ed by the parts of which it is composed" (p. 126). It cannot be understood by a piecemeal examination of its parts. "Accordingly, whenever a social phe-nomenon is directly explained by a psychological phenomenon, one may be sure that explanation is false" (p. 128). However, Durkheim provided little specific guidance concerning the observation of social units.

Thomas and Znaniecki (1918–1920) reflected a much less doctrinaire so-ciological orientation. They were acutely aware of the role of social units (partic-ularly the family), which they generally treated as supraindividual entities. But observation of such units was largely filtered through the reports of participants, and the reader of Thomas and Znaniecki's monumental work is likely to con-clude he has learned more about the acculturation of Polish peasants than about the observation and conceptualization of multiperson units.

Nowadays it is hard to find a social psychologist who endorses Durkheim's most extreme views. Even those who agree that social units sometimes seem to have a *sui generis* character are unlikely to agree that psychological explanations of social phenomena are inevitably wrong—inevitably incomplete, perhaps, but not inevitably wrong.

By contrast, some of Allport's extreme views are still supported by social psychologists. Thus, for example, Konečni (1979) asserts that "there is no group—only individuals exposed to, and continuously changing as a function of social influence" (p. 88). Moreover, Konečni refers to groups as "pseudo-entities" and protests the claim that "a groups is somehow 'more' than its component individuals." Allport's conclusion that the actions of a group turn out to be the behaviors of its individual members also has its advocates:

> Dealings between groups ultimately become problems for the psychology of the indi-vidual. Individuals decide to go to war; battles are fought by individuals, and peace is established by individuals. (Berkowitz, 1962, p. 167)

Although most contemporary social psychologists are not very explicit about their acceptance of Allport's early views of the group, their research and writings often indicate they believe it is the individual who can and should be observed, and who really matters. Consensus falls far short of unanimity, but if pressed to discuss the issue, most social psychologists would probably agree that the whole is nothing more than the sum of its parts and that everything that happens in groups will ultimately be explained by the psychology of its indi-vidual members.

At least one of Allport's early views seems unassailable: what we can observe is the individual and his actions. Groups do not ordinarily constitute a strong Gestalt; they rarely register in our direct experience as entities or things.

· As Allport said, "Groups are not denotable." In this respect they are more like solar systems than like individual human beings; their existence and properties must be inferred from observations of their parts. But as Durkheim contended, a piecemeal observation of parts is not sufficient; the wholeness of a group (or a solar system) is likely to be revealed only when the observer obtains information about the functional interdependence and mutual responsiveness of parts.

Imagine that it were possible for us to segregate the sun and each of the planets in separate areas in space. Piecemeal examination of the isolated components would be a very difficult way of discovering that they are normally parts of a larger whole or of learning how that larger whole operates. Durkheim's appraisal of the futility of applying psychological principles to groups was undoubtedly too harsh, but it was not without some merit. Psychological principles that are derived from observation of individuals in isolation from one another, or in highly contrived situations, are not likely to provide a very complete or wholly accurate picture of the groups in which these individuals periodically participate. As George Mead (1934) noted, a full understanding of groups and the individuals who populate them may require that we observe the complex group activity and then deduce the processes and capacities of creatures who engage in such intricate interactions.

Allport was only partly right in suggesting that everything a group does is really the action of the individual members. He was correct in the sense that I would be right if I proclaimed that everything a person does is really performed by one or more parts of his body. But saying that a single member of a group is a self-sufficient producer of acts may be no more realistic than saying that it is not you but your eyes that are reading this page.

Psychologists have recently become aware of people's pervasive tendency to believe that an actor's behavior is self-prompted. This neglect of external, situational factors has come to becalled "the fundamental attribution error" (Ross, 1977, p. 184). But psychologists, and even social psychologists, have generally remained somewhat insensitive to their own proclivity to assume that their subjects are self-determining organisms whose actions will ultimately be explained by probing ever more deeply within people's cognitions, viceras, or nervous systems.

The continuing appeal of Allport's early views is ironic, for he rejected many of them during the postretirement period of his life. In 1961 he acknowledged that " . . . any 'entity' or 'thing' at whatever level we find it, always seems to break down into a collection at a lower order" (p. 27). And he concluded that the objections he had raised against regarding groups as entities could, with almost equal validity, be leveled against individuals and atoms as well. Wholeness he had decided was a consequence of the mutual interdependence of acting parts, and it was the team rather than the individual player who had scored a touchdown. Allport's earlier views tend to be quoted profusely in textbooks and journal articles, but his recantations in 1961 and 1962 are rarely mentioned.

Although most social psychologists undoubtedly argue that it is individuals, not groups, that register in our direct experience, they disagree concerning the locale in which individuals should be observed. The majority probably subscribes to Allport's early contention that people behave the same way in groups as they do alone, only perhaps more so. If that is the case it doesn't really matter much whether individuals are observed alone or in groups. But a minority of social psychologists, and perhaps it is a very small one, would maintain that only by observing the continuing interaction of group members can one "perceive" and understand the group. These protesters would have a modicum of sympathy for Durkheim and an ideological loyalty to repentant Allport.

2. Good Gestalts and the Limits of Human Perception

In 1924 Allport called for denotable referents instead of good Gestalts. The word Gestalt was not yet an important part of the psychologist's language. But Allport's early argument concerning the reality of groups might have been expressed as follows: unless a collection of persons forms a good Gestalt, it cannot be regarded as anything more than the sum of its parts. Campbell (1958) applied parallel logic in an attempt to decide whether social units require a level of analysis that differs from that which is appropriate to the study of individuals. Unless social units qualify as entities, he contended, "the possibility of a social science representing a separate level of analysis from the biological or psychological will be eliminated" (p. 24). And, according to Campbell, the "entitativity" of social units could be assessed by applying the criteria by which entities in the physical world are identified. Thus collections of people can legitimately be regarded as entities to the degree that they manifest the qualities of a good Gestalt (Wertheimer, 1923): proximity and similarity of parts, common fate of parts, and good pregnance. Although multiple tests were desirable, Campbell emphasized the importance of common fate and good pregnance.

When he applied his criteria to human aggregations Campbell concluded that some social units fared better than others, but almost none manifested the level of entitativity that is typical of biological organisms. Indeed, when viewed as a *psychological* being, even the human individual turned out to have somewhat marginal "entitativity" because his psychological boundaries were generally rather indistinct. But Campbell's reservations concerning the scientific status of the single psychological being were small in comparison with his doubts about the appropriateness of treating groups as distinct objects of scientific inquiry.

It is probably true that constellations of events that form a good, clearly denotable Gestalt tend to be seen as entities. If we can assume that human intellectual and sensory equipment functions faultlessly, such constellations are, in fact, functioning entities. Given this crucial assumption, Allport's early views, and Campbell's later ones, are correct; whatever is perceived to be a functioning entity *is* one, and whatever is not so perceived is not a functioning entity. But a prime reason why science is needed to supplement and correct conclusions gleaned from everyday experience is that our intellectual and sensory equipment *does not* function faultlessly. As Stuart Rice (1928) concluded, "All data from the perceptual world turn out to be evidences about reality, but not reality itself" (p. 24).

Of course, our senses are the primary means by which we gain information about reality, but they are far from perfect tools. Indeed, Gerard (1942) has suggested that they are not just susceptible to random error, but are actually biased. During the course of human evolution our ancestors undoubtedly stood to gain more from an ability to perceive the presence and actions of saber-toothed tigers and members of their own species than they might have profited from a capacity to see the universe or subatomic particles.Over thousands of generations survival value dictated that our progenitors became capable of seeing entities and events of "intermediate size" for these were the aspects of their environment to which they might respond adaptively. For ourselves, as for ancient cavemen, there are myriad events that cannot be perceived because they are too large or too small, too fast or too slow, or too compressed or too dispersed for our senses. It is not surprising that people and catfish were judged to be real long before molecules and solar systems were. If, by some accident of nature, humans had come equipped with microscopic, X-ray eyes, perhaps we would now be debating whether people and catfish are illusions, and would long since have established the "entitativity" of subatomic particles and chicken livers. In any event, what we regard as a genuine functioning entity, and what we insist is only the sum of its parts, must reflect the way our sensory equipment is tuned as well as what is really out there to be seen and evaluated.

Hereditary bias is not the whole story. Cultural bias has also been evident, at least since the publication of Bartlett's (1932) classic studies on remembering. And as the appeal of positivism has faded, fewer and fewer scholars have been willing to contend that the senses provide a theory-neutral data base.

3. Postulating the Large and the Small

Increasing awareness of the fallible nature of the human senses should have permitted scholars to rely more heavily than before on the "mind's eye," and to some extent it seems to have had that effect. But its emancipating role has been quite uneven: thorists have found it more legitimate to postulate the existence of small, rapid, condensed events than to conceive large, dispersed patterns of events. To be sure, there have been fierce debates about the reality of molecules, atoms, germs, and subatomic particles, but those debates eventually subsided when the utility of postulating such unobservables was demonstrated, or when technology produced instruments that made them observable. But the contention that people are parts of larger wholes has been slow to gain widespread acceptance. Perhaps it has been a case of failing to see the forest because we find the individual trees so interesting, or maybe "we create an illusion of freedom by attributing more internal control to ourselves, to the individual, than actually exists" (Zimbardo, 1972). Moreover, it seems likely that some of the extreme versions of collectivist theorizing by Durkheim and others departed so markedly and defiantly from the world of observables that they undermined faith in postulated social units. Certainly research has not so convincingly demonstrated the utility of postulating societies, organizations, or groups, and technology has not yet provided tools by which such units can somehow be made to seem more denotably visible. (Perhaps computers will someday be helpful in this regard, but such assistance cannot come until much more extensive observational data are available to be processed.)

Cultural anthropologists (e.g., Benedict, 1934; Kluckhohn, 1954; Mead, 1930) have reported stimulating investigations of the individual's embeddedness in his society, and scholars from several disciplines (e.g., Barnard, 1938; Katz & Kahn, 1967; Parsons, 1951) have charted the actions of organizations. But these studies can hardly be said to have proved beyond a reasonable doubt that social units are anything more than a collection of interacting individuals, or that much is gained by treating the social unit, instead of the individual, as the actor. Nowadays, no informed person argues that it is futile or fanciful to postulate the existence of subatomic entities, some of which have never been directly observed. But lots of informed people question the utility or parsimony of assuming that groups or organizations act. Many of the doubters are social psychologists.

4. Early Interest in Social Units

Certain early developments in the history of social psychology suggested the discipline might become focused on the operations of social units. G. H. Mead (1934) argued that the search for understanding of social behavior must be anchored on observation of interacting organisms; the dog fight or a human conversation is a unitary thing in which the action of each participant is at the same time both response to, and stimulus for, the other participant(s).

> We are not in social psychology building up the behavior of the social group in terms of the behavior of the separate individuals composing it, rather we are starting out with a given social whole of complex group activity, into which we analyze (as elements) the behavior of each of the separate individuals composing it. (Mead, 1934, p. 7)

For reasons that were never entirely clear to this author, Mead's many insights were seldom very well received by psychologically trained social psychologists. When left to those who were sociologically trained they became the foundation for what is nowadays called "symbolic interactionism," a school of thought that retains Mead's concern for interaction in naturalistic settings, but is antagonistically opposed to experimental and/or quantitative nonexperimental methods.

In 1902 Charles Cooley (1902–1964) maintained that "A separate individual is an abstraction unknown to experience, and so likewise is society when regarded as something apart from individuals" (p. 1). Forty-five years later, Murphy (1947) offered behavioral scientists almost the same prescription.

> The individual organism can no more be considered an isolated object than it can be considered homogeneous with its environment, for either its complete isolation or, on the other hand, the loss of its boundaries would equally signify its obliteration. It is a region of relatively high structuring in a field of complex and ever-changing relations. (Murphy, 1947, p. 30)

Neither Cooley's nor Murphy's version of the message seems to have had a very marked effect on the development of social psychology. Kurt Lewin proposed an orientation that was much more enthusiastically received.

5. Lewin and the Life Space

Before coming to America Lewin had been a member of the Gestalt group in Berlin. So it is not surprising that his theorizing had a wholistic flavor. Explanations of human behavior, he contended, must take account of the total field of forces operating on the individual at the moment his actions occur. Many of these forces were presumed to have been instigated by external events (e.g., the presence or actions of other persons). But the significance of external events depended on the manner in which they were interpreted by the actor, and on the valences they acquired as a consequence of interpretation. The positive and negative valences of perceived or expected events were said to interact with tensions within the individual to create a configuration of forces, some pushing one way and some another. When competing forces were unbalanced the individual was presumed to respond in a manner that tended to restore equilibrium.

The forces in the field were, for the most part, thought to be represented in the "life space," the individual's cognitive map of goal regions toward which he might locomote, barriers to be traversed, and negative regions he would prefer to avoid. The observed and anticipated actions of other persons were also included in the life space and were said to be responsible for "induced forces." Finally, it was acknowledged that forces sometimes originated in the "foreign hull" of the life space, a region populated by events that were not perceived, thought about, or expected. However, Lewin devoted little attention to the foreign hull.

By comparison with cognitive theorists of more recent vintage, Lewin was not very prone to question the validity of the individual's cognitions. Perhaps he applied Gestalt theory's principle of isomorphism to an extremely wide range of phenomena. In any case, the life space was generally assumed to be a rather faithful reflection of the events it represented. Consequently, it could be manipulated by exposing experimental subjects to altered external conditions, and its major features could be inferred from observation of those conditions. Moreover, because the individual could be assumed to be aware of many of his important cognitions, information about his life space could also be gleaned from his self-reports.

In a general sort of way Lewin's conception of a field of forces harmonized with the thinking of Cooley and Murphy. But neither of the latter contended that an actor's conception of his total situation is likely to be very accurate, and neither tended to emphasize the actor's phenomenology while downplaying the kind of events Lewin assigned to the foreign hull. Lewin brought the external situation, including the group in which an actor might be functioning, into the head of the actor. Because the really important aspects of the group were represented in the actor's life space, an investigator could largely avoid difficult and tedious observational processes; major features of the group could be inferred from the actions of the member who was the investigator's primary interest, and/or from the self-reports of that member. Certainly Lewin did not object to the use of outside observers, but his emphasis on the situation as it is experienced by the actor himself made their use less imperative.

Although Lewin (1935) vigorously protested the reduction of psychological phenomena to the level of biology, he tended to reduce groups to the level of the individual member's thought processes. His theory can be seen as a prescription for the study of *the individual in the group*—but the group is whatever the individual perceives or imagines it to be. Lewin had little to say about the continuing sequences of human interaction by which members maintain the kind of interdependence he regarded as the essence of the group. His theory did not deal very explicitly with the processes by which members of groups *collectively* perform tasks or cope with their environments, and it was not very informative concerning what Deutsch (1954) has called "group spaces" or the external relations of groups.

In spite of these limitations, Lewin's thinking had a considerable impact on group research, and enabled him to make major contributions (Lewin, 1947-a,b,c, 1948) to the field. At a time when groups were still commonly regarded as "fallacies" he legitimized their study, and he attracted and trained many very competent young colleagues. His emphasis on the "life space" rather than upon the events actually transpiring in the group, and his faith in laboratory research (as well as field studies), made the investigation of groups seem quite manageable. Furthermore, his contention that the life space is a "dynamic whole" was a major step in the direction of a systems theory of groups in which "a change in the state of any subpart changes the state of any other subpart" (Lewin, 1948, p. 54).

6. The System as a Model

Although different theorists have offered different definitions of a system, most would probably agree with Parsons (Parsons & Shils, 1951), who maintained that the "most fundamental property of a system is the interdependence of parts and variables. Interdependence consists in the existence of determinate relationships among the parts or variables as contrasted with randomness of variability" (p. 107). In the case of "abstract" or "conceptual" systems (Miller, 1955), determinate relationships may be asymmetrical: variable A may affect variable B, though B has no effect on A. But when systems are "concrete," determinate relationships are usually symmetrical or mutual. Thus social systems, being concrete in the sense of Miller's distinction, are considered to consist of a set of mutually responsive components: what any one component does depends on what other components, singly or collectively, are doing or have done in the recent past.

In addition to mutual responsiveness of parts, social systems are said to have other defining characteristics. Some theorists (e.g., Bales, 1950; Parsons, 1951) suggest that the mutual responsiveness of the components maintains the system in a state of equilibrium, while others (e.g., Buckley, 1967; Homans, 1950) contend that, at least in the case of social–cultural systems, structural change and elaboration are completely normal and may be responsible for departures from equilibrium. Although systems are assumed to have boundaries that separate their components from outside events, factors that may be responsible for such separation are not routinely specified. In the case of social systems, boundaries may be presumed to include any condition that inhibits the free interaction of an included component with an excluded one (e.g., spatial isolation or the existence of walls, language barriers, segregation, organizationally prescribed communication channels, intergroup competition, ethnocentric bias, or social roles and norms).

While Lewin was inclined to treat the group as an aspect of its members' life spaces, and thus to regard it as an experiential matter, system theorists give the group a status that is largely independent of its members' awareness. Like the solar system, a group can exist without any of its parts regarding it as a unit or identifying the properties that qualify it to be treated as a system. Thus, according to system theorists, groups are "out there," available to be studied by observers who are not their members and whose observations can be subjected to the same kinds of tests of validity and reliability as are employed when assessing observations of the single individual. The social systems approach does not require that the cognitions of individual participants be ignored, but neither does it demand that such cognitions be accorded the special status Lewin gave them.

F. H. Allport did not become a system theorist when, during his postretirement period, he acknowledged that a group might be as real as an individual or atom. But his new way of thinking had some of the qualities of system theorizing. Thus, to the naked eye, groups may seem to be nothing more than the sum of their separate members, but they nevertheless achieve a degree of denotability if one focuses his attention on "event structures," the interdependencies of members when doing tasks or being social (Allport, 1962). By the use of a completely legitimate "intellectual artifice" one could see in his mind's eye what is not otherwise apparent. When Allport watched his college football team score touchdowns he became aware of a productive unity in which the total behavior pattern was more than a sum of the separate players' actions; it was also the precise timing of acts, the location of acts in space, and the elicitation of each player's acts by the acts of others (Allport, 1961).

The intellectual artifice by which system theorists detect wholeness in groups is quite different from that by which many other scholars separate the individual from the social unit. But, as the statements of Cooley, Murphy, and Lewin suggest, discovering the self-sufficient individual may require no less intellectual agility than discovering the invisible group. Whether one of these discoveries is more meritorious or legitimate than the other will presumably be determined by the research each generates and by the understanding each ultimately produces. It is much too early in the game to render a verdict at this point.

That actions are performed by individuals rather than by social systems is perhaps the most universally and habitually accepted paradigmatic assumption of contemporary social psychology. Although faith in groups is often affirmed, that faith seldom is manifested in contemporary theory or research. Thus, what passes as the study of group dynamics nowadays is likely to examine the impact of a collection of people called "the group" on the thoughts, feelings, and actions of the individual; it is unlikely to be very much concerned with the system-like interpersonal transactions of the people who are called a group (Tajfel, 1972b). The individual is ordinarily represented as reacting to "the group" without participating in it. Gordon Allport (the brother of F. H. Allport who is widely cited in this paper) has accurately concluded that,with few exceptions, social psychologists regard their discipline as "an attempt to understand how the thought, feeling and behavior of individuals are influenced by the actual, imagined or implied presence of others" (1968, p. 3). The *responding individual* is the social psychologist's favorite protagonist.

B. OBSERVING EVENTS

1. The Search for Indicants

If social psychology is a discipline that studies the effects of the real or imagined presence of other persons on the individual's thoughts, feelings, and behaviors, one might surmise that social psychologists spend a good deal of effort and time observing human interaction. But that is not what usually happens, for the emphasis is often on what the individual imagines or reads into the presence of others. For psychologically trained social psychologists there is likely to be more interest in what goes on inside individuals than in charting the lawful patterning of observable sequences of acts. Consequently, they devote a good deal of attention to the discovery of indicants of internal processes or states. Thus, attitudes are inferred from observation of the individual's responses to events in his environment, or, more often, from observation of consistent reactions to belief statements. Measured changes in skin resistance have been treated as indicants of emotion, and dilation of the pupils has sometimes been alleged to index approval or, at least, interest. Intelligence is calibrated to success in performing tasks, and personality has been inferred from reactions to inkblots, cartoons, and word-association tests. Social psychologists have been looking for clues to the internal man ever since F. H. Allport (1924a,b) told them their job was to identify the mechanisms that prompt the overt act and Thomas and Znaniecki (1918) assured them that social psychology *is* the study of attitudes.

Stevens (1951) contended that "We know about psychological phenomena only through effects, and the measuring of the effects themselves is the first trudge on the road to understanding" (p. 48). But effects on whom? The person whose internal processes one wishes to infer, or the investigator who wishes to infer those processes? It is often the former, but sometimes investigators project their own "internal responses" (effects) onto their subjects. Thus, for example, dissonance research thrived for several years before skeptics began to ask whether logical inconsistencies that were so apparent to the investigator were also apparent to his subjects and, if so, whether his subjects really experienced any distress as a consequence of being caught in the inconsistency.

Of course, acts are also observed for reasons other than their possible value as indicants. Radical behaviorists contend that they deal with operant acts and reinforcing acts, and aren't much concerned about the symbolic meanings those acts may have. Social psychologists rarely take such an extreme stance, though they sometimes attempt to observe stimulus and response sequences without inferring much by way of intervening process. However, even when they try to observe and record sequential series of acts by a single person or by several persons, they generally concern themselves with rather short sequences. In Section III,C,2, we will note that social psychological theorizing tends to emphasize the importance of proximal antecedents, and to minimize the importance of distal connections.

2. Who Shall Do the Observing?

Traditional psychology offered two distinctly different answers to this question. The introspectionists conceived their task to be that of exploring the mind, and they relied upon the "actor" to observe and report his own sensations and mental processes. But by 1920 this strategy had been strongly attacked by the behaviorists who contended that only those events that could be independently noted and reported by two or more observers could serve as scientific evidence. The individual's reports concerning his own sensations, perceptions, or thoughts dealt with a private realm that was not amenable to scientific inquiry.

A third answer to the question was provided by sociologists, anthropologists, and other social scientists who made extensive use of public documents. Census data, police records, and newspaper accounts might report either the observations of actors themselves *or* those of one or more witnesses to the act. In neither case were the observations made for the purpose of promoting scientific inquiry, and their authenticity was often somewhat suspect. Nevertheless, the value of public documents had been demonstrated by a number of published works, including Durkheim's (1897/1951) classic study of suicide.

From the outset social psychologists used all three kinds of "observers," sometimes two or all three in a single study. Observational procedures of the kind recommended by the behaviorists were employed in studies of a social psychological character long before Watson (1919) came upon the scene, and well before social psychology was regarded as a distinct discipline. Independent, nonparticipating observers continue to be used in certain kinds of social psychological research—particularly those dealing with individual and group performance, helping behavior, social learning, or aggression. But research in which major dependent variables are assessed by the use of outside observers is not really plentiful in social psychological journals; a book (Hartmann, 1982) on the use of such observers drew most of its content from research of the kind published in *Behavioral Assessment*. Today direct observation by nonparticipating observers is often left to the neobehaviorists.

The use of public documents has never been a primary tool of social psychologists, especially those whose roots are more strongly embedded in psychology than in sociology.

By the late 1920s self-reporting actor–observers had become the modal source of data. Perhaps this development can be understood as a consequence of the fact that the movement into social psychology was, in part, a reaction against the strictures imposed by behaviorists within psychology departments. Social psychology offered the opportunity to study "private" as well as "public" events. By the 1930s attitudes had become the foremost concern of the new field (McGuire, 1969), and when their popularity began to wane, increasing attention was given to other hidden, internal states, processes, or propensities: personality variables, interpersonal perception and attraction, attribution, dissonance. Self-report was not the only means by which such variables were assessed, but it was, and it remains, the most convenient method, and the one that is generally employed. Nowadays emphasis is placed on the development of increasingly sophisticated ways of eliciting and processing self-reports; observation by outside observers tends to be regarded as a duty one must perform from time to time in order to claim that one's self-report data are valid.

Social psychology is a discipline that relies primarily, though by no means exclusively, on self-reports to assess "private" events. To a lesser degree "public" behavioral events are also observed and reported by persons who participate in them.

C. RELATING OBSERVATIONS TO ONE ANOTHER

Although "raw perception" may sometimes confer a degree of understanding, scientific explanations are usually obtained by comparing, organizing, and relating observed events (Cassirer, 1923; Hume, 1961). The search for constancy of relationships among events is a major aspect of all science, but different investigators may attempt to understand event A by linking it to quite different patterns of other events.

1. Aristotelian "Few-Factors" and Galilean Patterns

Lewin (1935) described two ways of explaining human behavior. One of them attempts to identify causes within the actor himself, while the other relates the actor's behavior to a cluster of interacting environmental events. Needless to say, the latter is much more congenial than the former to a systems approach. But both kinds of explanations are generated by linking the actor's behavior to other variables (observed events or conditions).

Employing a strategy Lewin called Aristotelian (the first of the two mentioned above) one may note that all people seem to produce response A with more than chance frequency (i.e., response A is correlated with being human) and conclude that it is just human nature to behave that way. Instinct theories were generally based on presumed constancies across all people, but were gradually discarded as additional observations by anthropologists and others revealed the existence of societies in which the critical behavior rarely occurred. Alternately, one may conclude that behavior A is physiologically determined because it is regularly associated with persons in one age, sex, racial, or nationality category but not those in other categories. Or, one may decide behavior A is a manifestation of personality (or attitude) because it is produced by individuals who also give responses X, Y, and Z, but not by other persons. Each of these interpretations of behavior A holds that it is somehow prompted by something inside the individual who produces it; for this reason each may be regarded as an Aristotelian understanding of behavior A.

Lewin (1935) called the second pattern of explanatory thought Galilean. It endeavors to deal simultaneously with as much of the total situation (including the actor) as possible, and to recognize the possibility that all variables may be mutually responsive to one another. Thus, except at the convenience of the investigator, there are no independent and dependent variables, and no sharp beginnings or endings to the actions one may choose to study. The Galilean paradigm harmonizes well with the notion of systems, and it was the approach Lewin attempted to applywhen he conceptualized the life space. Unfortunately, Lewin's version of the Galilean model was almost totally restricted to the phenomenological world of the individual. Unless one were willing to assume that human cognitions were highly accurate, it had little to say about the ebb and flow of reality outside the individual, or about groups that might exist beyond the individual's imagination.

Behaviorists from Watson to Skinner have tended to be rabid anti-Aristotelians; they link observed acts to stimuli in the actor's situation, or to events of the past (the actor's reinforcement history). According to Skinner (1975), the task of scientific analysis "is to explain the hitherto inexplicable and hence to reduce any supposed inner contribution which has served in lieu of explanation" (p. 47). Behaviorists not only minimize the role of "inner" determinants of behavior; they also tend to concentrate their attention on a very limited range of external determinants. Thus they can hardly be regarded as Galileans. A large portion of the behaviorist's research is designed to demonstrate that he can engineer situations in which a single stimulus or class of stimuli is sufficient to evoke a desired response. The underlying thinking has sometimes been said to assume "one factor—one result"; it does not necessarily deny that a multiplicity of factors may operate, but it applies John Stuart Mill's canons in ways that, at the very least, must be expected to limit the real-life generalizability of the findings.

Clearly, social psychology has employed its share of Aristotelian thinking. The somewhat socialized instincts of McDougall or Freud never gained a strong foothold in the field, but more thoroughly learned determinants have had their day of prominence. Personality has been strongly touted, especially during and following World War II when the authoritarian personality was a prime explanation of many unhappy events. And it should be noted that social psychologists tend to be lumped with personality theorists both in journals and in administrative structures. As we remarked earlier, attitudes have sometimes been recommended as the most promising explanation of human social behavior, and during the 1970s a compelling and ubiquitous need to reduce dissonance became social psychology's newest obsession.

Neither Skinnerian nor any other version of behaviorism has ever dominated social psychology. But those of us who entered the ranks during the 1950s were exposed to other kinds of "one factor—one result" thinking. Indeed, a strong reason for the optimism among our generation of social psychologists was the belief that important research would be easily conducted and would identify *the cause* of this or that perplexing social problem (Elms, 1975). Those of us who did not accept the notion of internal, Aristotelian causes might nevertheless find it easy to imagine we would soon identify the single external factor that could be manipulated to cure one or another social illness. When early findings did not replicate very well we learned how to use analysis of variance (ANOVA) designs to sort out some of the complexities that bedeviled our simple world. But interaction effects were everywhere, and linear, "few-factors" models seemed never to produce answers that remained credible for very long. A couple of decades later Gergen (1973) interpreted the poor replication record of our findings to mean that there are few if any underlying laws of social behavior that retain their validity across time. But the replication record across time may not have been much worse than the record during a single month or year. Stability of findings should not be expected unless "comparable studies" are really comparable, which means that in all such studies experimenters and/or nature have induced *all* important variables to operate within the same ranges. In spite of the virtues of factorial designs, only a few variables are manipulated in any study, only a few of the remaining variables are experimentally controlled, and we have no assurance that nature has not tampered with the remainder which we have so carefully randomized across treatment categories. (Randomization does not compensate for changes in the level at which a variable exists within the pool from which cases are drawn.) Only the latter of these three possible reasons for the inconsistency of experimental findings is likely to become much more serious with the passage of time, and none of them can be regarded as indicating that social behavior is somehow historical but not lawful. Inconsistency of findings across factorial studies is more likely to be a function of the inadequacies of "few-factors" designs than an indication of chaotic determination of the behaviors studied.

During the past few years something called "macro-analysis" has been employed in an effort to infer the "average" finding of many "few-factors" studies that have reported the effect of variable A on variable B. Such an approach assumes that the disparities among findings are due to "chance" and that a measure of central tendency will somehow reveal the "true" relationship between A and B. But the troublesome disparities may be due to the fact that different investigators, or nature itself, have manipulated, controlled, or sampled variables at different levels. If reciprocity of variables is the rule, and if interaction effects are almost everywhere (Cronbach, 1975), the "average" of the findings yielded by several "few-factors" studies may be a commentary on the settings within which experimenters have examined a relationship, but will have little to say about the existence of a "true" and immutable relationship between variables A and B. Indeed, the notion that there is a true and immutable relationship between A and B suggests that we are still in a pre-Galilean stage of thinking.

Gergen's (1973) pessimistic interpretation of our poor replication record led him to conclude that "social psychology is primarily an historical inquiry" (p. 310) and that "the continued attempt to build general laws of social behavior seems misdirected" (p. 316). Social psychology studies "facts that are largely non-repeatable and which fluctuate markedly over time" (p. 310). A Galilean interpretation of the same record would say that replication studies that take explicit account of only a few of many potentially important variables are bound to be disappointing. We are doing poor history if we say that any two revolutions, political conventions, or physics experiments are alike because they are identical with respect to two or three critical variables. And if one of these two revolutions, political conventions, or physics experiments has an outcome that differs from that of its alleged counterpart, failure to replicate probably says more about our poor history than about the lawfulness of the events themselves.

An apparent failure to replicate would prompt a Galilean to question the accuracy and completeness of the two historical accounts he is dealing with, and to launch a search for differences between the two episodes that have yielded different outcomes—a search that might identify important variables that have not received appropriate attention. Galilean thinking would say we need better, more complete history in order to discover the underlying lawfulness of nature.

But a more complete history of events is not easy to obtain, and, as Thorngate (1976) has pointed out, a complete history may not be a very parsimonious explanation. A paradigm that requires us to specify every condition that surrounds the occurrence of an event ends up demanding a thorough description of that particular event—which nature may never again match in every detail. So it behooves us to seek a less extensive description which nevertheless subsumes the most important elements of the one that may be too difficult to obtain. Schlenker (1976) has suggested that this will require us to move to a higher level of abstraction, a step which would presumably be guided by careful experimental exploration. If it should turn out that the many critical circumstances surrounding a specific occurrence cannot be satisfactorily subsumed by a limited number of factors, Gergen's contention that social psychology can be nothing but history would be correct. But the success with which scientists have dealt with other complex constellations of variables suggests that the context of human action may eventually be represented by a limited number of abstract variables—more than are measured or manipulated by the "few-factors" approach, but many less than are likely to be operating in any concrete situation.

What seems to be needed is a practical compromise between the dolorous task implied by true Galilean thinking and Gergen's (1973) suggestion that the search for general laws of social behavior is futile. As a small beginning social psychologists might spend more effort trying to understand why seemingly parallel studies have yielded different outcomes, and less effort trying to assess the *mean* effect that variable A has had on variable B in several such parallel studies. They might also divert *some* of their energies away from the search for dispositional explanations of social behavior and invest it, instead, in research that examines the covariation of "situational influences" on social behaviors. The latter endeavor would recognize that one of the most non-Galilean aspects of traditional experimental design is the "fixing" or "holding constant" of "process variables" which might otherwise be expected to covary with manipulated or dependent variables. Other obvious steps toward a Galilean approach would include efforts to reduce the experimental constraints on what subjects can do; this means that the common practices of chopping behavior sequences into "trials" or "turns," of using experimental accomplices to structure the behavior of subjects, or of curtailing the sensory input available to subjects should be minimized. As a general rule investigators who wish to be labeled "Galilean" should probably avoid thinking or speaking about the single cause of any single effect, and should suppress the tendency to regard some variables as independent and others as dependent.

Needless to say, these and other steps we might propose call for more self-discipline and patience than most of us possess, and for a more adventurous spirit than our colleagues and journal editors are likely to tolerate. Even if a substantial fraction of the faithful could be induced to move toward a more Galilean form of social psychology, the positive effects, if any, would be unlikely to show up during the time period funding agencies are willing to contemplate. During the foreseeable future social psychologists seem likely to retain their paradigmatic preferences for Aristotelian explanations and "few-factors" experimental research.

It should be acknowledged that social psychologists who study organizations (e.g., Katz & Kahn, 1967) have been more inclined than others to employ Galilean models. Perhaps the fact that organizational processes are often highly structured by rules of various sorts, and that extensive records of those processes are sometimes available, have made a Galilean approach seem less formidable. Then too, the task-oriented character of many organizations probably inclines investigators to take a "wholistic" view of their operations, while, with a few exceptions (e.g., Davis, 1973; Steiner, 1972), students of the group have generally focused their attention on the processes by which individual members are influenced by their colleagues. The latter approach has not often required investigators to consider the group as a functioning unit.

At the level of the group, where a Galilean model seems especially appropriate, there have been few serious attempts to cope with the multiplicity of simultaneously operating variables, the continuing flow of process, and the mutual impact of variables and actors upon one another. In a somewhat primitive but highly commendable series of studies, Bales (1950) endeavored to observe, record, and analyze the ongoing actions of groups, but nobody has come very close to dealing effectively with the continuity (Barker, 1963) and reciprocity (Mead, 1934) of action that transpires when groups have several active participants. Bales's early attempts were hampered by the absence of recording instruments that are commonplace today. But it was my impression that his painstaking efforts met with little enthusiasm on the part of social psychologists during the 1950s—especially those with a psychological ancestry. Then, as now, most social psychologists preferred to conceptualize the world in Aristotelian or "few-factors" terms.

2. *Examining Sequences of Events*

No matter whether a social psychologist's inclinations are Aristotelian or Galilean, he will almost certainly agree that event A is a consequence of other events or conditions occurring at the same moment or at an earlier time. Probably he will also agree that the events or conditions that prompted event A were themselves triggered by other events or conditions. If pressed, he may concede that event A will have consequences of its own, either singularly or in collaboration with other events. There is an underlying consensus that events that have occurred in the past have somehow caused or cleared the way for those occurring now, and that events of the present have a determining impact on those of the future. But agreement on these propositions still leaves plenty of room for idiosyncrasy.

In their studies of the Polish peasant Thomas and Znaniecki (1918–1920) examined very long sequences of events that sometimes reached from the European background to the attitudes that prompted the immigrant settler to behave as he did. F. H. Allport (1924a) dealt with a much shorter span of events. Although he was concerned with the impact of co-workers on the individual's performance of tasks, and even conducted some of the earliest research on conformity, he contended that the true task of the social psychologist was to identify the internal mechanisms that are the immediate determinants of people's behaviors. Freud attempted to link his clients' present actions with their childhood experiences, while Lewin, though acknowledging that the distant past has structured the present, contended that it is the life space at the moment action occurs (or immediately preceding the action) that determines behavior.

The dominant practice in recent and contemporary social psychology is to concentrate on very small segments of an ongoing series of events. Attribution processes, dissonance reduction, social cognition, the dynamics of personality, and attitude and prejudice are all conceived to be rather immediate "causes" of behaviors that call for explanation. Questions concerning what happens inside the organism as a consequence of stimulation from outside are regarded as more crucial than those concerning how the outside stimuli happened to occur, or whether they are likely to occur again. One may have to observe some slightly distal events in order to infer the more proximal ones, but it is the latter that are really interesting and important. The proximal events are also more likely to be "internal," and to fit nicely within an Aristotelian view of the world. And they harmonize well with monadic traditional psychology which likes to find its explanations of behavior within the actor himself. As Sears (1951) noted:

> Psychologists think monadically. That is, they choose the behavior of one person as their scientific subject matter. For them, the universe is composed of individuals. These individuals are acted upon by external events, to be sure, and in turn the external world is modified by the individual's behaviors. However, the universal laws sought by the psychologist almost always relate to a single body. They are monadic laws and are stated with reference to a monadic unit of behavior. (pp. 478–479)

Sears might have added that the monadic tradition also legitimizes the practice of shutting the behavior sequence off as soon as the individual produces the response the investigator is looking for. There is little interest in the stimulus value that particular response might have for other persons or its possible role in sustaining or shaping a long sequence of collective action. The individual is pictured as a reacting, rather than a participating, agent.

Social psychologists who are less wedded to the monadic tradition are nevertheless likely to examine very small segments of what would ordinarily be a continuing sequence of events. Experimental subjects are required to repeat the same tiny task many times, each replication being regarded as a separate trial. Thus we had the conformity studies of the 1950s, the prisoner's dilemma research of the 1960s, and the investigation of choice shifts, which continued into the 1970s. And throughout these decades continuing interpersonal episodes were experimentally modeled by staged encounters in which accomplices effectively chopped the whole into small pieces, or the experimenter dictated who could speak to whom and when. Such practices revealed a faith that the whole is the sum of its parts, no matter how small or contrived the parts may be.

It must be acknowledged that not all departures from the monadic psychological model have been flawed in the ways indicated above; some studies (see Davis, Laughlin, & Komorita, 1976; McGrath, 1984; Shaw, 1971) have examined fairly long, naturalistic series of interpersonal events. Nevertheless, social psychology as a whole is an enterprise that weights proximal "causes" much more heavily than distal ones, examines small segments of ongoing process, and tends to employ monadic explanations.

3. The Impact of Experimental Methodology

A researcher becomes an experimenter whenever he intrudes on nature and observes the consequences of his actions on the customary course of events. But most experiments also entail some attempt to prevent unwanted simultaneous intrusions that might obscure the linkage between the experimenter's action and any observed change. After all, a good experiment is intended to provide the strongest possible evidence that event A "causes" the occurrence of event B. By comparison, correlational techniques always leave one with troublesome doubts about causation.

Wilhelm Wundt is sometimes called the founder of experimental psychology (cf. Boring, 1957), but Wundt did not believe that experimentation was the appropriate method for all kinds of psychological investigation. Indeed, he contended that it was not at all suitable for the study of longitudinal processes. But Oswald Külpe and other students of Wundt were less cautious than their mentor had been, and the Wundtian legacy that reached American shores during the early 1900s was rather thoroughly experimental.

The American rationale for the experimental method was based partly on the belief that it improved the accuracy of observation. As Titchener (1929–1972) explained in a posthumously published book:

> The universal and peculiar method of science is observation. Since the phenomena to be observed are both complex and elusive, and since human capacity is variously limited, observation is difficult. Science therefore calls in the aid of experiment, which prolongs the time of observation, rules out disturbing and irrelevant phenomena, and allows variation of circumstances. Experiment, which is observation under favorable conditions, is in so far simply an extension of the universal method of science. (p. 70)

However, F. H. Allport (1924a,b) and other early social psychological exponents of the experimental method were probably less attracted by the prospect of improving observational accuracy than by the possibility of charting causal connections among obserations. This at least appears to have been Allport's major aim when doing his pioneering studies on social facilitation and co-worker effects. And causal connections were a pervasive theme in his attempts to provide an associationist's explanation for a wide range of social behaviors.

Most sociologists and anthropologists of this period preferred to obtain their data in naturalistic, field settings, and made little or no attempt to manipulate specific variables while holding others constant. Thus, for example, the landmark studies by Thomas and Znaniecki (1918–1920) relied heavily upon observations of Polish peasants in their own environments, interviews with them, and documentary reports of various kinds; there were no experimental manipulations or attempts to establish experimental controls.

The publications of social psychologists during the 1920s and 1930s do not reveal an eager acceptance of experimentalism. To be sure, work on group performance, social facilitation, and cooperation versus competition tended to be experimental, but most of the early research on attitudes, prejudice, and socialization was not. Murchinson's *Handbook of Social Psychology*, published in

1935, contains only one chapter with an unmistakable experimental flavor. But by 1954 a new edition of the *Handbook,* edited by Gardner Lindzey, presented an orientation that was predominately experimental. The proportion of experimental investigations published in the *Journal of Abnormal and Social Psychology* and its successor, the *Journal of Personality and Social Psychology,* increased from approximately 30% in 1949 to 87% in 1969 (see Rosnow, 1981). Although recent years have brought increasing awareness of the limitations of the experimental approach, contemporary social psychology is an overwhelmingly experimental enterprise.

Common criticisms of the experimental method have by now been expressed and reexpressed in many places; they need not be detailed here. (Any reader who has been mysteriously insulated from the controversy will find an account of many of the criticisms of experimental social psychology, as well as the arguments that are advanced to refute them, in Volume 2 of the *Personality and Social Psychology Bulletin,* 1976.) Suffice it to say that some of the criticisms are directed at practices that are not inherent components of the experimental method. Thus social psychology experiments do not have to examine the reactions of college sophomores, rely upon self-report measures to assess dependent variables, employ instructions that are highly reactive, use manipulations that are flagrantly atypical of real-life counterparts, concentrate on issues that have little practical or theoretical importance, or engage in other activities that Ring (1967) has called the "fun and games" approach to social psychology. Probably a modicum of deception will always be required of those who do certain kinds of social psychology experiments, but even this loudly lamented practice can be minimized.

Unfortunately, there are other complaints that seem to concern fundamental limitations of the experimental method. Much of the alleged artificiality of laboratory experiments stems from the fact that human subjects, unlike atoms and rats, realize they are being studied and may be motivated to impress the investigator, or to assist or confound him. Problems traceable to human awareness and sensitivity can largely be avoided by doing a "field experiment" in which subjects do not realize they are being observed, but this strategy sacrifices the standardization of the laboratory experiment and leaves the investigator open to the charge of having violated the privacy of his subjects—a charge that may have more substance than the ubiquitous complaint about laboratory researchers deceiving innocent college students.

Probably the most serious criticism of experimental methods for studying human groups is the one voiced by Wundt himself: experimental methods do not deal very comfortably with lengthy, longitudinal processes. As McGuire (1973) has noted, both cognitive and social organizations involve parallel processing, bidirectional causality, and reverberating feedback, all features that may easily be obscured by research in which some, or even a few, process-related variables are held constant. Indeed, McGuire suggested that many laboratory experiments have not so much served to reveal anything new as they have demonstrated the stage-managing abilities of investigators who have wished to display the validity of conclusions to which they were already unalterably committed. Other critics (e.g., Helmreich, 1975; Manicas & Secord, 1983; Silverman, 1971) have also contended that traditional experimental methods have sometimes been an impediment to progress in the field. Regardless of how justified such bleak assessments may be, it seems fair to say that applying laboratory methods to the complexities of group processes has proved to be much more difficult and troublesome than Lewin assumed it would be. And the temptation to tailor the group to fit the method has often seemed irresistable.

However, one variety of group experiment, sometimes called "group simulation," minimizes the restraints created by the use of experimental controls. A number of persons are brought together, and after a brief or lengthy "get acquainted" session, are asked to work on a task, discuss an issue, or play a game. The manipulated variable may be the size of the group, the nature of the task or discussion topic, the manner in which rewards are to be distributed, or the assignment versus nonassignment of specific roles. After manipulations have been accomplished the experimenter and his assistant(s) become as inconspicuous as possible while observing the behaviors that ensue. Interaction, which may continue for only a few minutes or for more than an hour, proceeds without any further intervention by the experimenter.

Employing this model Bales (1950) manipulated little more than the size of ad hoc groups, but observed numerous effects of that variable on the ongoing course of interaction among students who were discussing human relations problems. Bakeman and Dabbs (1976) have described the use of analytic tools by which the overwhelming mass of data generated by experiments dealing with a stream of collective action can be reduced to manageable proportions, and Davis (1973) and Laughlin (1980) have described and demonstrated strategies by which important aspects of interpersonal process can be inferred from data concerning individual competencies and group outcomes. Although these and other studies indicate that laboratory-experimental methods can be used profitably to examine the processes of social systems, they do not suggest that a reasonable "fit" is easily achieved. Nor do they disprove the contention that the method may sometimes (or very often) lead to unfortunate adjustments in what is studied. It is undoubtedly easier to defend the merits of laboratory experiments if one is an Aristotelian at heart than if one is infused with Galilean fervor.

It is pertinent to ask why investigative social psychology, whose early growth was in part a reaction to the rigid experimentalism of behaviorist psychology, came eventually to admire experimental designs. A partial answer to this question may lie in the emergence of two extremely persuasive leaders during the period following World War II. Kurt Lewin and Carl Hovland were inspiring teachers and impressive models who influenced the thinking of a generation of social psychologists. Lewin advocated *both* a laboratory-experimental and a field-descriptive approach to data gathering, but his emphasis on the importance of the "pure case" legitimized attempts to create replicas of complex social phenomena within the laboratory, and most of his many highly productive students built their reputations by doing laboratory research. Hovland realized that his laboratory experiments failed in important ways to mirror the conditions that are likely to prevail in "real life" (Hovland, 1959). But he nevertheless concentrated his major efforts on experimental research, and popularized the laboratory approach to studies of attitude change.

Of course, one cannot be entirely sure to what extent Lewin and Hovland made their times, *or* were made by their times. But they were at least strong catalysts in the development of an experimentally oriented social psychology. A reasonable alternative (or supplement) to a "great man" explanation is implied by House (1977), who noted that both psychologically and sociologically trained social psychologists tended to retreat toward their points of origin following the adventurous and affluent 1950s. Psychology was much more firmly tied to experimental methods at that time than was sociology, and it was the psychologically reared members of the flock who most thoroughly accepted the experimental paradigm.

D. SUMMARY: DOMINANT PARADIGMATIC PREFERENCES OF SOCIAL PSYCHOLOGY

As we have noted earlier, social psychology can hardly be said to have settled upon a single, universally acclaimed paradigm. But our brief historical review has identified a number of goals, priorities, and practices that have become characteristic of the field.

Most social psychologists agree that things are not always what they seem to be, and that truth and understanding can sometimes be reached by using an intellectual artifice that shifts attention from that which is directly apprehended to that which is too small, fleeting, hidden, or obscure to register in direct experience. But most social psychologists are much less willingto explore the notion that what is perceived as a "whole" may, in fact, be a fragment from an interacting system. Social psychology is a discipline that attempts to reduce observed phenomena to unobserved elements but which is generally loath to construct unobservable wholes from observed parts.

Given this preference, it is not surprising that investigative social psychology has almost always regarded the single individual as the "actor" whose behavior is to be understood, predicted, and possibly controlled. Sometimes the object under examination is the individual in the midst of other real, live individuals, but often it is the individual in the midst of his own thoughts, memories, and imaginings about other individuals. Although conceiving the group as an acting unit has not often been branded as completely illegitimate, such departures from individualism have been comparatively rare and have sometimes been regarded as nonscientific flights into fantasyland.

The individual examined by social psychologists responds to the proximate acts of real or imagined others, but his response is unlikely to become a stimulus for other persons or an event in a continuing series of events. He functions as though he has been allotted a series of trials, each ending when he has done something an investigator finds noteworthy. Explanations of the individual's noteworthy acts usually highlight the impact of some other event in the immediate situation, thoughts or perceptions prompted by the immediate situation, or dispositional qualities of the individual himself.

Although events in the individual's immediate situation are regarded as instigating stimuli, the real field of action is thought to lie within the individual. As Sampson (1981) put it:

> Behavioristic accounts give us the person as a passive receptacle upon which an active world writes its messages; cognitivism has reversed this view by giving us a passive reality upon which the cognitively active person writes. (p. 734)

Contemporary social psychology features cognitivism and the active internal arena it implies.

Consistent with their strong preference for proximal explanations, social psychologists rely heavily on observed indicants of processes or states within the individual. Many of these indicants are, in fact, self-reports which are accorded a surprisingly high level of validity even when they are retrospective accounts of emotion-laden events of the distant past.

There seems to be no clear consensus concerning which internal factors provide the "best" explanation of the individual's social behavior, but many social psychologists are still looking for the internal mechanism(s) or dispositional qualities that will simultaneously account for alleged *high consistency of the individual* across families of situations and observed *inconsistency across individuals* in the same situations.

Single-factor explanations are preferred over few-factors explanations. Multifactor explanations of the kind required by a systems theory approach are likely to be interpreted as suggesting that social psychology is not a predictive science; if outcomes are determined by the reciprocal actions of many factors we are doomed to function as historians who study unique, non-reoccurring events.

Many social psychologists complain about the restrictive impact of experimental designs, but social psychology remains an overwhelmingly experimental endeavor, strongly dominated by laboratory research. Although the merits of field experiments have often been extolled, and sometimes overstated, published accounts of field research increased by only about 10% during the period 1961– 1974 (Mark, Cook, & Diamond, 1976). Descriptive, nonexperimental studies, such as those published by Cantril (1941) during the 1940s, have few advocates and seem to have lost ground to more highly controlled empirical studies.

IV. What Has Become of Social Psychology?

My colleague's prediction seems to have been on target; the 1990s are still several years away and already social psychology is hard to recognize. Most of what is published in the *Journal of Personality and Social Psychology* or *Journal of Experimental Social Psychology* is equally monadic as other brands of psychology, and equally experimental and cognitive. Textbook definitions stress social psychology's focus on responses to social stimuli, but that is not a very strong claim to distinctiveness. Much of what the personality theorist does is also concerned with the individual's responses to other persons, as is the work of the neobehaviorists. Although psychologists who concentrate on learning processes, child development, abnormal behavior, or one or another brand of cognitive processes are not quite so thoroughly committed to *social* stimulation as are people who call themselves social psychologists, their work would be drastically impoverished if responses to other humans were somehow withdrawn from it. Furthermore, sociology, anthropology, and other social sciences are also concerned with the kinds of stimulation that textbooks claim as the special province of social psychology.

During recent decades social psychology has not even validated the textbook claim very consistently. In 1957, Festinger presented his theory of cognitive dissonance, in which motivating inconsistencies did not have to involve anyone but the actor himself. Very much of the vast literature generated by that theory focused on the internal or external activities of an actor who, presuming himself to be a rational, consistent person, struggles to reconcile his own overt behaviors with his personal beliefs and preferences. Dissonance research, which dominated the social psychological journals during the late 1960s and much of the 1970s, often had nothings very explicit to say about responses to the real or imagined actions of anyone but the actor himself. It is not surprising that Festinger is quoted (Tajfel, 1972a) as having said he ceased to be a social psychologist long before he embarked on his more recent research on vision. What is surprising is that very many persons who called themselves social psychologists spent several years avidly exploring every nook and cranny of dissonance theory.

During February 1985 I encountered three intriguing newspaper/magazine articles that seem to have something to say about the elusive identity of social psychology. In one of them a social psychologist from University X is quoted as contending that IQ tests are in the model-T stage and do a very poor job assessing intelligence. In another article a social psychologist from University Y is said to have concluded that there are no discernable differences between the creativity of males and females. And in the third report a social psychologist from College Z proposed that people who become political dictators have had especially troubled childhoods. I am not sure how valid any of these three generalizations may be, but I am even less sure how being a social psychologist qualifies one as an authority on these matters. More importantly, I wonder what is, and what is not, social psychology.

The careful reader will have detected a note of regret in my description of the route social psychology has followed. But that reader will also have noticed that I have not said the route was wrong or useless—only that it led to a loss of identity and did not nurture the study of groups. Social psychologists have undoubtedly increased people's understanding of attitudes, social cognitions, and motives. Assimilation back into other branches of psychology has probably enriched the parent discipline and made the psychologist's *Homo sapiens* a little less like a hermit, robot, or rat. If that has indeed been the case perhaps it is enough; social psychology can be said to have had a commendable career.

But one may nevertheless regret that social psychologists have increasingly examined phenomena that are already being researched by other branches of psychology, and from perspectives that are rarely unique. The early appeal of social psychology was due in no small measure to its willingness to raise questions that were not already being investigated, or to make new methodological or substantive assumptions when seeking answers to old questions. Needless to say, such innovative steps were not always successful, but they gave the field an aura of freshness that seems to have faded during recent decades.

V.   Does the Group Have a Future
in Social Psychology?

New questions and perspectives need not necessarily be focused on groups. But if one wishes to reconstruct a social psychology that is social as well as psychological, the group is a good place to commence renovations.

A.   WHO SHOULD BE CONCERNED ABOUT SOCIAL SYSTEMS?

A dominant paradigmatic assumption of social psychology holds that social behavior is produced by individuals, not groups. Consequently, the ''dependent variable" in most social psychological theory and research concerns some aspect of the individual's actions, perceptions, or feelings. Other persons may separately or collectively affect that dependent variable, but the major concern is usually the single responding individual, and little attention is paid to the network of events by which persons in the stimulus group are influencing one another. Thus the prevailing perspective focuses on small, segregated parts of a much larger pattern of ongoing action. It leaves little room for a systems approach to the understanding of social behavior.

Any attempt to treat the group as a system will presumably require that we temporarily replace the psychologist's little black box with a whole cluster of little black boxes, each with its own flashing lights, turning wheels, and chirping tones. The first stage of our task will entail the meticulous observation of the sequential and concurrent behaviors of those boxes. Like astronomers studying the skies we will need to search for relationships among the observable actions of the "separate parts" while maintaining the belief that they may actually constitute a larger "whole" that has not yet registered in our direct experience. Video tape machines may be helpful in documenting our observations, and computers may be useful in locating subtle interrelationships within the vast array of data we accumulate. But we must beware of the temptation to regard computers as easy substitutes for observation; after all, Johann Kepler's mathematical ingenuity could not have revealed the solar system until other astronomers had spent thousands of hours mapping the migrations of celestial bodies.

So long as social psychology is guided by its current paradigmatic assumptions there is little reason to believe it will mount or support a research program of the kind I am describing. But there are minor currents, both within and outside of social psychology, that might possibly combine to do the job. Perhaps the most promising is a stream of research on *expressive behavior* (cf. Cappella, 1981) and *nonverbal communication*. Scholars who investigate these forms of interpersonal behavior usually rely heavily on outside observers; they do not assume that actor(s) can or will report their own behaviors accurately. The observations of such scholars ordinarily focus on at least two actors simultaneously and typically extend over a somewhat protracted period of time (i.e., more than a few minutes). Unfortunately, observations of units larger than the dyad are comparatively rare, and as Simmel (1950) and others have noted, the dyad does not reveal many of the complexities that are found in larger assemblages. Moreover, concentration on "expressive" and "nonverbal" behaviors means that limited attention may be given to human beings' most powerful tool for constructing social systems: their capacity to employ purposeful, semantic language.

Other psychologists who are not in the mainstream of social psychology, and who may not even regard themselves as members of the guild, have also observed interaction processes. As McClintock (1983) has noted, these persons have not ordinarily been interested in discovering how overt acts of interaction are organized. Instead, they have observed interaction in order to address specific substantive or theoretical issues. Thus, for example, Gottman (1979) was attempting to differentiate between distressed and nondistressed marital pairs, Patterson (1979) wished to change the dysfunctional relationships between aggressive children and their mothers, and Raush (1965) wanted to identify the determinants of friendly versus unfriendly acts of children in social settings. In these and numerous other studies, observation has been focused on specialized kinds of acts occurring in the interaction of specialized dyads or larger sets of people. By themselves they provide only limited data concerning the organization of ongoing interaction; but the data are useful and the methods and conclusions may prove to be essential to a broader understanding of groups.

The study of "close relationships" (cf. Kelley, Berscheid, Christensen, Harvey, Houston, Levinger, Peplau, & Peterson, 1983) is another line of research that might contribute to a social systems approach to groups. Although the data are often obtained through one or another form of self-report, the focus is on relationships between members of dyads over comparatively long periods of time, and the reciprocal nature of dyadic interaction is stressed.

With a shift of emphasis symbolic interactionists might also become strong contributors to a social systems approach. This would require that they focus more intently on observable box-to-box actions and would entail some postponement of their attempts to chart the internal processes by which boxes infer symbolic meanings. It would also demand a more willing acceptance of hardnosed empiricism.

Whether these, and possibly other, rather disparate research traditions will ever combine to support a full-scale investigation of group processes remains to be seen.

B. WHO SHOULD DEAL WITH QUESTIONS CONCERNING
    GROUP EFFECTIVENESS?

Although much of the work of the world is done by crews, teams, and committees, and although society often dispenses rewards to effective social units rather than to effective individuals, neither social psychology nor any other discipline has made a whole-hearted attempt to determine what makes groups perform well or poorly. Because the dominant paradigmatic preference of contemporary social psychology is to focus on the performance of individuals, it is not surprising that questions concerning group effectiveness have generally been left to students of business or industrial management, athletic coaches, or military planners. To be sure, a small minority of social psychologists (e.g., Bales, 1950; Davis, 1973; Davis *et al.*, 1976; Janis, 1972; Laughlin, 1980; McGrath, 1984; Steiner, 1972) have concerned themselves with the issue of group performance, but the questions that are yet to be raised almost certainly outnumber those that have been formulated and researched.

It is difficult to believe that a problem area that is so fraught with practical consequences will continue to go unclaimed. But whether it will be claimed by social psychology or by some other discipline remains in doubt.

C. WHERE SHOULD THE INDIVIDUAL'S SOCIAL BEHAVIOR BE OBSERVED?

The dominant paradigmatic preference of contemporary social psychology is to rely upon individuals to report their own social behaviors, or to observe the individual's conduct in rather specialized, contrived situations. The latter procedure has yielded interesting evidence concerning social facilitation, conformity, and obedience. But when investigators have examined situations in which individuals function as members of teams working toward a common goal, social facilitation, conformity, and obedience have sometimes been replaced by social loafing, nonconformity, and disobedience. These and other findings indicate that social behavior is influenced by many factors: whether the situation is "information reducing," how readily deindividuation can be achieved, whether the resources of coparticipants seem adequate to accomplish the "group's goal," and other considerations that reflect the nature of the task, the composition of the group, and the value and divisibility of the goal (cf. Kerr, 1983). Thus, even if one were interested only in the social behavior of individuals, one could not expect to gain a very representative sample of such behaviors without observing individuals in the social systems in which they are from time to time embedded. This is a conclusion that denies the validity of F. H. Allport's early contention that individuals in groups behave just as they would alone, only more so. It is a conclusion that Allport himself would probably have accepted during his later years, but one that does not harmonize well with the current paradigmatic preferences of social psychology.

Whether there is a future for the group within social psychology remains to be seen. My own hunch is that the group is too important to an understanding of human behavior and the workings of society to be forever neglected. If social psychologists do not research the group, someone else surely will.

VI. A Disclaimer

Nothing in this article should be construed to imply that all social psychologists should stop studying the isolated individual, or that attitudes, emotions, and cognitive processes are irrelevant to an understanding of social behavior.

People do not cease being people when they function as parts of social systems. But they often function quite differently than they would alone (cf. Konečni, 1979), and the actions of interacting persons are likely to be intertwined in ways that are difficult to infer from a study of isolated individuals. Perhaps it will someday be demonstrated that everything important about groups and human interaction could have been deduced from a burgeoning knowledge of single individuals. But that day is, at best, somewhere in the distant future, and there is no assurance that studying individuals alone is the most fruitful way of learning about groups. If the proper study of man is man perhaps the proper study of groups is groups. In any event, studying groups is worth the try, and there is reason to believe that it will yield information that would be extremely difficult to obtain by focusing on individuals.

Consider, for example, Bales's (1953) findings concerning the kinds of acts that follow other kinds of acts when individuals function as group members. Even if such statistical regularities could have been deduced from an examination of individual behaviors, someone would have had to observe group actions in order to confirm those deductions. The same can be said about Stephan and Mishler's (1952) demonstration that the participation rates of group members (in at least certain kinds of groups) can be described pretty accurately by an exponential curve. Even post hoc attempts to account for such patterning as a consequence of individuals' propensities have proven to be less than satisfactory. A third example of the merits of studying groups has been provided by Bavelas, Hastorf, Gross, and Kite (1965), whose findings indicated that reinforcement of a single member of a group was not sufficient to increase his participation rate; to achieve a change it was necessary to administer simultaneous negative reinforcements to other members. While this conclusion might conceivably have been deduced from literature concerning typical "one-on-one" reinforcement procedures, the authors apparently did not deduce it from the findings of such research, and they proceeded to observe ongoing interaction before reaching their conclusion.

The author is neither affirming nor denying that all phenomena at the group level can be reduced to the individual level. Instead, he is contending that the prediction that all group phenomena can be so reduced (when and if we get around to deciding what those phenomena are) puts the cart before the horse. Until we know more about what happens at the group level that prediction cannot possibly be tested, and its popularity as an item of social psychological folklore probably inhibits the careful observation of groups.

It seems reasonable to expect that what happens at the group level cannot contradict what we accurately understand to happen at the individual level, and that what happens at the individual level cannot contradict what we accurately understand to happen at the group level. Increased understanding of either level may augment or correct our understanding of the other. In 1985 the group is the neglected member of this partnership; it urgently needs attention.

VII. Conclusions

If the evidence and interpretations set forth in this article are basically correct two conclusions seem justified. Substantively and methodologically the contemporary version of social psychology so thoroughly overlaps other areas of psychology that it has little claim to distinctiveness, and social psychology has failed to provide a very supportive intellectual environment for the study of groups. Because these characteristics of the discipline reflect the dominant paradigmatic preferences of the field they are unlikely to change very rapidly in the near future.

That social psychology has not provided a very nurturing environment for the study of groups seems self-evident. A discipline that highlights the proximal (often internal) antecedents of the individual's behavior in experimental situations, focuses on specific acts of individuals rather than upon sequences of acts, and relies heavily on self-report data is not likely to encourage scholars who wish to examine the system-like qualities of groups. I am led to conclude that the circumstances I described in earlier publications (Steiner, 1974, 1983) were not the only reasons why the group became an endangered species; the intellectual climate within the discipline was probably at least as important a reason.

It is not my contention that individualistic social psychology should somehow be suppressed and replaced by a more ''groupy'' variety. But individualistic social psychology should be combined and coordinated with an almost nonexistent social psychology of *collective* behavior, without which it often provides a distorted picture of the individual's functioning. We should heed the admonitions of Cooley, Mead, and Murphy cited earlier in this article: there are no groups without individuals, and there are very few individuals who are not also functioning parts of groups. To conceive either without the other is to create an abstraction that ought to be checked periodically against the reality of their combined existence.

Of course, the evidence and interpretations presented above may be inaccurate. My brief historical review has drawn selectively and perhaps injudiciously on the record of the past, and my interpretations may sometimes have been no more wise than those that led me (Steiner, 1974) to predict a revival of the group by 1980. If errors of either kind have flawed my analysis, they reflect limited knowledge and understanding rather than self-serving bias. I have no personal reason to criticize social psychology which, after all, has been good to me. Indeed, my criticisms of the course social psychology has followed are criticisms of myself as well, for I have rarely deviated very far from the mainstream, and my occasional pleas for a more ''groupy'' social psychology have seldom been matched by actions to promote that end. Now that I am on the verge of retirement I have no reason, other than my candid appraisal of past and present events, to criticize the discipline in which I have participated for more than 30 years. I am aware that criticisms will not improve my golf score or protect me from the future ravages of inflation.

ACKNOWLEDGMENTS

The author is indebted to Seymour Berger and George Levinger for comments concerning an early draft of this article. However, responsibility for the interpretations and conclusions expressed on these pages rests solely with the author.

REFERENCES

Allport, F. H. (1924a). *Social psychology*. Boston: Houghton-Mifflin.
Allport, F. H. (1924b). The group fallacy in relation to social science. *Journal of Abnormal and Social Psychology*, **19**, 60–73.
Allport, F. H. (1961). The contemporary appraisal of an old problem. *Contemporary Psychology*, **6**, 195–197.
Allport, F. H. (1962). A structuronomic conception of behavior: Individual and collective. *Journal of Abnormal and Social Psychology*, **1**, 3–30.
Allport, G. W. (1954). The historical background of modern social psychology. In G. Lindzey (Ed.), *Handbook of social psychology* (Vol. 1). Reading, MA: Addison-Wesley.
Allport, G. W. (1968). The historical background of modern social psychology. In G. Lindzey & E. Aronson (Eds.), *Handbook of social psychology*, (Vol. 1, 2nd Ed.). Reading, MA: Addison-Wesley.
Altman, I. (1976). Environmental psychology and social psychology. *Personality and Social Psychology Bulletin*, **2**, 96–113.
Bakeman, R., & Dabbs, J. M. (1976). Social interaction observed: Some approaches to the analysis of behavior streams. *Personality and Social Psychology Bulletin*, **2**, 335–345.
Bales, R. F. (1950). *Interaction process analysis: A method for the study of small groups*. Cambridge, MA: Addison-Wesley.
Bales, R. F. (1953). The equilibrium problem in small groups. In T. Parsons, R. Bales, & E. Shils (Eds.), *Working papers in the theory of action*. New York: Free Press.
Barker, R. (1963). *The stream of behavior*. New York: Meredith.
Barnard, C. I. (1938). *The function of the executive*. Cambridge, MA: Harvard University Press.
Bartlett, F. C. (1932). *Remembering: A study in experimental and social psychology*. London & New York: Cambridge University Press.
Bavelas, A., Hastorf, A. H., Gross, A. E., & Kite, W. R. (1965). Experiments in the alteration of group structure. *Journal of Experimental Social Psychology*, **1**, 55–70.
Benedict, R. (1934). *Patterns of culture*. Boston: Houghton-Mifflin.
Berkowitz, L. (1962). *Aggression: A social psychological analysis*. New York: McGraw-Hill.
Boring, E. G. (1957). *A history of experimental psychology*. New York: Appleton-Century-Crofts.
Buckley, W. (1967). *Sociology and modern systems theory*. Englewood Cliffs, NJ: Prentice-Hall.
Campbell, D. T. (1958). Common fate, similarity, and other indices of the status of aggregates of persons as social entities. *Behavioral Science*, **3**, 14–25.
Cantril, H. (1941). *The psychology of social movements*. New York: Wiley.
Cappella, J. N. (1981). Mutual influence in expressive behavior:Adult–adult and infant–adult dyadic interaction. *Psychological Bulletin*, **89**, 101–132.
Cassirer, E. (1923). *Substance and function*. (Transl. by W. C. Swabey and M. C. Swabey). Chicago & London: Open Court.

Cooley, C. H. (1964). *Human nature and the social order.* New York: Schocken (originally published in 1902).

Cronbach, L. J. (1975). Beyond the two disciplines of scientific psychology. *American Psychologist,* **30,** 116–127.

Davis, J. H. (1973). Group decision and social interaction: A theory of social decision schemes. *Psychological Review,* **80,** 97–125.

Davis, J. H., Laughlin, P. R., & Komorita, S. S. (1976). The social psychology of small groups: Cooperative and mixed-motive interaction. In M. R. Rosenzweig & L. W. Porter (Eds.), *Annual review of psychology* (pp. 501–541). Palo Alto, CA: Annual Reviews.

Deutsch, M. (1954). Field theory in social psychology. In G. Lindzey (Ed.) *Handbook of social psychology* (Vol. 1, pp. 181–222). Reading, MA: Addison-Wesley.

Durkheim, É. (1895). *Les régles de la méthode sociologique.* Paris: F. Alcan.

Durkheim, É. (1897). *Le suicide.* Paris: F. Alcan. Transl. (1951). Glencoe, IL: Free Press.

Elms, A. C. (1975). The crisis of confidence in social psychology. *American Psychologist,* **30,** 967–976.

Festinger, L. (1957). *A theory of cognitive dissonance.* Evanston, IL: Row, Peterson.

Gerard, R. W. (1942). Higher levels of integration. In R. Redfield (Ed.), *Levels of integration in biological and social systems* (Biological Symposia No. 8, pp. 67–87).

Gergen, K. J. (1973). Social psychology as history. *Journal of Personality and Social Psychology,* **26,** 309–320.

Gottman, J. M. (1979). *Marital interaction: Experimental investigation.* New York: Academic Press.

Hartmann, D. P. (Ed.) (1982). *Using observers to study behavior: New directions for methodology of social and behavioral science.* San Francisco: Jossey-Bass.

Heider, F. (1958). *The psychology of interpersonal relations.* New York: Wiley.

Helmreich, R. (1975). Applied social psychology: The unfulfilled promise. *Personality and Social Psychology Bulletin,* **1,** 548–560.

Homans, G. C. (1950). *The human group.* New York: Harcourt, Brace, Jovanovich.

House, J. S. (1977). The three faces of social psychology. *Sociometry,* **40,** 161–177.

Hovland, C. I. (1959). Reconciling conflicting results derived from experimental and survey studies of attitude change. *American Psychologist,* **14,** 8–17.

Hume, D. (1961). *A treatise of human nature.* New York: Doubleday.

Janis, I. L. (1972). *Victims of groupthink.* Boston: Houghton-Mifflin.

Katz, D., & Kahn, R. (1967). *The social psychology of organzations.* New York: Wiley.

Kelley, H., Berscheid, E., Christensen, A., Harvey, J., Houston, T., Levinger, G., Peplau, L., & Peterson, D. (1983). *Close relationships.* San Francisco: Freeman.

Kerr, N. L. (1983). Motivation losses in small groups: A social dilemma analysis. *Journal of Personality and Social Psychology,* **45,** 819–828.

Kluckhohn, C. (1954). Culture and behavior. In G. Lindzey (Ed.),*Handbook of social psychology* (Vol. 2). Reading, MA: Addison-Wesley.

Konečni, V. J. (1979). The role of aversive events in the development of intergroup conflict. In W. Austin & S. Worchel (Eds.), *Social psychology of intergroup relations.* Monterey, CA: Brooks/Cole.

Kuhn, T. S. (1962). *The structure of scientific revolutions.* Chicago: University of Chicago Press.

Laughlin, P. R. (1980). Social combination processes of cooperative problem-solving groups on verbal intellective tasks. In M. Fishbein (Ed.), *Progress in social psychology.* Hillsdale, NJ: Erlbaum.

Lewicki, P. (1982). Social psychology as viewed by its practitioners. *Personality and Social Psychology Bulletin,* **8,** 409–416.

Lewin, K. (1935). *A dynamic theory of personality.* New York: McGraw-Hill.

Lewin, K. (1947a). Frontiers in group dynamics, I. *Human Relations,* **1,** 5–41.

Lewin, K. (1947b). Frontiers in group dynamics, II. *Human Relations,* **1,** 143–158.

Lewin, K. (1947c). Group decision and social change. In T. M. Newcomb & E. Hartley (Eds.), *Readings in social psychology* (pp. 330–344). New York: Holt.

Lewin, K. (1948). *Resolving social conflicts.* New York: Harper.

Lindzey, G. (Ed.) (1954). *Handbook of social psychology* (2 Vols). Reading, MA: Addison-Wesley.

Manicas, P. T., & Secord, P. F. (1983). Implications for psychology of the new philosophy of science. *American Psychologist,* **38,** 399–413.

Mark, M. M., Cook, T. D., & Diamond, S. S. (1976). Fourteen years of social psychology: A growing commitment to field experimentation. *Personality and Social Psychology Bulletin,* **2,** 154–157.

McClintock, E. (1983). Interaction. In H. Kelley, E. Berscheid, A. Christensen, J. Harvey, T. Huston, G. Levinger, E. McClintock, L. Peplau, & D. Peterson (Eds.), *Close relationships.* San Francisco: Freeman.

McGrath, J. E. (1984). *Groups: Interaction and performance.* Englewood Cliffs, NJ: Prentice-Hall.

McGuire, W. J. (1969). The nature of attitudes and attitude change. In G. Lindzey & E. Aronson (Eds.), *Handbook of social psychology* (Vol. 3). Reading, MA: Addison-Wesley.

McGuire, W. J. (1973). The yin and yang of progressin social psychology: Seven Koan. *Journal of Personality and Social Psychology,* **26,** 446–456.

Mead, G. H. (1934). *Mind, self and society.* (C. Morris, Ed.). Chicago: University of Chicago Press.

Mead, M. (1930). *Growing up in New Guinea.* New York: Morrow.

Miller, J. G. (1955). Toward a general theory for the behavioral sciences. *American Psychologist,* **10,** 513–531.

Murchinson, C. (Ed.) (1935). *A handbook of social psychology.* Worcester, MA: Clark University Press.

Murphy, G. (1947). *Personality.* New York: Harper.

Parsons, T. (1951). *The social system.* Glencoe, IL: Free Press.

Parsons, T., & Shils, E. (Eds.) (1951). *Toward a general theory of action.* Cambridge, MA: Harvard University Press.

Patterson, G. R. (1979). A performance theory for coercive family interaction. In R. B. Cairns (Ed.), *The analysis of social interaction: Methods, issues, and illustrations.* Hillsdale, NJ: Erlbaum.

Pepitone, A. (1976). Toward a normative and comparative biocultural social psychology. *Journal of Personality and Social Psychology,* **4,** 641–653.

Proshansky, H. M. (1976). Comments on environmental and social psychology. *Journal of Personality and Social Psychology,* **2,** 359–363.

Raush, H. L. (1965). Interaction sequences. *Journal of Personality and Social Psychology,* **2,** 487–499.

Rice, S. A. (1928). *Qualitative methods in politics.* New York: Knopf.

Ring, K. (1967). Experimental social psychology: Some sober questions about some frivolous values. *Journal of Experimental Social Psychology,* **3,** 113–123.

Rosnow, R. L. (1981). *Paradigms in transition.* London & New York: Oxford University Press.

Ross, L. (1977). The intuitive psychologist and his shortcomings: Distortions in the attribution process. In L. Berkowitz (Ed.), *Advances in experimental social psychology* (Vol. 10). New York: Academic Press.

Sampson, E. E. (1977). Psychology and the American ideal. *Journal of Personality and Social Psychology,* **35,** 767–782.

Sampson, E. E. (1981). Cognitive psychology as ideology. *American Psychologist,* **36,** 730–743.

Schlenker, B. R. (1976). Social psychology and science: Another look. *Personality and Social Psychology Bulletin,* **2,** 384–390.

Sears, R. R. (1951). A theoretical framework for social behavior and personality development. *American Psychologist,* **6,** 476–482.

Secord, P. F. (1976). Transhistorical and transcultural theory. *Personality and Social Psychology,* **2,** 418–420.

Shaw, M. E. (1971). *Group dynamics: The psychology of small group behavior.* New York: McGraw-Hill.

Silverman, I. (1971). Crisis in social psychology: The relevance of relevance. *American Psychologist,* **26,** 583–584.

Simmel, G. (1950). *The sociology of Georg Simmel* (Transl. by K. H. Wolff). Glencoe, IL: Free Press.

Skinner, B. F. (1975). The steep and thorny way to a science of behavior. In R. Harre (Ed.), *Problems of scientific revolution.* London & New York: Oxford University Press.

Steiner, I. D. (1972). *Group process and productivity.* New York: Academic Press.

Steiner, I. D. (1974). Whatever happened to the group in social psychology? *Journal of Experimental Social Psychology,* **10,** 94–108.

Steiner, I. D. (1983). Whatever happened to the touted revival of the group? In H. Blumberg, A. Hare, V. Kent, & M. Davies (Eds.), *Small groups and social interaction* (Vol. 2). New York: Wiley.

Stephan, F. F., & Mishler, E. G. (1952). The distribution of participation in small groups: An exponential approximation. *American Sociological Review,* **17,** 598–608.

Stevens, S. S. (1951). Mathematics, measurement, and psychophysics. In S. S. Stevens (Ed.), *Handbook of experimental psychology.* New York: Wiley.

Stokols, D. (1976). Social-unit analysis as a framework for research in environmental and social psychology. *Personality and Social Psychology Bulletin,* **2,** 350–358.

Tajfel, H. (1972a). Experiments in a vacuum. In J. Israel & H. Tajfel (Eds.), *The context of social psychology.* New York: Academic Press.

Tajfel, H. (1972b). Individual, inter-individual and social psychology. In J. Israel & H. Tajfel (Eds.), *The context of social psychology.* New York: Academic Press.

Thomas, W. I., & Znaniecki, F. (1918–1920). *The Polish peasant in Europe and America* (5 Vols). Boston: Badger.

Thorngate, W. (1976). "In general" vs. "It depends": Some comments on the Gergen–Schlenker debate. *Personality and Social Psychology Bulletin,* **2,** 404–410.

Titchener, E. B. (1972). *Systematic psychology: A prolegomena.* Ithaca, NY: Cornell University Press. Originally published (1929). New York: Macmillan.

Watson, J. B. (1919). *Psychology from the standpoint of a behaviorist.* New York: Lippincott.

Wertheimer, M. (1923). Untersuchungen Zur Lehre von der Gestalt. II. *Psychologich Forschung,* **4,** 301–350.

Zimbardo, P. G. (1972). Pathology and imprisonment. *Society,* **9**(6).

SOCIAL CATEGORIZATION: IMPLICATIONS FOR CREATION AND REDUCTION OF INTERGROUP BIAS

David A. Wilder

DEPARTMENT OF PSYCHOLOGY
RUTGERS, THE STATE UNIVERSITY
OF NEW JERSEY
NEW BRUNSWICK, NEW JERSEY

ADVANCES IN EXPERIMENTAL
SOCIAL PSYCHOLOGY, VOL. 19

Copyright © 1986 by Academic Press, Inc.
All rights of reproduction in any form reserved.

Between two hawks, which flies the higher pitch;
Between two dogs, which hath the deeper mouth;
Between two blades, which bears the better temper;
Between two horses, which doth bear him best;
Between two girls, which hath the merriest eye;
     (Shakespeare; Henry VI Part I, Act II, Scene IV)

All disciplines struggle with the tension between painstaking cultivation of theory and desire to see its fruits in immediate practice. No discipline wrestles with the theory–practice dialectic more strongly than social psychology. And within social psychology no subject has provided a richer field for theoretical and empirical jousts than intergroup bias, whether it be the study of attitudes toward (prejudice), beliefs about (stereotypes), or behaviors directed at (discrimination) social groups (e.g., Allport, 1954; Austin & Worchel, 1979; Billing, 1976; Stephan, 1985). For those seeking to understand human behavior, intergroup bias is an attractive topic because it encompasses the major areas of person perception, attitudes, and group dynamics. For those seeking to change human behavior, intergroup bias exists as a vexing, omnipresent obstacle to social harmony.

Numerous attempts have been made to explain intergroup bias (e.g., Allport, 1954; Ashmore, 1970a). Some explanations focus on characteristics of either the biased party or the target of bias. Voltaire put it forcefully and succinctly: "Prejudice is the reasoning of the stupid" (*Sur la Noi Naturelle IV*). Others examine conflict over limited resources or mutually exclusive objectives. Still others cite normative demands from the social system of which the groups are a part. These approaches range in levels of analyses from the intraindividual to the intergroup. They are, consequently, more often complementary than contradictory, though frequently less than complimentary to each other. It is unlikely that any single explanation is totally misguided, and certainly no one alone can account for the many forms and degrees of intergroup bias. All explanations do share, however, an implicit assumption that bias is imposed on the origanism. That is, persons either learn their biases (e.g., from role models or negative experiences with outgroup members) or develop a deficient style of thought that disposes them to be biased (e.g., authoritarian personality, dogmatism). The underlying assumption is that we all begin as unbiased individuals. This assumption is false. In this article I argue that the mere categorization of persons into different groups engages a series of assumptions that foster intergroup biases. Certainly, other factors can and do exacerbate bias, but the argument here is that categorization, per se, propels the individual down the road to bias. Tactics for reducing bias must, therefore, consider the implications of categorization processes if they are to be maximally effective.

In recent years the application of cognitive research to person perception has surged into the void created by a decline in interpersonal and group research (e.g., Carroll & Payne, 1976; Hamilton, 1979, 1981; Harvey, Ickes, & Kidd, 1976, 1978, 1981; Hastie, Ostrom, Ebbesen, Wyer, Hamilton, & Carlston, 1980; Steiner, 1974; Wyer & Carlston, 1979). Findings from the realm of attention, categorization, and memory have been applied vigorously to more molar actions including intergroup relations. A cognitive approach to intergroup bias views bias as a product of the ways individuals select, structure, and process social information. This orientation is structural and can be thought of as a context in which more specific, often functional explanations may operate (e.g., frustration–aggression, incompatible goals). For instance, competition for limited resources may create ill will between specific individuals. That antagonism is likely to generalize to the groups of which they are members because of assumptions of uniformity within groups. Furthermore, generalization will be greater to the extent that frustrating members appear to be highly representative of their group.

I. Perceiving Persons as a Group

A. CATEGORIES AS CONSTRUCTS: CRITERIA FOR INCLUSION

On the simplest level, groups may be defined as categories of persons subject to the same principles of organization and inference attributed to any category. Like any object category, a person's representation of a social group should approximate the actual organization of the environment (Rosch, 1977, 1978). (Consult Lingle, Altom, & Medin, 1985, for a discussion of similarities and differences between social and natural object categories.) Categories emerge as a consequence of observing correlations between objects and attributes. But simple positive associations are not, however, sufficient to give a category utility. There must also exist elements that do not show the correlation. In other words, "we are what we are because 'they' are not what we are" (Tajfel, 1979). Thus, all humans belong to the category *Homo sapiens,* yet this common membership is unlikely to be invoked unless a comparison is made with a nonhuman entity, such as an animal or extraterrestrial. Use of a category is dependent on both the existence of similarity among members and differences between members and nonmembers. Olson and Attneave (1970) made a similar point about visual perception, employing an analysis of variance (ANOVA) analogy. If the variance (dissimilarity among elements) between two regions of the visual field significantly exceeds the variance within regions, then we conclude that the regions differ.

Boundaries that demarcate category members from nonmembers may vary in their explicitness. At one extreme are boundaries based on *fixed* criteria that specify enduring attributes, impervious to the specific situational context. For instance, the category *mammal* requires certain characteristics for including an organism. At the other extreme are *relational* boundaries determined by the configuration of the immediate field (Lewin, 1935); in other words, by the relations among the elements at that time. Changes in relationships in the field may alter the categories even though the elements themselves remain the same. Gestalt principles of perceptual organization (e.g., common fate, similarity, proximity, frequency of association, "good" figure) are examples of field-dependent boundaries (Campbell, 1958; Pomerantz, 1981). Similarity of a stimulus to a prototype of the category is a field-dependent boundary. Stimuli that are somewhat similar may be assigned to the category in the absence of better matches but omitted when better fitting stimuli are available. One may also look to the perceiver for idiosyncratic or *personal* criteria for the creation and use of categories (Levine, Chein, & Murphy, 1947; Postman & Brown, 1952). Categories may be imposed by individuals according to their assumptions about what should go together given their values and needs. For instance, an individual who is set or primed for a particular category is likely to select and recall information relevant to that category (e.g., Hastie, 1980).

Whether by satisfying fixed, relational, or personal boundary criteria, stimuli are organized into categories. And categorization has predictable consequences. To begin with, categorization accentuates perceived intracategory similarity and intercategory dissimilarity beyond what may actually exist. Tajfel and Wilkes (1963) provide a good demonstration of this with object categories. They showed subjects a series of lines; each line differed from an adjacent line by a constant amount. When the lines were categorized into two groups (A and B) by splitting the series in half, subjects tended to underestimate differences in lengths within the A and B categories while overestimating differences between adjacent lines across categories.

Turning to the person perception literature, an enormous amount of research has examined distortions in the encoding and retrieval of information that is either consistent or inconsistent with categorical expectations (e.g., Cohen, 1981; Hastie, 1980; Wyer & Srull, 1980). Much of this research has demonstrated systematic biases in the direction of assimilating stimuli to expectations of the category to which the stimuli have been assigned. Nevertheless, other evidence indicates that information discrepant with expectations about the category can be accurately recalled. Discrepant information may be scrutinized more carefully to understand why it exists. Such special attention may facilitate later retrieval (Hastie & Kumar, 1979; Wyer & Hartwick, 1980). Clearly, categorical blinders pose limited rather than totalitarian restrictions.

B. SOCIAL GROUPS AS CATEGORIES

Do we perceive social groups as little more than categories of people not very different from categories of animals, vegetables, or minerals? In an intensive comparison of social and object categories, Lingle *et al.* (1985) concluded that they do differ in several ways. For instance, in comparison with object categories, social categories have a greater variety of structures, are less likely to be organized hierarchically, and exhibit greater stability within than between persons. To these I would add two more differences that are especially relevant for intergroup relations.

First, social groups are reflexive in that they can act upon and change themselves (Wilder & Cooper, 1981). Through interaction (or the prospect of interaction) group members can influence one another, thereby changing the group. The extent to which groups do evolve varies widely. Consider, for example, an experiential group whose climate varies as members drift in and out versus a social club whose traditions rigidly guide behavior regardless of who the members are.

Second, the perceiver's self-concept may be intertwined with the social category. Three possibilities exist: (1) no relationship between the perceiver and the group, (2) membership in the group (ingroup), and (3) membership in a complementary group (ingroup/outgroup).

Relevance of social categorization for the perceiver's identity suggests that different persons may look at the same social situation and categorize persons in different ways. The grouping or carving reflects the perceiver's cognitive schemas as well as any external cues that force a particular organization. As an illustration, a student enrolled in a large lecture course may regard his or her class and another section of that course as aggregates; two separate collections of individuals. To use Olson and Attneave's (1970) terminology, the between-class variance (heterogeneity) is not different from the within-class variance. Another student may categorize some members of the class who appear to interact frequently, (outgroup). Yet another student may interact with a few others on a project and define herself or himself as a member of that group (ingroup). Finally, a fourth student may compare her or his ingroup with another group in the class (ingroup/outgroup).

Moreover, a perceiver may regard identical collections of persons as groups or independent aggregates depending on the situational context. For example, I may consider the category "male" to be a collection of relatively heterogeneous individuals linked by a common sex but of little importance to my sense of self. I interact with other males not as a male but as a colleague, a parent, and so forth. But if a woman addresses me as a "man" or behaves toward me in a manner that defines me by my membership in the male group, I should experience a sense of identification with the category and should either act in accord with my expectations of how males should behave or attempt to communicate a different identity.

C. SUMMARY

Two questions were considered in the preceding discussion: (1) What is the essential feature of a social group and (2) do groups differ from more general object categories. I have argued that the critical feature of a group is a boundary; that which distinguishes members from nonmembers. Groups have little utility if they are so inclusive that nonmembers cannot be found. As an illustration, anthropologists have reported that isolated social groups are not likely to harbor characteristics (e.g., tribal name and symbols) indicating a strong sense of in-group identity (Mead, 1937). Representations of social groups differ from object categories in that (1) we must allow for change in groups as members come and go and influence one another and (2) groups help to determine our self-identities.

II.   Consequences of Social Categorization

What are the assumptions persons have about others who are categorized as a social group? Does the mere act of categorizing actors into a group lead to a different set of inferences than if they are perceived to be unrelated to one another? We can look across several levels of analyses to examine effects of social categorization: (1) assumptions of similarity among group members (Section II,A), (2) perceived meaningfulness of their behavior (Section II,B), (3) attributions of causality for their actions (Section II,C), (4) persuasiveness or social impact of their actions (Section II,D).

A.   ASSUMPTIONS OF SIMILARITY AMONG GROUP MEMBERS

If social categorization follows the principles of object categorization, then persons should be viewed as more similar to one another if they are thought to be a group. Wilder (1978e) showed subjects a videotape of four individuals who were depicted as either members of a group or unrelated individuals (aggregate). In the group tape the actors sat at a common table and wore tags identifying their group. In the aggregate condition the actors were seated separately and wore no group symbol. (Distance between actors and actors' behaviors were held constant across tapes.) After listening to one actor's opinions, subjects predicted how similar another actor's opinions and actions would be to those of the first actor. As expected, subjects assumed greater similarity of beliefs and behaviors between group members than between persons in the aggregate. To quote Allport's gustatory summation: "The category saturates all that it contains with the same ideational and emotional flavor" (Allport, 1954, p. 20).

Assumption of intragroup similarity may bias recall about group members so that homogeneity is overestimated. Research on prototypes has shown that persons significantly distort their recollections about category members so as to make them more similar to the prototype of that category (Cantor & Mischel, 1977; Cohen, 1981; Snyder & Uranowitz, 1978). For example, Cohen (1981) reported that persons were more likely to recall having seen "librarianlike" qualities in the behavior of a stimulus person when she was allegedly a librarian than when she was presented as a waitress. Taylor, Fiske, Etcoff, and Ruderman (1978) found subjects to be less accurate in distinguishing among members of a social category (race or sex) than between members of different categories when asked to recall the speakers from a conversation they heard.

B. INFORMATION CONVEYED BY GROUP MEMBERS

When we observe objects, we do not see a continuous field of light. Rather, we chunk or organize some portions of the field into distinct patterns and figure–ground relationships (Pomerantz, 1981). Similarly, Newtson and others (e.g., Barker, 1963) have argued that perceivers organize the actor's "behavioral stream" into discrete chunks or units. Newtson (1973) showed subjects a video tape of an actor and asked them to divide the actor's behavior into units by pushing a button attached to an event recorder whenever the actor produced a meaningful act. The number of units a person used to partition the actor's behavior appears to be determined by both the nature of the actor's behavior and the perceiver's set. As Newtson (1973, 1976) and Wilder (1978a,b) have shown, unpredictable behavior is segmented into more meaningful units and is judged to be more dispositional (actor generated) than is predictable behavior. Ebbesen (1980) and Cohen (1981) have reported that persons instructed to form an impression (as compared to persons instructed to memorize) employed a finer grain analysis (i.e., more units) of the actor's behavior.

Behavior by members of a group should be divided into fewer meaningful units than the same behavior performed by an aggregate of individuals. This prediction follows from the assumptions of within-group similarity discussed in the last section. If group members are expected to act similarly, then similar behavior will be less informative about them than the same behavior among persons not categorized as a group. In most circumstances unanimity among group members does not tell us much about them because consensus can be attributed to a variety of factors—common situation (similarity of environment), common category membership (normative pressures), or common dispositions.

An experiment was designed to test this hypothesis using Newtson's methodology (Wilder, 1984). Subjects were asked to focus on the behavior of one person among four on a video tape and to divide his behavior into meaningful units of action. For some subjects the confederates on the video tape were called a group; they sat at a common table and wore group identification tags on their shirts. For other subjects the confederates were presented as an aggregate of four persons whose presence together was due to chance; they sat in separate chairs and wore no group insignia. The behavior of the confederates was identical on the group and aggregate video tapes. (Actors performed two tasks: continuous assembling of booklets and judgments of responsibility for an accident in a mock civil suit.) As expected, subjects divided the group member's behavior into fewer units than the individual's behavior. Moreover, subjects were more likely to make a dispositional attribution for the actor's behavior when he was among an aggregate (85% made a dispositional attribution) than when he was a group member (58% made a dispositional attribution).

Several interpretations are possible. The larger units used to segment the group member's actions suggest that observers were employing a more molar analysis in processing his behavior. Anticipating interactions (or at least reactions) among group members, observers may not have considered much of the solo behavior of the actor as meaningful. Alternatively, initial organization of the actors as a group set the range of relevant stimuli to monitor at a wide level (i.e., all four persons on the tape). The group as a whole was taken as the unit for monitoring. In the aggregate condition the unit for observation was the individual. Observers could focus closely on his behavior while ignoring the others. In a similar vein Pomerantz (1981) argued that object categorization using Gestalt principles of organization decreases attention to individual members of the unit. But a different group member stands out better when others are grouped than when there is no organization imposed on the objects. Extrapolating to social categories, we would expect deviant group members to provoke close attention.

Results of a recently completed study supported this interpretation (Wilder, 1984). Subjects viewed a video tape of a group and were asked to focus on the behavior of one member. Half way through the tape another group member performed a series of unexpected actions. He began performing the task (construction of booklets) in reverse order. In the aggregate condition the actor behaved the same without the group categorization. Control conditions were included in which all actors behaved the same, yielding a 2 (aggregate, group categorization) × 2 (uniform, different behavior) design. Analysis of the unit data netted an interaction; subjects divided the actor's behavior into fewest units when observing the uniform group. When the actor dissented in the group condition, subjects divided his behavior into as many units as when he was among the aggregate. Dissent in the group individuated the different member whereas dissent among the aggregate had little effect. The dissenter's behavior stood out in the group condition because subjects employed a broader scope (the entire group) in monitoring the actor. As evidence for this, subjects in the group condition were more likely to recall the actions of all persons on the video tape than were subjects in the aggregate condition. These data suggest that perceivers cast a broader attentional net when monitoring the behavior of a group member than when monitoring an individual thought to be independent of others about her or him.

C. CAUSAL ATTRIBUTIONS FOR GROUP MEMBERS

If social categorization affects judgments of similarity among group members and the meaningfulness of their behavior, then we might expect to find categorization effects for attributions of causality as well. The classic assumption in the attribution literature is that we seek to determine whether an actor's behavior was caused by internal or external forces because such information makes our world more predictable (Heider, 1958; Jones & Davis, 1965; Kelley, 1967). When observing the behavior of an actor among others, causal attributions may be made to either the actor's disposition (internal), task requirements (external), or the relationship among the actors such as conformity pressure (external). The plausibility of this last causal agent should be affected by social categorization. Common behavior among group members may reflect expectations or norms of agreement. No such social expectations exist among an aggregate, so that external cause is not as plausible an explanation of common behavior. Consequently, consensus among group members should be attributed more to situational causes (in particular, presence of one another) than the same actions taken by an aggregate. On the other hand, a dissenting group member should evoke a more dispositional attribution because that behavior is out of role (socially undesirable; Jones & Davis, 1965) and focuses attention away from the group as a whole (Wilder, 1984).

In a test of these hypotheses (Wilder, 1978c), subjects observed the behavior of an actor who either agreed or disagreed with three others. The four stimulus persons were either categorized as a single group, categorized as two separate groups, or not categorized at all (aggregate). Subjects indicated the extent to which the actor's behavior was due to dispositional versus situational causes, to personality, to ability, to task characteristics, and to the presence of the others. When a member of a group, the actor was perceived to be more influenced by the situation, by the task, and by the presence of other group members when in agreement than when in disagreement with the others. But agreement or disagreement did not affect attributions when there was no social relationship among the actors (aggregate conditions). Moreover, in the agreement conditions, a significantly stronger situational attribution was made when the actor was a group member than among an aggregate.

D. SOCIAL IMPACT OF GROUP MEMBERS

If social categorization influences assumed similarity among group members, perceived informativeness of their actions, and causal attributions for those actions, then we should expect categorization to have an impact on their potential for social influence. Certainly, persuasiveness of a source depends, in part, on attributions made about the credibility of that source (e.g., Ross, Bierbrauer, & Hoffman, 1976).

Considering that a group member is assumed to be similar to and relatively dependent on fellow members, I reasoned that persons categorized as a group would be less persuasive than persons in an aggregate (Wilder, 1977, 1978d). In a test of this prediction, subjects viewed a video tape of six persons who were categorized either as a single group, two groups of three persons each, three groups of two, or as an aggregate of six unrelated individuals. Subjects heard the actors express their reactions to a legal case that the subjects had just read. The actors' opinions were designed to differ substantially from the common response given by naive subjects to the civil suit. After viewing one of the four tapes, subjects expressed their reactions to the case. Results showed a linear relationship between influence and the number of social units in opposition to the subject. Even though subjects in all conditions heard the same messages from the same confederates, influence was greatest when the actors were not categorized into groups (aggregate of six). Among the group conditions, three groups of two were more influential than two groups of three who, in turn, were more persuasive than a single group of six.

In a subsequent study (Wilder, 1978d), subjects viewed a video tape of a jury deliberation among eight confederates. Race (black, white) and alleged occupation (white collar, blue collar) of the jurors were systematically varied resulting in (1) four single group conditions where all were either black–white collar, black–blue collar, white–white collar, or white–blue collar employees, (2) four two groups conditions where half the jurors were black and half were white with occupation held constant, or half were white collar and half were blue collar with race held constant, and (3) a four groups condition where two jurors fit each of the four combinations of race and occupation (black, white crossed with white collar, blue collar). All subjects heard the same deliberation regardless of what combination of jurors they saw. Social influence varied directly with the number of groups in opposition. Jurors organized as four groups of two were more persuasive than two groups of four. The latter were more influential than a single, homogenous group of eight. In addition, subjects rated the jurors as more independent and less similar to each other as the heterogeneity of the jury increased from one to two to four groups. Note that unlike earlier studies (Wilder, 1977) the experimenter did not explicitly categorize the jurors into one or more groups. Rather, cues (race, occupation) were provided that encouraged subjects to categorize the jurors into the various groups.

In a final experiment in this series, subjects received social support from one actor while three others tried to influence them (Wilder, 1977). The four actors were either presented as a single group, two groups of two, or an aggregate of four. Not surprisingly, social support effectively reduced the impact of the majority in all conditions (Allen, 1975). But social support was more effective in reducing conformity when the opposition was categorized as a group than when perceived to be an aggregate. Dissension within a group may cause one to question the validity of the entire group whereas disagreement among independent individuals "spills over" less from one to another.

Harkins and Petty (1981) found very similar effects. Three persons making three different arguments were more persuasive than three persons making the same argument or one person making three different arguments. If the three persons were identified as members of a committee they had less impact than if no common grouping was mentioned. Two explanations appear quite plausible. When communicators are perceived to be members of a common group, we suspect collusion and doubt the independence of their judgments. In addition, to the extent we assume similarity among group members, we suspect that they cannot provide the different perspectives that independent communicators can. In other words, we suspect more redundancy in expertise and experience among group members and consequently a smaller sum than among independent individuals.

An additional finding from the Harkins and Petty research is quite intriguing. Informing subjects that the communicators were members of a group (committee) did not decrease their persuasiveness when that information was withheld until after subjects had heard the messages. This suggests that social categorization acts as an early screen in diminishing the impact of the group members. That role would be quite consistent with the research summarized in the preceding sections where categorization diminished perceived meaningfulness of the individual group members' actions and resulted in attributions of behavioral causality to the influence of the group.

E. SUMMARY

Consequences of social categorization have been examined for four interdependent topic areas: assumptions of similarity among group members, information conveyed by the behavior of group members, attributions of causality for group members, and social influence of group members. The pattern that emerges from this literature is clear. When categorized as a group, persons are thought to possess relatively similar beliefs and to exhibit similar behaviors; their actions are viewed as less informative about them as individuals; causal attributions reflect the likelihood that category or group membership rather than personal dispositions guide their behavior; and their persuasiveness is less than that of individuals not categorized as a group.

III.   Ingroup–Outgroup Categorization

In the work reviewed thus far, social categorization of stimulus persons had no direct implications for the subject's social identity. For instance, in most of my studies, subjects passively viewed a video tape of others. There was no prospect of interacting with them, and in some cases subjects never expected to perform the same tasks as those on the tape. This constrained situation was created to examine effects of mere categorization of others. Needless to say, in most social settings, groups into which we categorize others have relevance to our social identity. Section III,A considers the association between ingroups and outgroups. Subsequent sections examine consequences of ingroup–outgroup categorizations. These include assumptions of similarity within and dissimilarity between groups (Section III,B), preferences for information about ingroups and outgroups (Section III,C), assumptions of homogeneity among outgroup members (Section III,D), and discrimination between groups (Section III,E).

A.   SOCIAL IDENTITY OF THE PERCEIVER

Categorizing others as a group should prime or increase the probability of activating cognitions about associated groups. Moreover, activation of a social dimension that includes a group to which the perceiver belongs should prime that ingroup. If a person's social identity is a "library of scripts" (Bruner, 1958), then salience of an outgroup serves as a calling card directing the person to the book most appropriate for that setting. Salience of an outgroup should make the perceiver's corresponding ingroup salient. Certainly the presence of fellow ingroup members and physical symbols of the ingroup ought to be sufficient to make the ingroup salient. The ingroup should also be salient when members of an outgroup treat one as a member of one's ingroup. On a more subtle level, a strong link between cognitions about the ingroup and outgroup can be demonstrated if mere salience of an outgroup enhances an individual's sensitivity to ingroup cues. This hypothesis was examined in two experiments (Wilder & Shapiro, 1984).

In one study subjects viewed a symbol of either an ingroup, an outgroup relevant to the subjects' ingroup, or an irrelevant outgroup. Subjects in a control condition viewed no group cues. Subjects were students at Rutgers University. We selected Princeton University as a relevant outgroup because of its proximity and rivalry. A professional baseball team, the New York Yankees, was chosen to be the irrelevant group. Relevance of the outgroup refers to whether the outgroup lies on the same dimension as the ingroup (in this case universities) and is, therefore, an appropriate comparison group.

Ostensibly participating in a verbal learning study, subjects entered a cluttered room and sat in separate booths. The experimenter mentioned that the room was being used for several experiments. A pennant was taped to the wall facing subjects. All subjects (except controls) saw either a Rutgers, Princeton, or Yankees pennant. Following a brief introduction, subjects viewed a list of 50 words. After completing filler tasks, they checked those words that had appeared in the learning session from a longer list of items. Included in the checklist were words associated with the ingroup (Rutgers), the relevant outgroup (Princeton), and the irrelevant outgroup (Yankees). These cue words were selected by pretesting Rutgers students for words associated with the three groups.

Of primary interest to us was the number of group cues subjects recognized given that none of those words had actually appeared in the learning session. We made two predictions: (1) Salience of a group should increase the likelihood of erroneous reports of cues associated with that group; (2) Salience of an outgroup should make salient the relevant ingroup. Thus, words associated with Rutgers should be selected more frequently in the Princeton condition than in either the Yankee or control conditions. Results supported both hypotheses. Not surprisingly, subjects in each condition were more likely to report words associated with the salient group than the nonsalient groups. More importantly, selection of Rutgers words was nearly as great when Princeton was the salient cue as when Rutgers was the salient cue. Salience of the outgroup (Princeton) aroused the relevant ingroup (Rutgers) so that subjects were primed for words associated with either category. This did not occur when the Yankee outgroup was salient because Rutgers is not a relevant ingroup for a professional baseball team.

In a second experiment (Wilder & Shapiro, 1984), subjects were randomly assigned to one of two groups. Each group deliberated several legal cases independently. Subjects received bogus feedback indicating that their group favored the plaintiffs while the outgroup favored the defendants. Then subjects were divided into different groups for the second phase of the study. Again they deliberated several cases. This time, however, the ingroup favored the defendants, and the outgroup favored the plaintiffs. In the third phase of the study, subjects deliberated several cases individually in the presence of cues associated with either the outgroup from the first or the second phases. When the first outgroup was salient, subjects awarded pro-plaintiff decisions (consistent with the norm of the first ingroup), and when the second outgroup was salient, they made pro-defendant decisions (in agreement with the norm of the second in-group). Thus, salience of an outgroup made the relevant ingroup salient and resulted in behavior consistent with past actions of that ingroup.

If the presence of an outgroup helps to define a person's social identity by making salient the corresponding ingroup, then reactions to an outgroup should not be independent of one's cognitions about the associated ingroup. Cognitions about the outgroup and ingroup may very well be organized as a unit; but access to this package is probably unidirectional. Salience of the outgroup is sufficient to evoke relevant ingroup associations and may determine the individual's social identity in that context (Allen, Wilder, & Atkinson, 1983). It is less likely, however, that ingroup salience makes a particular outgroup salient. While a person usually belongs to only one group on any given social dimension, there often exists multiple outgroups. (Exceptions would be categories having only two groups such as sex.) Thus, in our first study, salience of an ingroup (Rutgers) did not make cues associated with the relevant outgroup (Princeton) any more salient than cues associated with the irrelevant outgroup (Yankees).

In related research McGuire and colleagues reported that persons' self-concepts reflect the social situation in which they are immersed (McGuire & Padawer-Singer, 1976; McGuire, McGuire, Child, & Fujioka, 1978; McGuire, McGuire, & Winton, 1979). In these studies ethnic ingroup identity was more likely to be salient to the extent children were in the ethnic minority in their classrooms. And sex was more likely to be mentioned as a self-descriptor when members of the opposite sex were in the majority in the child's family. It appears, then, that the presence of outgroup members is particularly likely to make the relevant ingroup salient when the outgroup members dominate the social field. With increasing presence of the outgroup, intergroup contact becomes more likely, thereby enhancing the salience of the ingroup–outgroup categorization.

Dion and Earn (1975) reported that a lone Jew in a group of Gentiles, whom he thought knew his religious affiliation, attributed task failure more to bias than did a Jew in a group that did not know his religion. Jews rated themselves more positively on traits consistent with the Jewish stereotype when their identity was made salient. In another study Dion (1975) employed sex as the ingroup–outgroup category. He manipulated female students' perceptions of the sex prejudice of male opponents. Females who failed to prejudiced males evaluated themselves more favorably on positive traits associated with stereotypes of women than did women with unprejudiced opponents.

These studies support the hypothesized link between cognitive representations of the ingroup and outgroup. Salience of an outgroup is sufficient to stimulate cognitions associated with the relevant ingroup and can accentuate ingroup identity (e.g., Dion's and McGuire's works). And certainly overt conflict with an outgroup enhances ingroup identity (Dion, Earn, & Yee, 1978; Doise, 1978; Sherif, 1967).

B. ASSUMED SIMILARITY WITHIN AND DIFFERENCES
    BETWEEN GROUPS

As argued in Section I,A, people expect group members to be relatively similar to one another even in areas that have little to do with the criteria for group membership. Research with object categories indicates that similarities within and differences between categories are exaggerated. Extrapolating to an intergroup setting, we would expect persons to assume differences between groups as well as similarities within groups. In a test of this hypothesis, Allen and Wilder (1979) divided subjects into two groups on the basis of a trivial task (alleged preferences for paintings). Subjects completed a questionnaire assessing their beliefs on a range of topics, pertaining to art, politics, and college life. Then they were asked to complete the questionnaire a second time as if they were another ingroup or outgroup member. Analyses showed that they expected their beliefs to be more similar to a fellow ingroup member than to an outgroup member. This assumption held across all items whether relevant (art) or irrelevant (politics) to the criterion for categorization. (These findings have been replicated in an experiment using a similar methodology; Wilder, 1985).

In one of the control conditions subjects were told that all preferred the same paintings, so there was no outgroup. When asked to predict the beliefs of an anonymous ingroup member, subjects again assumed significant ingroup similarity with themselves (as compared to a control condition involving no social categorization). But subjects expected greater similarity within the ingroup when an outgroup existed than when all belonged to the same ingroup. Salience of an outgroup restricted the range of positions imputed to ingroup members. This finding is reminiscent of the assimilation–contrast predictions from accentuation theory (Eiser & Stroebe, 1972; Tajfel & Wilkes, 1963). When a dichotomous classification (ingroup/outgroup) is imposed on a continuous dimension (range of beliefs), differences within each category are underestimated while differences between the two are overestimated.

Doise, Deschamps, and Meyer (1978) conducted two experiments demonstrating accentuation of perceived intergroup differences and underestimation of intragroup differences. In the first study subjects were divided into groups and were asked to rate three ingroup and three outgroup members on several trait adjectives. Half the subjects initially expected to rate only three others (either ingroup or outgroup members) and did not learn about the additional three ratings until the first three had been completed (no anticipation condition). Other subjects were told at the outset that they would rate three members of each group (with anticipation condition). Results indicated that subjects in the with anticipation condition showed larger intergroup differences and smaller intragroup differences in their ratings than subjects in the no anticipation condition. As Allen and Wilder (1979) reported, simultaneous consideration of the ingroup and outgroup appeared to have accentuated perceived differences between and similarities within groups.

In a second experiment (Doise *et al.*, 1978), Swiss school children (14 years of age) described three groups on a set of 16 positive and negative traits. Some subjects evaluated three ethnic Swiss groups: German Swiss (GS), French Swiss (FS), and Italian Swiss (IS). Others evaluated two of the Swiss groups and another nationality: GS, FS, Italians or GS, IS, French or IS, FS, Germans. Overall, differences in ratings of the ethnic Swiss groups were less in the presence of another national outgroup.

In another nationality study, Tajfel, Sheikh, and Gardner (1964) assessed the stereotypes a sample of Canadians possessed about Indians. Two Indians were interviewed before another group of Canadians. They were judged to be more alike on stereotype-relevant characteristics (e.g., submissive, religious, family-oriented) than on characteristics not part of the stereotype (e.g., sociable, optimistic).

Howard and Rothbart (1980) divided subjects into two groups on the basis of a simple task. (The subjects estimated numbers of dots on slides; groups were composed of consistent underestimators and overestimators.) Subjects were given a list of positive and negative traits to be assigned to the ingroup and outgroup. Subjects assigned more positive items to the ingroup and more negative traits to the outgroup.

Assumptions of ingroup similarity and outgroup differences from oneself can affect recall of information about ingroup and outgroup members. Howard and Rothbart (1980) conducted two experiments in which subjects were given positive and negative traits about the ingroup and outgroup. When later asked to recall which traits belonged with which group, they recalled more negative statements about the outgroup and fewer negative statements about the ingroup than were actually presented. In other research Rothbart and colleagues reported that subjects better recalled statements that confirmed their expectations about group than statements that disconfirmed or were irrelevant to their expectations (Rothbart, Evans, & Fulero, 1979). But more confirming than disconfirming information was available to subjects in those studies, and examination of the proportion of items recalled indicates that disconfirming information was better remembered than the confirming information.

Wyer and Gordon (1982) held constant the amount of confirming and disconfirming information. Subjects were asked to form an impression of either a single person or a group using a list of trait adjectives and behaviors. The behaviors varied in their consistency (both evaluative and descriptive) with the traits. Subjects recalled more behaviors under the person impression than under the group impression set; recall of traits did not differ significantly although more were recalled in the group than person condition. Considering that the trait information was more general (e.g., "talkative") than the behavioral information (e.g., "Told a lot of funny stories at a party"), superior recall of the latter in the person memory condition parallels the findings for attention to behavior reviewed earlier (Section I,B). If persons use a more molar level of analysis for organizing information about groups, then recall of specific behaviors about a group should suffer relative to individuals. Turning to the consistency variable, information that was only evaluatively inconsistent was not recalled better than consistent information in the group condition. But information that was both descriptively and evaluatively inconsistent was recalled better than consistent information. Although we expect members of a group to be similar to one another, some variability is not disconcerting because we realize that individual group members do differ in the degree to which they possess characteristics we impute to the group. It may be easy (and efficient), therefore, to dismiss small deviations from expectations about group members. But large deviations (e.g., both descriptive and evaluative inconsistencies) command explanation. Explanation, in turn, requires examination of the discrepancy and increases our likelihood of later recalling it.

Persons often assume similarities within groups and differences between groups to a greater degree and across a broader range of characteristics than is warranted by objective evidence. Whether persons selectively recall information consistent with these assumptions is open to question and may depend on the relative amounts of consistent versus inconsistent information, the extremity of the inconsistencies, and the presence of competing responses that may facilitate or interfere with learning the information. There is, however, clearer evidence that persons prefer information consistent with expectations about social categories. This evidence is discussed in the next section.

C. PREFERENCE FOR INFORMATION ABOUT INGROUPS
   AND OUTGROUPS

Theories of cognitive consistency posit that information consistent with expectations is desired because it compliments us as accurate naive scientists, it stabilizes and provides a good figure to our representation of the world, and it allows superior prediction (e.g., Heider, 1958). By implication, members of a group should prefer information that indicates ingroup similarity and outgroup dissimilarity to themselves.

In a test of this prediction, Wilder and Allen (1978) categorized subjects into groups on the basis of their preferences for paintings; actually random assignment. They completed a general attitude inventory and were later given the opportunity to see the responses of others (either ingroup or outgroup members) who responded either similarly or dissimilarly to them on the inventory. Subjects rank ordered the four types of information in terms of their preference for

viewing. Subjects significantly preferred information indicating ingroup similarity and outgroup dissimilarity to themselves. Consistent with these findings,
Campbell (1967) suggested that behavior an ingroup member would be punished
for is likely to be noticed and integrated into the outgroup stereotype. Preference
for information that confirms one's expectations about groups is a small step
away from acting to confirm those expectations.

Snyder and associates (e.g., Snyder, 1981; Snyder & Swann, 1978; Snyder,
Tanke, & Berscheid, 1977) conducted an interesting series of experiments demonstrating that persons confirm their expectations by subtly shaping the behavior
of others to fit those expectations. For example, in the Snyder *et al.* (1977)
study, subjects who expected to interact with an attractive (or unattractive) other
behaved in a telephone conversation so as to shape responses in the other supportive of what the subjects expected of an attractive (or unattractive) other in a
phone conversation.

In a classic demonstration of the self-fulfilling prophecy, Word, Zanna, and
Cooper (1974) had white subjects interview both white and black job applicants.
When interviewing black applicants, subjects made more speech errors and
concluded the session sooner than when interviewing white prospects. In a
second experiment white confederates interviewed white applicants while mim-
icking the interview styles displayed in the first study. Applicants who were
interviewed by the confederate employing the style used by white subjects interacting with black applicants in the first study performed relatively poorly and
appeared nervous. Putting the two experiments together, the expectations persons have about outgroup members influences the style of interaction in contact
settings so as to fulfill those expectations. Because we are not aware of these
subtle influences, we use the apparently confirming behavior of the outgroup
member as evidence for the accuracy of our expectations.

D. ASSUMED HOMOGENEITY OF OUTGROUPS

Far from being a blatant example of bigotry, the expression "they all look
alike" may reflect a lack of differentiation and richness of one's representation
of the outgroup. Several arguments can be generated to support the contention
that persons often assume that outgroup members are relatively more homogeneous than ingroup members. To begin with, because we interact more frequently with ingroup than with outgroup members, we are likely to encounter
greater diversity among the former.

Secondly, the quality of interaction with outgroup members is likely to be
more superficial and more constrained by social norms (e.g., minimum civility).
Thus, interaction with outgroup members may lack the intimacy that reveals
individual uniqueness.

Thirdly, we may assume heterogeneity in the ingroup as a means of asserting our uniqueness (Fromkin, 1973). When compared with members of an outgroup, our ingroup membership may provide a sense of individuality. But our ingroup membership provides no differentiation between other ingroup members and ourselves; we must, therefore, rely on more idiosyncratic differences to distinguish ourselves (e.g., subgroups, personal peccadillos).

Fourthly, intergroup comparisons are likely to be made between the ingroup and outgroup as a whole whereas comparisons within the ingroup are made among individuals (Tajfel & Turner, 1979). Intergroup comparisons focus attention on differences between the ingroup and outgroup while minimizing differences within the outgroup. But intragroup comparisons focus on differences between individuals.

Finally, assuming outgroup homogeneity enables us to deindividuate members of the outgroup. As discussed more fully in Section IV,A, deindividuation of the outgroup can justify and encourage ingroup favoritism (Brewer, 1979; Wilder, 1978c).

Some support for the homogeneity hypothesis was reported by Linville (1979). Young subjects showed greater complexity in their descriptions of other young males (ingroup) than in their descriptions of older males (outgroup). Linville and Jones (1980) argued that persons have a more complex schema for ingroups than for outgroups. Consequently, judgments of outgroup behavior should be more extreme or polarized than judgments of ingroup behavior. In support of this prediction, white subjects evaluated a black applicant for graduate school more positively (or negatively) than a white applicant when the black's credentials were strong (or weak). Taylor *et al.* (1978) reported more errors within categories (e.g., confusion of which male made a statement on a tape they listened to) than between categories (e.g., whether a male or a female made a statement).

In more direct tests of the homogeneity hypothesis, Quattrone and Jones (1980) had subjects observe the behavior of either an ingroup (same college as subject) or outgroup (rival college) member. When asked to predict the percentage of others who would behave the same, subjects predicted more similarity among outgroup than among ingroup members' actions. But when asked to predict the behavior of a specific other, the homogeneity hypothesis was not supported. Finally, Park and Rothbart (1982) reported assumed outgroup homogeneity using sex and sororities as categories. They found support for the outgroup homogeneity hypothesis for attributions of both socially desirable and undesirable traits.

In the preceding studies investigators tapped expectations about natural groups. Assumptions of outgroup homogeneity may, therefore, have reflected actual experiences with those outgroups rather than an expectation about outgroups in general. To test for the latter Wilder (1985) divided subjects into laboratory groups and asked them to make predictions about the range of beliefs within the ingroup and outgroup. After arriving for the experiment, subjects privately expressed their preferences among a series of paintings. Then they gave their opinions about several issues relevant to art and to politics. They also read a summary of a legal case. Pretesting had indicated that these topics (art, politics, legal case) formed a continuum of decreasing relevance to the categorization criterion (artistic tastes). Then they were either divided into two groups (ingroup/outgroup condition), assigned to one group (ingroup only), or not assigned to groups at all (control). Following categorization, subjects estimated the range of opinions held by others on each kind of item. Results supported the homogeneity hypothesis. Subjects attributed a greater range of artistic preferences and political beliefs to members of the ingroup than to members of the outgroup in the ingroup/outgroup condition. But attributions about the legal case did not differ among conditions. Furthermore, the ingroup was thought to be more homogeneous when an outgroup was present (ingroup/outgroup condition) than when it was absent (ingroup only condition). The latter finding is consistent with research reviewed earlier (Section II,B) indicating that presence of an outgroup restricts the range of positions attributed to ingroup members.

Overall, intergroup categorization fostered assumptions of outgroup homogeneity relative to the ingroup on items that were correlated (political beliefs) as well as directly relevant (artistic beliefs) to the categorization criterion. In this experiment nothing was known about the outgroup other than its difference in painting preferences from the ingroup. In most situations, however, we have more information about both groups. A more versatile test of the homogeneity hypothesis requires that subjects be presented with information about the groups. Then they would predict the beliefs of an anonymous ingroup or outgroup member. If differential assumptions of homogeneity occur despite base rate information, then we would have evidence that the assumption of outgroup homogeneity is a relatively powerful expectation.

In a second experiment subjects were divided into two groups. They completed a set of attitude measures and received false feedback about the responses of some of the others in the session. Then subjects predicted how another person in the session responded to the items. Note that subjects were not asked to recall information presented about those individuals. Rather, this procedure is analogous to situations in which persons generalize from their impression of a group to a specific member whom they have never encountered. Differences between subjects' predictions about the unseen target person and the available base rate information provided a test of the homogeneity hypothesis. To the extent they predicted similarity between the target and the base rate information, they were assuming greater homogeneity. As expected, when an outgroup member, the target person was predicted to possess more similar beliefs to the base rate information provided about the outgroup. Greater hetereogeneity was expected for the target ingroup member vis-á-vis the ingroup as a whole. In sum, these laboratory experiments combined with the studies using natural groups provide strong support for the outgroup homogeneity hypothesis.

E. INTERGROUP BIAS

An extensive literature indicates that the mere categorization of persons into an ingroup and outgroup is sufficient to foster bias (i.e., ingroup favoritism at the expense of the outgroup). The most frequently used paradigm was developed by Tajfel and his colleagues (e.g., Tajfel, 1970; Tajfel, Billig, Bundy, & Flament, 1971). Subjects are assigned a code number and divided into groups on the basis of a trivial task (i.e., preferences for paintings, estimation of the number of dots on slides). Subjects are separated before receiving this information so that they do not know who are the members of each group. Actual assignment is random. At this point one or more tasks may be interjected. At the conclusion of the session subjects are given a series of reward matrices to distribute points (usually worth some monetary amount) between various combinations of persons (i.e., between ingroup members, between outgroup members, between ingroup and outgroup members). The subject's code number does not appear in a matrix, so that self-serving bias cannot occur. In variations of this paradigm, investigators have employed different, but equally trivial, methods of categorization (e.g., experimenter's whim, Rabbie & Horwitz, 1969) and different dependent measures (e.g., trait ratings, Rabbie & Horwitz, 1969; Wilder, 1978e; Thompson, 1983; Wilson & Miller, 1961).

Regardless of specific measures used, these studies have shown that subjects assign more positive traits and rewards to the ingroup than to the outgroup (e.g., Allen & Wilder, 1975; Billig & Tajfel, 1973; Brewer & Silver, 1978; Doise, Csepeli, Dann, Gouge, Larson, & Ostell, 1972; Doise & Sinclair, 1973; Kahn & Ryan, 1972; Rabbie & Wilkens, 1971; Tajfel & Billig, 1974). (See Brewer, 1979, for more thorough review.)

Several interesting findings have emerged from this literature. Most obviously, intergroup bias may be fostered by very minimal conditions. The mere existence of mutually exclusive groups appears to be sufficient. But there is a limit to how minimal this categorization can be. Thus, Rabbie and Horwitz (1969) failed to find bias when groups were explicitly created by chance (coin flip). But discrimination did occur when the experimenter stated that he was arbitrarily creating the group assignments. In the latter case subjects may have supposed that the experimenter had a hidden reason for dividing them as he did, and that reason reflected a significant difference between the groups. Billig and Tajfel (1973) reported that simply assigning subjects different sets of code numbers (half in the 40s and half in the 70s) did not lead to ingroup favoritism unless the experimenters explicitly referred to the subjects as "groups." Explicit reference to "groups" may trigger subjects' expectations about how group members are likely to be similar, are likely to interact with one another, and so forth.

Secondly, bias observed in this research occurs even when subjects cannot directly benefit from their behavior. Subjects divide rewards between anonymous others in the groups. Thus, ingroup favoritism truly reflects a desire to benefit the ingroup rather than a means of maximizing gain for oneself. Ingroup favoritism vicariously rewards the self to the extent one's social identity is invested in the group.

Thirdly, subjects act not simply to reward the ingroup but to create a relative advantage for the ingroup over the outgroup (Allen & Wilder, 1975; Billig & Tajfel, 1973; Tajfel et al., 1971). Subjects sometimes reward the ingroup less than they might in order to ensure that the outgroup receives even less. For example, in one of the reward matrices subjects are given a choice between rewarding 7 points to the ingroup and 1 point to the outgroup or 12 points to the ingroup and 11 points to the outgroup. Subjects prefer the 7/1 choice to the 12/11 combination even though the latter nets more for the ingroup. The 7/1 choice, however, retains a greater advantage for the ingroup. Rewarding the ingroup may be important, but so is differentiating between the ingroup and outgroup.

Finally, as a qualification, it must be pointed out that ingroup favoritism observed in this literature is tempered with fairness. Subjects rarely maximize positive outcomes for the ingroup. Overall, ingroup favoritism is a consistent, significant, and modest consequence of social categorization that occurs accross gender, age, and nationalities.

F. SUMMARY

1. Deindividuation within Groups

The consequences of social categorization reviewed above comprise an interdependent set of cognitive and behavioral phenomena. It is difficult to discern which are causally related and what the directions of causality may be. What follows is one reasonable sequence: Categorization of persons into a social group leads me to assume extensive similarities among the beliefs and behaviors of group members. I use the group as my unit of analysis in monitoring their behavior and deciding what constitutes informative action. That may lead me to emphasize the impact of group level variables (interpersonal influence, normative pressure as opposed to individual actions) in making attributions about the causes of a member's behavior. Such an attribution reduces the credibility of group members as sources of information and fosters an overestimation of perceived similarity within the group. In this picture the individual tree is lost in the group forest. Categorization deindividuates group members as reflected in less differentiated responses toward them.

2. *Differentiation between Groups*

When categorizing others creates an ingroup–outgroup relationship, we must consider between as well as within group expectations. The existence of both an ingroup and outgroup invites comparisons that often bode poorly for intergroup relations. "Comparisons are always odious and ill taken" (Cervantes; *Don Quixote* II,i). "Comparisons are odorous" (Shakespeare; *Much Ado About Nothing* III,v). Perceivers not only assume differences between ingroups and outgroups (both in terms of belief similarity and homogeneity) but also act to create those assumed differences (information preference and intergroup bias). Differentiating between social groups parallels accentuation of intercategory differences reported in the object categorization literature (e.g., Doise & Sinclair, 1973; Eiser & Stroebe, 1972; Tajfel & Wilkes, 1963). But an accentuation explanation cannot easily account for the consistent direction of differences in evaluating ingroups and outgroups (i.e., ingroup favoritism). Additional factors must be postulated to explain ingroup favoritism when no apparent reason exists to justify bias (such as actual differences in group performances). Three explanations are offered: cognitive consistency, social identity, and social script.

G. EXPLANATIONS OF BIAS INDUCED BY CATEGORIZATION

1. *Cognitive Consistency*

Social categorization divides the environment into two mutually exclusive entities, the ingroup and outgroup. In general, persons should experience a positive sentiment toward the ingroup as a result of their association with it (Heider, 1958). Consequently, when differentiating between the groups, persons should favor the ingroup over the outgroup in order to maintain cognitive consistency. This rationale has not been directly tested. Support derives chiefly from its conceptual similarity to the large literature on cognitive consistency.

2. *Social Identity*

Ingroup favoritism reflects a desire for a favorable social identity (Billig & Tajfel, 1973; Tajfel, 1982; Tajfel & Turner, 1979). Questing a positive sense of self, persons compare their group with relevant other groups and act to create a favorable distinction between the groups. It is crucial, therefore, that the ingroup's outcomes (e.g., rewards, evaluations) be better than those of the outgroup, so relative superiority is more important than the absolute level of out-comes. Consistent with this hypothesis, several researchers have shown that subjects discriminate in favor of the ingroup even when the payoffs are arranged so that favoritism of both groups can occur and net more for the ingroup (e.g., Allen & Wilder, 1975; Brewer & Silver, 1978; Tajfel *et al.*, 1971; Turner, Brown, & Tajfel, 1979). Note that the social identity interpretation focuses on the perceiver's search for her or his niche in the social structure cleaved by the categorization.

If ingroup favoritism is produced from a search for a positive social identity, then an individual's self-esteem might increase following the opportunity to discriminate. Oakes and Turner (1980) tested this hypothesis using the minimal group procedure discussed earlier. Subjects were divided into two groups. Half of the groups completed reward matrices that divided points between members of the groups. The remaining groups worked on an irrelevant task. Then all subjects completed three measures of self-esteem. As expected, when given the oppor-tunity to discriminate, subjects showed the typical pattern of ingroup favoritism. Moreover, subjects reported significantly higher self-esteem on two of the mea-sures (20-sentence test, Kuhn & McPartland, 1954; semantic differential, Julian, Bishop, & Fiedler, 1966) when they had the opportunity to discriminate. There was no difference between conditions on the third measure (Rosenberg's, 1965, scale).

3. Social Scripts

The nearly universal existence of ingroup favoritism (e.g., LeVine & Campbell, 1972; Sumner, 1906) suggests a normative component to intergroup bias. Persons favor ingroups because that is expected, socially approved behav-ior. We learn a script (Abelson, 1976) that advocates ingroup favoritism. This script arises out of our experience in groups where ingroup favoritism is re-warded both through participation in payoffs and approval from fellow ingroup members for benefiting the whole. Furthermore, most cultures teach that soli-darity with ingroups, varying from families to nations, is an honorable value. Socialization of this script begins early and can be seen in the preferences children have among nations of which they know precious little (Tajfel, 1979). Because ingroup favoritism is part of our script for intergroup behavior, we are likely to invoke it in an intergroup setting, whether or not we can materially benefit by biased behavior. Note that the script explanation does not require that bias be a means of establishing social identity. Indeed, one may have little sense of identity invested in the simple categorization imposed by the experimenters. Yet one favors the ingroup because that is what one should do. Two points of possible confusion warrant comment.

First, one's script for intergroup behavior may contain contradictory ele-ments—both an expectation for ingroup favoritism and the belief that persons ought to treat one another equally. Favoritism of the ingroup is what we expect others to do even though we might wish that everyone be treated equally. In an intergroup categorization study, Allen and Wilder (1975) reported that subjects expected others in both groups to behave as they did; that is, to show ingroup favoritism in the division of rewards between groups. Nevertheless, they also stated that they would have preferred to divide the rewards equally. Indeed, in that study as well as others employing reward matrices (Branthwaite, Doyle, & Lightbrown, 1979), subjects did show a significant preference for fairness in the distribution of rewards. On some matrices the typical subject divided points equally between groups; on others the subject showed significant bias. The behavior of subjects in these laboratory studies suggests a juggling of competing expectations from their scripts governing intergroup behavior and self-presentation before strangers (other subjects and experimenter).

Second, a social script interpretation should not be confused with an experimental demand interpretation. According to the latter ingroup favoritism in laboratory experiments is an artifact; a consequence of conformity to perceived expectations of the investigator (Orne, 1962). (See Tajfel, 1978, for a detailed refutation of the demand hypothesis.) Research indicates that most subjects are concerned with preserving a good image of themselves (e.g., Weber & Cook, 1972). Given that discrimination is openly condemned in most educational settings, any demands should be in the direction of minimizing intergroup bias, particularly when the bias does not materially benefit the subjects. Like conformity research, I suspect that the bias found in these laboratory studies underestimates what would be observed in field settings.

Clearly, several conflicting expectations may guide behavior following social categorization. A script calling for ingroup favoritism is likely to be tempered when subjects are in a laboratory setting by (1) norms of fairness in the absence of concrete reasons (e.g., superior performance) to favor the ingroup and (2) the subjects' realization that their behavior is under observation. It should not be surprising, therefore, to find that subjects display a combination of evaluative "strategies" when given several opportunities to behave in a biased manner (e.g., multiple reward matrices, multiple trait scales). They display significant ingroup favoritism and significant fairness. They do not simply maximize ingroup benefits, but rather show relative preference for the ingroup over the outgroup.

4. Summary

Accentuation of between group differences and within group similarities is a product of categorization. Simple extrapolation of categorization principles to social groups can account for intergroup differentiation but not consistent ingroup favoritism. Three hypotheses have been offered, none of which excludes the others. According to the consistency hypothesis, we favor ingroups because such action supports our cognitive association with the ingroup. It feels good (both in terms of "good figure" and any tangible outcomes) to benefit those associated with us. According to the social identity hypothesis, ingroup favoritism provides us with a distinct and positive social identity. According to the social script hypothesis, ingroup favoritism is an expected response that is part of our script for intergroup behavior. Each explanation addresses a different function—organization of social cognitions (consistency), definition of self (social identity), and presentation of self to others (social script).

IV. Reducing Intergroup Bias by Altering the Ingroup–Outgroup Representation

Regardless of which explanation one favors, the implication for lessening bias based on categorization is clear. If we can reduce the perceived accuracy of an intergroup categorization, then the perceiver may be less likely to act on the basis of that categorization. Three tactics for reducing bias are discussed in this section: (1) individuation of the outgroup (Section IV,A), (2) diminishing intergroup boundaries (Section IV,B), and (3) decreasing the contribution of the ingroup to one's social identity (Section IV,C).

A. INDIVIDUATION OF THE OUTGROUP

When categorized as a group member, a person's behavior is judged to be less informative about her or him, is attributed less to dispositonal and more to situational causes, is considered more homogeneous and similar to other group members, and is perceived to be less credible and less independent of the others in the group (Section I). In essence, the group member is deindividuated relative to a person uncategorized. Observations from several field studies indicate that outgroup members are deindividuated (LeVine & Campbell, 1972). Middleton (1960) and Swartz (1961) reported that unfamiliar outgroups were regarded as less human than more familiar groups. For example, the Trukese categorize remote groups of New Guinea with loathesome animals such as sharks (Swartz, 1961). In a similar vein, outgroups are frequently regarded as immoral people who do not observe conventional standards of civilized behavior (Dollard, 1938).

Certainly, when intergroup conflict is great, deindividuation of outgroup members dehumanizes them, increases their threatening nature, and facilitates aggressive responses toward them. Propaganda during wars evoke the humanity of the ingroup and inhumanity of the enemy. Consider the World War I posters of the Allies in which innocent Belgian and French children were bayoneted by ominous, hulking "Huns." Or consider a scene from Eisenstein's classic film of the Russian revolution, *Potemkin,* in which government troops march toward hapless peasants. The former are obscured by their uniformity of dress and march; they are a faceless, "inhuman" machine. By contrast, close-up shots of the civilians emphasize their unique identities and very human emotions. But without direct experimentation, it is unclear whether deindividuation of the outgroup is a cause or a consequence of intergroup bias. As Gibbon tersely observed, "Our sympathy is cold to the relation of distant misery" (*The Decline and Fall of the Roman Empire* XLIX).

Deindividuation of an individual increases the likelihood that he or she will be a target of aggression. For example, in Milgram's (1965) obedience research, subjects gave more severe shocks when the victims were out of sight in the next room than when they could see or touch them. Worchel and Andreoli (1978) presented evidence for the reverse relationship. When anticipating an agressive interaction, subjects deindividuated the target by recalling less unique information about him than when a more friendly encounter was expected.

If deindividuation of outgroup members lessens our regard for them, then individuation of those persons may enhance our evaluation of them. Although direct experimental evidence is scant, some anecdotal evidence suggests that individuation fosters a more favorable response. For instance, Zimbardo (1970) reported that guards of Nazi concentration camps treated Jews less harshly when they knew their names than when they were anonymous members of the outgroup.

As another example, consider the case of Gerard Vaders, who was a passenger on a train commandeered by South Moluccans in the Netherlands in December 1975 (Ochberg, 1977). When negotiations were going poorly, the captors decided to execute Vaders as an example. Before doing so they allowed him to dictate a final letter to his family. In that letter Vaders reflected on his life, dwelling on both accomplishments and shortcomings. The letter was directed to his family and did not contain pleas for sympathy. After completing the letter, his captors decided not to execute him. Instead they shot. another hapless hostage without allowing him to compose a parting letter.

Although supportive anecdotes are comforting, they are seldom convincing. Several arguments based on experimental evidence can be marshaled to support the individuation hypothesis. Individuation of the outgroup shatters the assumptions of outgroup homogeneity and similarity. The situation shifts from an intergroup to an interpersonal one in that the simple ingroup–outgroup categorization becomes a less meaningful means of ordering the social environment (Tajfel & Turner, 1979). As a result, the perceiver's identity is less dependent on positive differentiation of the ingroup from the outgroup. From this line of reasoning, bias is reduced because it is no longer functional for the perceiver's quest for a positive identity.

Secondly, arguing from the similarity–attraction literature (e.g., Byrne, 1969), individuation of outgroup members focuses attention on those persons and enables one to notice similarities with them. Any perceived similarities should promote a positive evaluation.

Thirdly, individuation of outgroup members should make it easier to take their perspectives and even empathize with them. Role-taking responses should encourage a more positive, self-like response to them (Gould & Sigall, 1977; Regan & Totten, 1975). Note that the similarity and role-taking hypotheses do not necessarily extend to the perceiver's evaluation of the outgroup as a whole. Generalization of a positive reaction to the outgroup as a whole may depend on other conditions such as how typical the individuated members appear to be of the others in the outgroup. On the other hand, the interpretation based on a change from an intergroup to an interpersonal situation predicts less differentiation between the groups as a whole because intergroup comparisons are less relevant for one's social identity.

Tactics that individuate outgroup members may emanate from two sources: the behavior of the outgroup members and actions of the perceiver.

1.   Individuation through Actions of the Outgroup

If homogeneity is expected of outgroup members, then individuation may occur through unexpected hetereogenity. Dissimilar behavior among outgroup members and information emphasizing personal idiosyncrasies may decrease the utility of the outgroup category.

a.   Dissimilar Behavior.   When consensus is expected in a group, dissent should individuate outgroup members and result in less reliance on the ingroup–outgroup categorization in evaluating outgroup members. This hypothesis was examined in an experiment in which subjects were arbitrarily categorized into two groups by the experimenter (Wilder, 1978c). The groups were physically separated and adjudicated two legal cases. Feedback from the outgroup indicated that either all members agreed on both cases or one member dissented on both cases. (In control conditions feedback was obtained from only one person to control for the specific positions taken by the dissenting and majority members in the experimental conditions.) Subjects then divided earnings between group members using six matrices of the kind employed by Tajfel (1970). Ingroup favoritism was significantly greater when the outgroup was unanimous than when there was a dissenter. Subjects in the dissent condition divided rewards nearly equally between the groups and were more likely to describe the outgroup as an aggregate of independent individuals than as a single unit. Comparisons with control conditions indicated that the effect of dissent could not be attributed to the specific positions taken by the dissenter. The disruption of unanimity compromised the adequacy of the simple intergroup categorization.

b. Distinctive Attributes. Disclosure of unique information about outgroup members should encourage a more complex and differentiated view of them. Some information may be individuating because it violates expectations about the outgroup (e.g., a tall person in a social club may be more likely to stand out and be focused on as an individual than the same person on a basketball team.) Other personal information is sufficiently idiosyncratic to be individuating regardless of the group context (e.g., name, family, aspirations).

In two experiments Wilder (1978c) individuated outgroup members through the disclosure of personal information. Subjects in both experiments were divided into groups and performed several problem-solving tasks. On one of these tasks they received critical feedback from the outgroup to create a negative relationship between the two. Later, subjects requested assistance from the outgroup to complete a task. At this point groups were assigned to one of four conditions. Some received all the help they had requested (cooperative condition); others received no help at all (uncooperative condition); others received partial help from half of the outgroup acting as a unit (partially cooperative–group condition); and some received partial assistance from half of the outgroup acting as individuals (partially cooperative–individual condition). Feedback in the partially cooperative–group condition came from the entire outgroup; there was no indication of the identities of the outgroup members. In the partially cooperative–individual condition assistance came in individual notes signed by those helping. Subjects divided earnings between the two groups. Not surprisingly, the greatest ingroup favoritism occurred when the outgroup was uncooperative and the least when it was fully cooperative. The partially cooperative conditions fell in between. Subjects displayed significantly less ingroup favoritism when the outgroup members were individuated (partially cooperative–individual condition) than when they responded as a unit (partially cooperative–group condition) even though the amount of aid was the same in both conditions. Bias against the individuated outgroup did not differ substantially from the amount of bias (virtually none) observed when the outgroup cooperated fully.

2. Individuation through Changes in the Perceiver

Individuation is successful because it reduces the perceiver's reliance on the group category as a determinant of his or her behavior. The tactics examined in the last section may be effective because they force the perceiver to examine the outgroup members individually. More generally, conditions that cause a perceiver to adopt a careful, deliberate examination of outgroup members should result in a less uniform and automatic response to them. On the other hand, when highly aroused or under extreme demand, the perceiver should be more likely to overlook individuating information and respond to the outgroup as a homogeneous unit.

a. Careful Examination of Outgroup Behavior.   Wilder (1984) hypothesized that close monitoring of an outgroup member's behavior would result in differentiation of the person from the outgroup. This prediction was tested using the behavioral units paradigm discussed in Section I,B (Newtson, 1973). Subjects observed a video tape of four persons and partitioned one actor's behavior into what they judged to be meaningful units of action. The four persons were either identified as members of a common group (group condition) or unrelated to each other (aggregate condition). Subjects were instructed to focus on one actor and to either divide that actor's behavior into fine units (i.e., look for many meaningful acts) or to partition the behavior into naturally occurring units (i.e., whatever they felt was appropriate). This yielded a 2 (group/aggregate categorization) × 2 (close/normal focus of attention) design.

Subjects in the group condition were more likely to perceive the target actor as independent of the others and recalled more specific information about the actor when they focused closely (fine unit condition) than when they did not scrutinize so well (normal unit condition). Subjects in the group–fine unit condition did not differ from subjects in the aggregate conditions in their response to the target person. Thus, the impact of social categorization can be reduced if perceivers focus closely on individual group members. Increased attention to a group member necessitates decreased attention to others in the group. The monitored member may appear more unique because few comparisons are made with the others. In addition, focusing closely on one group member may have enabled perceivers to notice cues that actually differentiated the actor from the others, thereby weakening the categorization.

b. Perceiver's Level of Arousal.   Given a limited capacity for attention, increasing arousal should restrict attention to external stimuli as more capacity is spent monitoring and coping with the arousal (Kahneman, 1973). Under conditions of high arousal a perceiver should be less able (and willing) to make fine differentiations among stimuli, preferring instead to rely on simple categorical expectations to guide behavior. If a person expects negative interaction with members of an outgroup, then the person may perceive positive contact less favorably when arousal is high. This hypothesis was examined in three experiments (Wilder, Thompson, & Cooper, 1983). The first study demonstrated that positive contact is regarded as less pleasant when persons expect a negative interaction. The second and third studies indicated that anxiety restricts the range of attention during intergroup contact.

In the first experiment subjects were categorized into groups and expected a cooperative or a competitive interaction with an outgroup. Three of the four outgroup members evaluated an ingroup product negatively while one gave a positive rating. The pleasant outgroup member was rated less favorably and his actions were perceived less positively in the competitive condition. In addition, subjects in the competitive condition rated themselves as more anxious prior to interaction with the outgroup.

Experiments 2 and 3 directly mainpulated subjects' levels of arousal (operationally defined as anxiety at the prospect of performing an embarrassing act). Subjects in the high anxiety condition expected to either make a speech about their bodies (Experiment 2) or have their pictures taken wearing infant apparel (Experiment 3). Subjects in the low anxiety condition expected to either make a speech about school policy (study 2) or have their pictures taken wearing a mask that disguised their identities (study 3). Then subjects viewed an interaction among four members of a group, one of whom displayed a different style of behavior from the others. Anxious subjects in both experiments rated the different group member more similarly to the others than did less anxious subjects. The anxious subjects failed to make as fine and as accurate discriminations among the group members.

Results of these investigations suggest that the perceiver's level of arousal will color the intergroup relationship. Anticipation of an unpleasant interaction may increase arousal, resulting in greater emphasis given to expectation–confirming behavior among outgroup members. Positive aspects of the outgroup may be overlooked or misinterpreted. Moreover, anxiety may foster guarded behavior that elicits a similar response in the outgroup, to the detriment of the relationship. On the other hand, lowering anxiety may permit processing of more individuating information about the outgroup.

3. *Extensions and Limitations of Individuation*

Findings from several studies are consistent with the individuation hypothesis even though none has tested it directly. In a study of the belief congruence theory of prejudice, Byrne and McGraw (1964) reported that white subjects liked a black stranger more when a photograph of the stranger accompanied a written protocal of him or her. The photograph was an individuating cue giving flesh and uniqueness to an otherwise stereotypic image of the group.

Chadwick-Jones (1962) investigated majority–minority relations in Britain. Attitudes of Britons toward a group of Italian workers varied with the type of contact. Persons who had little contact with the Italians expressed disapproval; those who had frequent fact-to-face contact with individual Italians displayed positive reactions. The latter persons also differentiated among individual outgroup members.

Several of Kelman's (1966) suggestions for improving international attitudes through interpersonal contact spotlight the importance of individuation. For successful contact he argues that the foreign visitor needs to be regarded as an individual, not as a member of a category; needs to be involved in on-going activities, not treated specially or ignored; and needs to be able to develop personal relationships, not restricted to formal, surface interactions.

In many situations, however, merely individuating outgroup members may be insufficient to promote favorable role taking or empathic responses to them.

For a favorable reaction it may be necessary for individuating tactics to ensure that ingroup members are aware of the "scripts" members of the outgroups are employing (Abelson, 1976). Ostensibly pleasant contact may be ineffective if the participants misinterpret the meanings behind the actions of one another. Thus, Sager and Schofield (1980) reported that blacks and whites in desegregated schools frequently have opposite perceptions of one another. Blacks perceive whites to be prejudiced and conceited. Whites view themselves as unprejudiced and helpful, and angry when their offers of help are rejected. What is needed in such situations is not simply contact but an appreciation for the different interpretations given to the same actions by the different parties. When the whites are able to take the perspective of the blacks and vice versa, contact should be more successful.

Triandis (1976) recognized this problem in his cultural assimilator technique for modifying intergroup relations. Ingroup members are taught the scripts that outgroup members employ in contact situations so that their intentions can be construed accurately by the ingroup. This research points to one reason why the belief congruence hypothesis (Rokeach, 1960) has received mixed support. Even when different groups share similar beliefs and values, they may differ in the means they choose to implement those beliefs and values. Differences in actual behavior and interpretations of behavior can mask underlying similarities; similarities that are often more easily made salient in a laboratory setting.

The individuation research suggests that intergroup contact between a few individuals may be superior to contact between groups of persons. The former encourages specific, personal reactions to outgroup members as separate entities. The latter, however, encourages categorization of the individuals into larger units, thereby deindividuating them. Recall from Section I that multiple persons grouped together have less impact than separate individuals. Thus, favorable behavior by "groups" of outgroup members may be less effective in reducing intergroup bias than favorable behavior by individual outgroup members who are not "chunked" together (e.g., contact with different members on different occasions and across different situations).

There are also potential drawbacks to the individuation tactic. Might not individuation of outgroup members increase their perceived dissimilarity from the outgroup category and, consequently, decrease their relevance for evaluations of the outgroup as a whole? As specific members become more individuated, it should be easier to point to ways in which they differ from stereotypes of the outgroup. As a result, responses to those individuals may become more positive without generalizing to the outgroup as a whole. This may not have been a problem in my studies because very little was known about the groups. Individuating information could not be compared with expectations about the outgroup and used to conclude that the individuated members were atypical. (I shall return to this quandry in Section VI,A.)

4. Summary

Research reviewed in this section demonstrates that individuation of the outgroup can lessen ingroup favoritism. Individuation appears to foster interpersonal as opposed to intergroup comparisons, thereby reducing the need for ingroup favoritism as a means of achieving a positive identity. In addition, individuation may encourage taking the role of outgroup members and, perhaps, empathic responses to them. Individuation can occur through the behavior of outgroup members (e.g., dissent when consensus is expected; revealing personal information) and through changes in the perceiver (e.g., increased attention to individual members; change in arousal).

In many situations it may be impossible to individuate members of an outgroup. The social categorization may be too entrenched because of frequent use or because it is central to the perceiver's self-concept. In these situations perceived differences between the groups may be reduced even though the ingroup–outgroup categorization remains. The next section examines such tactics.

B. DIMINISHING INTERGROUP BOUNDARIES

Several tactics can be suggested to lessen reliance on a particular intergroup categorization in ordering the social environment. These tactics assume that an ingroup–outgroup category is less likely to be used to the extent boundaries become less clear. For instance, the ingroup–outgroup boundary may be weakened by increasing perceived similarity between members of the two groups. Secondly, an outgroup may become more acceptable when compared to a more different outgroup. Thirdly, evidence that the groups overlap on some dimension of comparison may weaken the division between ingroup and outgroup. Fourthly, intergroup boundaries may be effectively removed by creating a common group to which both belong. Finally, simply removing cues that reinforce the intergroup boundary may lesson reliance on the ingroup–outgroup division as a guide for behavior.

1. Similarity of Beliefs and Behaviors

Assumed belief dissimilarity (Allen & Wilder, 1979) reinforces the boundary between groups and increases any perceived threat posed by the outgroup (Rokeach, 1960). Extrapolating from the extensive literature on similarity and attraction (e.g., Byrne, 1969), an increase in perceived similarity between the ingroup and outgroup should foster a more positive evaluation of the outgroup. Intergroup similarity may be increased either by the removal of cues that indicate dissimilarity (e.g., differences in status), by the introduction of cues that indicate similarity (e.g., opinion agreement), or by both removing dissimilar cues and introducing similar ones (e.g., replacement of a competitive relationship with a cooperative one).

An examination of the literature reveals that lessening dissimilarity between group members sometimes, but not always, lessens bias. (See reviews by Ashmore, 1970b; Billig, 1976; Brewer, 1979; Brown, 1984a; Brown & Turner, 1981.) Likewise, information indicating belief similarity between group members sometimes results in a reduction of bias (e.g., Brewer & Campbell, 1976; Byrne & Wong, 1962; Rokeach, 1960), but again not always (Allen & Wilder, 1975; Brown, 1978; Tajfel et al., 1971; Triandis, 1961; Turner, 1978). Direct attempts to reduce assumed dissimilarity between groups may falter when persons perceive them for what they are—attempts to manipulate their cognitions (Brehm, 1972).

Apart from any problem posed by reactance, Brown (1984a; Brown & Turner, 1981) has questioned the propriety of generalizing from interpersonal research on the similarity–attraction relationship to the realm of intergroup conflict. At the risk of making a simple categorization (with the attending consequences discussed earlier), Brown's concerns are shared by several European social psychologists who see American social psychologists as too willing to leap from the individual to the group level of analysis (e.g., Billig, 1976; Tajfel & Turner, 1979). They argue that individuals differentiate between groups to maintain a positive social identity in an intergroup setting. An outgroup that is highly similar to the ingroup threatens the latter's uniqueness and may also be a competitor for ingroup goals. Thus, information indicating the outgroup is similar to the ingroup could exacerbate bias.

Turner (1978) divided subjects into groups and varied the attitudinal similarity, status similarity, and stability of the status manipulation. Results were generally consistent with the social identity position. Ingroup favoritism was greatest when the outgroup was similar in status and when the similarity appeared to be stable.

Brown (1984b) divided subjects into groups and manipulated the attitudinal and status similarity of the outgroup. The social identity hypothesis received support on only a competitive measure constructed in the prisoner's dilemma style. In a second study Brown explicitly manipulated the competitiveness of the intergroup environment. Because the manipulation of competitiveness was not effective, Brown performed an internal analysis, dividing subjects into cooperative and competitive conditions based on their subjective impressions of the experiment. When the outgroup was similar in status to the ingroup, competitive subjects displayed more ingroup favoritism.

At minimum, the relationship between outgroup similarity and bias is a complex, multivariate one. Simple extrapolation from interpersonal research will not suffice. Some mediating variables to consider include (1) whether a similar outgroup poses a threat to the ingroup (e.g., competition); (2) whether the ingroup–outgroup boundary is permeable; similarity between open groups with "soft" boundaries poses a greater threat to group identity than if the boundaries are "hard" (Ziller, 1965); (3) how much persons rely on their group for a sense of identity; and (4) the breadth and importance of the similarity information (beliefs, values, goals, physical appearance, and so forth).

2. Relative Similarity Following a Change in Social Context

Evidence from a variety of sources indicates that evaluation of a stimulus changes with changes in the situational context. Praise (or criticism) from a previously critical (or complimentary) source may seem more rewarding (or harsh) because of the juxtaposition of the opposite response (e.g., Aronson & Linder, 1965; Berkowitz, 1960). Shakespeare phrases it more eloquently in this passage from Sonnet LXXXIX:

> If thou wilt leave me, do not leave me last
> When other petty griefs have done their spite,
> But in the oneset come; so shall I taste
> At first the very worst of fortune's might;
> And other strains of woe, which now seem woe,
> Compared with loss of thee will not seem so.

With less eloquence than Shakespeare, we may argue that evaluation of an outgroup can be affected without directly changing the characteristics ascribed to that group. A change can be induced by introducing another outgroup, one that is more different from the ingroup than the first outgroup. In comparison to the second outgroup, the first seems more palatable to the ingroup. Three experiments examined this hypothesis.

a. Contrast Effect. In the first study we randomly assigned subjects to one of four conditions in a laboratory setting (Thompson, Wilder, & Cooper, 1979). Depending on condition, subjects were divided into two or three groups. In separate rooms each group discussed a mock civil suit and received feedback indicating that the outgroup disagreed with their position. The case was constructed so that all subjects decided for the plaintiff. In the extreme-outgroup condition, the outgroup rendered the opposite decision, absolving the defendants from all responsibility. In the moderate-outgroup condition, the outgroup blamed all parties equally and awarded partial compensation to the plaintiff. In this manner the moderate outgroup assumed a stance midway between that advocated by the subjects' ingroup and the extreme outgroup. The third condition (divided outgroup) was a composite of the moderate and extreme conditions. Half of the outgroup members differed moderately and half differed extremely from the ingroup's position. Finally, in the two-outgroups condition, subjects were divided into three groups. (Additional subjects participated in this condition, so group size was constant across all conditions.) One outgroup differed moderately, and one differed extremely from the ingroup. (Two additional conditions were included to control for the presence of the second outgroup in the two-outgroups condition. Subjects were divided into three groups in both of the extra conditions. In one, both groups assumed the moderate position; in the other both advocated the extreme position. There were no differences between these two conditions and the corresponding single moderate and extreme conditions on any of the dependent measures.)

Subjects were given the opportunity to divide a $30 bonus between members of the ingroup and members of the outgroup(s). We expected a significant reduction of ingroup favoritism at the expense of the moderate outgroup when the more extreme outgroup was present (two-outgroups condition). But bias directed against the outgroup was not expected to decrease in the divided-outgroup condition, even though subjects were exposed to the same range of opinions as in the two-outgroups condition. Given that moderate and extreme factions in the divided group were both members of the same entity, the moderate members could not be easily separated from the more extreme members and contrasted in the direction of the ingroup.

Results supported these predictions. Significant ingroup favoritism occurred in the moderate-, extreme-, and divided-outgroup conditions. But subjects divided rewards almost equally between the ingroup and moderate outgroup in the two-outgroups condition. They awarded an average of $16 to the ingroup and $14 to the moderate outgroup when the more extreme outgroup was present. But when the moderate outgroup was alone, subjects gave $21 to the ingroup and only $9 to the outgroup.

Hensley and Duval (1976) reported similar findings in an experiment they interpreted using Helson's (1970) theory of adaptation level. Subjects viewed the opinions of others on two issues. The others' positions were constructed to cluster in two groups. The opinions of Group S were moderately similar to the subjects and did not vary across conditions. The experimenters manipulated the distance of Group O's opinions from those of Group S across five levels. Perceived similarity and correctness of Group S's opinions, as well as liking for Group S, increased as Group O became more dissimilar to Group S and the subjects. It is interesting to note that the contrast of Group S away from Group O did not occur in a smooth, continuous manner. There were virtually no changes in judgments of Group S between the first and second levels of Group O's discrepancy from the subjects. At the third level, subjects showed a marked change in evaluation of Group S. This favorable shift did not, however, increase substantially with further increases in Group O's distance from Group S. Evidently, the contrast effect found by Hensley and Duval was an all-or-none phenomenon.

Doise et al. (1978) reported evidence for a contrast effect in the judgment of groups when a more different outgroup was salient. In their study Swiss children perceived several Swiss ethnic groups to be more similar when they were evaluated along with a non-Swiss group (i.e., either Germans, French, or Italians) than when they were rated alone.

Burnstein and McRae (1962) placed a member of a social outgroup in the subjects' experimental group. Subjects displayed less prejudice against the outgroup member when the ingroup was externally threatened than when no threat was evident. Several interpretations are possible; one is that the outgroup member appeared to be less heinous in the presence of the external threat.

b. Assimilation Effect. Findings from these experiments are comparable to the contrast effect reported in the judgment literature (Eiser & Stroebe, 1972; Sherif & Hovland, 1961). But the judgment literature also allows for assimilation, whereby a moderate outgroup may be judged to be similar to the extreme outgroup and even more different from the ingroup. In this case one would expect greater bias against the moderate outgroup following the introduction of the extreme outgroup. Most of us can cite circumstances in which an outgroup is damned because of its perceived similarity to a more extreme outgroup. For example, some conservative groups brand liberals and socialists as indistinguishable radicals while some environmentalists fail to see substantive differences among business groups, and so forth.

A neglected theory of attitudes may be helpful in sorting out assimilation and contrast effects in groups. Sherif and Hovland (1961) argued that persuasive communications are assimilated toward the perceiver's position when the message is deemed to be not too discrepant (latitude of acceptance). The message is contrasted away and rejected when it is relatively distant (latitude of rejection). The net product should be a curvilinear relationship between message discrepancy and attitude change.

Eiser (1971) and Stroebe (1971) challenged a central tenet of the social judgment argument. Although assimilation and contrast effects have been reported in the psychophysical literature (e.g., Eiser & Stroebe, 1972), for any given set of judgments, either all stimuli are assimilated toward or contrasted away from the anchor. To obtain simultaneous assimilation and contrast effects within a single stimulus array, one must superimpose a discrete category on the stimulus series. (A more complete exposition of this thesis can be found in Doise, 1978; Deschamps, 1977; Tajfel, 1957; and Tajfel & Wilkes, 1963.) Thus, in the attitude change studies of social judgment theorists, subjects rate a series of positions that vary both in favorability to the issue and acceptability to themselves. The former is a relatively continuous gradation; the latter is a discrete category of acceptance or rejection. Imposition of the acceptance–rejection category on the range of possible positions should result in an exaggeration of differences between members of different categories (contrast) and underestimation of differences within categories (assimilation).

Returning to intergroup perception, whether an outgroup is assimilated toward or contrasted away from the ingroup may depend on how distant the outgroup is perceived to be from the ingroup. Outgroups that are not too different are more likely to benefit from the introduction of an extremely different outgroup whereas outgroups that are quite different may be judged even more unacceptable when an extreme outgroup is salient.

Evidence for assimilation was found in a partial replication of the moderate- and extreme-outgroup study (Wilder, Thompson, & Cooper, 1981). We employed a different civil suit and different measures. As in the Thompson *et al.* (1979) investigation, subjects were arbitrarily categorized into groups, discussed a civil suit, and received differing opinions from the outgroup(s). In the extreme-outgroup condition, the outgroup took an extreme and clearly unacceptable position relative to the ingroup. The position of the outgroup in the moderate-outgroup condition was closer to that of the ingroup, yet still unacceptable based on pretesting. In the moderate- and extreme-outgroups condition, one outgroup assumed the moderate position and the other advocated the extreme verdict. On the postexperimental questionnaire, subjects rated the outgroup on a series of positive and negative traits and indicated their desire to join the outgroup.

Subjects gave a significantly more negative evaluation to the extreme outgroup than to the moderate outgroup when the moderate outgroup was alone. But when the moderate outgroup was evaluated in the company of the extreme outgroup, ratings of both were equally unfavorable. Desire to join the outgroup for a later task decreased significantly when the moderate outgroup was viewed in the context of the extreme outgroup than when the moderate outgroup was alone. Finally, the moderate outgroup's position was judged to be less acceptable in the moderate-and-extreme condition than in the moderate-only condition.

c. Assimilation and Contrast Effects. In a third study Thompson (1983) attempted to generate both assimilation and contrast effects in the same context. He employed a mock civil suit in which a plaintiff sued an automobile manufacturer following an accident. Pretesting had established that subjects favored the plaintiff. With a pilot group Thompson established latitudes of acceptance and rejection for a range of outcomes—from a wholly favorable judgment for the plaintiff to one totally favorable to the defendant. Two adjacent positions of moderate disagreement were selected for the main study. One position was rated unattractive but acceptable; the other was judged unattractive and unacceptable. These adjacent positions formed the boundary between the latitudes of acceptance and rejection. After completion of the pretest, a different set of subjects was placed in the ingroup–outgroup paradigm described in Thompson *et al.* (1979) and Wilder *et al.* (1981). Subjects rated the outgroup(s) on the measures used in Wilder *et al.* (1981).

In one condition one outgroup took the unattractive but acceptable position, and a second outgroup advocated an extremely rejected opinion. Subjects rated the moderate outgroup significantly more favorably in the presence of an extreme outgroup than when alone (i.e., contrast of the moderate outgroup away from the extreme outgroup toward the ingroup). This finding echoed that reported by Thompson *et al.* (1979). In another condition subjects received feedback from two outgroups—one that advocated the adjacent and slightly more unacceptable position and one that took the extreme position. Here the moderate outgroup was discriminated against more in the presence of the extreme outgroup than when no other outgroup was salient (i.e., assimilation of the moderate outgroup toward the extreme outgroup and away from the ingroup). This outcome replicated that reported by Wilder *et al.* (1981).

Overall, results from this series of studies indicate that both assimilation and contrast effects can be obtained in intergroup evaluations. The key appears to be how dissimilar the moderate outgroup is judged to be initially. Outgroups that are different yet not totally unacceptable may benefit from the salience of a more extreme, clearly rejected outgroup. Outgroups that are unacceptable to begin with may be viewed as less distinguishable from the extreme outgroup and damned all the more by its company. The rub is to predict a priori when an outgroup is likely to be contrasted toward the ingroup or assimilated toward the more distant outgroup. Sherif and Hovland (1961) proposed that the importance of an issue affects the sizes of the latitudes. The more important an attitude, the smaller is the region of acceptance and the larger is the region of rejection. Extrapolating to the group level, the more important (e.g., greater involvement, lack of alternatives) a social identity is for an individual, the more likely a moderate outgroup will be assimilated toward extreme outgroups and rejected.

A second variable that should affect the latitudes is the range of groups to which the perceiver has been exposed. As the judgment literature indicates (Eiser & Stroebe, 1972), introduction of a novel stimulus beyond the range of an individual's experience precipitates a contrast effect; perceived distance between older stimuli decrease relative to the new one. Analogously, introduction of an extreme outgroup that expands the judgment scale should cause a shift in moderate outgroups toward the ingroup. Even the most distant ethnic outgroup might be judged palatable in comparison to a group of extraterrestrials. As Brewer and Campbell (1976) conclude from their study of ethnic relations in East Africa, one may feel psychologically closer to the "familiar enemy" than to the little-known stranger.

The effectiveness of diminishing intergroup "distance" probably depends on maintaining the salience of the more extreme outgroup. It is small wonder that groups often exert energy to remind members of the existence of distant outgroups. Countries with a tradition of acrimonious factions may unite in response to the external, "extreme" enemy. A ceaseless struggle or a constant stream of external threats may be necessary to overcome the less extreme, yet continually simmering, divisions within the nation. Consider the recent history of Iran following the deposition of the Shah. First, there was conflict with the United States

and then Iraq. Those different conflicts shared a common effect of focusing
hostility outward, away from intragroup tensions. Chekhov acidly remarked,
"Love, friendship, respect do not unite people as much as a common hatred for
something" (*Notebooks*).

3. Overlapping Group Memberships

Differences between groups may also be reduced by indicating how members of the groups share common identities on other social dimensions, even
though the groups are mutually exclusive on the dimension at hand. Doise (1969)
examined the overlapping membership hypothesis. Doise created overlapping
memberships by crossing ethnic groups with a laboratory manipulation of group
membership. For some subjects group membership and ethnicity coincided
whereas for others the two categories overlapped. Less intergroup bias was found
when group membership overlapped. Doise (1978) reported similar findings in
an experiment in which children were assigned to groups on the basis of two
criteria (sex and an arbitrary color label). Again, bias was more pronounced
when the ingroup–outgroup categorizations coincided for each dimension than
when some ingroup members were outgroup members on one dimension and
vice versa on the second criterion.

In a review of ethnocentrism research, LeVine and Campbell (1972) cited
several studies indicating less intergroup bias in societies characterized by overlapping social groups (cross-cutting structures) as compared with societies where
groups were relatively independent of one another (pyramidal structures). For
example, the Mundurucu of Brazil have a matrilocal society; following marriage,
men reside with the families of their brides (Murphy, 1957). As a result, a man
has ties among many homes; ties with his parents, with his wife's family in-
asmuch as he is now living with them, and with his brothers who also may be
married and living with new families. Thus, a complex network of familial bonds
arises among men in the matrilocal society. On the other hand, in a patrilocal
system a man remains with his parents following marriage, so fewer ties are
formed outside his family. Interestingly, Murphy (1957) reported more conflict
generated by males between groups using the patrilocal arrangement.

Commins and Lockwood (1978) also reported evidence relevant to the
overlapping categories hypothesis. They divided subjects into groups cutting
across two dimensions: religious affiliation (Catholic, Protestant) and performance on an ambiguous dot estimation task (overestimators, underestimators).
Subjects were selected from Protestant and Catholic schools in Northern Ireland.
Given this location, one suspects that religious affiliation would be a salient and
important category for these subjects. Subjects were assigned to one of three
conditions. In the Catholic condition all subjects were Catholics and were divided into groups solely on the basis of the dot estimation task. The same procedure

was used to create groups in the Protestant condition. In the mixed condition half of the subjects were Catholics and half were Protestants. Because subjects did not know the identity of fellow ingroup members, those in the mixed condition could not tell how many Protestants and Catholics were in each group. Following categorization, subjects completed a set of matrices dividing money between the groups. Those in the Catholic and Protestant conditions displayed the same amount of ingroup favoritism. But subjects in the mixed condition were some-what less biased. For the Catholic and Protestant conditions, religion was irrele-vant because members of both groups shared the same religious affiliation. In the mixed condition, however, categorization on the bases of religion and dot es-timation overlapped. Outgroup members on one dimension may have been in-group members on the other dimension.

Deschamps and Doise (1978) crossed a real category (sex) with an experi-mentally concocted one (color) using 9 and 10 year olds. Subjects in the crossed condition sat around a table with boys on two adjacent sides and girls on the complementary adjacent sides. Half of each sex group was labeled "red" and half "blue." In the simple condition subjects were partitioned into groups on the basis of sex only. All subjects individually worked on a number of puzzles and rated each other's performance. Same-sex persons were rated significantly better than opposite-sex persons in the simple condition; there were no differences in the crossed categorization condition. In effect, bias favoring one's own sex was cancelled by tendencies for bias on the basis of one's color category.

Brown and Turner (1979) criticized the preceding research on two grounds. First, the categorization dimensions were not of equal value in the Commins and Lockwood (1978) and Deschamps and Doise (1978) studies. One category had a history and significance beyond the laboratory (religion and sex, respectively), whereas the other had significance only within the narrow confines of the study (dot estimation and color). In addition, they argued that subjects in crossed conditions were faced with a more complex task (consideration of two sets of categories) than those in the simple conditions. To control for these possible artifacts, Brown and Turner crossed subjects on two artificial categories (prefer-ence for two fictitious countries and two photographers). After division into groups (either a simple division where preferred country and photographer coin-cided or a crossed division into four groups), subjects estimated the performance of members from each group on a "perceptual ability" task. To control for complexity of cognitive demand, some subjects in the crossed conditions rated everyone (as in the Deschamps & Doise study) while others only rated members of one group. Results were mixed. When asked to rate all members of the outgroups in the crossed condition, subjects showed no significant bias, con-sistent with the Deschamps and Doise findings. But when rating only one out-group member, subjects displayed significant ingroup favoritism when the out-group members differed on both dimensions and in one of the conditions where the outgroup was an ingroup on one dimension but an outgroup on the other. But there was no significant difference between ingroup and outgroup ratings in the other condition where the outgroup member was in an ingroup on one dimension but not on the other.

It seems fair to conclude that intergroup bias cannot always be eliminated by crossing or overlapping group memberships. Whether overlapping groups is effective in diminishing intergroup boundaries may depend on a number of factors including the individual's degree of anonymity (e.g., surveillance by one of the ingroups should increase pressure to favor that group), the relative importance of the categories for the individual's social identity (Brown & Turner, 1979) and for the task at hand, and the presence of cues that make one ingroup category more salient than the other(s) (Wilder & Shapiro, 1984).

Returning from this speculative sojourn, findings provide some support for the overlapping membership hypothesis. Ingroup favoritism can be lessened when ingroup and outgroup members are also members of overlapping groups. In those situations intergroup boundaries become somewhat nebulous as members of an ingroup may also be members of an outgroup, and outgroup members may surface as ingroup members. Overlapping categories discourage a simplistic "we–they" representation of the groups. Overlapping categories may also encourage individuation of outgroup members. With increasing overlap between ingroups and outgroups across social categories, perceivers must generate more subgroups to accommodate for the multiple combinations, with each subgroup being smaller than the one from which it was derived. Taken to the extreme, complete overlap of the ingroup and outgroup eliminates the distinction between the two, netting a single group.

4. Elimination of Intergroup Boundary

Both the "assimilation–contrast" and "overlapping" tactics attempt to reduce the effects of social categorization while maintaining the ingroup and outgroup as distinct entities. The most effective tactic may also be the most audacious—complete elimination of intergroup boundaries.

The outgroup may become part of the ingroup by several means. First, the groups may be merged by an agent controlling them or by a change in social convention. For example, two separate work groups in a company may be combined to labor on a project, either formally by management directive or less formally by mutual consent. A mandated merger may not, however, be accepted by the group members. Attitude change research and intuition suggest that a merger will be more effective if the group members believe they have had some input in the process. Furthermore, imposed consolidation of the groups may have limited generality. Consider Minard's (1952) classic study of coal miners. Black and white miners interacted well beneath the surface, but they exhibited racial prejudice above ground. In the subterranean environment they were united as a single group by their employer and a common task. Rising from darkness to light, they returned to a community divided into multiple groups (e.g., families, social class), one of which was race.

Secondly, one group may annex the other. The difficulty with this option is that the group that is swallowed may be stigmatized as weak and assigned a low status position in the combined group. Any such stigma will create a new category, that of dominant and subordinate subgroups within the combined group.

Thirdly, a change in the categorization dimension may bring the outgroup into the ingroup. As Brewer and Campbell (1976) suggest, changes in ingroup–outgroup groupings are likely to occur to the extent intergroup boundaries are based on multiple dimensions that do not converge. The more dimensions that do not corroborate the salient ingroup–outgroup dimension, the more likely that any changes in the salient dimension will shift the outgroup to ingroup status. Consider Heider's (1958) example of the Kansian who boasts of the Empire State Building to a foreigner. The presence of the foreigner makes the United States–foreign nation category salient; for that grouping even New York is part of the Kansian's ingroup. But for other categories (e.g., political orientation), New York may be an outgroup to Kansas. The ingroup–outgroup dimension may also be altered by a change in group goals. Goals compatible with those of the outgroup may encourage a merger of the two, especially in the case of a superordinate goal where each group needs the other (e.g., Sherif, 1967).

5. Removing Outgroup Cues

The four tactics discussed above share the goal of reducing the salience of the ingroup–outgroup boundary. Worchel (1979) showed in a series of clever experiments that cooperative contact between groups is most effective when accompanied by a reduction in the salience of intergroup boundaries. The salience of group boundaries may be influenced by (1) distinctive physical or visible differences between the groups, (2) outcome of intergroup interaction, (3) intensity of any previous conflict, (4) frequency and duration of cooperation between the groups, and (5) disparities in power and status between the groups.

Worchel, Axsom, Samaha, & Schweitzer (1978) reported that cooperation between groups led to greater intergroup attraction when the groups were dressed identically than when dressed distinctively. Distinctive dress reinforced the differences of the groups, thereby diminishing the effect of cooperation. Worchel, Andreoli, and Folger (1977) found that cooperative success increased attraction to the outgroup. But failure at a cooperative task increased attaction to the outgroup only when the groups had not previously competed. Prior competition may have strengthened intergroup boundaries so that frustration stemming from failure on the cooperative task was visited on the outgroup.

6. Summary

Tactics that discourage a simple "we–they" representation diminish the role of social categorization in fostering ingroup favoritism. Increasing the belief similarity between the groups may be effective when increased similarity does not pose a threat to ingroup identity. Increasing perceived similarity by way of a "common enemy" or more extreme outgroup may be a more effective tactic. Appeals to overlapping group memberships on other dimensions or to common, broader ingroups ought to be effective in that either tactic voids a simple dichotomous representation of the ingroup and outgroup. And clearly tactics that literally reduce the presence of cues indicating the ingroup–outgroup division have been shown to be helpful. None of these tactics guarantees success, partly because intergroup bias is often determined by factors other than social categorization and partly because the effects of categorization are most likely more difficult to reverse than to create.

C. DIMINISHING DEPENDENCE ON THE INGROUP FOR SOCIAL IDENTITY

Tactics explored thus far for reducing bias resulting from categorization have focused on either making the outgroup more sympathetic or minimizing intergroup boundaries. A third approach focuses on the perceiver's relationship to the ingroup. If desire for a positive social identity fosters bias, then reducing the ingroup's role in providing one's identity may lessen ingroup favoritism.

The most obvious tactic is to discourage an individual from developing a strong association with the ingroup (Heider, 1958; Section IV,C,1). Secondly, one might introduce information that creates dissimilarities and conflicts between the individual and the ingroup (Section IV,C,2). Thirdly, one might provide means to satisfy the individual's goals without dependence on the ingroup (Section IV,C,3). Finally, social support for dissent may lessen a person's dependence on the ingroup (Section IV,C,4).

1. Association with the Ingroup

Intuition suggests a direct relationship between favorable interaction with fellow members of an ingroup and strong identification with that group. If such is the case, then minimizing ingroup contact should result in weak identification with the ingroup and thus lessen the resultant ingroup favoritism.

John Thompson and I tested this hypothesis in a study of intercollege bias (Wilder & Thompson, 1980). Subjects were recruited from two undergraduate colleges among the several making up Rutgers University. Douglass College is a women's institution whereas Rutgers College is coeducational. Pretesting had revealed several stereotypes that members of each college held about the other group. Rutgers women assumed Douglass students were overly concerned with their physical appearance, studies, and academic evaluation. Douglass women believed Rutgers women were interested in having fun and were relatively unfeminine.

Five subjects from each college participated in an experiment allegedly comparing the performance of Douglass and Rutgers students on a variety of cognitive tasks. Groups of subjects were randomly assigned to one of five conditions. They either interacted for one or for two half-hour sessions with the ingroup and for one or two sessions with the outgroup. In addition, some subjects were assigned to a control condition in which they interacted only with the ingroup. In each of the contact sessions subjects confronted a problem-solving task designed to promote cooperative interaction. Following the contact session(s), subjects evaluated members of both groups and divided earnings between the groups.

Analysis of the reward distribution indicated main effects for both ingroup and outgroup contact. Decreasing contact with the ingroup significantly reduced ingroup favoritism. Bias was also reduced by increasing cooperative contact with the outgroup. Parallel results emerged for the trait evaluations of the groups. Hence, independent of contact with the outgroup, less contact with the ingroup lessened ingroup–outgroup bias. By reducing ingroup contact (at least with newly formed groups), one may diminish the role of the ingroup as a source of social identity.

2. Similarity and Attraction to the Ingroup

An individual's relationship with an ingroup may be affected by altering the similarity between them. As mentioned earlier (Section III,B,1), the extensive interpersonal attraction literature suggests less ingroup favoritism to the extent persons perceive themselves to be dissimilar to the ingroup. (Reservations mentioned in Section III,B,1 about generalizing from interpersonal attraction research to intergroup relations are less applicable here because an individual's relationship with the ingroup is interpersonal; no group boundaries are crossed.)

In an examination of the role of ingroup similarity, Allen and Wilder (1975) categorized subjects into two groups on the basis of an arbitrary criterion (painting preferences). Subjects also responded to a set of items tapping their opinions on a variety of topics including art, politics, and college life. Later they were given an opportunity to view information about the beliefs of fellow ingroup and outgroup members. The information they saw indicated either ingroup similarity and outgroup similarity to themselves; ingroup similarity and outgroup dissimilarity; ingroup dissimilarity and outgroup similarity; or ingroup dissimilarity and outgroup dissimilarity. Subsequently, subjects divided earnings between anonymous members of the groups. Overall, they displayed ingroup favoritism regardless of the belief similarity manipulation. The magnitude of ingroup favoritism, however, was significantly less when the ingroup was thought to be dissimilar to the subjects.

Consistent with this finding, Brewer's (1979) extensive review of the group categorization literature indicates that similarity within the ingroup may be a better predictor of ingroup favoritism than similarity between the ingroup and outgroup. Note that while ingroup similarity enhances ingroup favoritism, ingroup dissimilarity does not completely eliminate bias. Although a dissimilar ingroup may be less preferred, it may also be the only social identity available in the setting. When alternative ingroups are available, individuals may use one of them as a referent, thereby furthering distancing them from the dissimilar ingroup.

Reducing cohesiveness (attraction to the ingroup) should lessen one's identification with the ingroup and consequent desire to differentiate it favorably from outgroups. Dion (1973) reported a significant relationship between ingroup cohesiveness and intergroup behavior. Subjects displayed ingroup favoritism when the ingroup was highly cohesive but failed to discriminate when ingroup cohesiveness was low. Ferguson and Kelley (1964) reported similar findings in a study in which subjects evaluated ingroup and outgroup products. Subjects who were more attracted to the ingroup evaluated the ingroup's product more favorably.

Others, however, have reported that increased attraction to the ingroup is associated with increased attraction to the outgroup as well (Stephan & Rosenfield, 1978; Wilson & Kayatani, 1968). Absence of a simple relationship between ingroup cohesiveness and intergroup bias suggests that the role of cohesiveness is tempered by other factors. One candidate is the degree of incompatibility between the groups (Holms, cited in Dion, 1979). In cooperative settings ingroup cohesiveness should correlate negatively with intergroup bias while a positive relationship is likely to exist under competitive conditions. In the former case satisfaction with the ingroup generalizes to the positively associated outgroup whereas in the latter instance satisfaction with the ingroup may be threatened by the adversary outgroup.

3.   Social Mobility versus Social Change

Regardless of whether an individual likes the ingroup, one may identify with that group if (1) there are no alternative ways of constructing one's social identity in that setting or (2) alternatives exist but adoption of one is not possible.

If the ingroup is closed (Ziller, 1965) so that movement is not possible, the individual has little choice but to define himself or herself through that ingroup (particularly if others will react to the individual as a member of that group). If the ingroup is disliked, a coerced ingroup identity can result in "self-hatred" (Lewin, 1948). Alternatively, constrained membership can foster a strong sense of ingroup identity. Fate interdependence among group members is high because individuals cannot disguise their identity and have little prospect of publicly adopting another. In such cases a positive identity is dependent on group, rather than individual, success; in other words through social change (movement of groups) rather than social mobility (movement of individuals across groups; Tajfel, 1982). Social networks based on rigid castes and classes (e.g., apartheid) fall into this camp. On the other hand, members of open ingroups are less dependent on any one group to attain a favorable social identity. Any specific ingroup, therefore, becomes less important in defining oneself, and ingroup favoritism should decline.

Two examples should make this argument clear. Social mobility has been an option for most members of white ethnic groups in the United States, in part, because public education has provided tools to overcome language and cultural castes and because there are few physical differences that prevent passing from one group to another. But black Americans cannot shed their group membership. Compared to other ethnic groups, blacks appear to have a strong sense of identity with their ingroup. Conflict between a social mobility orientation (that decreases ingroup identity) and a social change orientation (that increases dependence on the ingroup) can be seen in the debate among blacks over integration (social mobility—lessening of intergroup boundaries) versus separatism (social change—strengthening of intergroup boundaries) as goals for black–white relations. The social change and social mobility positions gather strength from the failures of each other.

As another example consider differences in "class consciousness" between European and American workers. The former are more likely to be organized into labor unions and to show solidarity (e.g., general strikes). Traditionally, European workers have expected little social mobility; individual success comes through group movement (Tajfel, 1978). American workers, however, are more likely to believe that individuals may move across social classes ("evolutionary individualism," Hirschman, 1972). Consequently, groups are less likely to be viewed as necessary for individual success. Note that this difference carries over to our explanations of social behavior. At the risk of oversimplification, European social psychologists seem to be more concerned with the impact of social groups on the individual while their American colleagues look from the individual to the group.

To the extent individual mobility is slight, ingroup identity should be strong and potential for ingroup favoritism should be great. Actual bias may be tempered by a number of factors, two of which are the perceived legitimacy and stability (possibility for change) of the categorization. Categorization that offers little individual mobility, that is perceived to be illegitimate, and that is unstable should engender the strongest ingroup favoritism. That combination of factors fosters maximum ingroup identity, grievance, and hope for social change (Brown & Turner, 1981). Ingroup favoritism should be minimized when persons either (1) believe in social mobility and are not dependent on the ingroup for social identity or (2) believe in the legitimacy of group differences and the unlikelihood of social change. In the latter case group members may accept a subservient relationship with the outgroup.

4. Surveillance and Social Support

Dependence on the ingroup for social identity may be weakened when an individual is alone and has no support from fellow ingroup members. A vast literature attests to the efficacy of social support in maintaining independence in the face of conformity pressure (Allen, 1965, 1975). Similarly, presence of fellow ingroup members helps to maintain the salience of the ingroup and the individual's social identity as defined by that group.

In a study bearing on this argument, Boyanowsky and Allen (1973) provided white subjects with social support from either a black or a white ally. Both supporters were effective in reducing conformity to the majority on tasks involving perceptual judgments and general opinions. But for self-referent items, subjects high in prejudice conformed more with the black ally than with the white ally. This effect was increased when they were under surveillance by the white majority (racial ingroup). To cite another example from a different literature, Stephenson and Brotherton (1975) reported that bargaining sessions between four persons (two on each side) were more acrimonious and polarized than sessions between two persons. The presence of a fellow ingroup member on each side made compromise more difficult.

For the marginal and half-hearted members, surveillance serves an additional function—an Orwellian reminder of their link to the ingroup. Absence of surveillance allows these members to shed behavioral allegiance to their ingroup identity.

5. Summary

Intergroup bias based on social categorization may be decreased by severing the individual's dependence on the ingroup for positive social identity. Most directly, one may reduce the association between the individual and ingroup. But what might occupy the void if contact with the ingroup were reduced? Replacement with positive contact with the outgroup would be a means of knotting both ends of the rope—decreasing dependence on the ingroup and increasing positive cognitions about the outgroup. Reliance on the ingroup can also be reduced by evidence that the ingroup is a dissimilar, ill-suited referent and by evidence that the individual can attain a positive self-identity without reliance on the ingroup.

Finally, removal of cues associated with the ingroup (especially surveillance by ingroup members) should reduce the salience of the ingroup and any conformity pressures.

V. Reducing Intergroup Bias by Changing the Categorization Process

The bias reduction tactics I have discussed involve a change in cognitions about the outgroup (individuation tactics), the ingroup (tactics to reduce dependence on the ingroup for social identity), or the distinction between the two (tactics that diminish intergroup boundaries). All are post hoc attempts to ameliorate undesirable consequences of social categorization.

Alternatively, one might try to change the categorization process itself; that is, alter the manner in which we form social categories and draw bias-producing inferences. Interference with the social categorization–intergroup bias chain may occur at two points. At the earliest stage we may try to prevent social categorization. However, to the extent that social categorization follows the general principles of object categorization, this would be a difficult and, perhaps, ultimately undesirable effort. More reasonably, we might devise strategies to make individuals less vulnerable to the biased inferences they often make following social categorization. At minimum, we might educate them to acknowledge that these biases occur.

As an opening ploy, suppose we encourage persons to rely less on social categories and more on the larger situational context when evaluating others. Reliance on social categories encourages a loss of information about individual members of the outgroup. Categorical expectations color the ways we monitor and interpret behavior. We generalize quickly from categories to individual instances. The likelihood of error should increase as the social category becomes more removed from the perceiver. Evaluation of remote outgroups is probably based largely on category information as opposed to direct experience with them. This is where contact between individual members of different groups can be valuable. Contact under favorable conditions can provide both a positive experience with the outgroup and rich, individuated information about outgroup members. (See Amir, 1969, 1976, for discussion of the "favorable" circumstances in which contact can be successful.) Favorable contact lessens one's dependence on abstract and often secondhand social stereotypes when evaluating outgroup members. Favorable contact may not change attitudes toward the outgroup immediately, but it may soften or "unfreeze" (Lewin, 1948) cognitions so that the outgroup is represented in a more differentiated manner, thereby permitting a more individually tailored response to specific outgroup members.

A half century ago, Lewin (1935) challenged social psychologists to seek a Galilean rather than an Aristotelian conceptualization of lawfulness. In choosing those names, Lewin posited a radical change in thought between the physics of Aristotle and Galileo. The Aristotelian view of lawfulness creates categories on the basis of *frequency* and phenotypic similarities among elements. In a circular fashion the Aristotelian mode treats criteria that categorize objects as the end states to which the objects evolve *(teleology)*. Thus, similarities among elements of a category serve as both causes and effects; criteria for inclusion and consequences of being included. For example, an object is classified as heavy because it falls rapidly, and it falls rapidly because it is heavy. Frequency is a criterion for a law. The infrequent is an accident and does not vitiate the law. Consequently, laws change only when a large number of "exceptions" occur.

The Galilean perspective eschews frequency as a criterion for lawfulness. Single exceptions can invalidate a law. Category membership is insufficient information for prediction. Rather, the relationship of the object to the total field determines its properties and causal relationships. The rate with which a "heavy" object falls is not a property of the object, per se, but an outcome of the total field—object and situation in which it is observed. Thus, the Galilean representation is both richer and more complex than the Aristotelian alternative.

Turning to social categories, our representations of outgroups are largely Aristotelian while our representations of ingroups tend to be more Galilean. I suspect this difference is due in part to the greater familiarity we have with most ingroups relative to outgroups. On an interpersonal level, this Aristotelian–Galilean difference is manifested by differences in the interpretation of our actions versus those of others. Again, our interpretation of others' behavior tends to be Aristotelian while explanations of our own actions are Galilean. Because we have a portion of our social identity invested in ingroups, ingroups and outgroups are "group level" analogs of self and others (Tajfel, 1982). Differences in interpreting ingroup and outgroup actions parallel those reported between self and others (Pettigrew, 1979). Dispositional attributions to the behavior of outgroup members is Aristotelian in that attributions are made on the basis of phenotypic properties (group membership), often with little regard for the broader context in which the behavior occurs. Attention appears to be narrowly focused on the actor rather than on the interaction between actor and setting. Attribution theorists have repeatedly commented on this bias for underemphasizing the role of the situation in determining others' actions (e.g., Jones & Nisbett, 1970; Jones, 1979; Ross, 1977). But if attention is directed toward the context of the actor's behavior, perceivers make more self-like attributions (e.g., Storms, 1973). Encouraging perceivers to empathize with the actor also nets a more self-like interpretation of the actor's behavior (e.g., Regan & Totten, 1975).

By the same token, relatively more situational interpretations of one's own actions reflect a Galilean mode of thought. Explanations of one's own actions (even when "incorrect"—see Nisbett & Wilson, 1977; and White, 1980) demonstrate a richer, broader consideration of situational impact with less reliance on a priori traits which are often Aristotelian descriptions implying a narrow teleology. (Indeed, we may find it uncomfortable to describe ourselves using dispositional traits as they connote a lack of behavioral freedom.) Consider that inconsistencies between our own beliefs and actions are not dismissed as aberrations; rather, we attempt to find a lawful interpretation in terms of the unique, dynamic relationship between ourselves and the environmental presses in those specific settings. Relying on a more Aristotelian view of others, however, we regard inconsistencies as unreliable data, as exceptions to their traits, and by their very infrequency, as testimony to the lawfulness of those characteristics.

Aristotelian reasoning encourages deindividuation of outgroup members, thereby nurturing the likelihood of bias. By contrast, developing a Galilean view of outgroups should promote a more supportive, self-like response to them. How, then, do we shift from an Aristotelian to a Galilean view of outgroups? Several of the tactics for bias reduction discussed in this article move the individual away from an Aristotelian representation of the outgroup. Individuation of the outgroup (Section IV,A) and diminishing the ingroup/outgroup boundary (Section IV,B) encourage the perceiver to take the perspective of the outgroup, to examine contextual factors other than category membership, and ultimately to make a more ingroup-like response to the outgroup.

VI. Bias Reduction: Benefits to the Individual or to the Group

Most of the research reviewed in this article has focused on small laboratory groups. Bias-reduction tactics have usually involved groups as a whole. When dealing with large groups, however, information about a small subset of the group may not be easily generalized to the group as a whole. The ease with which information about a subgroup can be generalized to the larger group ought to be influenced by the perceived typicalness of the subgroup. In addition, generalization from a sample to the whole group ought to be more likely as the size of the sample increases.

A. TYPICALNESS OF SUBSET

In a series of studies I arranged contact sessions between members of two undergraduate colleges (Douglass and Rutgers) that form part of Rutgers University (Wilder, 1984). Rutgers is coeducational while Douglass is a women's college. Members of each college generally prefer their ingroup and possess a few uncomplimentary stereotypes of the outgroup school. In the first experiment subjects interacted with a member of the outgroup college. The latter was a confederate who either behaved in a positive or negative manner, and who appeared to be either typical (matched the stereotypes of the outgroup) or atypical of the outgroup. Following the contact sessions, subjects evaluated both the contact person and the outgroup as a whole. As one might expect, the contact person was evaluated more favorably when she behaved in a positive, cooperative manner regardless of how typical she appeared to be. But evaluation of the outgroup as a whole interacted with the typicalness manipulation. When the confederate appeared to be typical of the outgroup, positive contact resulted in a significantly more favorable evaluation of the outgroup than negative, unpleasant contact. But positive contact with the atypical member was no more beneficial than unpleasant contact. Additional measures assessed subjects' stereotypes of the outgroup college to see if these had been affected by the contact experience. Analyses showed no significant differences among conditions.

Overall, the effectiveness of favorable contact with an outgroup member on evaluations of the outgroup as a whole depended on how typical the contact person was of the outgroup. In addition, changes in evaluation of the outgroup may occur without changes in stereotypes (Brigham, 1971). Contact with the helpful, typical member may reinforce some stereotypes because the contact person matches them. But something about this rationale does not seem quite right. If outgroups are disliked, in part, because they are thought to possess undesirable characteristics, then typical members should also have some of those characteristics. Moreover, traditional wisdom recommends that the behavior of an outgroup member be contrary to stereotypes (e.g., Ashmore, 1970b; Deutsch & Collins, 1951). The key to this dilemma may lie in the specific stereotypes the outgroup member displays in the contact setting. Some beliefs about the outgroup directly involve the ingroup (e.g., "they think themselves better than us") while others do not (e.g., "they are indolent"). The manipulation of typicalness in the above experiment employed beliefs that did not bear directly on the ingroup (e.g., outgroup member's appearance, studiousness). Furthermore, the outgroup member did not make explicit comparisons between the groups.

In a second experiment (Wilder, 1984) the manipulation of typicalness involved a direct comparison between groups. Pretesting had indicated that members of each college believed the outgroup thought their own college provided a better education. Employing the methodology of the first study, subjects had a cooperative, pleasant interaction with a typical outgroup member. In addition, for some subjects, the typical contact person made an unfavorable comparison between the groups, alleging superiority of her college. Although subjects in both conditions rated the interaction favorably, those who interacted with the confederate who made the "typical" unfavorable comparison between the groups evaluated the outgroup less positively than those who had contact with the same confederate behaving the same way but without the intergroup comparison. In the former condition the contact person, although helpful and generally pleasant, reinforced an expectation about the outgroup that had negative implications for the ingroup. Hence, increasing the typicalness of a contact person will be counterproductive if that increase is purchased by the display of negative stereotypes involving the ingroup.

A third experiment (Wilder, 1984) gathered evidence relevant to several possible explanations of the "typicalness" finding. Only one received support; subjects judged the typical outgroup member's personality and behavior to be more indicative of how others in the outgroup would act in the contact setting. Because she behaved positively, there was a good chance that others in her group would behave likewise. But positive behavior on the part of less typical members was not readily generalized to the outgroup as a whole.

As an illustration, consider an early study of intergroup contact that netted mixed findings. Young (1932) took a class of graduate students studying race relations and had them interact over the semester with blacks who were quite favorable models, yet I suspect quite atypical of existing stereotypes (e.g., doctor, wealthy and cultured couple, pianist). Despite the favorable contact, attitude change was mixed. Some students showed little change while others became less and some even more prejudiced toward blacks in general. Quite likely many of the students discounted their contact experiences because the outgroup members were so atypical of their expectations.

On the other hand, Hamill, Wilson, and Nisbett (1980) reported a strong impact of atypical information on categorical judgments. They provided subjects with a description of an humane prison guard who was atypical of guards in general. Subjects given this information judged prison guards to be more humane than a control group not provided with the exception to the rule. On reflection, however, this finding does not contradict the typicalness hypothesis. In the Hamill et al. (1980) studies, subjects were asked to make judgments about groups with which they had had few contact experiences, if any. Contrast that situation with those in which we have had many contacts with both ingroup and outgroup members (e.g., racial groups, adjacent college populations). One would expect the impact of any one contact experience to be less in the latter situations than in the former, in which little is known about the outgroup. Even the exception may have some impact on attitudes toward the whole outgroup when experiences with members of the outgroup is minimal.

The relationship between typicalness and evaluation of the outgroup presents a quandary for the individual outgroup member who desires both a favorable evaluation of self and of the outgroup as a whole. Both responses may be difficult to realize together. Benefit from positive contact will accrue to the outgroup to the extent the contact person is perceived to be typical. But maximum benefit for the contact person may result from being dubbed an exception, particularly if that implies a more favorable status than other members of the outgroup (e.g., greater abilities or effort to overcome obstacles inherent in membership in the outgroup). Linville and Jones (1980) presented whites with a description of an applicant to law school who was either white or black and either well or poorly qualified. The black applicant was rated more favorably when well qualified and more unfavorably when poorly qualified than the comparable white applicant. Assuming white subjects have a narrower range of expected performance for blacks than whites (which would be consistent with the assumption of outgroup homogeneity discussed in Section III,D), one interpretation is that the qualified black was judged to be an exception whereas the unqualified black was viewed as more consistent with expectations. Consequently, evaluations of them were more polarized than ratings of the ingroup members (whites) about whom greater heterogeneity was anticipated in the first place.

The fact that contact situations can become self-fulfilling prophecies further complicates the dilemma of self-presentation. To the extent the outgroup member is judged to be highly typical, expectations about the outgroup may influence the manner in which information is selected and recalled about that individual (e.g., Snyder, 1981). Clearly positive behavior, such as that performed by the outgroup member in Wilder's (1984) typicalness studies, may be difficult to distort. But motives behind behavior can always be questioned. For this reason it is not uncommon to find individual outgroup members attempting to maximize positive evaluations of themselves by distancing themselves from the outgroup. Thus, some members of minority groups eschew characteristics thought by the majority group to be typical of them.

From this discussion of typicalness and contact, it appears that a member of a negatively evaluated outgroup is in a trap. On the one hand, information that strengthens the member's association with the outgroup enhances the generalizability of a favorable contact experience to the outgroup as a whole. But to the extent that an outgroup member appears to be typical of the outgroup, he or she risks confirming stereotypes unfavorable to the perceiver's ingroup. On the other hand, information that weakens an outgroup member's association with the outgroup enhances the impact of his or her favorable behavior on self-evaluations. But to the extent the person appears to be atypical of the outgroup, favorable contact has less impact on evaluation of the outgroup as a whole.

B. SIZE OF SUBSET

Intuition suggests that the more favorable information one has about an outgroup, the greater should be the likelihood of changing one's evaluation of that group. Ever fickle, intuition also suggests the absence of any simple continuous relationship between amount of favorable information and overall evaluation of the outgroup. As argued earlier (Section II,D), the impact of favorable contact with multiple members of an outgroup will depend on how one organizes those members. To the extent all are perceived to be highly similar, they may be categorized as a peculiar subgroup of the outgroup. Generalization of a favorable response to the outgroup as a whole should suffer. But to the extent they are perceived to be somewhat different from one another yet still highly representative (or typical) of the outgroup, favorable actions on their part are most likely to improve evaluation of the whole outgroup. In short, positive experiences with individual outgroup members should most affect cognitions about the entire outgroup when they are perceived to be (1) typical rather than exceptions to the rule and (2) sufficiently heterogeneous so that as a subgroup they cannot be dismissed as an exception to the rule. In addition, consistency over time and location ought to maximize the impact of the outgroup members (Allen & Wilder, 1978).

VII. Final Remarks

Between two hawks, which flies the higher pitch;
Between two dogs, which hath the deeper mouth;
Between two blades, which bears the better temper;
Between two horses, which doth bear him best;
Between two girls, which hath the merriest eye;
(Shakespeare: Henry VI, Part I, II.iv.)

This article began with the observation that persons organize their social environment by categorizing themselves and others into groups. Categorization serves at least two functions, enabling us to simplify the present social environment and to predict future social behavior. Although reliance on categories is efficient, we risk errors when we use a category based on phenotypic similarities to infer genotypic properties. (Thus, members of a group may share similar opinions on matters relevant to the group but that similarity may not reflect an underlying similarity of motives or dispositions.) Categorizing others into ingroups and outgroups produces a set of consistent and quite logical effects, including assumptions of similarity within and dissimilarity between groups, assumed homogeneity of the outgroup, and overreliance on information that supports these assumptions. In short, these effects foster deindividuation of outgroups and identification with ingroups. Not surprisingly, categorization leads to intergroup comparisons and ingroup favoritism over outgroups even when no obvious justifications are present for bias.

Strategies that reduce bias generated by social categorization involve some combination of individuating the outgroup, reducing the salience of intergroup boundaries, and reducing the perceiver's identification with the ingroup. The first two strategies attack the categorization process by making the ingroup–outgroup representation a poor way of organizing the environment. In the case of individuation tactics, the outgroup is portrayed as relatively heterogeneous, so a simple categorical representation cannot be sustained. In the case of boundary tactics, the distinction between the ingroup and outgroup is blurred so that a particular categorization loses predictive utility. Finally, reducing the perceiver's identification with the ingroup mitigates ingroup favoritism based on a desire for a positive social identity derived through membership in that ingroup.

But if one social categorization is rendered impotent, will not another replace it? If we are set to make categorizations, will not less reliance on one increase dependence on another? While this may be true, clearly some social categories are more benign than others. For instance, some categorizations do not imply intergroup competition or do not have powerful implications for one's social identity. Use of these categories may minimize the likelihood of bias based on categorization. Unfortunately, precisely because such categories are less self-involving, they may not be the categories of choice in constructing social reality.

Bearing this last statement in mind, when is it possible to have a strong, positive identity without denigrating outgroups? First, one can cultivate characteristics of the ingroup that are positive in an absolute sense, regardless of the outgroup. Second, when comparisons are made with outgroups, multiple dimensions can be examined so that differences favorable to the ingroup on some are offset by superior outcomes for the outgroup on others. The dynamics of juggling multiple comparisons (across several dimensions with several groups) has not been studied, although common experience indicates that it occurs.

This article has sought to identify effects of social categorization and to generate tactics to lessen one effect—intergroup bias. Implicit in this approach is the desire to return the perceiver to the "unbiased" state that preceded the act of categorization. But, of course, the categorization did occur. We cannot take a phenomenon, change it, and then return it to its "original" state again. We are not like the mechanical pendulum of Newton's physics whose movements are reversible. Although psychological processes may repeat themselves, they cannot reverse themselves; we cannot go back. Returning to social categorization, although the consequences of categorization for intergroup relations may be minimized by the tactics discussed here, once a social category has been employed it cannot be erased. It will remain a means of organizing the social environment, of differentiating among the hawks, dogs, blades, horses, and girls. Nevertheless, we can struggle to minimize the undesirable and to nurture the beneficial consequences of social categorization.

REFERENCES

Abelson, R. P. (1976). Script processing in attitude formation and decision-making. In J. S. Carroll & J. W. Payne (Eds.), *Cognition and social behavior*. Hillsdale, NJ: Erlbaum.

Allen, V. L. (1965). Situational factors in conformity. In L. Berkowitz (Ed.), *Advances in experimental social psychology* (Vol. 2). New York: Academic Press.

Allen, V. L. (1975). Social support for nonconformity. In L. Berkowitz (Ed.), *Advances in experimental social psychology* (Vol. 9). New York: Academic Press.

Allen, V. L., & Wilder, D. A. (1975). Categorization, beliefs similarity, and intergroup discrimination. *Journal of Personality and Social Psychology, 32,* 971–977.

Allen, V. L., & Wilder, D. A. (1978). Perceived confidence and persuasiveness as a function of consistency across belief and time. *European Journal of Social Psychology, 8,* 289–296.

Allen, V. L., & Wilder, D. A. (1979). Group categorization and attribution of belief similarity. *Small Group Behavior, 10,* 73–80.

Allen, V. L., Wilder, D. A., & Atkinson, M. L. (1983). Multiple group membership and social identity. In T. R. Sarbin & K. E. Scheibe (Eds.), *Studies in social identity*. New York: Praeger.

Allport, G. W. (1954). *The nature of prejudice*. Reading, MA: Addison-Wesley.

Amir, Y. (1969). Contact hypothesis in ethnic relations. *Psychological Bulletin, 71,* 319–341.

Amir, Y. (1976). The role of intergroup contact in change of prejudice and ethnic relations. In P. A. Katz (Ed.), *Towards the elimination of racism*. Oxford: Pergamon.

Aronson, E., & Linder, D. (1965). Gain and loss of esteem as determinants of interpersonal attractiveness. *Journal of Experimental Social Psychology, 1,* 156–171.

Ashmore, R. D. (1970a). The problem of intergroup prejudice. In B. E. Collins (Ed.), *Social psychology*. Reading, MA: Addison-Wesley.

Ashmore, R. D. (1970b). Solving the problem of prejudice. In B. E. Collins (Ed.), *Social Psychology*. Reading, MA: Addison-Wesley.

Austin, W. G., & Worchel, S. (Eds.) (1979). *The social psychology of intergroup relations*. Monterey, CA: Brooks/Cole.

Barker, R. G. (Ed.) (1963). *The stream of behavior*. New York: Appleton-Century-Crofts.

Berkowitz, L. (1960). The judgmental process in personality functioning. *Psychological Review, 67,* 130–142.

Billig, M. (1976). *Social psychology and intergroup relations*. New York: Academic Press.

Billig, M., & Tajfel, H. (1973). Social categorization and similarity in intergroup behaviour. *European Journal of Social Psychology, 3,* 27–52.

Boyanowsky, E. O., & Allen, V. L. (1973). Ingroup norms and self-identity as determinants of discriminatory behavior. *Journal of Personality and Social Psychology, 25,* 408–418.

Branthwaite, A., Doyle, S., & Lightbrown, N. (1979). The balance between fairness and discrimination. *European Journal of Social Psychology, 9,* 149–163.

Brehm, J. W. (1972). *Responses to loss of freedom: A theory of psychological reactance*. Morristown, NJ: General Learning Press.

Brewer, M. B. (1979). In-group bias in the minimal intergroup situation: A cognitive–motivational analysis. *Psychological Bulletin, 86,* 307–324.

Brewer, M. B., & Campbell, D. T. (1976). *Ethnocentrism and intergroup attitudes: East African evidence*. Washington, D.C.: Halsted.

Brewer, M. B., & Silver, M. (1978). Ingroup bias as a function of task characteristics. *European Journal of Social Psychology, 8,* 393–400.

Brigham, J. C. (1971). Ethnic stereotypes. *Psychological Bulletin, 76,* 15–38.

Brown, R. J. (1978). Divided we fall: An analysis of relations between sections of a factory workforce. In H. Tajfel (Ed.), *Differentiation between social groups: Studies in the social psychology of intergroup relations.* New York: Academic Press.

Brown, R. J. (1984a). The role of similarity in intergroup relations. In H. Tajfel (Ed.), *The social dimension: European developments in social psychology.* London: Academic Press.

Brown, R. J. (1984b). The effect of intergroup similarity and cooperative vs. competitive orientation on intergroup discrimination. *British Journal of Social Psychology,* **23,** 21–33.

Brown, R. J., & Turner, J. C. (1979). The criss-cross categorisation effect in intergroup discrimination. *British Journal of Social and Clinical Psychology,* **18,** 371–383.

Brown, R. J., & Turner, J. C. (1981). Interpersonal and intergroup behavior. In J. C. Turner & M. Giles (Eds.), *Intergroup behavior.* Oxford: Blackwell.

Bruner, J. S. (1958). Social psychology and perception. In E. E. Maccoby, T. M. Newcomb, & E. L. Hartley (Eds.), *Reading in social psychology.* New York: Holt.

Burnstein, E., & McRae, A. V. (1962). Some effects of shared threat and prejudice in racially mixed groups. *Journal of Abnormal and Social Psychology,* **64,** 257–263.

Byrne, D. (1969). Attitudes and attraction. In L. Berkowitz (Ed.), *Advances in experimental social psychology* (Vol. 4). New York: Academic Press.

Byrne, D., & McGraw, C. (1964). Interpersonal attraction toward Negroes. *Human Relations,* **17,** 201–203.

Byrne, D., & Wong, T. J. (1962). Racial prejudice, interpersonal attraction and assumed dissimilarity of attitudes. *Journal of Abnormal and Social Psychology,* **65,** 246–253.

Campbell, D. T. (1958). Common fate, similarity, and other indices of the status of aggregates of persons as social entities. *Behavioral Science,* **3,** 14–25.

Campbell, D. T. (1967). Stereotypes and perception of group differences. *American Psychologist,* **22,** 812–829.

Cantor, N., & Mischel, W. (1977). Traits as prototypes: Effects on recognition memory. *Journal of Personality and Social Psychology,* **35,** 38–48.

Carroll, J. S., & Payne, J. W. (Eds.) (1976). *Cognition and social behavior.* Hillsdale, NJ: Erlbaum.

Chadwick-Jones, J. K. (1962). Intergroup attitudes: A stage in attitude formation. *British Journal of Sociology,* **13,** 57–63.

Cohen, C. E. (1981). Person categories and social perception: Testing some boundaries of the processing effects of prior knowledge. *Journal of Personality and Social Psychology,* **40,** 441–452.

Commins, B., & Lockwood, J. (1978). The effects on intergroup relations of mixing Roman Catholics and Protestants: An experimental investigation. *European Journal of Social Psychology,* **8,** 383–386.

Deschamps, J.-C. (1977). *L'Attribution et la categorisation sociale.* Bern: Peter Lang.

Deschamps, J.-C., & Doise, W. (1978). Crossed category memberships in intergroup relations. In H. Tajfel (Ed.), *Differentiation between social groups: Studies in the social psychology of intergroup relations.* London: Academic Press.

Deutsch, M., & Collins, M. E. (1951). *Interracial housing: A psychological evaluation of a social experiment.* Minneapolis: University of Minnesota Press.

Dion, K. L. (1973). Cohesiveness as a determinant of ingroup–outgroup bias. *Journal of Personality and Social Psychology,* **28,** 163–171.

Dion, K. L. (1975). Women's reactions to discrimination from members of the same or opposite sex. *Journal of Research in Personality,* **9,** 294–306.

Dion, K. L. (1979). Intergroup conflict and intergroup cohesiveness. In W. G. Austin & S. Worchel (Eds.), *The social psychology of intergroup relations.* Monterey, CA: Brooks/Cole.

Dion, K. L., & Earn, B. M. (1975). The phenomenology of being a target of prejudice. *Journal of Personality and Social Psychology,* **32,** 944–950.

Dion, K. L., Earn, B. M., & Yee, P. H. N. (1978). The experience of being a victim of prejudice: An experimental approach. *International Journal of Psychology*, **13**, 197–214.

Doise, W. (1969). Intergroup relations and polarization of individual and collective judgments. *Journal of Personality and Social Psychology*, **12**, 136–143.

Doise, W. (1978). *Groups and individuals: Explanations in social psychology*. London & New York: Cambridge University Press.

Doise, W., Csepeli, G., Dann, H., Gouge, C., Larsen, K., & Ostell, A. (1972). An experimental investigation into the formation of intergroup representations. *European Journal of Social Psychology*, **2**, 202–204.

Doise, W., Deschamps, J.-C., & Meyer, G. (1978). The accentuation of intra-category similarities. In H. Tajfel (Ed.), *Differentiation between social groups: Studies in the social psychology of intergroup relations*. London: Academic Press.

Doise, W., & Sinclair, A. (1973). The categorization process in intergroup relations. *European Journal of Social Psychology*, **3**, 145–147.

Dollard, J. (1938). Hostility and fear in social life. *Social Forces*, **17**, 15–25.

Ebbesen, E. B. (1980). Cognitive processes in understanding ongoing behavior. In R. Hastie, T. M. Ostrom, E. B. Ebbesen, R. S. Wyer, D. L. Hamilton, & D. E. Carlston (Eds.), *Person memory: The cognitive basis of social perception*. Hillsdale, NJ: Erlbaum.

Eiser, J. R. (1971). Enhancement of contrast in the absolute judgment of attitude statements. *Journal of Personality and Social Psychology*, **17**, 1–10.

Eiser, J. R., & Stroebe, W. (1972). *Categorization and social judgment*. New York: Academic Press.

Ferguson, C. K., & Kelley, H. H. (1964). Significant factors in over-evaluation of own group's products. *Journal of Abnormal and Social Psychology*, **69**, 223–228.

Fromkin, H. L. (1973). *The psychology of uniqueness: Avoidance of similarity and seeking of differences*. West Lafayette, IN: Krannert Graduate School of Industrial Administration, 1973.

Gould, R., & Sigall, H. (1977). The effects of empathy and outcome on attribution: An examination of the divergent-perspective hypothesis. *Journal of Experimental Social Psychology*, **13**, 480–491.

Hamill, R., Wilson, T., & Nisbett, R. (1980). Insensitivity to sample bias: Generalizing from atypical cases. *Journal of Personality and Social Psychology*, **39**, 578–589.

Hamilton, D. L. (1979). A cognitive-attributional analysis of stereotyping. In L. Berkowitz (Ed.), *Advances in experimental social psychology* (Vol. 12). New York: Academic Press.

Hamilton, D. L. (Ed.) (1981). *Cognitive processes in stereotyping and intergroup behavior*. Hillsdale, NJ: Erlbaum.

Harkins, S. G., & Petty, R. E. (1981). The multiple source effect in persuasion: The effects of distraction. *Personality and Social Psychology Bulletin*, **7**, 627–635.

Harvey, J., Ickes, W., & Kidd, R. (Eds.) (1976). *New directions in attribution research* (Vol. 1). Hillsdale, NJ: Erlbaum.

Harvey, J., Ickes, W., & Kidd, R. (Eds.) (1978). *New directions in attribution research* (Vol. 2). Hillsdale, NJ: Erlbaum.

Harvey, J., Ickes, W., & Kidd, R. (Eds.) (1981). *New directions in attribution research* (Vol. 3). Hillsdale, NJ: Erlbaum.

Hastie, R. (1980). Memory for information which confirms or contradicts a general impression. In R. Hastie, T. M. Ostrom, E. E. Ebbesen, R. S. Wyer, D. L. Hamilton, & D. E. Carlston (Eds.), *Person memory: The cognitive basis of social perception*. Hillsdale, NJ: Erlbaum.

Hastie, R., & Kumar, A. P. (1979). Person memory: Personality traits as organizing principles in memory for behaviors. *Journal of Personality and Social Psychology*, **37**, 25–38.

Hastie, R., Ostrom, T. M., Ebbesen, E. E., Wyer, R. S., Hamilton, D. L., & Carlston, D. E. (Eds.) (1980). *Person memory: The cognitive basis of social perception.* Hillsdale, NJ: Erlbaum.

Heider, F. (1958). *The psychology of interpersonal relations.* New York: Wiley.

Helson, H. (1970). Adaptation-level theory. In M. H. Apply (Ed.), *Adaptation-level theory.* New York: Academic Press.

Hensley, V., & Duval, S. (1976). Some perceptual determinants of perceived similarity, liking, and correctness. *Journal of Personality and Social Psychology, 34,* 159–168.

Hirschman, A. O. (1972). *Exit, voice and loyalty: Responses to decline in firms, organizations and states* (2nd ed.). Cambridge, MA: Harvard University Press.

Hovland, C. I., Janis, I. L., & Kelley, H. H. (1953). *Communication and persuasion.* New Haven, CT: Yale University Press.

Howard, J. W. & Rothbart, M. (1980). Social categorization and memory for in-group and out-group behavior. *Journal of Personality and Social Psychology, 38,* 301–310.

Jones, E. E. (1979). The rocky road from acts to dispositions. *American Psychologist, 34,* 107–117.

Jones, E. E., & Davis, K. E. (1965). From acts to dispositions: The attribution process in person perception. In L. Berkowitz (Ed.), *Advances in experimental social psychology* (Vol. 2). New York: Academic Press.

Jones, E. E., & Nisbett, R. E. (1970). *The actor and the observer: Divergent perceptions of the causes of behavior.* Morristown, NJ: General Learning Press.

Julian, J., Bishop, D., & Fiedler, F. C. (1966). Quasi-therapeutic effects of intergroup competition. *Journal of Personality and Social Psychology, 3,* 321–327.

Kahan, A., & Ryan, A. H. (1972). Factors influencing the bias toward one's own group. *International Journal of Group Tensions, 2,* 33–50.

Kahneman, D. (1973). *Attention and effort.* Englewood Cliffs, NJ: Prentice-Hall.

Kelley, H. H. (1967). Attribution theory in social psychology. In D. Levine (Ed.), *Nebraska symposium on motivation, 1967* (Vol. 15). Lincoln: University of Nebraska Press.

Kelman, H. C. (Ed.) (1966). *International behavior.* New York: Holt.

Kuhn, M. H., & McPartland, T. S. (1954). An empirical investigation of self-attitudes. *American Sociological Review, 19,* 68–76.

LeVine, R. A., & Campbell, D. T. (1972). *Ethnocentrism: Theories of conflict, ethnic attitudes, and group behavior.* New York: Wiley.

Levine, R., Chein, I, & Murphy, B. (1947). The relation of intensity of a need to the amount of labeling bias. *Journal of Consulting and Clinical Psychology, 13,* 283–293.

Lewin, K. (1935). *A dynamic theory of personality.* New York: McGraw-Hill.

Lewin, K. (1948). *Resolving social conflicts.* New York: Harper.

Lingle, J. H., Altom, M. W., & Medin, D. L. (1985). Of cabbages and kings: Assessing the extendibility of natural object concept models to social things. In R. Wyer, T. Strull, & J. Hartwick (Eds.), *Handbook of social cognition.* Hillsdale, NJ: Erlbaum.

Linville, P. N. (1979). *Dimensional complexity and evaluative extremity: A cognitive model predicting polarized evaluations of outgroup members.* Unpublished Ph. D. dissertation, Duke University, Durham, North Carolina.

Linville, P. N., & Jones, E. E. (1980). Polarized appraisals of out-group members. *Journal of Personality and Social Psychology, 38,* 689–703.

McGuire, W. J., McGuire, C. V., Child, P., & Fujioka, P. (1978). Salience of ethnicity in the spontaneous self-concept as a function of one's ethnic distinctiveness in the social environment. *Journal of Personality and Social Psychology, 36,* 511–520.

McGuire, W. J., McGuire, C. V., & Winton, W. (1979). Effects of household sex composition on the salience of one's gender in the spontaneous self-concepts. *Journal of Experimental Social Psychology, 15,* 77–90.

McGuire, W. J., & Padawer-Singer, A. (1976). Trait salience in spontaneous self-concept. *Journal of Personality and Social Psychology, 33,* 743–754.

Mead, M. (1937). *Cooperation and competition among primitive peoples.* New York: McGraw-Hill.

Middleton, J. (1960). *Lugbara religion.* London: Oxford.

Milgram, S. (1965). Some conditions of obedience and disobedience to authority. *Human Relations, 18,* 57–76.

Minard, R. D. (1952). Race relationships in the Pocahontas coal fields. *Journal of Social Issues, 25,* 29–44.

Murphy, R. F. (1957). Intergroup hostility and social cohesion. *American Anthropologist, 59,* 1018–1035.

Newtson, D. (1973). Attribution and the unit of perception of ongoing behavior. *Journal of Personality and Social Psychology, 28,* 28–38.

Newtson, D. (1976). Foundations of attribution: The unit of perception of ongoing behavior. In J. Harvey, W. Ickes, & R. Kidd (Eds.), *New directions in attribution research* (Vol. 1). Hillsdale, NJ: Erlbaum.

Nisbett, R. C., & Wilson, T. D. (1977). Telling more than we know: Verbal reports on mental processes. *Psychological Review, 84,* 231–259.

Oakes, P. J., & Turner, J. C. (1980). Social categorization and intergroup behaviour: Does the minimal intergroup discrimination make social identity more positive? *European Journal of Social Psychology, 10,* 295–301.

Ochbert, F. (1977). The victim of terrorism: Psychiatric considerations. *Terrorism An International Journal, 1,* 1–22.

Olson, R. K., & Attneave, F. (1970). What variables produce similarity grouping? *American Journal of Psychology, 83,* 1–21.

Orne, M. T. (1962). On the social psychology of the psychological experiment: With particular relevance to demand characteristics and their implications. *American Psychologist, 17,* 776–783.

Park, B., & Rothbart, M. (1982). Perception of out-group homogeneity and levels of social categorization. *Journal of Personality and Social Psychology, 42,* 1051–1068.

Pettigrew, T. F. (1979). The ultimate attribution error: Extending Allport's cognitive analysis of prejudice. *Personality and Social Psychology Bulletin, 5,* 461–476.

Pomerantz, J. R. (1981). Perceptual organization in information processing. In M. Kubovy & J. R. Pomerantz (Eds.), *Perceptual organization.* Hillsdale, NJ: Erlbaum.

Postman, L. & Brown, D. R. (1952). The perceptual consequences of success and failure. *Journal of Abnormal and Social Psychology, 47,* 213–221.

Quattrone, G. A., & Jones, E. E. (1980). The perception of variability within ingroups and outgroups: Implications for the law of small numbers. *Journal of Personality and Social Psychology, 38,* 141–152.

Rabbie, J. M., & Horwitz, M. (1969). Arousal of ingroup–outgroup bias by a chance win or loss. *Journal of Personality and Social Psychology, 13,* 269–277.

Rabbie, J. M., & Wilkens, G. (1971). Intergroup competition and its effect on intragroup and intergroup relations. *European Journal of Social Psychology, 1,* 215–234.

Regan, D. T., & Totten, J. (1975). Empathy and attribution: Turning observers into actors. *Journal of Personality and Social Psychology, 32,* 850–856.

Rokeach, M. (1960). *The open and closed mind: Invistigations into the nature of belief systems and personality systems.* New York: Basic Books.

Rosch, E. (1977). Human categorization. In N. Warren (Ed.), *Advances in cross-cultural psychology* (Vol. 1). New York: Academic Press.

Rosch, E. (1978). Principles of categorization. In E. Rosch & B. Lloyd (Eds.), *Cognition and categorization.* Hillsdale, NJ: Erlbaum.

Rosenberg, M. (1965). *Society and the adolescent self-image*. Princeton, NJ: Princeton University Press.

Ross, L. (1977). The intuitive psychologist and his shortcomings: Distortion in the attribution process. In L. Berkowitz (Ed.), *Advances in Experimental Social Psychology* (Vol. 10). New York: Academic Press.

Ross, L., Bierbrauer, G., & Hoffman, S. (1976). The role of attribution processes in conformity and dissent: Revisiting the Asch situation. *American Psychologist*, **31**, 148–157.

Rothbart, M., Evans, M., & Fulero, S. (1979). Recall for confirming events: Memory processes and the maintenance of social stereotypes. *Journal of Experimental Social Psychology*, **15**, 343–355.

Sager, H., & Schofield, J. (1980). Racial and behavioral cues in Black and White children's perceptions of ambiguously aggressive acts. *Journal of Personality and Social Psychology*, **39**, 590–598.

Sherif, M. (1967). *Social interaction process and products*. Chicago: Aldine.

Sherif, M., & Hovland, C. I. (1961). *Social judgment: Assimilation and contrast effects in communication and attitude change*. New Haven, CT: Yale University Press.

Snyder, M. (1981). On the self-perpetuating nature of social stereotypes. In D. L. Hamilton (Ed.), *Cognitive processes in stereotyping and intergroup behavior*. Hillsdale, NJ: Erlbaum.

Snyder, M., & Swann, W. B. (1978). Behavioral confirmation in social interaction: From social perception to social reality. *Journal of Experimental Social Psychology*, **14**, 148–162.

Snyder, M., Tanke, E. D., & Berscheid, E. (1977). Social perception and interpersonal behavior: On the self-fulfilling nature of social stereotypes. *Journal of Personality and Social Psychology*, **35**, 656–666.

Snyder, M., & Uranowitz, S. W. (1978). Reconstructing the past: Some cognitive consequences of person perception. *Journal of Personality and Social Psychology*, **36**, 941–950.

Steiner, I. D. (1974). Whatever happened to the group in social psychology? *Journal of Experimental Social Psychology*, **10**, 94–108.

Stephan, W. G. (1985). Intergroup relations. In G. Lindzey & E. Aronson (Eds.), *The handbook of social psychology* (3rd ed.). Reading MA: Addison-Wesley.

Stephan, W. G., & Rosenfield, D. (1978). Effects of desegregation on racial attitudes. *Journal of Personality and Social Psychology*, **36**, 795–804.

Stephenson, G. M., & Brotherton, C. J. (1975). Social progression and polarisation: A study of discussion and negotiation in groups of mining supervisors. *British Journal of Social and Clinical Psychology*, **14**, 241–252.

Storms, M. (1973). Videotape and the attribution process: Reversing the actor's and observer's points of view. *Journal of Personality and Social Psychology*, **27**, 165–175.

Stroebe, W. (1971). The effect of judges' attitudes on rating of attitude statements: A theoretical analysis. *European Journal of Social Psychology*, **1**, 419–434.

Sumner, W. G. (1906). *Folkways*. New York: Ginn.

Swartz, M. J. (1961). Negative ethnocentrism. *Journal of Conflict Resolution*, **5**, 75–81.

Tajfel, H. (1957). Value and the perceptual judgement of magnitude. *Psychological Review*, **64**, 192–204.

Tajfel, H. (1970). Experiments in intergroup discrimination. *Scientific American*, **223**, 96–102.

Tajfel, H. (1976). Exit, voice, and intergroup relations. In L. Strickland (Ed.), *Social psychology in transition*. New York: Plenum.

Tajfel, H. (1978). *The social psychology of minorities*. London: Minority Rights Group, Report No. 38.

Tajfel, H. (1979). Individuals and groups in social psychology. *British Journal of Social and Clinical Psychology*, **18**, 183–190.

Tajfel, H. (Ed.) (1982). *Social identity and intergroup relations.* London & New York: Cambridge University Press.

Tajfel, H., & Billig, M. (1974). Familiarity and categorization in intergroup behavior. *Journal of Experimental Social Psychology, 10,* 159–170.

Tajfel, H., Billig, M., Bundy, R., & Flament, C. (1971). Social categorization and intergroup behavior. *European Journal of Social Psychology, 1,* 149–178.

Tajfel, H., Sheikh, A. A., & Gardner, R. C. (1964). Content of stereotypes and the inferences of similarity between members of stereotyped groups. *Acta Psychologica, 22,* 191–201.

Tajfel, H., & Turner, J. C. (1979). An integrative theory of intergroup conflict. In W. G. Austin & S. Worchel (Eds.), *The social psychology of intergroup relations.* Monterey, CA: Brooks/Cole.

Tajfel, H., & Wilkes, A. (1963). Classification and quantitative judgment. *British Journal of Social Psychology, 54,* 101–114.

Taylor, S. E., Fiske, S. T., Etcoff, N. L., & Ruderman, A. J. (1978). Categorical and contextual basis of person memory and stereotyping. *Journal of Personality and Social Psychology, 36,* 778–793.

Thompson, J. E. (1983). *Assimilation and contrast effects in the judgment of outgroups: An application of social judgment theory to intergroup relations.* Unpublished Ph. D. dissertation, Rutgers University, New Brunswick, New Jersey.

Thompson, J. E., Wilder, D. A., & Cooper, W. E. (1979). *Shift in judgment of an outgroup following the introduction of a more different outgroup.* Paper presented at the meeting of the American Psychological Association, New York, September 1979.

Triandis, H. C. (1961). A note on Rokeach's theory of prejudice. *Journal of Abnormal and Social Psychology, 62,* 184–186.

Triandis, H. C. (1976). Methodological problems of comparative research. *International Journal of Psychology, 11,* 155–159.

Turner, J. C. (1978). Social comparison, similarity and ingroup favouritism. In H. Tajfel (Ed.), *Differentiation between social groups: Studies in the social psychology of intergroup relations.* New York: Academic Press.

Turner, J. C., Brown, R. J., & Tajfel, H. (1979). Social comparison and group interest in ingroup favoritism. *European Journal of Social Psychology, 9,* 187–204.

Weber, S. J., & Cook, T. D. (1972). Subject effects in laboratory research: An examination of subject roles, demand characteristics and valid inference. *Psychological Bulletin, 77,* 273–295.

White, P. (1980). Limitations on verbal reports of internal events: A refutation of Nisbett and Wilson and of Bem. *Psychological Review, 87,* 105–112.

Wilder, D. A. (1977). Perception of groups, size of opposition, and social influence. *Journal of Experimental Social Psychology, 13,* 253–268.

Wilder, D. A. (1978a). Effect of predictability on units of perception and attribution. *Personality and Social Psychology Bulletin, 4,* 281–284.

Wilder, D. A. (1978b). Predictability of behavior, goals, and unit of perception. *Personality and Social Psychology Bulletin, 4,* 334–338.

Wilder, D. A. (1978c). Reduction of intergroup discrimination through individuation of the outgroup. *Journal of Personality and Social Psychology, 36,* 1361–1374.

Wilder, D. A. (1978d). Homogeneity of jurors: The majority's influence depends upon their perceived independence. *Law and Human Behavior, 2,* 363–376.

Wilder, D. A. (1978e). Perceiving persons as a group: Effects on attributions of causality and beliefs. *Social Psychology, 1,* 13–23.

Wilder, D. A. (1981). Perceiving persons as a group: Categorization and intergroup relations. In D.

L. Hamilton (Ed.), *Cognitive processes in stereotyping and intergroup behavior*. Hillsdale, NJ: Erlbaum.

Wilder, D. A. (1984). *Effects of perceiving persons as a group on the information conveyed by their behavior*. Unpublished manuscript, Rutgers University, New Brunswick, New Jersey.

Wilder, D. A. (1985). Predictions of belief homogeneity and similarity following social categorization. *British Journal of Social Psychology*, in press.

Wilder, D. A., & Allen, V. L. (1978). Group membership and preference for information about other persons. *Personality and Social Psychology Bulletin*, **4**, 106–110.

Wilder, D. A., & Cooper, W. E. (1981). Categorization into groups: Consequences for social perception and attribution. In J. Harvey, W. Ickes, & R. Kidd (Eds.), *New directions in attribution research* (Vol. 3). Hillsdale, NJ: Erlbaum.

Wilder, D. A., & Shapiro, P. (1984). The role of outgroup salience in determining social identity. *Journal of Personality and Social Psychology*, **47**, 342–348.

Wilder, D. A., & Thompson, J. E. (1980). Intergroup contact with independent manipulation of ingroup and out-group interaction. *Journal of Personality and Social Psychology*, **38**, 589–603.

Wilder, D. A., Thompson, J. E., & Cooper, W. E. (1981). Shift in judgment of one outgroup toward a less acceptable second outgroup. Unpublished manuscript, Rutgers University, New Brunswick, NJ.

Wilder, D. A., Thompson, J. E., & Cooper, W. E. (1983). Anxiety as a mediator of unsuccessful contact between groups. Unpublished manuscript, Rutgers University, New Brunswick, New Jersey.

Wilson, W., & Kayatani, M. (1968). Intergroup attitudes and strategies in games between opponents of the same or a different race. *Journal of Personality and Social Psychology*, **9**, 24–30.

Wilson, W., & Miller, N. (1961). Shifts in evaluation of participants following intergroup competition. *Journal of Abnormal and Social Psychology*, **63**, 428–431.

Worchel, S. (1979). Co-operation and the reduction of intergroup conflict: Some determining factors. In W. G. Austin & S. Worchel (Eds.), *The social psychology of intergroup relations*. Monterey, CA: Brooks/Cole.

Worchel, S., & Andreoli, V. A. (1978). Facilitation of social interaction through deindividuation of the target. *Journal of Personality and Social Psychology*, **36**, 549–556.

Worchel, S., Andreoli, V. A., & Folger, R. (1977). Intergroup cooperation and intergroup attraction: The effect of previous interaction and outcome of combined effort. *Journal of Experimental Social Psychology*, **13**, 131–140.

Worchel, S., Axsom, D., Ferris, F., Samaha, C., & Schweitzer, S. (1978). Factors determining the effect of intergroup cooperation on intergroup attraction. *Journal of Conflict Resolution*, **22**, 429–439.

Word, C. O., Zanna, M. P., & Cooper, J. (1974). The nonverbal mediation of self-fulfilling prophecies in interracial interaction. *Journal of Experimental Social Psychology*, **10**, 109–120.

Wyer, R. S., & Carlston, D. E. (1979). *Social inference and attribution*. Hillsdale, NJ: Erlbaum.

Wyer, R. S., & Gordon, S. E. (1982). The recall of information about persons and groups. *Journal of Experimental Social Psychology*, **18**, 128–164.

Wyer, R. S., & Hartwick, J. (1980). Information retrieval, syllogistic reasoning and social inference. In L. Berkowitz (Ed.), *Advances in experimental social psychology* (Vol. 13). New York: Academic Press.

Wyer, R. S., & Srull, T. K. (1980). The processing of social stimulus information: A conceptual integration. In R. Hastie, T. M. Ostrom, E. E. Ebbesen, R. S. Wyer, D. L. Hamilton, & D. E. Carlston (Eds.), *Person memory: The cognitive basis of social perception*. Hillsdale, NJ: Erlbaum.

Young, D. (1932). *American minority peoples*. New York: Harper.

Ziller, R. C. (1965). Toward a theory of open and closed groups. *Psychological Bulletin, 64,* 164–182.

Zimbardo, P. (1970). The human choice: Individuation, reason, and order versus deidividuation, impulse, and chaos. In W. Arnold & D. Levine (Eds.), *Nebraska symposium on motivation, 1969* (Vol. 17). Lincoln: University of Nebraska Press.

INDEX